Marketing Environment 1999–2000

The Chartered Institute of Marketing/Butterworth-Heinemann Marketing Series is the most comprehensive, widely used and important collection of books in marketing and sales currently available worldwide.

As the CIM's official publisher, Butterworth-Heinemann develops, produces and publishes the complete series in association with the CIM. We aim to provide definitive marketing books for students and practitioners that promote excellence in marketing education and practice.

The series titles are written by CIM senior examiners and leading marketing educators for professionals, students and those studying the CIM's Certificate, Advanced Certificate and Postgraduate Diploma courses. Now firmly established, these titles provide practical study support to CIM and other marketing students and to practitioners at all levels.

 The Chartered
Institute of Marketing

D1742422

Formed in 1911, The Chartered Institute of Marketing is now the largest professional marketing management body in the world with over 60,000 members located worldwide. Its primary objectives are focused on the development of awareness and understanding of marketing throughout UK industry and commerce and in the raising of standards of professionalism in the education, training and practice of this key business discipline.

Marketing Environment 1999–2000

Mike Oldroyd

Published on behalf of
The Chartered Institute of Marketing

BUTTERWORTH
HEINEMANN

OXFORD AUCKLAND BOSTON JOHANNESBURG MELBOURNE NEW DELHI

Butterworth-Heinemann
Linacre House, Jordan Hill, Oxford OX2 8DP
225 Wildwood Avenue, Woburn, MA 01801-2041
A division of Reed Educational and Professional Publishing Ltd

A member of the Reed Elsevier plc group

First published 1999

British Library Cataloguing in Publication Data
A catalogue record for this book is available from the British Library

ISBN 0 7506 4368 4

Set by Avocet Typeset, Brill, Aylesbury, Bucks
Printed and bound in Italy

FOR EVERY TITLE THAT WE PUBLISH, BUTTERWORTH-HEINEMANN
WILL PAY FOR BTCV TO PLANT AND CARE FOR A TREE.

Contents

higher employment – Control of inflation – Economic indicators – Economic policies – Trade and exchange rate policies – Balance of payments – The impact of international trade – The basis for trade: at the micro level – Frictions in the international environment – Summary – Activity debrief – Examination hints and specimen questions

A quick word from the Chief Examiner

I am delighted to recommend to you the new series of CIM workbooks. All of these have been written by authors involved with examining and marking for the CIM.

Preparing for the CIM exams is hard work. These workbooks are designed to make that work as interesting and illuminating as possible, as well as providing you with the knowledge you need to pass. I wish you success.

Trevor Watkins
CIM Chief Examiner,
Deputy Vice Chancellor,
South Bank University

Preface

This workbook has been written to help you understand how businesses and their marketing environments relate and interact. Social, legislative, economic, political and technological environments affect virtually every organizational function and activity, not least those concerned with marketing.

The primary objective, however, is to provide a student-centred framework for studying this Certificate level subject, the Marketing Environment. This integrative subject, first launched by The Chartered Institute of Marketing in 1994, was the product of an extensive consultation process with relevant stakeholders such as students, teaching centres and employers. Following five years of examination experience this process has been repeated using representative focus groups to ensure that the new syllabus is even more relevant to the current and future needs of marketing practitioners.

The new syllabus retains the same essential philosophy and objectives but is more streamlined and future orientated. Treatment of both the legislative and economic environments are now more on a par with other equally important environments. All are intended to be covered at the 'appreciation' level rather than in-depth, with emphasis consistently placed on the influence of these environments on, and implications for, the marketer.

Coverage of the international environment has also been re-shaped with the introduction of a new section called Managing the Future Environment. The content is dynamic, future orientated and action centred with its focus on understanding the nature of a turbulent and ever-changing environment, applying a toolbox of appropriate methodologies and assessing the significance of emerging environmental challenges.

The main aims and objectives of the Marketing Environment syllabus and this workbook are as follows:

- To enable students to understand the nature of the marketing environment and its relevance for the organization and marketing practice (see unit 1).
- To examine the interface between marketing, internal functions and external influences (see unit 2).
- To encourage students to recognize the importance of building relationships with relevant stakeholders and publics (see units 3–4).
- To enable students to identify and interpret the marketing implications of significant changes in the organization's wider environment (see units 5–9).
- To appreciate the complex, dynamic and uncertain nature of the external environment and how it might be best managed in marketing terms (see units 9–10).

The approach taken in this workbook is to provide a blend of academic knowledge, common sense understanding and practical applications/activities which will meet the needs not only of marketers, but also of many other types of students. This is particularly the case for students studying for professional qualifications, such as IPD, or those on BTEC HNC/D equivalent-level courses studying for qualifications requiring a broad appreciation of the business environment within their curricula.

The author has had considerable experience in teaching various levels of students in this area, and the methodology adopted should be ideally suited to the needs and requirements of both tutors and students in the subject. The workbook material and activities have been designed to have more general application even though the specific focus taken has been concentrated on the activities of marketing departments.

This workbook provides you with the means of making sense of the complex relationships that exist between an organization and its environment. It heightens your awareness of changes that are taking place and their implications for your day-to-day work activities. The environment is by its nature dynamic, and any text might easily become quickly dated. Every effort has been made to minimize this process of 'decay' by generalizing the concepts discussed and many of the activities related to them. The new syllabus places added weight on current and future environmental challenges and this gives added significance and immediacy to the syllabus. The challenges highlighted will change as time goes by in order to retain the freshness of the text and its relevance to marketers. Both the syllabus and the workbook will be revised on a rolling annual basis to ensure that they are up to date with environmental changes. Particular stress will be given to the currency of examination questions and model answers. The emphasis throughout, however, is to reinforce the intention of the CIM that students should be given every encouragement to relate their knowledge to understanding, and that understanding to marketing applications.

As Senior Examiner/author of the Marketing Environment syllabus I have tried to design a workbook that is sufficiently comprehensive so that candidates are not confronted with the necessity to consult and purchase myriad sources in order to complete their studies. Only a few texts are currently available in this area, or provide the necessary breadth and level of coverage required. Books that do exist either fall into the category of being academic with limited or no examples and activities, or provide a succession of activities and rapidly dating newspaper clippings with very little explanatory text. I hope you find that this workbook has achieved a more balanced blend that would be equally valuable to the marketer at certificate level as it would to a stage one DMS or even non-business background MBA student.

Writing this workbook with a clearly identified group of students in mind has served to simplify the structure into ten similar-sized study units. A final unit concerns the important area of guidance on examinations and revision. Learning outcomes expected as a result of undertaking this course of study are highlighted beneath the relevant units:

The first four units concentrate on the organization and its micro-environment. Students will be able to:

- Distinguish between the types of organization within the public, private and voluntary sectors, understand their objectives and the influences on them.
- Recognize organizations as open systems and explain the importance of relationships between the organization and its suppliers, market intermediaries, customers and other key stakeholders.
- Appreciate the concept of societal marketing and social responsibility.
- Access relevant sources of information on the marketing environment, undertake a competitor analysis and systematically evaluate forces impacting on market share and profitability.

The final six study units focus on the wider macro environments and managing the future environment. Students will be able to:

- Undertake an environmental audit for an organization and assess the probable impact of significant opportunities and threats
- Recognize and assess the potential impact of key trends in the social, technical, economic, environmental, political, legal and ethical environments.
- Understand the complex nature of the marketing environment in order to discuss the significance of a number of current and future environmental challenges.
- Draw on a toolbox of techniques to meet the challenge of change and communicate the concepts and implications of the marketing environment in a variety of relevant business communication formats.

The units must not, however, be seen as separate compartments of knowledge but rather as interlocked pieces of an intricate jigsaw.

The layout of what follows is designed to be as student-friendly as possible. The text is broken up into digestible chunks by definitions, questions and activities. Debriefs are provided to many of these at the end of each unit, but have been purposely limited to encourage maximum contribution from you! All the questions provided are actual examples from past CIM papers or specimens of the likely form of questions in new sections of the syllabus. You should use them to cement your understanding of the subject matter to the applications of the knowledge in question.

One topsy-turvy recommendation I hope you will consider implementing before you progress very far in this workbook is that you carefully read and digest the first five pages of Unit 11 where guidance on revision and examinations is provided. Waiting until you have completed all ten workbook units will probably be too late to obtain maximum benefit from this section with the examination just around the corner.

To conclude, this workbook is intended to be a resource; a source of information and explanation as well as a framework for study. It is designed to be a one-stop solution for your professional development in this challenging subject area. Use it systematically and use it well and I am confident you will meet with the examination success you deserve.

Mike Oldroyd

Acknowledgements

Very special thanks are due to my darling wife Karen for her good humour and hard work in preparing and editing the manuscript; to Martin Murphy for the benefit of his considerable legal expertise and very useful comments in the development of Unit 5; to the team at Butterworth-Heinemann for expediting the manuscript so efficiently; and finally to my good friend Angela Hatton for her creative stimulus in helping me get to grips with effective workbook format. All their assistance was invaluable but any deficiencies that remain are entirely my own.

Regarding this new 1999–2000 edition, I wish to add my thanks once again to those tutors and students who provided such invaluable comments through their inspection copies. I welcome objective feedback from my own particular marketing environment in order to further refine the product. I would also like to acknowledge the contributions of those who participated in the focus groups providing critical feedback on the deficiencies of the old syllabus and the needs of the new. The input from my fellow certificate examiners and the staff at the CIM was also positive and supportive. Dr Heather Davison, in particular, provided welcome drive and coordination at critical points in the process.

Finally, I would like to acknowledge the contribution of my own students, past and present, at the Huddersfield University Business School. For their sins they are regularly required to keep me and their peer group briefed on business cases and environmental developments. They help me to keep my finger on the pulse of the ever-changing marketing environment in often interesting and creative ways. To them I owe a debt of gratitude, but with a disclaimer of any implied entitlement to a percentage of the royalties!

How to use your CIM workbook

The authors have been careful to structure your book with the exams in mind. Each unit, therefore, covers an essential part of the syllabus. You need to work through the complete workbook systematically to ensure that you have covered everything you need to know.

This workbook is divided into ten units. Each unit contains the following standard elements:

Objectives   tell you what part of the syllabus you will be covering and what you will be expected to know having read the unit.

Study guides   tell you how long the unit is and how long its activities take to do.

Questions   are designed to give you practice – they will be similar to those you get in the exam. You will find at least one or two recent ones at the end of each unit.

Answers   give you a suggested format for answering exam questions. *Remember* there is no such thing as a model answer – you should use these examples only as guidelines.

Activities   give you the chance to put what you have learnt into practice.

Exam hints   are tips from the senior examiner or examiner which are designed to help you avoid common mistakes made by previous candidates.

Definitions   are used for words you must know to pass the exam.

Extending activity sections   are designed to help you use your time most effectively. It is not possible for the workbook to cover *everything* you need to know to pass. What you read here needs to be supplemented by your classes, practical experience at work and day-to-day reading.

Summaries   focus on the key learning points you should have picked up from reading the unit.

In addition you will find the following:

The **syllabus** is reproduced as an appendix at the back of the workbook so that you can tick off sections as you complete them and double check you are fully prepared for the examinations. Remember the syllabus is the basic building block in every examination paper.

A **glossary** of terms provides definitions of all key terms found in the syllabus and past examination papers and many more besides. This is found near the back of the workbook and should be regularly referred to as most questions require clear definitions of the terms used.

Index for easy location and cross-referencing of information on particular topics.

The organization and its environments

In this introductory unit on organizations you will:

❏ Examine the diversity of organizational types.

❏ Understand the meaning and importance of an organization's mission.

❏ Appreciate the nature and significance of organizational objectives.

❏ Consider the organization as a open system responding to changing situations.

By the end of this unit you will:

❏ Recognize the strengths and weaknesses of different forms of organization.

❏ Appreciate the diversity of organizational objectives.

❏ Understand the nature of open systems and the interface between marketing and other important sub-systems.

❏ Apply systems and contingency thinking to managing organizations in a changing environment.

Covering the organizational section of the CIM syllabus this first unit of the Marketing Environment Workbook will provide you with a framework and organizational setting within which you may explore the dynamic interrelationships between businesses and the various environments in which they operate. The material is relatively straightforward but of critical importance to an understanding of subsequent units, since it provides a foundation upon which the others are built.

Since the marketing environment is broad and ever changing it is essential that you constantly work to relate the course material to current developments. Acquire the habit of 'scanning' the quality press for up-to-date articles, reviews and surveys relating business to its environments. Supplement this by tuning in weekly to a serious news analysis programme on TV or radio. Use the internet, if it is available at work or college, to access various websites with databases related to the environment. As you will see under 'Examination hints' later in this unit, you will need to be prepared for broad questions which test your grasp and general appreciation of the evolving marketing environment.

I would expect you to take 2–3 hours to work through this first unit, since it is larger than most, and suggest you allow around 5–6 hours to undertake the various activities suggested. These are very important since examiners will expect you to relate understanding to application. Besides your notepad and writing equipment you will need the following to complete this unit:

- Open a file section under the heading of 'Organization'.
- Annual reports of two or three large public limited companies (plcs)/public corporations, e.g. the BBC.
- Newspaper cuttings.
- Any available feedback or group discussion notes.
- Obtain a written statement of your organization's objectives and those of your department.

This first unit will also help you to familiarize yourself with the approach and style of our workbooks. It has been developed to ensure that you acquire not only the knowledge necessary for examination success but also the skills to apply that knowledge both in the examination and in your work as a professional marketer. You will find the boxed panels clearly signposted to help you practise, evaluate and extend your knowledge and these will be used throughout this workbook so that you can manage your own learning in terms of both pace and depth.

Study Tips

Start as you mean to go on in the organization of your study materials. From the very beginning of the course it is sound advice to:

- Use file dividers to index broad topic area notes.
- Add relevant materials, activity output, articles and clippings.
- Summarize related articles which may provide current examples for illustrating examination answers. The examiner *will* expect this!
- Cross-reference to other sections of the file since questions may address more than one part of the syllabus.
- Produce a set of implications for the marketer and/or the organization for every aspect of the syllabus.
- Incorporate past questions, examiner reports, model answers and revision notes when available.
- Edit and summarize into bullet points for easy memorizing.

In this way your file sections will be complete and facilitate ease of revision prior to the examination.

The importance of the marketing environment

The CIM defines marketing as:

> ... the management process which identifies, anticipates and supplies customer requirements efficiently and profitably.

This focuses attention on the importance of the marketing environment for practitioners and students alike. Identifying and anticipating customer requirements is impossible unless the organization looks outward from itself, to understand its external environment and the implications of changes taking place on its current and future profitability. Few businesses can afford to adopt a 'production orientation' and fail to respond to the evolving opportunities and threats in its marketplace.

Question 1.1

List the elements of the external environment you consider most important to the marketers' understanding of:

(a) Its potential customers
(b) Its potential profitability

Provide *four* different examples of external factors where you feel 'change' seems fastest.

Probably your initial thoughts were of existing and potential markets. The changing tastes and preferences of customers, their disposable incomes and the price and availability of substitutes will clearly be important, as will the size, strength and numbers of competitors. Less obvious are the changes in the broader environment which influence these market conditions. Demographic changes alter the population of various market segments while tax adjustments affect their purchasing power. Cultural and technical developments may exert even more powerful influences on the longer-term supply, demand, profitability and life cycle of different goods and services. Rising concern with the green environment, for example, has caused many businesses to modify their product offerings and methods of production.

No organization, whether small or large, public or private, profit or non-profit making can afford to ignore its environment. As the strategist H. I. Ansoff observed,

> the firm is a creature of its environment. Its resources, its income, its problems, its opportunities and its very survival are generated and conditioned by the environment.

Activity 1.1

Interpretation of this quotation formed part of the December 1998 paper. Better candidates demonstrated their understanding of each aspect of it in turn. Can you develop the idea of the organization as a creature of its environment? Themes could include:

- Must exist in an environment full of threats and opportunities.
- Must adapt to the unexpected.
- Environment full of rivals, competitors and allies – how do you relate to them?
- Pressure to adapt – survival of the fittest.
- Must be constantly aware of surroundings and understand what is going on.
- What are your strengths and weaknesses relative to others in the environment?
- Do you rely on size, or speed and flexibility, as your defensive strategy?

Can you brainstorm a list of themes for each of the other elements of the firm conditioned by the environment, i.e. resources; income(revenue); problems; opportunities and survival?
How will the analysis vary according to the size and nature of the firm?

(**Note** – this will be discussed in more detail in Unit 2.)

Societal concerns are often translated through the legislative process to impact on the freedom of business to manage. The marketer must always therefore be aware that the environment reflects the pressures from a range of interested groups to which a positive response may be called for. It is also the domain of actual or potential competitors, and is consequently ignored at the organization's peril.

Large firms, particularly multinationals, may be able to exert greater influence over their business situation but small firms may have the advantage in responding to the need for change more flexibly.

Definition 1.1

A *multinational* has operations in many host countries, but control and decision making remains in the parent country. The worldwide annual turnover of companies such as Exxon (Esso) and General Motors exceeds the gross domestic product of many of the smaller West European countries.

Before exploring the nature of this environment and the marketer's approach to it, we need to study the different forms of business organization involved in the economy.

Question 1.2

Can you identify a named example of each of the following forms of business organization?

Legal form   *Your example*
- Sole trader
- A partnership
- A cooperative
- A limited company
- A public limited company (plc)
- A nationalized industry - *Post Office*
- A municipal/local authority enterprise
- A franchisor - *McDonalds*
- A multinational - *ICI*
- A quango - *National Parks*
- A holding company

The purpose of organizations is to bring together people with common interests in a systematic effort to produce goods and services which they could not readily have produced as individuals. Organization allows for specialization and division of labour. This saves time and raises productivity. Organizations are also social in nature providing mutual support and opportunity for development. We all come into contact with organizations when we buy goods, attend lectures, deposit funds or go to the doctor's. Your list of examples should reflect this *diversity*. Whatever the form or purpose of the organization it will have common characteristics such as:

- A framework of written or tacit rules (e.g. articles of association)
- A decision-making hierarchy (e.g. AGM, board of directors, the MD)
- A record of proceedings (e.g. minutes of meetings)
- A means of coordinating efforts and resources to determine what and how to produce, in what quantities and using what channels of distribution.

These matters are explored in the CIM workbook *Effective Management for Marketing* while we are concerned with the types of business organization and their environment.

Business classifications

As marketers, we need to understand the diversity of business:

- Each address potential customers in different ways due to their differing objectives, strengths and weaknesses.
- Each are buyers and sellers in their own right, but multinationals purchase in bulk using professionals whereas small firms tend to source and sell locally.
- The implications for competition, growth and innovation vary with each.
- Their relative importance is changing with the growth in small businesses and self-employment, a shrinking public sector and the rising importance of entrepreneurial non-profit makers such as charities.

To understand the diversity of business we must first classify the various types and form a framework for understanding their characteristics.

The formal and informal economy

An economy may be thought of as being made up of three parts: the public sector, the private sector and the informal economy.

The public sector

This comprises all those activities involving provision of goods and services by the state. Revenue to finance these is raised by:

- Taxation on the rest of the economy
- Fees and charges
- Government borrowing.

These resources are then allocated to the various spending departments who plan provision according to government objectives rather than market forces. These may involve socially desirable objectives embracing some concept of fairness and civil rights and achieved through redistribution of income and wealth. The state has taken responsibility in a number of areas where provision by the private sector was not seen as adequate or appropriate. *Public goods* such as defence, law, order and emergency services comprised one major category while *merit goods* such as health, education and other social services provided the other. A number of other industries might come into the domain of the state for a variety of reasons including: strategic considerations, natural monopolies; job preservation and national security.

In post-war Britain direct government expenditure has accounted for 20–25 per cent of gross domestic product (GDP) although this has fallen recently with the privatization of many businesses. The government has also sought to introduce market disciplines into its remaining activities through various initiatives to make public services accountable to their users (e.g. hospital trusts, local management of schools opting out of local authority control and compulsory competitive tendering for local authority services). This is encouraging a degree of marketing orientation into a wide cross section of previously producer-oriented public services. More and more are realizing that only by relating their offering to the needs of the client will the necessary contract, budget or funding be forthcoming.

Public organizations of all types are becoming facilitators of services instead of direct providers. Rather than use directly employed labour to provide building, maintenance and waste disposal/refuse services, as in the past, these will now be purchased from private sector contractors. The role of public sector managers is to award the contracts, monitor quality, ensure cost and performance targets are met and above all secure value for money for the rate or tax payer. A recent example is the contracting of the first commercially run school following the pattern for privately operated facilities already set in the prison service. This general approach then allows the public agencies to concentrate on core services which no other sector can sensibly or willingly supply.

Powers are also devolved, through a large number of executive agencies known as quangos, to supervise a wide variety of activities. Appointed by ministers these are non-elected bodies with considerable powers over disposal of resources and important regulatory activities. They have expanded rapidly in recent years to number around 6000 and together they are estimated to control over one third of public spending. The public sector therefore owns or controls a complex variety of organizations but the distinction between these and organizations in other sectors are becoming increasingly blurred as more and more competition is introduced into their environment. Examples of public sector organizations who provide marketable goods and services are seen in Figure 1.1.

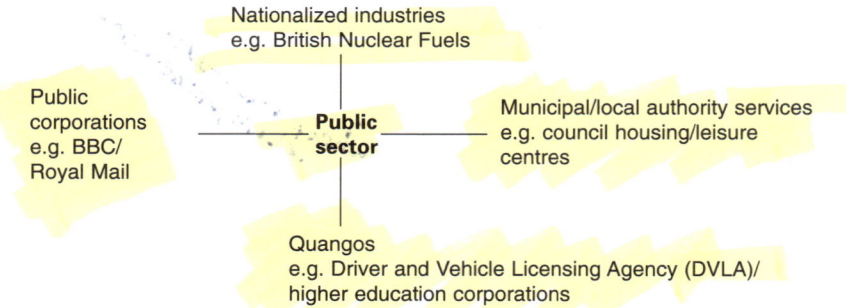

Figure 1.1
Public sector organizations providing marketable goods and services

The private sector

Sole trader
e.g. Pearson's Builders

Partnership
e.g. Dobson & Reed, Solicitors

Limited
company
e.g. C.R. Longley & Co. Ltd

**Private
sector**

PLC
e.g. Tesco plc

Cooperative
e.g. CRS

Franchise
e.g. Body Shop

Multinational
e.g. BP

Figure 1.2
Elements of the private sector

This sector accounts for the majority of domestic output and exports. It also produces most of the investment goods. Resources are privately owned and businesses compete to satisfy consumer wants and needs. Most are profit motivated and decide on what and how to produce by identifying and anticipating market demands, on the one hand, while combining and converting resource inputs efficiently, on the other. As you can see in Figure 1.2, a number of different trading organizations may be identified and we will explore their strengths and weaknesses below. Non-profit-making organizations include trade unions and employer associations, e.g. Confederation of British Industry (CBI).

Activity 1.4	Before you consider the advantages and drawbacks of these various types of private business organization spend a few minutes comparing the relative strengths and weaknesses of the public versus the private sector – use headings and bullet points to set these out. (**See** Activity debrief at the end of this unit.)

The informal economy

The activities of the public and private sectors constitute the formal economic activities of a country and their combined output is measured by GDP. However, three other sectors should be recognized and understood by the marketer. These are shown in Figure 1.3.

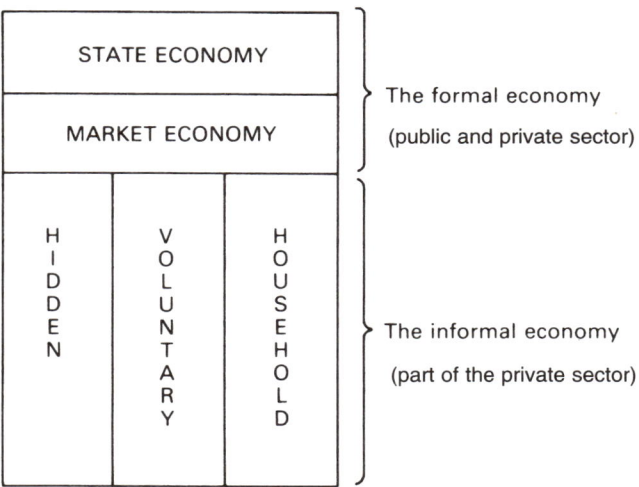

Figure 1.3
The formal and informal economies

The *household* economy includes the unpaid domestic services of wives and mothers (e.g. childcare, cooking and cleaning). This economy has undergone significant changes in recent years with women's liberation and increasing employment in the formal economy.

Do-it-yourself activities are also undertaken here and gardening, prop-

7

erty improvements, maintenance and repair have increased rapidly. None of these activities are, however, counted in the GDP statistics since no market transactions occur.

Marketers are clearly interested in the shifting patterns within this 'economy' because of the demand for goods and services to support activities within it, as well as the implications of the changing lifestyles and tastes of the various household members.

The *voluntary* economy includes those services undertaken by individuals and organizations for which no money payment is normally involved (i.e. non-commercial). It includes the activities of various unions, clubs and associations who act to promote the common interests of their membership. Many of these organizations have a special status and services are performed out of friendship or as acts of charity focused on the most needy in society. As such, they satisfy important needs and generate considerable social welfare but are not counted in the statistics on national output. Charities are controlled by the Registrar of Charities and attract generous tax concessions. Charities such as Oxfam, Help the Aged, Imperial Cancer Research and Scope seek to protect and assist the deprived and disadvantaged within society. They operate on very different principles to the private or public sector, with dedicated staff often working for little or no monetary reward. Rational economic calculation may not be the primary driving force but their performance has, through competition for funding, had to become more professional and marketing informed. Effectiveness may be measured in terms of the gross value of the contributions they raise, the degree of suffering they are able to alleviate and their success in raising the public profile of the cause that they represent. Their skill in marketing communications is clearly a determinant of the latter, while in Britain their trading activities have been reflected in the increasing presence of 'charity shops' on the high street. As such, they constitute an element of choice and competition with established retailers.

The *hidden* or shadow economy involves transactions and activities which are 'undeclared' for tax purposes. Moonlighting workers perform services outside their normal work for cash in hand and no questions asked! The marketer cannot afford to ignore this economy in terms of either hidden purchasing power or as low-cost competition. Small and medium businesses in the formal economy paying tax and national insurance, charging VAT and conforming with legislation may be at a considerable disadvantage compared to so-called 'cowboy operators'.

Estimated to account for as much as 10 per cent of GDP, this economy tends to grow with self-employment, high taxation and unemployment. Other elements of this hidden sector include pilferage, fiddles and outright illegal activities such as drug dealing and stolen goods. A new crackdown on tax avoidance and evasion was announced in the 1996 Budget targeted on this shadowy economy.

Extending Activity 1.1	Brainstorm the implications of the trend towards more working wives for • Retailers • Food suppliers • Household appliance manufacturers. Why has DIY increased and which businesses are most affected by this 'self-service' trend. Can you think of 'business opportunities' that have arisen from this? Is the hidden economy growing or shrinking? Justify your answer. (**See** Activity debrief at the end of this unit.)

Another important way of classifying business is according to the sector it operates in. The government has a comprehensive framework which places businesses into classes, groups and activities as part of its annual measurement of national output. Table 1.1 gives an indication of the significant changes in the relative importance, in terms of employment, of different sectors over a comparatively short period of time.

The primary sector includes agriculture, fisheries and forestry. Industrialization brought about a dramatic decline in its share of employment as seen in the shift of the 60 per cent across the chart. By the start of this century the majority were employed in industry which included manufacturing, energy and construction, but again this had fallen considerably by 1981 as service employment became dominant. Manufacturing had already shrunk to under 20 per cent of employment in 1997 and some, like Professor Stonier in his book *The Wealth of Information* predict a fall to as low as 10 per cent by early next century.

Table 1.1   Percentage sectoral change in employment patterns over time

Sector/Time	1801	1901	1981	2010	2041
Primary	60		4		
Secondary		60		10 est.	
Tertiary			60		
Quaternary					60

[handwritten margin note: agriculture/forestry — manufacturing — service — personal services —]

The quaternary sector involves personal rather than business services (e.g. health, education, leisure and other personal services). This may represent the areas where humans have a comparative employment advantage over computer-based technology in the next century.

Extending Activity 1.2	• Draw up a list of marketing employment specialisms which you consider will continue to exist as job opportunities in the year 2010 and those that will not, due to computer-based developments. • When you next visit your local convenience store or hairdressers ask the proprietors about the advantages and drawbacks of being a sole trader. Compare this with your expectations arising from reading the following sections. • Why do you think professional people and building contractors prefer partnerships to sole trader status? Check your answer the next time you have dealings with them.

The legal form of trading organizations

Sole trader

Characteristics
- Oldest type, simplest to form – self employment
- Unincorporated – business carried on in own name
- Ownership and control in a single person
- Individual assumes all rights/duties
- No separate legal existence – business = individual
- No disclosure of information bar to tax authorities.
- No limit on employees – may employ >100
- Farming/personal services/building/retail
- May originate in the hidden economy

Merits	Disadvantages
Minimum formalities/privacy	Unlimited liability for any debts
Complete control/no consultation	Raising capital difficult:
Favourable tax treatment	own funds/plough back/family
Highly motivated/single-minded	Specialized and risky – banks view
Least costly to form	Jack of all trades/narrow outlook
Close to customers/employees	Depend on health/lack continuity
Flexible/attend to detail	Self-exploitation – work long hours
Niches where limit to market	Competition from large/small
Exemption from legislation/VAT	Lack management skills
Personal satisfactions – status	No-one to share burden

Of over 3.7 million enterprises in Britain today (there were 2.5 million in 1979), 97 per cent employ less than 20 employees (equivalent to one third of total employed outside government) and an estimated 80 per cent are sole traders. Small firms and the sole trader are the predominant form in terms of numbers but not in terms of contribution to total output. However, all firms employing less than 100, outside government, now account for over 50 per cent of turnover, up from 40 per cent in 1979.

Found in sectors where entry barriers are low and capital requirements limited, few sole traders would be defined as entrepreneurial. Perhaps 10 per cent of the total might fall into this category and even here their inventiveness is not always sufficient to produce innovation. They will be weak compared to well-resourced companies so that even if new product developments make it to market they often face fierce competition and alternative offerings. Limited capital restricts their growth while excessive competition often requires hard work and long opening hours just to survive. Their social and economic lives tend to merge, and while they are motivated by self-interest they also bear all of the risks. They are often under pressure from larger businesses, e.g. according to *Verdict*, the share of specialist food retailers fell from 10.5 to 6.5 per cent between 1989 and 1996. Many are self employed in name only, working exclusively under contract.

It is difficult to know the precise number of such enterprises since they merge into the hidden economy.

Partnerships

Characteristics
- Unincorporated
- Two or more in common with a view to profit
- No more than 20, bar certain professions
- Form an agreement or are bound by 1890 Act
- Unlimited liability and jointly liable
- Share management/profits/losses
- No legal personality

Merits	Disadvantages
Able to raise more capital	Unlimited liability unless 'Limited'
Pool expertise/mutual support/funds	still must be at least one partner fully liable
More chance to specialize	Lack of legal identity – dissolves if
No corporation tax on business	death/disagreement = expense/trouble
	Potential disagreements
	Frozen investment

This form is much more attractive to the professions where capital requirements are limited in many cases and codes of conduct limit the risk of financial malpractice. Legal formalities are few and privacy is high. However, recent high profile and costly legal settlements involving poor financial advice given by accountancy firms to corporate clients (Ernst and Young and Merry-Go-Round Clothing, $4 billion US law suit) has caused at least one of the largest (KPMG) to opt for the company form. For most other businesses the company form is much more attractive.

Registered company

Characteristics

- Incorporated, separate legal entity – enter contracts, etc.
- Formed under 1985 Companies Act
- Confers various rights and duties
- Members contribute capital and own shares
- Dominant form
- Liability limited to amount invested or guaranteed

Public company (plc)
Two or more members
£50,000 and two directors
Offer shares to the public
Requires Business Certificate
before trading/borrowing
Similar legislation elsewhere (e.g.
'inc' in the USA/
'Sdn Bhd' in Malaysia)

Private company (Ltd)
Minimum two/£100 authorized
capital
One director plus a Secretary
Offence to offer shares to public –
friends OK
Trade once incorporation certificate
received
Typically family business
Raising additional bank funds
easier (personal guarantees may be
needed)

A registered company has a number of duties and must also submit to the Registrar of Companies:

- *Memorandum of association*: regulates external affairs/protects investors and suppliers/states name (registered versus business), liability, objectives and scope of business
- *Articles of association*: regulate internal administration – issue/transfer of shares, shareholder rights, directors' powers, accounting procedures, etc.
- *Statutory declaration of compliance* with the relevant Act
- *Independently audited annual accounts and directors report* (smaller firms of less than 50 employees provide a summary only)

Note: 'Unlimited liability' companies are exempt from filing accounting data.

Duty of care and trust on all directors

Public companies must also hold an AGM and comply with Stock Exchange regulations

Merits
Separate legal entity
Limited liability of owners
Greater financial capability
Easy transfer of ownership
Able to fund innovation/new
product development
Customers feel reassured

Disadvantages
Special and double taxation
Complex/costly to form
Disclosure requirements
Government regulations
Inflexibility of size
Impersonality

Many companies hold shares in other enterprises which they may have formed or acquired. If these exceed more than 50 per cent of the voting rights the business is termed a *holding company*. Such holdings may sometimes form a pyramid, with the *ultimate* holding company having overall control.

Activity 1.5	Keep your eye on the company section of a quality newspaper (e.g. *Financial Times*) for a company seeking plc status and offering shares for sale to the public. Read the preamble to the Offer and list the advantages of this course of action to the business. What are the potential drawbacks?
	Ask any friends, colleagues or family who own shares how often they have attended an AGM. Try and explain the answers they give and draw conclusions as to who exercises the real control.
	(**See** Activity debrief at the end of this unit.)

In undertaking this activity you might reflect on several factors:

- The ability to raise considerable amounts of capital is the main attraction of the plc but what about the 'costs' of raising funds this way?
- What are your feelings about the degree of scrutiny required by the Companies Act?
- Does a quotation on the Stock Exchange force the business to think short term rather than long term as some commentators suggest?
- Why have some public companies decided to buy back their shares (e.g. Virgin Group, the Body Shop)?
- Doesn't going public make you vulnerable to a takeover and what if the 'Offer' flops?
- Why have increasing numbers chosen 'Unlimited company' status since the law allowed exemption from filing accounts (i.e. financial affairs are kept private)?
- City institutions produce pressure to perform, and open trading of shares brings the danger of a hostile takeover bid.

Cooperative

Characteristics

- 1844 Rochdale pioneers in retailing
- Governed by Industrial and Provident Societies Act
- Worker ownership/control but falling numbers/mergers
- Limited liability but one member, one vote
- Self-help not profit maximizing via management committee
- Equitable distribution of dividend *if a surplus is made*

Comment

A significant but declining force in grocery retailing (food share fell from 7.6 to under 5 per cent between 1990 and 2000) in the face of competition from the better-managed and more focused multiples, the CRS has been forced to merge and specialize in other niches. There are other worker cooperatives among farmers and craft workers but these are not organized under the same Act. They tend to establish in times of recession or rapid structural decline in the industries concerned. Producer coops doubled in the 1980s but suffer weaknesses in attracting managers of the right calibre and raising capital for large-scale ventures. The Scott Bader Commonwealth, a chemical concern, is the most-quoted industrial example with an interesting constitution which includes among other things: a limit of 350 employees per unit, a maximum remuneration spread of 1:7 and no dismissals.

Franchising

Characteristics

- Franchisor sells the right to market a product under its name to a franchisee
- Separate entities but interdependent businesses
- Rapid growth especially retailing (e.g. McDonald's, the Body Shop)
- Ready-made opportunity for an entrepreneur with capital wishing to minimize risks of a new venture (90 per cent survive beyond three years)

Activity 1.6	• Identify a franchise business and a 'manager'-run outlet of a national company in your locality. • Observe the quality of service in the two outlets • Assess the relative strengths and weaknesses of the two • Consider *why* franchising has become such an important form of business organization and *what* makes it so customer orientated.

In undertaking this activity take account of a 'typical' agreement:

Franchisor agrees to	Franchisee agrees to
Provide business format/initial training	Pay an initial sum to franchisor
Supplies of product and quality control	Pay a percentage of profit to franchisor
Promotional support (e.g. advertising)	Buy supplies of product from franchisor
	Maintain standards laid down

The public services

The public corporations

- Publicly owned, controlled and accountable via Ministers to Parliament
- Separate legal entities created by Statute or Royal Charter (e.g. Royal Mint)
- Boards of management appointed by ministers
- Financed from revenue raised or central government funding
- Designed to be commercially independent but subject to ministerial control
- Intended to secure long-term strategic objectives and control of the economy
- Lack of competition and conflicting objectives led to inefficiency
- Susceptible to pressure group activity, especially trade unions

The regulated plcs

- The bulk of the nationalized industries were privatized in the 1980s and 1990s
- They were sold:

  Direct to the public (e.g. BT) or to management/employee buyouts (e.g. National Freight Corporation)
  To other companies (e.g. Rover to British Aerospace and subsequently to BMW)
  In parts (e.g. British Rail hotels, rolling stock)
- Those remaining are either unprofitable or unsaleable (nuclear) or ideologically difficult (Royal Mail, London Underground – though private investment allowed in 1998)
- The transfer of ownership to private shareholders was justified under:

Political factors	Economic factors
Reduced role of the state	Achieve efficiency improvements
Deregulation of the economy	Increased competition and choice
Encourage shareholding democracy among customers	Pressure on management to become marketing orientated
Enable worker share-ownership	Improve industrial relations
Provide freedom to manage	Exploit new opportunities
Cut borrowing (PSBR) and taxes	Supply side rises in productivity
Cut costs	

Public sector borrowing requirement

- The creation of private monopolies in water, electricity, gas and telecoms was counterbalanced by new regulators with considerable powers to enforce efficiency gains and improvements in service. Recent public concerns that some regulators have become increasingly influenced by the regulated (e.g. OFWAT, OFLOT) have, however, resulted in an enquiry by the Greenbury Committee on public standards.

Local authorities

Services provided by local government include, among others, fire and police, road maintenance, consumer protection, recreation, environmental health, education and even airports. They are managed by elected councillors through full-time professional officers. As in the rest of the public sector, they have been subject to radical structural and operational changes over the past decade. Central government control has increased, but authorities have been encouraged to forge mutually beneficial links with local business communities. Exposure to market forces through compulsory competitive tendering has transformed the council officer role into that of a 'facilitator' rather than a direct provider of local services.

Vision and the organization's mission

It is clear that most economies are composed of a diversity of organizational types each seeking to achieve their objectives within a challenging environment. Before considering the nature of that environment it is important to appreciate what organizations are trying to achieve and what is driving their behaviour. Buchanan and Huczynski defined organizations as social arrangements for the controlled performance of collective goals. The marketer needs to understand how goals are formulated and the importance of mobilizing the contribution of all those within the organization towards their achievement.

Every business organization, whether a sole trader or a multinational requires vision. Business vision may be defined as the ability to imagine or foresee the future prospects and potential for the organization. Effective vision is closely linked to the marketing environment since it requires the ability to discern future conditions in the industry or market concerned. It is a critical requirement at the strategic level of all organizations and is normally the responsibility of the board of directors. Vision, then, involves understanding the future, anticipating how markets, tastes and technologies will evolve and the mobilizing of resources to translate the vision into reality. It is key to business success and competitive advantage and explains why the marketing environment is so central to the marketer's role and importance. An early example of vision was the declaration by the chairman of Coca-Cola in 1927 that the product should *always be within an arm's length of desire*. The company is now in the global top ten by market capitalization. More recently Bill Gates formulated a vision of a *PC with Windows software on every desk*. In 1999 it became the largest company in the world.

The Coca-Cola vision was translated into a business mission to make the drink an integral part of consumer's lives. Management was also able to set clear objectives – that the brand be available everywhere the consumer seeks liquid refreshment. Converting a vision into a mission statement produces a strong sense of overall purpose and direction. It seeks to establish 'what is our business/what should it be' and distil the fundamental reason for the organization's existence. It encompasses the scope of its core activities and endeavours to distinguish itself from other organizations of its type by clearly defining its uniqueness. Finally, it may provide a set of corporate values intended to unify the various stakeholders in the organization and in effect generate a strong sense of mission.

A business mission statement would normally refer to a number of the following key elements:

- What is its philosophy, values, priorities and aspirations.
- What are its key strengths, competencies and competitive edge.
- Who are its main customers.
- What are the main products and services offered.
- What markets does it compete in.
- What core technology does it use.
- What are its responsibilities towards society.
- What is its position regarding key stakeholders.

Activity 1.7

Consider the following and decide if the elements would fit in a mission statement.

IBM principles

- The marketplace is the driving force behind everything we do.
- At our core, we are a technology company with an overriding commitment to quality.
- Our primary measures of success are customer satisfaction and shareholder value.
- We operate as an entrepreneurial organization with a minimum of bureaucracy and a never-ending focus on productivity.
- We never lose sight of our strategic vision.
- We think and act with a sense of urgency.
- Outstanding, dedicated people make it happen, particularly when we work together as a team.
- We are sensitive to the needs of all employees and to communities in which we operate.

Has your organization and/or college a formal mission statement? If so, how good do you consider it to be? If not, is there an informal/unwritten mission for the organization? Is the formal statement purely for 'public' consumption with other goals actually pursued in practice?

The importance of the mission statement is seen in a number of dimensions:

- As a clear statement of purpose it allows more specific, relevant and realistic objectives to be formulated.
- It defines a common purpose for the organization so mobilizing the loyalty and commitment of staff and management.
- It provides a clear statement for external stakeholders of the values and future direction of the business.
- It acts as a control or benchmark for comparison by senior managers in evaluating the success of the business in realizing its purpose.
- It can motivate employees where the stated values of the organization coincide with their own. The mission is part of the corporate culture and this is the glue that unifies contributions.
- With over three-quarters of larger companies with formal mission statements, there is strong evidence of corporate belief in their contribution and importance.
- The mission statement must not, however, be allowed to submerge the arrival of contradictory environmental information which demands immediate decisions in order to amend its purpose, e.g. IBM's mainframe dominance in the 1980s blinded it to the emerging reality of distributed computing power.

Study the following mission statement and statement of intent:

The University of Huddersfield's prime objective is to enable students to reach their full potential by equipping them with the knowledge, attitudes and skills they need to meet with confidence the requirements of work and society in the twenty-first century. It will draw its students from those seeking learning opportunities throughout their lives as well as from suitably qualified school leavers and postgraduates, from both the United Kingdom and from overseas.
The University will, over the period of the plan:

- Continue to provide students with programmes to equip them with the knowledge, skills and attitudes required for the twenty-first century.
- Continue to provide programmes leading to self-standing awards geared mainly to employment needs.
- Provide cost-effective higher education.
- Enrol 800 international, 400 research and 2200 students on postgraduate taught courses.
- Increase the number of home students from under-represented groups.
- Promote good practice in teaching and provide programmes that satisfy students' and employers' demands for content, delivery and outcome.
- Provide all staff and students with access to networked computer facilities at, or near to, their normal place of work.
- Achieve Investors in People Award in 2000 and balanced budgets that allowed planned investment in infrastructure.

(University of Huddersfield Strategic Plan 1996–2001)

- Distinguish mission statements from objectives for the university.
- Use this framework to draw up a mission statement for your own organization or one with which you are familiar.
- Compare and contrast the above mission statement for an educational institution with one for a business.

(**See** Activity debrief at the end of this unit.)

Whereas business vision refers to the future, mission represents the current generalized statement of intent and the means to realize it. Objectives by contrast are the ends to be achieved in order to fulfil the business mission. Organizations exist to pursue objectives. They are specific and more concrete guideposts by which the organization defines standards to be accomplished in key result areas such as profitability and customer service. Objectives can be classified into strategic, tactical and operational categories and each are linked into a planning process which seek to identify and implement effective strategies to achieve them:

- *Strategic objectives* are broad long-term goals set by senior management. Examples include:
  - Achieve and maintain a position of leadership in specified markets;
  - To maintain a product portfolio where those introduced less than three years ago account 25 per cent of sales;
  - To earn an average rate of return on capital of 20 per cent and earnings growth of 10 per cent p.a.
- *Tactical objectives* are set by middle managers and relate to functional areas like marketing. They tend to be more measurable, for example:
  - Open ten new stores this year;
  - Reduce operating costs by 5 per cent p.a.;
  - Achieve preferred supplier status with designated customers.
- *Operational objectives* are set by first-line management on a short-time horizon:
  - Daily production targets;
  - Reduce customer complaints by 5 per cent per month.

General organizational objectives

Your first task is to summarize your understanding of the various terms used so far:

- *Business purpose* This is the broad role defined for business by society (e.g. to manage scarce resources efficiently and effectively to maximize the society's welfare).
- *Business goals* These provide a broad sense of direction to organizational activities. Often used interchangeably with objectives, they normally have a longer time horizon. Goals are future outcomes to achieve (e.g. to become the leading consumer marketing company in the Far East).
- *Business mission* A fundamental statement defining the place and purpose of the organization's existence within its environment. Unique to the business, it usually refers to its primary market/product/technology.
- *Business vision* The ability to imagine or foresee the future prospects or potential for the organization.
- *Business values* Moral or ethical standards applied in the pursuit of business objectives (e.g. quality, honesty, customer satisfaction, etc.).
- *Business objectives* Targets or ends to be achieved in order to fulfil the goals and mission of the organization.
- *Strategies* These are large-scale programmes involving interaction with the environment in order to achieve objectives (e.g. become least-cost supplier in the market in order to achieve No. 1 position).
- *Plans* These are the means devised for implementing strategies.

In this part of the unit we will focus on organizational objectives in more general terms before considering the internal and external influences upon them. So far in Unit 1 we have studied the diversity of organizations across the business, public and voluntary sectors. In a mixed economy it is not surprising that the nature of objectives will vary. We may identify a number of orientations:

Organization	*Primary orientation*
Private business	Profit
Cooperative	Members' returns
Public corporation	Public service + profit
Social service	Public service
Interest group	Member self-interest
Charitable	Alieviating suffering

As we shall see, however, the actual objectives pursued by any one organization may be both diverse and complex. They will also be subject to considerable influence by the environment.

17

- List the main objectives you consider would be pursued by a competitive business. Your own organization would be ideal.
- Now list your own personal and career objectives.
- How do your objectives relate to those of the business?

Do they conflict? Or
Are they complementary?

- What are the objectives of the sales or marketing department in the business? Do they conflict with those of the business as a whole?

You will probably have put profit at the top of your business objectives list, but how many others could you think of? What about basic survival as a motive or the desire for growth? Did you think about the personal objectives of those who actually decide the strategies and allocate the resources in business? These might diverge from the interests of the shareholders.

What of your own goals? Do these include such things as a high and rising salary, plenty of perks, training and career development, promotion, job security and a satisfying job? If so then perhaps your ambitions would not be best served in a business pursuing maximum profits.

What of your marketing department? Is not its inclination to build sales and market share even at the expense of profitability? Should it be constrained by the financial director in this regard or is it the 'right' objective? Clearly, there are a number of difficult questions to be addressed here so we must approach it step by step.

Study Tips

Don't just accept at face value what you read in a text or a newspaper. Think through what is said, carefully and logically. Do not be afraid to have your own opinion, but be prepared to justify it to others. Critical awareness of the subject matter is something that is welcomed by the examiner but usually only evident among excellent candidates. Make the investment this needs in 'thinking' and 'discussion' time. It will repay handsome dividends.

Survival

This is a basic drive in all businesses and relates to the needs we have as individuals for security and the satisfaction of our economic wants. The jobs of management and workers depend on it, and this can lead to considerable sacrifices being made in times of economic hardship. The Japanese in particular are renowned for their willingness to accept cuts in salary and redouble efforts to restore corporate fortunes.

Many sole proprietors would continue in business even at the cost of exploiting themselves and family workers. The directors of public limited companies will also be aware of the need to avoid the possibility of a hostile takeover bid. These often lead to the removal of top management, especially where the bid arose due to their underperformance in the eyes of shareholders. The press frequently reports examples, such as Hilton Hotels' $6.5 billion hostile bid for ITT, who own the prestigious Sheraton chain, or Gucci's unwelcome approach by LV Moet Hennessy.

Society is faced with the reality of scarce resources relative to its needs and wants. It therefore requires that these are managed effectively and is prepared to see businesses fail so that their resources are released for use by the more competent managers.

Businesses must justify their use of resources over and over again if they are to survive and avoid possible takeover or liquidation. This means that they must make a profit!

Profit and profit maximization

This is the most-quoted business objective, although, strictly, it is more a motivation than an end in itself. It does, however, provide a *measurement system* for assessing business performance. Profit maximization implies that businesses seek to make not only a profit but the maximum possible profit through time. Profit, as shown in Figure 1.4, is the difference between revenue and cost.

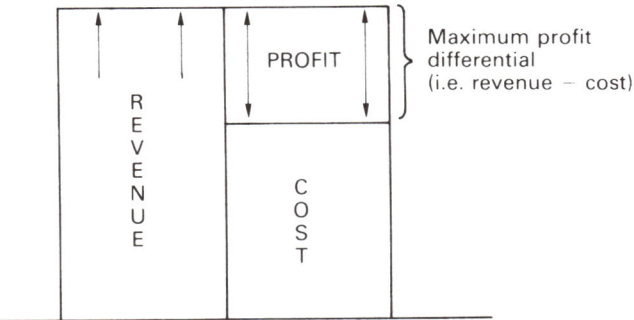

Figure 1.4
Pursuit of the maximum profit differential

Businesses are viewed as rational and self-interested in their decisions, seeking to allocate resources so as to maximize this profit differential by:

- *Supplying those goods that consumers most wish to buy.* Profit and marketing-orientated firms will carefully research customer needs, anticipate their changing preferences and supply whenever the addition to total revenue exceeds the change in costs.
- *Combine resource inputs to produce planned output at minimum possible cost* Business will not satisfy consumer wants to gain revenue irrespective of cost. They will cease to supply further units when additional cost exceeds the price received. At this output they will ensure that factor inputs are combined so as to produce at least cost.
- *Responding quickly to changes in supply and demand conditions* If consumer tastes change or input prices alter then it will profit the firm to adjust the marketing mix or production methods accordingly.

The pursuit of maximum profit therefore answers two of the basic economic problems arising from scarcity:

1 What to produce and in what quantities and
2 How to produce them

It also provides a dynamic growth incentive to the business system. As can be seen in Figure 1.5, business has the incentive not only to produce efficiently to satisfy existing preferences but also to:

- Innovate new and improved products that enhance value for money for consumers and revenue for the firm
- Invest in research and development of more efficient methods of production to reduce costs.

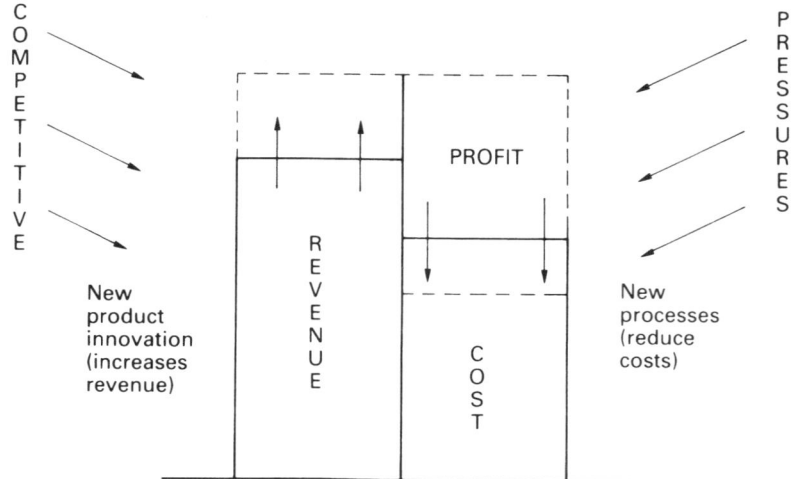

Figure 1.5
The carrot and the stick to profit maximization

Maximizing profit would appear to promise an ideal allocation of resources by rewarding those businesses that produce and market the right goods, in the right quantities, using the most efficient methods and ploughing back resources into producing economic growth through new products and better methods.

Activity 1.9	- Taking a business with which you are familiar, list practical suggestions which, if implemented, would improve profitability. - Review the suggestions on your list and consider this question: Why has the business not already taken steps to exploit this extra profit potential? - Is the profit objective/motive strong enough, by itself, to produce the outcome mentioned above?

What if businesses were content with just modest profits or decided to pursue other objectives? What if they are run by salaried managers, who stand to gain nothing from extra profit, rather than the shareholders? What if they are production-orientated and are not concerned with the consumers' real needs? These possibilities can only arise in the absence of *full and free competition*.

When competition is very strong, firms must market what consumers demand, otherwise their competitors will, reducing market share and threatening the very survival of the business. Firms must be efficient, otherwise they will be undercut by lower-cost rivals. They must provide excellent service because the consumer is sovereign in such a situation.

No firm, no matter how profitable, can afford to stand still. Much of the profit earned has to be ploughed back into new product development and improved methods if the firm is to retain a competitive edge. Customers will not give a second thought to a badly managed business, which will go bankrupt or be taken over by firms better fitted to manage the resources, e.g. Facia Group, second largest retailer chain into receivership in March 1996.

Business therefore appears to be very much a treadmill when competition is strong. Even if an innovative business succeeds in making extra profits, this will merely attract new competitors into the market to erode away the rewards. However, as we shall now see, the scope for pursuing other objectives will be much greater where market imperfections exist or large firms dominate.

Question 1.3	If managers are rational and they have the choice between making either 'maximum possible profits' in the short term or just modest profits, can you think of any sound business reasons why it might be sensible to choose the latter? (**See** Activity debrief at the end of this unit.)

Market share

Observation suggests that many businesses seek to maximize sales *subject to a profit constraint*. There may indeed be a positive correlation between profit and market share, but beyond a certain point extra share may only be 'bought' at the expense of profit. Prices and margins will be trimmed or extra promotional expense incurred. This objective has been at the forefront of cellular telephone companies such as Orange, Cellnet and Vodafone as they have vied to expand 'pay as you talk' sales. A similar picture can be seen in internet connections (BT have withdrawn charges) and digital TV. So long as sufficient profit is made to keep shareholders content, then management may see an advantage in the stability and security of a dominant position.

Japanese exporters have been accused of pursuing this objective in the short run in order to drive out domestic competitors prior to raising prices and profits in the longer term. *Long-run versus short-run profits* is an important consideration. It is suggested that many quoted British companies are under considerable pressure from 'the City' to deliver buoyant short-run profits even at the expense of longer-term investment. Japanese and German companies, by contrast, are able to give greater emphasis to the long run due to the support of shareholding banks.

Question 1.4	How would marketing differ between a business looking for short-run profit and one seeking long-run profit? Think about the different emphasis in the marketing mix as well as the nature of long-term marketing investment payoffs. What sales and marketing strategies will produce long-run profitability?

Business growth

Question 1.5	What are benefits to management of a growing company? Identify a fast-growing company and determine the primary cause of the growth.

While growth and profits may be positively related, again after a certain point this will cease to be the case. The rapid growth in out-of-town grocery superstores appears to be a case in point. Alternatively, growth may require takeovers and acquisitions and these may prove unsuccessful, especially if they represent diversification into unfamiliar areas. It will also put pressure on the scarce management resource.

Growth is, however, attractive for a number of reasons:

- It is easier to resolve conflicts between stakeholders.
- It provides opportunities for promotion and job satisfaction.

- It increases market power and management status.
- It raises morale in general.

Management objectives

If management is not under severe competitive pressure, it may decide to *satisfice*. That is, it will produce satisfactory performance and profits. Where there is a *separation of ownership from management* there is no automatic incentive for professional management employees to maximize profits for shareholders.

The organization may operate with what is termed *organizational slack*. This is the difference between the cost level which would maximize profits and actual costs. These excessive costs would finance a number of 'unnecessary expenditures', for example:

- Buy market share
- Management perks
- Pet projects
- Excess staff assistants

Question 1.6

Can you identify slack in your organization?

How does management respond to a downturn in sales?

Activity 1.10

Scan the papers for a business or public sector organization facing adverse change in its environment and look for evidence of efforts to reduce organizational slack.

The idea of slack suggests that management may choose to have their own satisfactions as an objective. They will manage the business so as to maximize their security, income, status, power and job interest. They can also take in the slack without threatening core activities and programmes in times of adversity.

The existence of slack has underpinned government efforts to improve productivity in a range of public services. Lack of competition, the absence of a profit incentive and powerful stakeholder groups led to an accumulation of slack in health, education, local authorities, nationalized industries and the civil service.

Public sector organizations are intended to maximize benefits to society given a budget resource constraint. To eliminate pursuit of self-interested objectives and reduce budget deficits the government, you will recall, has:

- Deregulated markets
- Introduced internal markets
- Made services client-driven
- Introduced citizens' charters – setting service standards
- Insisted on compulsory competitive tendering
- Weakened the power of trade unions
- Attracted better-calibre managers
- Appointed powerful regulators to set price/performance standards.

As the objectives have become more customer-orientated in the public sector so the nature of these organizations have been transformed. The skills of the marketer have also come to the fore in the quest for more focused customer benefits.

How are goals established?

To understand how business goals change we must understand how they are formed. The board of directors are responsible for deciding objectives and formulating plans and policies to secure their effective achievement. The managing director is appointed to implement policy while non-executive directors are often invited onto the board of public companies to provide an external dimension to formulating objectives.

The key influences may be summarized as internal and external influences.

Internal influences

- The memorandum of association sets limits in the objects clause to the powers of a company. Pursuit of purposes outside these limits will be deemed *ultra vires* and therefore legally void. In practice this clause will be broadly defined to allow the directors to diversify outside their traditional business.
- The personal values and objectives of senior management will exert significant influence, particularly where they are represented on the board, e.g. the marketing director.
- The expectations of the internal decision makers and their degree of aversion to risk.
- The limits set by resource availability – a minimum return on capital may be required in order to attract the necessary internal and external funds to finance other objectives.
- Key individual and institutional shareholders.
- The force of inertia and past successes may prevent serious internal review of objectives.

External influences

- Successful businesses recognize the importance of matching the capabilities of the organization to its environment. Internal strengths and weaknesses must be set against external threats and opportunities.
- There are a variety of connected and external stakeholders whose interests and attitudes must be considered before objectives are set. Their contribution will often be crucial to the effective implementation of the objectives.
- Conflict between the interests of shareholders and various stakeholders may require compromise to retain their contribution to the achievement of set objectives.
- The competitive environment may constrain what are achievable objectives within a given time frame.
- A change in government will alter the objectives set in local and central government, while changes in legislation will define what is, and is not, achievable for private businesses.
- External interests may be represented on the board, e.g. worker or consumer directors.

What causes the goals to change?

Virtually every organization must periodically review its objectives if it is to survive and succeed. There are compelling reasons to regularly consider changes to goals:

- Most organizations operate in a dynamic and constantly changing environment.
- As these environmental forces threaten to throw the business off-course, management must respond proactively by setting a new direction and a renewed focus to unify the organization's efforts.
- Changes in consumer wants must be anticipated and responded to with matching goals.
- Changes in production possibilities transform resource availability and technological options.
- Opportunities and threats from the various environments represent new realities and require new responses.
- Objectives are intended to be achieved and so require renewal as this occurs.
- If control processes show that objectives are not being realized then a change to more realistic goals will provide more effective motivation for management and staff.
- A change in the chief executive or perhaps a merger or acquisition will tend to change the strategic goals.

Larger organizations may adopt corporate planning to formalize the above process. According to Cole (G. A. Cole, *Management Theory and Practice*, DPP, 2nd edition, 1986):

> Corporate planning is the continuing process by which the long-term objectives of the organization may be formulated and subsequently attained by means of long-term strategic actions.

Strategic objectives are therefore the outcome of the above influences and considerations but on, say, a five- to ten-year rolling basis with on-going rigorous review and correction.

The organization as an open system

It is clear from the above section that the objectives of an organization must be reviewed and set by reference to internal and external considerations. Understanding this interplay between internal organization and the wider environment has led to the organization being viewed as an open system. This approach focuses on the interrelated activities which enable inputs to be converted into outputs and provides a very useful framework for gaining insight into the relationships that prevail between the organization and its marketing environment.

There are many different systems we could identify: ourselves, the marketing department, our organization, the business system, the marketing environment, wider society, the global economy, the eco-system, our galaxy and the solar system. Each has a boundary which represents its interface with the others. We will be particularly concerned with the interface between the organization and its environment. This is represented in Figure 1.6 and possesses the following common characteristics:

- Productive inputs and energy is received/obtained from the marketing environment.
- The organization adds value by converting these inputs into desired outputs.
- They discharge their outputs into their environment – both positive and negative.
- They apply control by monitoring for feedback on achievement of objectives.

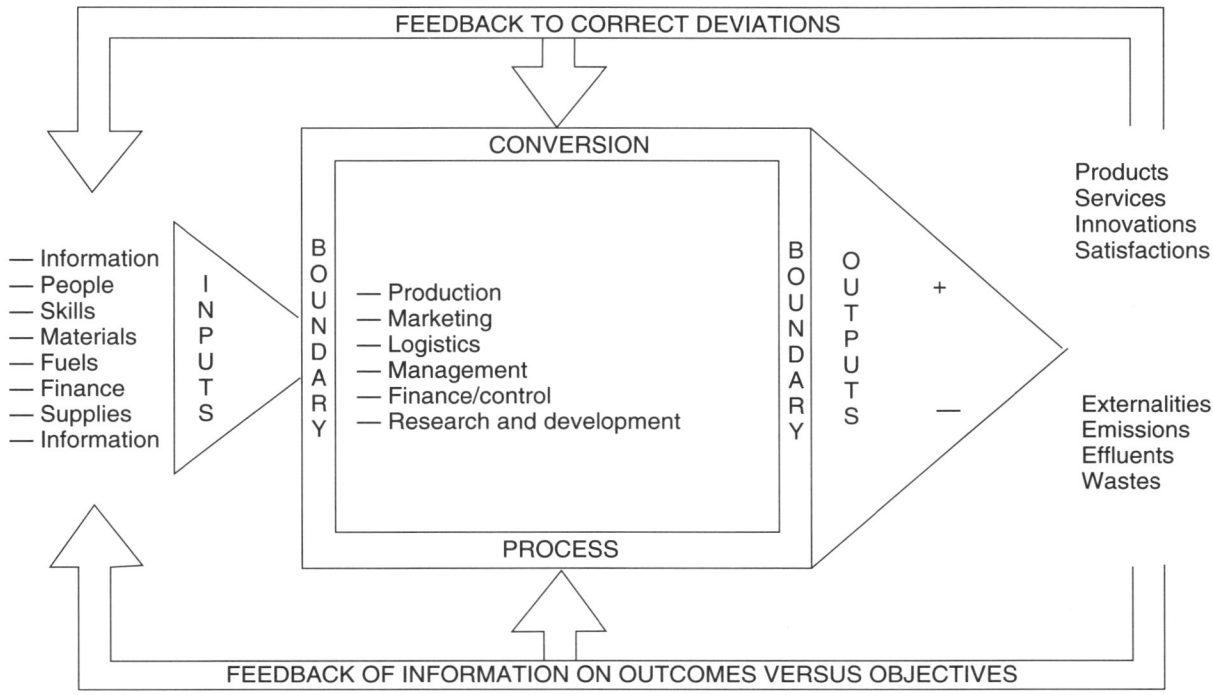

THE MARKETING ENVIRONMENT

FEEDBACK TO CORRECT DEVIATIONS

CONVERSION

— Information
— People
— Skills
— Materials
— Fuels
— Finance
— Supplies
— Information

INPUTS

BOUNDARY

— Production
— Marketing
— Logistics
— Management
— Finance/control
— Research and development

BOUNDARY

OUTPUTS

+

—

Products
Services
Innovations
Satisfactions

Externalities
Emissions
Effluents
Wastes

PROCESS

FEEDBACK OF INFORMATION ON OUTCOMES VERSUS OBJECTIVES

THE MARKETING ENVIRONMENT

Figure 1.6 Business as an open system

Open systems are interdependent with their marketing environment and must adapt to change if they are to survive and develop. Open systems are vital where the environment is unstable or uncertain. Closed systems on the other hand do not respond to change and only function well in stable conditions.

Open systems will also scan the external environment for opportunities and threats. When the organization adapts to this external environment it will impact on its *effectiveness* whereas when it adapts its internal structure and organization it will impact on its *efficiency*.

Activity 1.11

Spend a few moments applying systems thinking to the human body. Think about inputs/conversion and output and the interface between some of the sub-systems involved, e.g. nervous system, memory, digestion and the senses. How adaptive are you to your environment? How effective is your interface with your marketing manager?

The interface between marketing and other functions

Most systems also divide into sub-systems as can be seen in Figure 1.6. The boundaries between sub-systems are referred to as interfaces although the scope of departments, such as marketing, will vary. In some organizations, for example, purchasing or sales may be a separate function while in others they are integrated. Successful adaption requires that relationships are coordinated. Individual departments which seek to maximize their own outcomes inevitably detract from an optimum outcome for the system as a whole. Marketing is one function which clearly operates across the external boundary with the wider environment but must also establish and maintain effective relationships across the internal boundaries with key departments such as finance, research and development and production. Production is often more akin to a closed system and it falls to marketing to ensure their effective contribution to the evolving demands of the environment. We can identify three fundamental cases of business focus related to the environment:

1   Production orientation.
2   Sales orientation.
3   Marketing orientation.

Each one has implications for organizational effectiveness and the degree to which it is outward looking. Every business tends to evolve from an inward-looking focus on production efficiency and product quality through greater sales awareness to comprehensive operational emphasis on anticipating and satisfying changing consumer requirements.

Question 1.7	What is the orientation of your own organization or college? Justify your answer.

Where *production orientation* prevails the emphasis is on design and operations management. Technical or finance specialists will tend to dominate the hierarchy in which the sales function will be minor with no representation on the board. Examples are found in niche markets where demand far exceeds supply (e.g. Morgan cars) or in the public services like education and health before recent efforts to break their monopoly. The latter tended to be bureaucratic, dominated by professionals with little incentive to inquire into or respond to the real needs of their captive consumers.

In the absence of a seller's market and where competition is increasing, businesses soon learn that producing efficiently is not enough. A natural reaction was to focus on salesmanship and promotion to overcome consumer resistance. The sales director would gain equal status with operations and finance to ensure volume and market share.

Exam Tip	What orientation are you going to adopt in the examination?

- A technical orientation, where all your attention goes into getting the information down *you* feel is appropriate?
- A selling orientation with lots of gimmicks to try to convince the examiner you know what you are talking about but without that ring of confidence?
- Or a marketing orientation where you focus on what the examiner (i.e.) the customer really wants – a clear answer focused on what the question requires.

A *sales orientation*, however, gave no real thought to the needs and requirements of the final customer. The requirement was not just to change the name of sales to the marketing department but also to focus the efforts of the whole organization to this end. A marketing orientation is now recognized as a survival condition in a competitive and rapidly changing environment. As T. Levitt observed:

Selling focuses on the needs of the seller, marketing on the needs of the buyer. Selling is pre-occupied with the seller's need to convert his product into cash; marketing with the idea of satisfying the needs of the customer by means of the product and the whole cluster of things associated with creating, delivering and finally consuming it.

Activity 1.12

A marketing orientation places the customer at the centre of the whole organization's attention. With this in mind, make a list of desirable organizational characteristics that would achieve this.

Taking an organization of your choice, design an organizational form that would place it close to its customers.

(**See** Activity debrief at the end of this unit.)

The main difficulty confronting a business wishing to achieve a marketing orientation is the change in organization and culture implied. Functional divisions within the business create potential barriers, preventing a cohesive response to customer needs. Unless there is drive and strong leadership from the top to establish the philosophy throughout the organization they will fail to pull together, reverting instead to narrow departmental interests. If the organization is unable to get its own internal act together it is unlikely to respond successfully to environmental change.

Managing the marketing environment: a contingency approach

This approach to managing organizations renounces the idea of a universal formula and relies instead on tailoring the response to the specific situation encountered. Research by Lawrence and Lorsch (P. R. Lawrence and J. W. Lorsch, *Organization and Environment: Managing differentiation and integration*, 1969, Irwin) suggests that there is no one best means of managing organizations to meet their current objectives in an environment of uncertain or volatile change. Marketers must therefore identify and then adapt continuously to the conditions that are found to prevail in the present and the future.

Contingency management is the logical development of a systems perspective. This framework for analysing complex inter-dependency provides the basis for deciding appropriate responses to the challenge of environmental change (some of the techniques used to identify and meet this challenge will be explored in Unit 10 of this workbook). However, as the following table and conclusions suggest, the marketer must work hard to ensure that all departments are pulling towards a marketing orientation.

Function/criteria	Goal orientation	Time horizon	Inter-dept. relationships	Formality/structure
Marketing	Market share	Medium term	+++	Medium
Sales	Revenue max.	Short term	++	Medium
Production	Cost minimize	Short term	−/+	High
Research/dev.	New products	Long term	−/+	Low
Finance	Profit	Short term	+	High

The implications are:

- Differences in attitudes and departmental culture lead to potential conflicts.

- The more dynamic and complex the environment, the higher the degree of collaboration between departments that is required.
- High performance demands effective means of resolving conflicts.
- Marketing managers are important vehicles for integrating the work of the various functions in uncertain environments.
- Flexible and organic systems with open communications are most suited to changing conditions but large firms must still maintain a high degree of formality.

In conclusion we may note that many large organizations are under increasing global competitive pressure to become leaner, meaner and generally more innovative and responsive in the face of environmental change. A number of trends may be identified which are transforming the organization of such businesses:

- *Delayering* Reducing the number of levels in the organizational hierarchy. This speeds the flow of information to the top and decisions to the bottom of the chain of command.
- *Downsizing* Middle managers are stripped out of the organization and those who remain take over their duties, assisted by more effective information systems.
- *Outsourcing* Businesses focus on core activities and competencies while contracting third party operations to undertake peripheral activities.
- *Empowerment* Decision-making power is delegated to subordinates often operating in teamworking situations with day-to-day tactical matters determined without reference to higher authority.
- *Demerger* Reversing earlier trends towards conglomerate strength, Thorn-EMI, ICI-Zeneca, TransCo-British Gas and Hanson's four-way demerger is a vote for manageable focus.

Summary

In this unit we have seen that:

- A diversity of organizations exist in a mixed economy such as Britain's.
- The strengths of one form of organization are often the weaknesses of the other.
- An informal economy operates alongside the formally reported one.
- Organizational objectives are stepping stones along the road to achieving the corporate mission.
- Business objectives are varied and reflect different motivations.
- Objectives pursued reflect internal values as well as external influences and constraints.
- There is an important distinction between satisfying and maximizing behaviour.
- Businesses are open systems which rely on interaction with their environment for survival/growth.
- A major part of the work of the marketer is to manage the internal and external boundaries.
- The marketer should respond flexibly to the realities of the changing situation.
- A marketing-oriented structure is the key to effective achievement of objectives.

Study Tip

At the end of each unit you will find a summary of some of the main learning points to be found within it. If you don't fully understand a learning point then return to the relevant part of the unit and re-read it. Tick off the points as you feel you fully understand them.

Definition 1.2 5, 4, 6, 1, 2, 3.

Question 1.3 The case against profit maximization   Management may think twice about making as much profit as possible if:

- It involves taking high risks.
- It attracts new entrants to the market.
- It leads to an anti-monopoly investigation.
- It encourages wage demands which are unsustainable in the long term.
- It creates rising dividend expectations among shareholders.
- It is at the expense of sales and market share.
- It prejudices customers who perceive the profit as resulting from high prices and will turn to alternatives once available.

Activity 1.2 Ownership – private/public/mutual/cooperative; Legal form – limited company/sole proprietor/partnership; Control – directors/shareholders/workers/trustees; Sector – public/private/voluntary; Objectives – profit/public welfare/social responsibility; Accountability – to shareholders/ministers/customers; Activity – agriculture/manufacturing/services/utilities/construction; Size – small/SMEs/global.

Activity 1.3 One of your examples may have been your local DVLA. The marketing orientation of this quango might be questioned given the closure of many local offices and the need to queue for long periods at critical times of the month/year at regional centres. The service is often bureaucratic and far from customer focused with limited come-back available given the lack of democratic accountability. There are no alternative suppliers of licences. On the other hand, greater operational freedom has led to marketing initiatives to meet customer wants for personalized plates. It is closer to its customers than government departments and this may transform its culture.

Activity 1.4

Public sector	*Private sector*
Strengths (there are more)	
Provide essential but non-profit making services	Private ownership means initiative
Avoids wasteful duplication of expensive resources	Strong motivation to use resources well
Funds are easily raised through taxation	Funds are efficiently/effectively used
Can overcome failings in the market	Respond quickly to market signals
Employees are motivated by public service	Employees are paid by results
Weaknesses (again there are more)	
Tendency towards political interference/indecision	May mean ruthless exploitation of weak
Monopolies and bureaucracies don't serve public	Outcome of competition = monopoly?
Over-accountability limits entrepreneurship	Competitive over-investment wasteful
Unions tend to be powerful/taxpayers weak	Ignore costs that affect/damage society
Public expectations over level of 'free' services	Question values – everything has a price!

Activity 1.5 The vast majority of shareholders have not and will not attend an AGM unless their holding is very substantial. As one share in a portfolio, an AGM held during the working week and often a long way away, and with little or no influence over proceedings, the incentive is small.

Activity 1.2 Marketing orientation and organizational characteristics The need to be close to the customer, sensitive to change in the environment and coordinated to ensure quick response throughout the organization would require:

- Marketing representation at main board/MD level
- A flat decentralized structure
- Delegation of decision to those closest to the customer
- Open communications internally and externally
- Profit-centred general manager structure for coordination of all functions
- Integrated Management Information System (MIS)
- Customer service philosophy promoted by the organization

Extending activity 1.1 You should have considered implications from the employment and marketing side. For example, the increasing numbers of working wives is filling the gap left by declining numbers of school leavers. (Women are expected to account for 46 per cent of the workforce by 2006 and contribute the majority of employment growth, according to the 1997 *Social Trends* report.) This allows flexible staffing using part-time hours but demands changes in personnel policy as a result. Working wives alter the times of peak shopping hours and increases the demand for convenience and frozen foods.

Extending activity 1.4 Mission statement Unless the adoption of a mission statement changes organizational behaviour, it has little value. Yet its absence is like being a traveller without a destination with no way of determining progress. Organizational objectives must therefore be formulated which enables progress towards them to be measured.

A mission statement should differentiate the organization from others and establish its individuality, if not its uniqueness. As such, it defines what the organization 'wishes to be' and provides a unifying concept which both enlarges its view of itself and brings it into focus.

It should be relevant to all the direct stakeholders and motivate their commitment. Accordingly, it needs to excite and inspire, encouraging participation through a shared vision. Do your mission statements meet these criteria?

Examination hints and specimen questions

The material in this unit covers just over 10 per cent of the syllabus. It should enable you to attempt any question posed on the organization. There is no guarantee of a question in any particular examination but a full or a part question is to be normally expected. You should note that questions may be set which relate your understanding of organizations to other aspects of the syllabus. At least half of the material in this unit is newly introduced into the syllabus and it is reasonable to expect that questions will be posed on these aspects in the near future. Unfortunately there are no actual examples of possible questions in these areas so some 'suggested questions' are produced below for you to attempt alongside recent questions set on continuing sections of the syllabus.

1 (a) Indicate two benefits and one major drawback to trading as legally established partnerships. (6 marks)
  (b) How would corporate objectives differ between public and private sector organizations? (6 marks)
  (c) Outline, with an example, one method of managing the marketing environment used in either:
    (i) a public sector organization
    (ii) a voluntary sector organization (8 marks)

(CIM Marketing Environment paper, June 1998)

2 (a) '… the firm is a creature of its environment. Its resources, its income, its problems, its opportunities and its very survival are generated and conditioned by the environment.'

Using examples, fully explain your understanding of this quotation.

(15 marks)

(CIM Marketing Environment compulsory case question, December 1998)

3 You are to address a group of marketing trainees on the importance of viewing the organization as an open system. Makes notes for this address with particular reference to:

(a) the meaning of the term
(b) the importance of the concept in marketing terms
(c) the marketing interface with other sub systems

(20 marks)

(Sample question)

Question 1

- This three-part question format is candidate friendly because it conveniently divides up the marks.
- Plan out all three parts at the outset to ensure you don't overlap content.
- Stick to the precise question and write sufficiently for the marks on offer and no more.
- Don't be tempted into digressing, e.g. into legal form.
- Provide two distinct benefits in (a).
- Focus on how objectives differ, e.g. public service versus pursuit of profit.
- This is an example of a question which spans different parts of the syllabus.
- In (c) be sure to provide only an outline of a method and set it in the required context, e.g. a college might use a PEST analysis (see Units 5 and 10), a charity might use an environmental set (see Units 3 and 10).

Question 2

- The sample answer to this question may be found on pages 274–5.
- It is a question on the core meaning of the marketing environment.
- Providing content should be no difficulty but writing a concise, well-structured and focused answer is the challenge.
- You must ensure that relevant examples are provided to illustrate the points you make.
- The quotation provides a ready-made structure for the answer so use it.
- It is not an excuse to write down all you know or had revised about the marketing environment, this would be heavily penalized by the examiners.

- Be sure to adopt the required format since 10 per cent of the marks will be available for this.
- The question asks for notes, so provide them in bullet format and with evidence of recognition that the audience is composed of marketing trainees.
- Address all three aspects cited and consider a definition and a diagram to illustrate the meaning.
- Focus on the importance of systems thinking in the second part.
- Recognize the internal interface with other departmental sub-systems and the importance of communication, coordination and feedback across the boundary.
- Although there is sufficient content in Unit 1 to answer this question you will find relevant supplementary ideas and information as you progress through the units.

In this contextual unit you will:

❏ Examine the various environments of the business organization.

❏ Recognize the importance of the micro-environment in the context of the systems approach.

❏ Appreciate the significance of stakeholders and their contribution to the organization.

❏ Understand the importance of the micro-environment in the marketing process.

❏ Define societal marketing and increasing significance of ethical issues.

❏ Consider the importance of stakeholders and the debate regarding social responsibility.

By the end of this unit you will:

❏ Appreciate the complexity of the environment.

❏ Become aware of the important inter-relationships within the micro-environment.

❏ Be able to classify the various external elements and influences.

❏ Recognize potential conflicts in stakeholder expectations and the importance of coalitions.

❏ Assess the marketer's potential for influence in the micro-environment.

❏ Understand the pressures on organizations to adopt more responsibilities towards both primary and secondary stakeholders.

Study Guide

While this unit provides an initial overview of the marketing environment it is primarily concerned with the micro-environment. If you turn to the Glossary near the end of this workbook you will find this defined as including the groups and organizations that have a two-way operational relationship with the business and which are controlled and influenced by it to some degree. This glossary should be regularly used by you and particularly when you require an important term to be concisely defined. In this case it is clear from the definition that this unit is mainly concerned with an environment that is the work-a-day operational context for the organization. We saw in Unit 1 that the organization is an open system with boundaries to its immediate environment. Relationships must be established across these boundaries if supplies or credit, for example, are to be obtained. Similarly the organization must have effective linkages, through intermediaries, to the marketplace, or directly to the final customers themselves.

Competitors also inhabit this environment and it is important that the marketer understands the significance of relationships that prevail within the industry setting. These will be introduced in this unit and examined more fully in Unit 4.

Information is critical to understanding and the marketer must draw on a network of intelligence sources if successful adaption to change is to result. As the above definition suggests the organization must be proactive if it is to control or at least influence the behaviour of the various stakeholders to be found in the micro-environment.

This is a syllabus area to relate directly to your own experience. You are a consumer; you supply labour services to your employer; you will be aware of the competitors operating in your industry, you may deal directly with distributors or consumers as part of your job description and your functional specialism is marketing, which concerns itself with promoting profitable relationships across the system boundaries. You are in an ideal position to appreciate the micro-environment.

Working through this unit's content is expected to take 2–3 hours but activities may take up to twice this time if you undertake them thoroughly. This unit covers around 10 per cent of the syllabus and is the first of three units devoted to the micro-environment. It is introductory, but should be treated as an integral part of the overall section. It is suggested that you:

- Open a file section under the heading of 'The micro-environment'.
- Create sub-sections for subsequent elements of the micro-environment syllabus.
- Establish a section immediately for sources of information on this environment.
- Consult your own department regarding relevant sources used in your own organization.
- Brainstorm your own internal and external sources.
- Specify the source and briefly summarize the nature of the information and why it is useful.
- If the opportunity arises consult stakeholder group representatives about their expectations of the organization (note: this can also be applied to college stakeholders).

The business as a resource converter

All organizations seek, as Peter Drucker observed, *to make resources productive.* Every organization, irrespective of its specific objectives, has this as their common goal because resources are scarce and must be competed for and utilized efficiently and effectively. Various inputs, as seen in Figure 2.1 (this is a simplified representation of the open system depicted in Figure 1.6), are drawn by various means (e.g. paid/volunteer) from the environment and converted in time, place or form to create utility, value and satisfaction for the ultimate consumer.

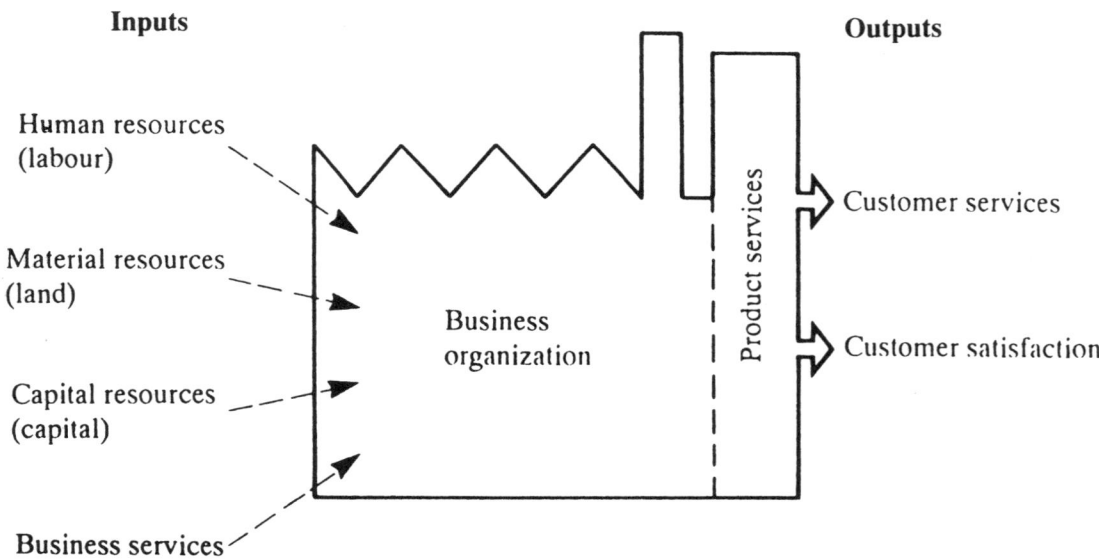

Figure 2.1 Business as a resource converter

In modern business, productive inputs are diverse and often complex entities in themselves, drawn from an interrelated global economy. The traditional economic classification of land, labour and capital is therefore simplistic. The human resource an organization requires may embody numerous skills, enterprise, creativity and an ability to adapt to changing circumstances.

Capital resources are often high technology and very specialized. They include not only buildings, equipment and transportation but also financial inputs to lubricate the process of resource conversion in advance of actual sales. Business services are important inputs as more and more firms contract-out provision of IT services, transport, catering, market research, etc. to focus their resources and attention on their core conversion activities.

Activity 2.1

Select a marketing resource and explain the process of making it productive.

(See Activity debrief at the end of this unit.)

The resource providers may also be viewed as stakeholders in the business. This idea will be developed later in this unit, where organizations are viewed as a coalition of stakeholders and it is the role of management to achieve a workable balance between the claims and interests of these groups. Shareholders, as the owners of the business, would seem to qualify as stakeholders but strictly speaking this term is reserved for the other providers of inputs or recipients of outputs namely:

- Employees
- Management themselves
- Suppliers
- Creditors
- Local community
- Distributors
- Customers

The environmental context of the organization

The environment of business has never been so complex and challenging as it is today. Marketers more than ever before are finding themselves confronted by increasing pressures and demands which they must seek to understand and respond to. As can be seen in Figure 2.2 at any given point in time organizations will be confronted by a confusion of environmental factors that may or may not constitute threats to, or opportunities for, the marketer. To assist you in dealing with the threats and exploiting opportunities involved, a classification is required of the persons, groups, trends and often turbulent events that occur, external to the firm's boundaries. You need a grasp of the big picture and the role of your organization and yourself within it.

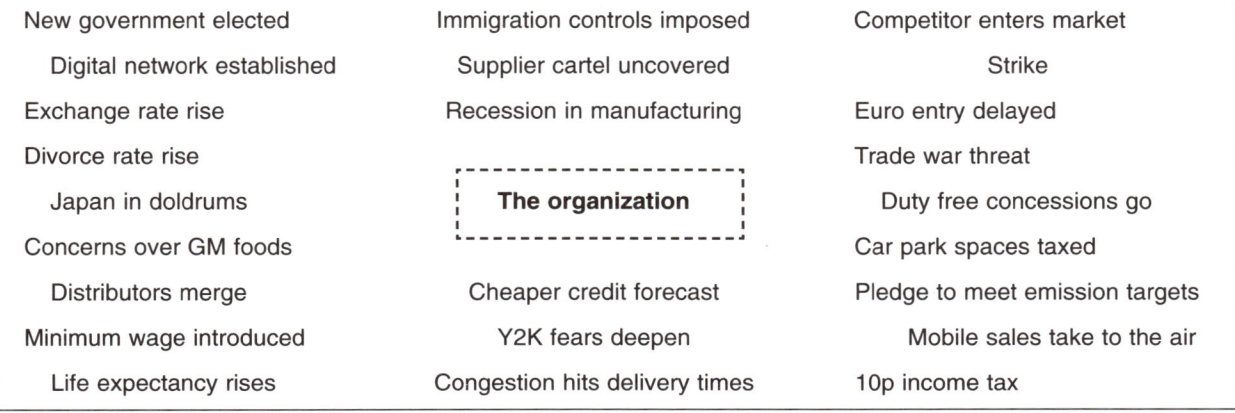

New government elected	Immigration controls imposed	Competitor enters market
Digital network established	Supplier cartel uncovered	Strike
Exchange rate rise	Recession in manufacturing	Euro entry delayed
Divorce rate rise		Trade war threat
Japan in doldrums	**The organization**	Duty free concessions go
Concerns over GM foods		Car park spaces taxed
Distributors merge	Cheaper credit forecast	Pledge to meet emission targets
Minimum wage introduced	Y2K fears deepen	Mobile sales take to the air
Life expectancy rises	Congestion hits delivery times	10p income tax

Figure 2.2

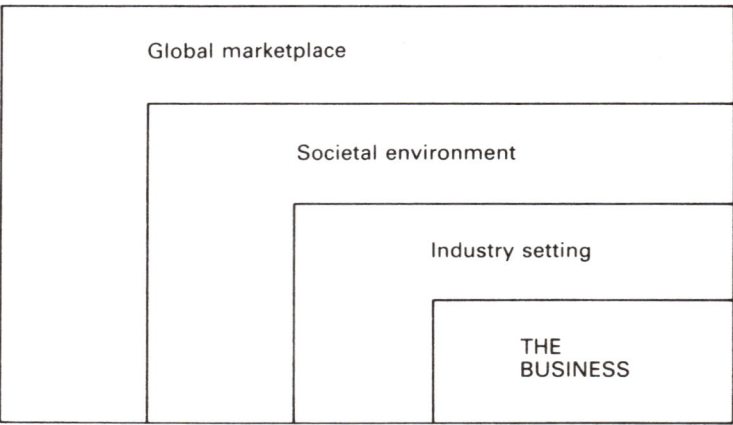

Figure 2.3
The environmental framework

Figure 2.3 provides a possible classification. The lines do not imply a solid separation between the various environments and the influence of each initially seeps and then cascades through into the business. The global environment appears very distant to marketers operating on a regional or even a national scale and yet with information technologies shrinking distances these multinational operations are extending into every corner of the marketplace. This aspect will be considered in Unit 10 of the workbook along with developments such as European Monetary Union (EMU).

To set the micro-environment in context we should also classify factors which are relevant to the societal or macro-environment. Within any society all businesses face a common political, economic, social and technological environment, although any one element will often impact differently according to the size and situation of the firm. The key characteristic, however, is the inclusion of forces that impact on the business, creating opportunities and threats, but over which it has no real influence or control.

The macro-environment

The wider environment (Figure 2.4) over which the organization can exert little influence is often referred to by the acronym PEST. The inclusion of a regulatory framework of laws, standards and customs converts the acronym to SLEPT while the addition of ethics and environment (natural) converts it to STEEPLE. These provide compartments into which we can sort the various trends, events, threats and opportunities which occur in the environment.

| **Definition 2.1** | Match up the following terms: |

Match up the following terms:

- Customs
- Laws
- Standards
- Regulations

1 Prescribed qualities and performances to which products must conform.
2 Rules or orders governing various business operations and procedures (e.g. health and safety).
3 Long-established business practices and modes of customer behaviour (e.g. half-day closing).
4 Enactments established by government authority.

(**See** Activity debrief at the end of this unit.)

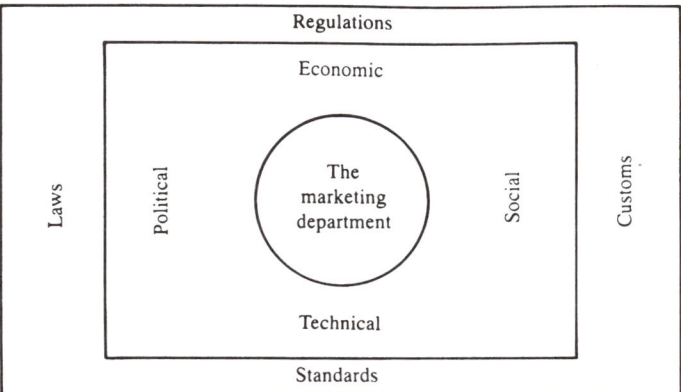

Figure 2.4
PEST factors and the regulatory framework

Units 5–9 will consider each of these macro-environments in detail, but we may increase our understanding of this unit with just a brief mention of each.

Political

The role and impact of the state on business extends far beyond the making of laws. The size of the public sector was mentioned earlier and all its organizations affect businesses whether as suppliers, customers, policy makers or regulators. The philosophy of the government in power sets the climate for business and a change of party in office can significantly alter the thrust and direction of all aspects of their policies.

Economic

This is closely linked with the political environment, and economic policies to achieve government objectives will impact on the costs, prices, competitiveness and profitability of businesses. The business pages of the quality press are therefore required reading for the serious marketer since an understanding of the key economic indicators provides the necessary information for anticipating developments in the marketplace. The economic horizons of businesses will vary greatly, as seen in Figure 2.5.

Many sole traders compete wholly in local markets and are therefore only interested in the local economy. However, the conditions experienced here will often have cascaded down from conditions in the world economy, which in turn influence national economies and regions within them. The importance of international factors has increased in recent years with the development of trading blocs, single markets and the formation of the World Trade Organization (WTO) following the successful conclusion of the GATT talks. The implications of EMU and a single currency currently confront Britain's politicians and businesses alike. Businesses who are reluctant to search out the opportunities presented by these developments may soon find their profitable niche markets exposed to new competition.

Extending Activity 2.1	'Prepare a regular business environment brief' Produce a summary of the main events and developments affecting a business of your choice over the past week. Use the elements in your micro- and macro-environment as your headings. Many companies appoint an executive to collate such information on an on-going basis in order to build up a moving picture of change in their environment. Perhaps you could organize weekly briefs in your CIM classes.

Social

This is perhaps the most difficult environment for the marketer to identify, evaluate and respond to. It includes changes in population characteristics, educational standards, culture, lifestyles, attitudes and beliefs. The way we think, live and behave is the outcome of complex cultural conditioning by

Figure 2.5
The four horizons

family, friends, school, church, work and the various media. It conditions who decides what we buy, where and when we buy it, whether we use credit or cash. Social and demographic change may often appear to change slowly, yet their impacts are likely to far outweigh the consequences of political decisions over the longer term. The trends towards lower and later births and the corresponding ageing of the population, for example, will generate massive changes over time in patterns of work and spending.

Technical

This environment is characterized by accelerating rates of change in the means, methods and knowledge that organizations utilize in the supply chain. It is the primary means by which the production possibilities of society and the productivity of scarce resources can be expanded, enabling more wants to be satisfied. It also constitutes threats to those organizations that fail to innovate new and better products and processes.

The lead time between invention, innovation and market introduction has shrunk significantly with the application of computer technology, while the development of telecommunications has combined to make the global economy a reality. All businesses face the challenges implied but only the more alert, flexible and proactive, such as Microsoft, 3M and Sony, will translate them into opportunities and profit.

Activity 2.2

Take a typical workday of a marketing executive and log occasions and actions which link your organization to its environment.

Hint: This should include items on news bulletins and in the local papers.

The micro-environment

The micro-environment is to be found within the industry setting of Figure 2.3. It has already been defined as those individuals, groups and organizations that have a two-way operational relationship with the business and may be controllable and influenced by it to some degree. It includes key stakeholder groups who are directly connected to the organization. Figure 2.5 represents the typical micro-environment of the firm and includes all those stakeholders that have a close and often day-to-day relationship. Each group with a significant effect on the marketing organization is summarized below. Some of the more important relationships will be explored in more depth in Units 3 and 4.

Question 2.1

Can you allocate the elements in Figure 2.2 to the appropriate global/macro/micro-environment?

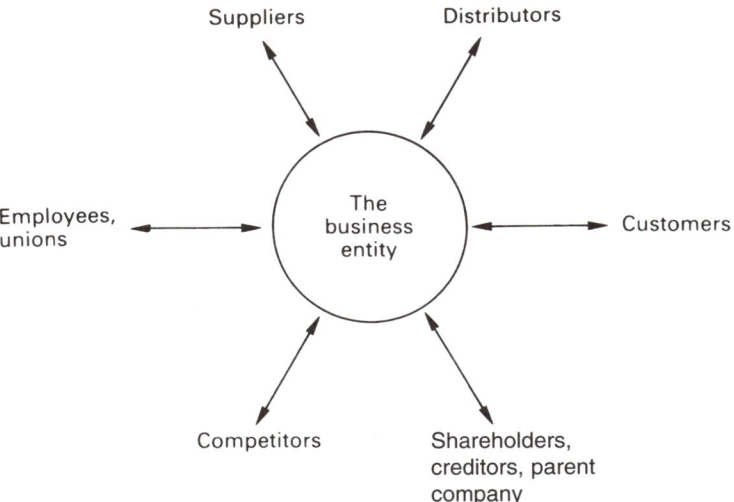

Figure 2.6
The micro-firm environment

Suppliers

No firm can supply all its own needs. Materials, components, fuel and a host of business services are necessary inputs. Suppliers are a critical link with the environment, a source of cost and also of possible partnership. A vehicle producer may have hundreds of suppliers but, as the arrows in Figure 2.6 suggest, it is a two-way dependence. Firms such as these are dramatically reducing their number of suppliers but demanding, in return for long-term contracts, total quality, just-in-time delivery, research and design support.

Dependence on one or two suppliers, however, has considerable risks, just as it is risky for the smaller business with only one or two customers. Any action or decision may have critical consequences.

Importance to the marketing process

- Key determinant of availability, delivery times and quality of the product.
- Cost of materials are an important factor in the total cost of many products.
- The supply chain may have many links back to primary producers and be susceptible to disruption.
- The relative power of suppliers is often critical and depends on size, substitutes and degree of actual competition between them.
- The quality of the supplier relationship is a crucial parameter in marketing effectiveness.
- Suppliers can assume the stockholding function allowing maximum space for selling operations.
- If partnership fails to deliver marketing benefits, backward integration may be considered.

Exam Tip	It is essential that you achieve a sound grasp of these basic environmental concepts. They will occur frequently as part of different questions referring to the environment.

Competitors

These are the exceptions in the micro-environment in that they continuously threaten rather than contribute to the survival of the business. As we will explore in a later unit, the reality of competition may be in the form of hundreds of similar rivals, as in corner-shop retailing or catering, or a handful of powerful multinationals, as in pharmaceuticals or oil refining.

The relationship is again two-way in that while competitors can constrain the achievements of the business, the marketing department can also

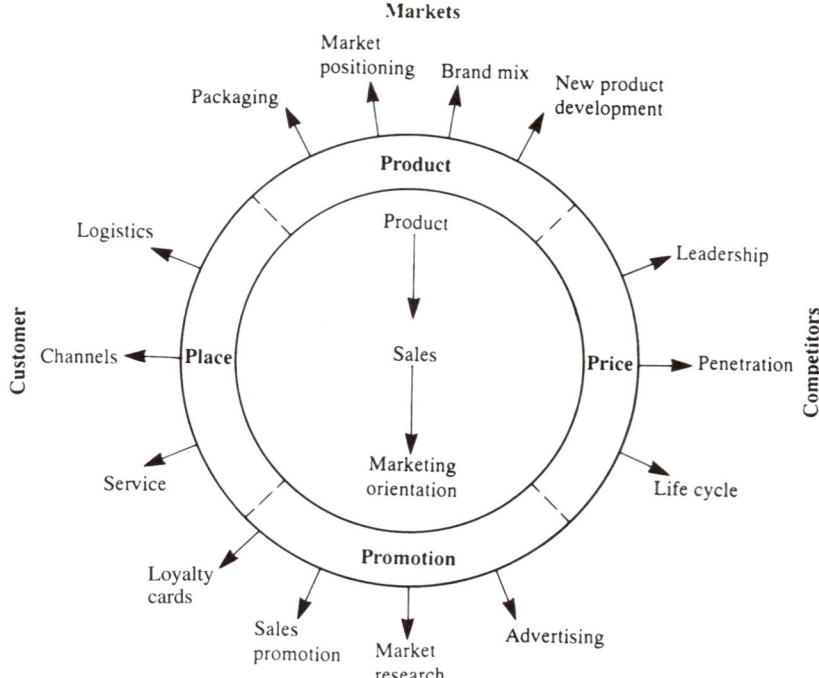

Figure 2.7
The marketing set

shape and influence the competitive environment. As can be seen in Figure 2.7, business has the discretion to adjust its marketing mix as conditions change. The truly marketing-orientated company will ensure that its strategies, plans, tactics and responses will be decided not in a vacuum but with careful reference to its changing threats and opportunities.

Importance to the marketing process

- No business can make decisions without reference to its competitive environment.
- Even a monopoly must be concerned about potential entrants or effective substitutes.
- Pricing must account for what the market will bear and the reactions of competitors.
- The more competitors there are and the closer their product offering the more sensitively will sales respond to a relative change in price.
- Price wars may erupt from time to time but non-price competition using branding and other product and promotional tactics shown in Figure 2.7 are the norm.

Customers

All businesses, as the marketer knows full well, have customers as the final link in the input–output chain. The idea that they are stakeholders is less familiar, although the choice of withdrawing their stake or not will determine the success or otherwise of the enterprise. The business will naturally be concerned with all the influences affecting that choice.

Importance to the marketing process

- Customers are the only source of revenue for most organizations.
- If they withdraw or transfer their custom to a competitor then survival is threatened.
- A dissatisfied customer tells many more of the experience than does a satisfied one.
- Customer retention is normally more cost effective than recruiting new ones due to the life-time revenue stream that is often involved.
- Customers are looking for value for money. This is a combination of the broadly defined satisfaction deriving from consumption of the product and its relative price.

- Customer preferences can change very quickly.
- Customer preferences and their buying rationality can be influenced through the marketing set.

Intermediaries/distributors

These must also be considered where the firm does not sell directly to the consumer. They are important elements of the marketing channel which makes the product available to the consumer or industry user. They may include wholesalers, retailers, dealers, agents and franchisees. Their power and position may be significant not least in respect of retailer brands which may be promoted aggressively at the expense of manufacturer offerings. Tying in distributors may provide a competitive edge over rivals.

Importance to the marketing process

- Distributors who are ineffective in delivering the product to the customer as, where and when they want it will negatively impact on the business.
- Effective partners deliver advantage in the form of transport, stock management, market knowledge, merchandizing and display, together with after sales service.
- The marketer must communicate with both the final customer and the distributor(s) delivering the product to this end user.
- Distributors have economic leverage arising from their strategic position.
- Distributors have mutual interests in common to form the basis of joint ventures and partnerships.

Exam Tip	Remember the course you are studying is first and foremost about the environment. Do not be tempted to answer questions in marketing terms alone.

Shareholders and creditors

Shareholders provide the longer-term capital while creditors such as banks and other financial institutions provide short- and medium-term funds. They can affect the business through the sale of shares or withdrawal of credit. Small businesses are particularly vulnerable to the latter in times of recession while institutional shareholders, such as pension funds, are becoming more active in their scrutiny of public company management.

Importance to the marketing process

- These are important constituencies to the organization so clear and timely communication with them based on an understanding of their needs is required.
- Adverse shareholder perceptions may lead to selling which drives down the market valuation of the company relative to its net asset value so risking unwelcome take-over bids.
- Trade and bank credit are critical to maintaining a healthy cash flow. Relationships with both must be nurtured and improved.
- The public image of the business is largely the responsibility of marketing.

Employees and unions

Most businesses have employees who contribute their time and skills for monetary and other rewards. They form part of the wider society and reflect the values and beliefs found there. They are clearly affected by company activities, including harmful ones, but again the effects are two-way. They can unionize, adversely affect productivity, leave or have equally positive effects on company fortunes. The decline in trade unions has clearly affected the freedom of many firms to manage but so too has increased legislation on health, safety, employment and pollution.

Importance to the marketing process

- As with customers, retention of skilled staff is normally more cost effective than the uncertainties of recruitment
- The image of the organization is an important determinant in the quality of applicant attracted.
- The business will attract the calibre of employees it deserves.
- Internal marketing to critical departments and employees is central to the achievement of goals.

Activity 2.3

Taking a business with which you are familiar, identify and rank its five most important suppliers, distributors, competitors, customers and creditors. What marketing mix does it employ to:

- Retain and motivate its distributors?
- Secure a competitive edge over its rivals?

(**See** Activity debrief at the end of this unit.)

The micro-environment as a whole is of general importance to the marketing process, for the following reasons:

- The marketer can utilize the marketing mix to influence and impact on all the stakeholders.
- The marketer must recognize that the same stakeholders can damage or advantage the business.
- The marketer must understand that the micro-environment includes not only actual customers, suppliers, intermediaries and competitors but potential ones as well.
- The marketing mix can also be deployed to convert potential customers, for example, into actual ones or to discourage potential competitors from entering the market.
- Writers, like Michael Porter, consider that successful businesses are those that are part of larger 'clusters' of collective activity. The Dutch bulb industry is a world beater because of the concentration of suppliers, research organizations, producers, competitors and intermediaries that complement, strengthen and support one another.
- The micro-environment provides a tension between competition and cooperation. Businesses compete for customers and sometimes compete for shelf space with distributors, but equally they may cooperate with suppliers over new product development or with intermediaries for joint promotions. The marketer must assess the pay-off associated with both approaches.
- It forms the immediate or operational environment for the marketer and drives tactical responses on a daily basis. It is often the longer term effects of macro-environment changes which condition strategic responses.
- The marketer operates across the boundary with the micro-environment and represents the critical interface between key stakeholders and the rest of the organization.

Question 2.2

Review questions
Review the section in this unit on the business as a resource convertor and consider the following question:

- What would an organization without stakeholders look like?

(**See** Activity debrief at the end of this unit.)

Stakeholder pressures

Having explored the micro-environment we can now reconsider the stakeholder concept in some detail. Stakeholders are defined as any group or individual who can affect or are affected by the achievement of the organization's objectives. Since they have a stake, a legitimate interest in the business, they can influence objectives. Management cannot hope to operate in isolation but must seek to satisfy their stakeholders' legitimate expectations if they are to contribute value in return.

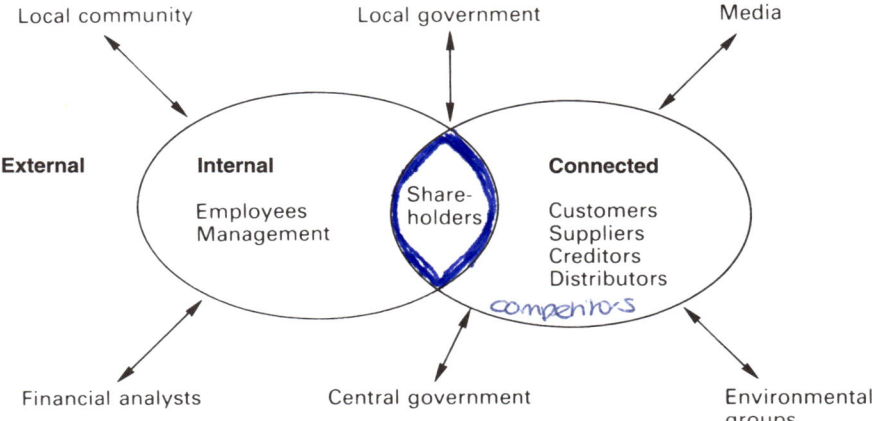

Figure 2.8
Internal, connected and external stakeholders

Direct or connected stakeholders are closely related to the core economic functions of the business. Together with the pressure exerted by competitors, they can change the goals and nature of the organization unless managed effectively.

Stakeholder	*Pressure exerted*	*Expectations*
Shareholders	Delegate decision power to board but recent increase in activism over remuneration and appointments. Selling shares is the real threat as a falling share price attracts takeover predators.	Above average return on equity, improving return on assets, share value rising.
Employees	Absenteeism, turnover, low morale, media leaks, unionization, poor productivity.	Above average remuneration, training and skill development, company growth/promotion, employment security/job satisfaction, improving conditions and wages.
Customers	Reduce purchases, buy from competitors, organize boycott, complain to other potential customers, press for legislation	Value for money, product safety/quality assurance, innovation/improved design, better service.
Creditors	Limit credit, withdraw credit, cut credit rating, charge higher rates.	Regular/timely repayment, early notification of problems.

43

Stakeholder	Pressure exerted	Expectations
Distributors	Stock and promote competing brands/own-label, integrate backwards, delay payment.	Reliable supplies, support in promotion, progressive product development, good communications.
Suppliers	Supply competitors, reduce priority, limit trade credit, poor-quality service, integrate forward	Reliable payment, regular supply schedules, development support, ability to interrogate stock/production systems.

Exam Tip

Any new course of study is hard going at the beginning. You do not know the terminology and you have studied too few pieces of the overall jigsaw to be able to see the overall picture unfolding.

However, remember that the more pieces you fit together, the easier it gets, not least because you move down your learning curve. Each question and activity you attempt provides experience you can apply to advantage when you address the next. So keep on going and develop some learning momentum!

There is a considerable potential for conflict of interest between the primary stakeholder groups. Higher wages for employees may conflict with shareholder profits or result in higher prices which upset customers. Local community concerns for health and safety may increase costs, reduce competitiveness and jeopardize jobs.

If any stakeholder considers they are not receiving sufficient return they may withdraw their contribution to the organization. For example, if customers no longer feel a product is value for money they will buy elsewhere. If workers consider their remuneration too low they will change jobs and their contribution will be lost.

Balancing these partly conflicting stakeholder expectations while achieving objectives of growth, market share and profitability is not easily achieved, not least in times of rapid change. *Internal marketing* is now widely recognized as an essential part of any manager's role. Implementation and fulfilment of business strategies requires that managers identify groups of internal as well as external stakeholders and market their plans to them.

Extending Activity 2.2

In the light of the above consequences of *failing* to attend to the interests of direct stakeholders, suggest how a business can best ensure that their contributions remain positive and add value.

Hint: One way of doing this might be to draw up a 'code of good practice' for each stakeholder.

Indirect or external stakeholder groups are not directly engaged in the business operations but can exert influence on and be seriously affected by their activities. A few of these are listed below for each group. Can you think of others?

- *Local government* Interested not only in the investment, jobs, prosperity, tax revenue and prestige the organization generates locally but also on its compliance with relevant legislation, planning requirements, etc.
- *Communities* Concerned with property values, quality of life, jobs and prosperity, congestion, links with local schools and charitable activities.

Can protest, mobilize the media, obstruct planning applications, etc.

- *Financial analysts* Assess past/future performance in financial and broader terms. Downgrade where suspicious of unethical behaviour and highlight undervalued assets/possible takeover. They have the ear of the shareholders.
- *Media* Can seriously enhance or damage the public image of the business. They publicize issues and corporate achievements and form a line of communication from the organization to the local/national community.
- *Central government* Governments often hold a controlling influence over many public sector organizations and so are direct stakeholders. Make, interpret and enforce laws, monitor compliance, levy taxes and implement economic policies. They also provide infrastructure, spend, protect, subsidize, rescue and restructure. The organization may seek influence through trade associations, lobbying, provision of information, joint projects and even political donations.
- *Environment groups* They can protest, resist development and generate considerable media attention. Trend until recently of rising membership and public concerns but clamour for more jobs and improved competitiveness together with the government's desire to cut red tape and regulations may actually reduce environmental pressures on firms, particularly in times of economic recession.

Not all stakeholders have the same degree of influence and power. As Brooks and Weatherston point out in their text *The Business Environment*, relevant environmental stakeholders need to be 'mapped' according to their level of interest in the organization's activities, on the one hand, and their real power to influence outcomes on the other. Figure 2.9 shows an application of this analytical tool to a college.

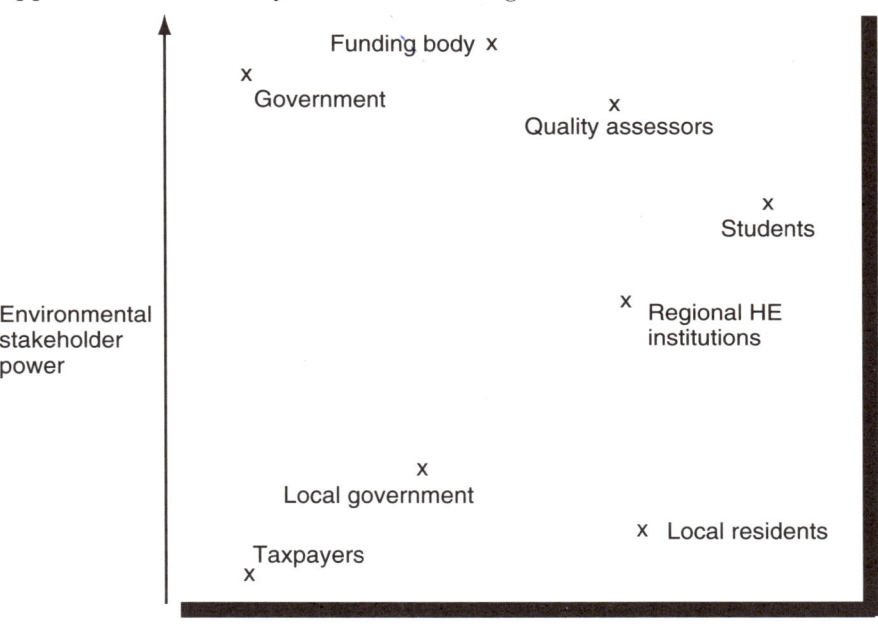

Source: The Business Environment: challenges and changes, I. Brooks and J. Weatherston 1997, Prentice Hall

Figure 2.9 Stakeholder mapping: college of higher education (HE)

Activity 2.4

Draw up a stakeholder map for your own organization or a local large employer of your choice.

Consider the criteria you are using in assessing the relative power and influence of each.

Stakeholders, as will be developed in Unit 3 will have differing and often conflicting viewpoints on the organizational objectives to be pursued. It is not surprising therefore that statements of objectives are frequently vague and generalized. The objectives clause in the Memorandum of Association is deliberately broad so as not to limit development and provide maximum flexibility for management. There will be a *hierarchy of objectives* rather than a single focus, and these will trickle down through the various functional areas of the business. Many may implement *management by objectives* (MBO) as a means of linking goals with planning and management at all levels. Managers commit themselves to achieving certain objectives and are appraised and rewarded according to their success in doing so.

Question 2.3	In what sense are you a stakeholder in CIM and how might you seek to influence the organization?

Societal marketing and ethical issues

The final section of this unit is concerned with the attitude of the organization towards its stakeholders and wider society. Societal marketing develops the concept of marketing orientation into the idea that an organization should not only anticipate and identify the needs and wants of target markets and deliver the desired satisfactions more profitably than competitors, but also this should be achieved in a manner that maintains or improves both the consumer's and society's welfare.

Many excellent companies have lost market share and profitability because they have failed to adapt successfully to a changing environment. Companies such as IBM and Phillips in the 1980s, Reebok and Laura Ashley in the 1990s have suffered in this way. However, societal marketing suggests that unless companies begin to consider wider concerns they may suffer even worse consequences. McDonald's, for example, has been attacked by consumerists in regard to the nutritional value of their product while environmentalists have focused on wasteful non-biodegradable packaging and damage to rain forests cleared for cattle grazing. There would appear to be a serious potential for conflict between satisfaction of short-run consumer wants and longer term welfare for organizations such as Coca-Cola and tobacco giant Phillip Morris to address.

The societal concept seeks to balance concern for satisfying consumer wants and human welfare with the organization making a profit. It embraces ethical notions in the sense of doing what is right in marketing terms and still achieving profitability. The Body Shop is an example of an ethical company placing stress on stakeholder values and animal rights. Other companys, like Norsk Hydro and Johnson and Johnson have exemplary records despite operating in high profile 'dirty' industries.

| Question 2.4 | Brainstorm a list of ethical issues confronting businesses today.

(See Activity debrief at the end of this unit.) |
| --- | --- |

Business ethics are a set of moral principles which govern the behaviour of the organization. They translate into standards of behaviour and conduct applied by managers and marketers in carrying out their activities. They normally involve a strong commitment to aligning business values to those of the stakeholders. Failure to make the 'right' decision in response to the ethical concerns of any of these groups may cause reactions which impact adversely on the business. Ethical issues are amongst the most difficult faced by managers. As Question 2.5 demonstrates it is difficult to formulate hard and fast rules to cover every situation. A number of standards or common sense guidelines may be formulated to reflect relevant values which underpin responsible business ethics. These include:

- *Obey the law* – profit only assumes importance once minimum legal requirements are achieved.
- *Above all do no harm* – very important in the area of product safety standards.
- *Tell the truth* – important where product recalls are required.
- *Respect for individuals* – part of the old M&S culture to treat employees well by industry standards.
- *Do unto others as you would have them do unto you* – provides a benchmark principle.

Ethical businesses act when their responsibility is clear and obey the spirit as well as the letter of the law. They often operate well in excess of minimum legal requirements, e.g. ethical retailers such as the Cooperatives developing a code of practice to govern sourcing from poorer countries.

Recent examples of doubtful ethics in Britain include:

- Mis-selling of personal pensions.
- Cases of insider share dealings.
- Formula 1 tobacco sponsorship.
- Rises in top executive salaries.
- Poor labelling of genetically modified foods.
- Arms sales to parts of Africa.

Activity 2.5

Scan the company news for examples of ethical organizations. Look for examples in different sectors, e.g. voluntary, cooperative, public and various business areas. Make a note of why you have defined them as ethical and what impact it has had on their ability to achieve their objectives.

Pressures to improve ethical standards in future

- *The threat of legislation* – may inhibit behaviour that society considers unethical.
- *More knowledgeable and educated consumers* – aware of their rights and increasingly critical of irresponsible behaviour. They are also more prepared to make legal claims which are costly in terms of time, money and bad publicity for the organization in question.
- *Rising affluence increases social and environmental concerns.*
- *Competitive pressure* – as businesses seek competitive advantage by emphasizing their ethical credentials. Customers or investors who value such behaviour will wish to be associated with such companies, e.g. ethical investment trusts.
- *Stakeholder pressure* – from those concerned with quality or their own corporate image. Many large companies insist their suppliers are millennium compliant or have implemented codes of good practice.
- *European Union directives* – ensure compliance with common standards across the single market. This produces a ratchet effect of higher standards in terms of food safety, packaging, recycling, etc.
- *Pressure group activity* – tend to crystallize these pressures and provide support and legal backing. Many thousand interest groups now exist ranging from the Consumers Association to Greenpeace.
- *The media* – provide focus and attention on many areas of corporate weakness. Recent examples include allegations concerning the use of child labour in the manufacture of products for *socially responsible* organizations such as M&S and the recent furore over genetically modified foods.
- *Demonstration effects* – of ethical businesses, e.g. Scandinavian companies, in many sectors.

Question 2.5

Ethical issue 1 – You discover that the process plant that you work for is exceeding permitted discharge levels into a nearby lake. Revealing the information would cost the company $40,000, create bad publicity and damage local tourism. It is unlikely that outsiders would find out and no danger is posed to humans. At worst it will kill some fish. Do you blow the whistle or not?

'Whistleblowers' are normally employees who divulge sensitive information to the media or authorities regarding actions or plans of their organization that they consider immoral. Why do they do this?

Ethical issue 2 – As marketing manager you are offered a 'token' gift of various wines and spirits as a Christmas present from an advertising agency. Do you accept?

Ethical issue 3 – You have responsibility for purchasing and stock control in the small company you work for. Your marketing director is applying pressure due to concern about missing stock. In the latest delivery from a long standing supplier you find they have inadvertently oversupplied items by 10 per cent. Do you return the stock or use it to cover those that are missing?

(**See** Activity debrief at the end of this unit.)

The concept of social responsibility

To what extent do you believe that business should have responsibilities to the rest of society? Should they incur extra costs in protecting the environment? Is it right that they sponsor community projects? Is it proper if their employment practices far exceed the requirements laid down by law? These are important questions which involve consideration of corporate social responsibility.

Social responsibility is acceptance by an organization of obligations to protect and improve the welfare of society as well as its own interests. It is part of the so-called 'third way' that presents an acceptable face of capitalism which, while not abandoning its primary economic mission, seeks to reconcile inescapable stakeholder demands. Stakeholder concerns, other than those of the shareholders, are accounted for and action goes beyond the minimum requirements of the law. Action is voluntary and may involve net cost and therefore the sacrifice of net profit. Socially responsible companies recognize that business and society are intertwined and interdependent. As worldwide expectations rise, so they must aim for a balance and pursue long-run rather than maximum profits. Such an approach, however, involves complex questions of ethics, legality, economic cost, risk and judgement.

Milton Friedman, the American market economist, argues that business is an economic not a social organization and exists *to maximize returns to shareholders*. This and competition ensures that society's scarce resources are most efficiently utilized. Its primary and only responsibility is as a wealth producer and allocator of these scarce resources. There is no such thing as a free lunch, Friedman maintains, and any avoidable costs incurred in pursuit of social objectives will inevitably be at the expense of one stakeholder or another, i.e.:

- Shareholders, if profits are reduced
- Customers, if prices have to be increased
- Employees, if jobs are lost or wages constrained
- Communities, if local plants have to be closed.

Social responsibility blurs management accountability and reduces competitiveness, not least with other countries, he argues. It also requires that business assumes authority in social areas where they have limited competence and where issues should rightly be left to the state. So, if an inefficient plant is kept open to protect the local community while competitors close and move offshore it will quickly be unable to compete causing all stakeholders to lose in the long term. Similarly, are social problems relevant to even a mega-company beyond the setting of appropriate policies. Only inter-governmental cooperation can deal with societal problems like the ozone layer or Aids.

Extending Activity 2.3

- Where does your government stand on this issue? Consider, for example, why the Conservative Party opposed the Social Chapter of the Maastricht Treaty, while New Labour supports it.
- List any areas where your organization acknowledges social responsibilities. What is its justification and what (if any) is the net cost?
- How would you convince your board of directors that social responsibility is the key to achieving competitive advantage?

Society's view of the role of business has changed as economies have prospered. The narrow role expressed by Friedman is no longer accepted by many commentators, who suggest that it is a fallacy that business can prosper or even exist without due regard to broader social concerns. They argue the following:

- Sanctions will be applied if stakeholder interests are ignored.
- Societal concern may represent enlightened self-interest since bad publicity damages sales, employee morale, corporate reputation and vice versa.
- Laws, as the expression of society's wishes, lag behind current attitudes and expectations, so compliance with minimum standards is insufficient.
- Social responsibility can be profitable (e.g. by materials recovery, recycling and energy conservation).

Activity 2.6

Can you think of how social responsibility might be profitable in

- Health and safety standards for consumers?
- Positive discrimination in favour of recruiting female marketers?
- An ethical code of practice for fair dealing with suppliers?

(**See** Activity debrief at the end of this unit.)

- Management is a leadership group with the capabilities and resources to create a better environment for both society and for business.
- Business has concentrated economic power and control over global resources. It must be accountable for the 'responsible' exercise of this power. Being efficient and profit-motivated is no longer sufficient, and business must account to its stakeholders for how products are produced, used and disposed of, how profits are distributed and their contribution to society.

Question 2.6

In fulfilling the needs of society for jobs and rising living standards it has been argued that business cannot divorce wealth creation from the means of producing it and the consequences for stakeholders. Our way of life must be *sustainable* into the future and there is clearly more to human welfare than additional goods and services, however efficiently they are produced. Society gives organizations their charter to exist, so if they diverge from fulfilling its wider purpose or behave irresponsibly, the charter may be revoked.

But is social responsibility a luxury that only large organizations with monopoly power can enjoy?

A final thought concerns whether socially responsible businesses still require laws and regulations. The Friedman arguments suggest that they do to provide guidance, a level playing field and universally applying standards. Social responsibility raises behaviour above this minimum to a level congruent with current values and expectations. Such behaviour is always one step ahead as new societal expectations are progressively codified into law.

Summary

- Business ignores its environment at its peril.
- Marketers have a key role in identifying environmental change.
- Organizations have a number of primary stakeholders and these make up its micro-environment where influence is two way.
- Business must also account and respond to opportunities and threats in its wider environment over which it has no control.
- Social responsibility is increasingly expected as public perceptions of the role of business change.
- The ethical performance of organizations is coming under closer scrutiny and a positive but practical approach is required to deal with the many issues arising.

Activity debrief

Definition 3, 4, 1, 2.

Question 2.2 A self-sufficient monastry? A lost tribe?

Question 2.4 Social disclosure; animal testing; profit sharing; industrial democracy; positive discrimination; community involvement; environmental sustainability; animal testing; animal welfare.

Question 2.5 Financial gain is seldom the motive and they often put their job on the line. A strong code of professional ethics is often the explanation. This overrides any sense of loyalty to management or the organization.

Activity 2.1 You might consider a resource such as market research, or information generated from loyalty cards. How would you fully exploit the information?

Activity 2.3 Product availability and promotion would be priorities for distributors while innovation, particularly in product and place, would be the probable means of achieving sustainable advantage.

Activity 2.6 Consider airline safety standards relative to sales; the untapped potential of an under-utilized gender noted for empathetic skills; availability in times of difficulty/shortage.

Examination hints and specimen questions

Since the marketing environment links the organization with external constraints, opportunities and threats, it is unsurprising that questions frequently arise requiring you to explore the relationship between the two. While the syllabus content of this unit is 10 per cent its significance extends much wider in terms of questions and part questions appearing at regular intervals on CIM papers. Since the content of this unit links into both of the following units as well as providing an introduction to the macro-environment it is one you must ensure you fully understand. The new syllabus gives greater emphasis to societal marketing and ethics so you must be prepared for more questions in this area of corporate social responsibility.

1 In the context of a business of your choice:

    (a) Produce a slide defining the micro environment.   (5 marks)
    (b) State the importance of three of its primary stakeholders. (6 marks)
    (c) Write a brief memorandum on the growing importance of relationship marketing with one of the primary stakeholder groups.
                                        (9 marks)
         (CIM Marketing Environment paper, June 1998)

2 You are to address a group of marketing trainees on the nature and importance of the marketing environment. Using a mixture of headings, illustrations and diagrams, prepare notes for this talk.   (20 marks)
(CIM Marketing Environment paper, June 1997)

3 In the context of a business of your choice:

(a) Identify **two** stakeholder groups and briefly assess the nature and terms of their stake in the organization. (10 marks)
(b) Prepare a brief for your marketing director outlining the concept of social responsibility and indicating how this might be applied to your customers and how it might be of overall benefit. (10 marks)
(CIM Marketing Environment paper, December 1994)

4 See the December 1998 paper in Unit 11 – Compulsory Question 1(c).

Hints: Indicative content and approach

Question 1

- This question draws on material from this unit and Unit 3.
- Be sure to use a business context and examples, e.g. your own/your bank/a large retailer, etc.
- Format marks are available for setting the material in a slide for (a) and a memorandum for (c).
- Provide 5 or 6 direct stakeholders and define the types, e.g. internal/connected/external, and the relationship, e.g. direct/two-way/controllable.
- There are clearly 2 marks for summarizing the importance of each in (b).
- Return to part (c) after you have completed Unit 3.

Question 2

- This appears to be a simple question but care is required.
- Format requirements must be rigorously observed.
- You must be concise since you only have 35 minutes available.
- Use headings and bullet points but don't spend too much time on the diagrams.
- Divide up your answer into:
    - the nature – descriptive and defining;
    - the importance – analysis and implications.
- Provide a conclusion drawing your main points together.

Question 3

- Note the need for a business context once again – ignoring this loses marks.
- 5 marks are available for each stakeholder discussed.
- 1 mark for identifying a relevant stakeholder and 2 marks each for the nature and terms of the stake, e.g. employees contribute time/effort/commitment and remain loyal so long as they are paid fairly/have good conditions/job satisfaction/training and opportunities.
- In (b) there are format marks for the brief. Be sure to make it concise/use bullets.
- Outline/define the concept; provide applications for customers, e.g. no quibble guarantee.
- Provide general/marketing benefits in the last part, e.g. improved image; loyalty, etc.

The organization and its 'publics'

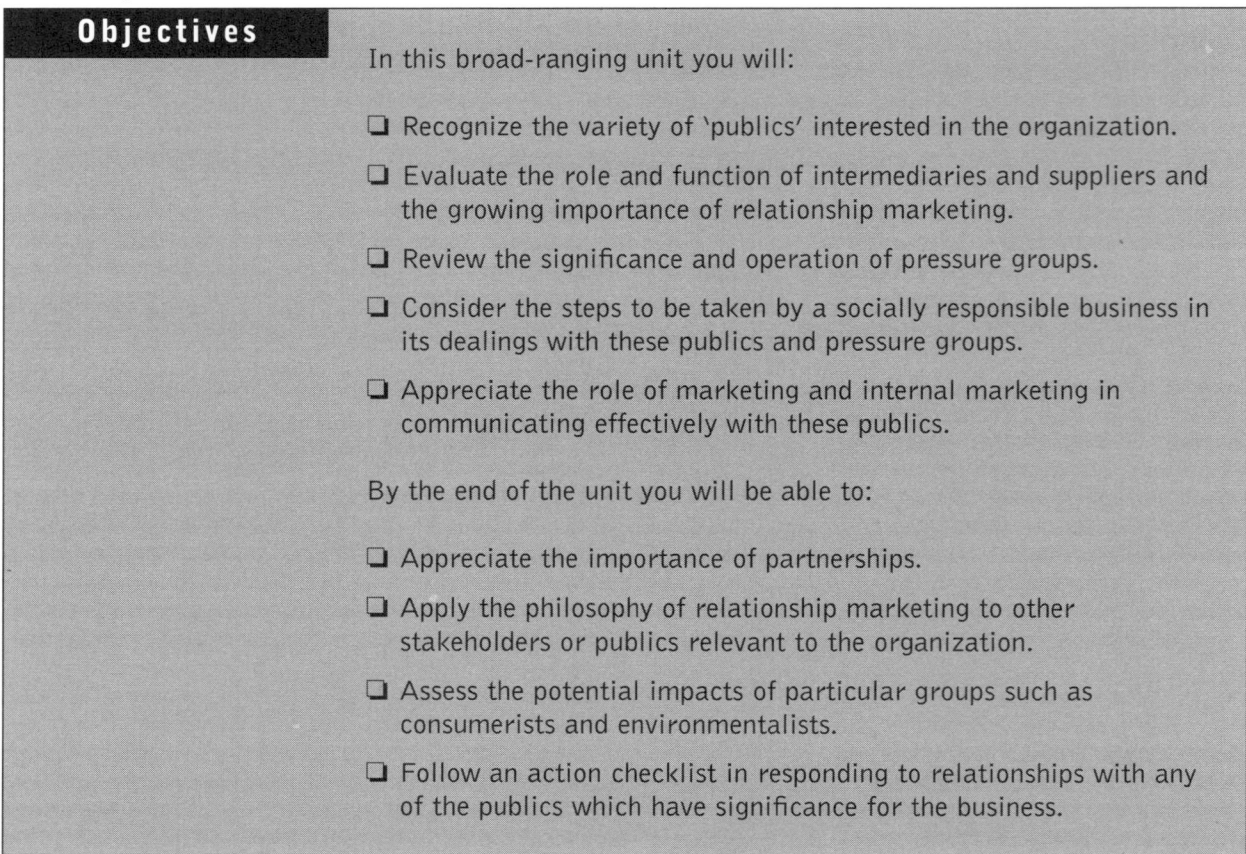

In this broad-ranging unit you will:

❑ Recognize the variety of 'publics' interested in the organization.

❑ Evaluate the role and function of intermediaries and suppliers and the growing importance of relationship marketing.

❑ Review the significance and operation of pressure groups.

❑ Consider the steps to be taken by a socially responsible business in its dealings with these publics and pressure groups.

❑ Appreciate the role of marketing and internal marketing in communicating effectively with these publics.

By the end of the unit you will be able to:

❑ Appreciate the importance of partnerships.

❑ Apply the philosophy of relationship marketing to other stakeholders or publics relevant to the organization.

❑ Assess the potential impacts of particular groups such as consumerists and environmentalists.

❑ Follow an action checklist in responding to relationships with any of the publics which have significance for the business.

Study Guide

This is an encompassing unit which considers the diversity of an organization's many publics. It is a development of the stakeholder concept introduced in Unit 1 and developed in more depth in Unit 2. You should therefore refresh your understanding of direct and indirect stakeholders and the pressure they can bring to bear on the organization. The potential for conflict of interest between stakeholder groups was another important theme considered.

Organizations, especially large ones with market power, are in a position to respond positively to the influence exerted by these various stakeholder groups. Most of this influence is a direct response to the impact such organizations have on publics far beyond the corporate base. However, as in the efficient allocation of scarce resources, so management will be aware that it can only afford to do so much, and must prioritize according to the pressures and their likely impacts.

This aspect of the syllabus ranges across all the stakeholder publics. While we have space to consider only one or two in some depth, you must try to keep abreast of developments in them all. The examiner may focus on one public in particular or may test your knowledge of their collective importance to the organization. It is at these stakeholders that the vast majority of marketing communications are directed. The customer is the main target, of course, but marketers will also be keen to influence and persuade other groups such as employees, investors, political decision makers and the broader community.

This unit should take only 2–3 hours to work through thoroughly, with a further 3 hours for the extending and other activities. As in previous units, you are advised to:

- Open a new file under the heading 'Stakeholders, the firm's many publics'.
- Subdivide this file into six sections on: responsibilities to direct stakeholders, responsibilities to indirect stakeholder publics, supplier/intermediary partnerships and relationship marketing, pressure group activities and methods, the management of stakeholder pressure and marketing to its publics.
- Open sub-sections in the first two for each stakeholder group and build up information and clippings on these. Pay particular attention to the consumerist and environmental lobbies.

Stakeholders: analysis of an organization's many publics

Publics may be defined as those groups with an actual or potential interest in, or impact on, the activities of the organization and its ability to achieve its objectives. Though the term is often used interchangeably with stakeholders, it mainly refers to the secondary or indirect groups as distinct from the primary actors, like customers and competitors, who compose the micro-environment.

Kotler distinguishes seven types of publics each with a two-way relationship with the organization. These may be summarized as follows:

1 *The general publics* This public collectively represents the nation's householders, consumers, workers, pensioners and many other sub-categories of wider society. Their attitudes and expectations are important and reflected in opinion polls. They are purported to be represented by various media and politicians. This public matters to organizations because their concerns and beliefs impact on their economic decisions. Companies recognize this and the need to market themselves effectively through public relations expenditure. Large companies like BT, BP and the BBC invest considerable time and resources in building and maintaining a positive public image.

2 *Community publics* Every organization has local publics it must take particular account of. This is clearly sensible in the case of the large chemical plant with its attendant risks and hazards. However, service organizations such as Oxford University or the Halifax Bank must establish close links with neighbourhood residents and community organizations given their relative size and impact. Sponsorship and openness will be two of the means deployed to maintain good relationships.

3 *Pressure group publics* The activities and decisions of the organization and its marketing function may be challenged by a variety of action groups concerned over specific causes or interests. Later in this unit we will consider the pressures applied by consumerists and the environmental lobby.

4 *Government publics* As the source of legislation, both central and local, together with its monitoring and enforcement there is a clear need to establish effective two-way dialogue between these publics and the marketing function. Note the inter-linkage between the above publics where the community or general public may put pressure on government to get their voice heard.

5 *Media publics* These include news, articles, features and editorials carried by television, newspapers, radio, journals, magazines and increasingly the internet. Again, these are the medium used by the other publics to make their point and marketers must seek to develop good relationships with media representatives so that the organizational case is also made.

6 *Financial publics* These include banks, analysts, market makers and shareholders. Public companies, in particular, need to be aware of the information needs of these publics and their influence on the company's ability to obtain funds. The organization must market itself effectively to

such groups to ensure that sentiment remains positive.

7 *Internal publics* Any organization will have a variety of internal publics ranging from the board of directors through management, operatives, support staff and even part-timers. They are important constituencies who represent the organization to the outside world. Appropriate and regular communication is clearly important through newsletter and meeting, as well as representation and consultation.

Exam Tip

Are you remembering to think of at least one or two more examples for each one cited in the text? The examiner is going to be more impressed with your orginal examples, rather than re-reading his/her own!

The days when organizations could safely 'mind their own business' are no longer! The behaviour of companies and the managers that run them, like politicians, have become everybody's business nearly all of the time. Organizations must recognize that they are under the watchful gaze of all the above publics from time to time. Pressure groups are exerting two types of pressure:

1 *Legislative,* which will be the concern of Unit 6, and
2 *Ethical,* which seeks to change business objectives, policies and behaviour in various ways.

For example, large firms should pay smaller ones more promptly, top executives should set an example in their remuneration practices and all businesses should employ a higher proportion of women and minority groups in senior positions.

The stakeholder publics of any organization are unique but may either threaten and challenge its objectives and operations or support them. It is therefore vitally important that the business 'knows its stakeholders', since from knowledge comes the power to deal with them effectively.

Overlooking the potential power of these publics may inflict untold damage as the recent experience of M&S shows. Supplier criticisms, poor trading results and boardroom battles soon after the announcement of an ambitious £2.2 billion expansion programme up to the year 2001, first disenchanted financial and media publics, followed by internal and general publics. As profits and the share price fell sharply and jobs at headquarters were cut by a fifth, the company slipped from the top to the bottom of an corporate image survey. The speed at which the mighty can fall provides a clear lesson for others to learn. Positive reaction from such publics over time requires care and a planned and proactive approach from the marketer.

At a more general level, the political importance of stakeholder-publics has been emphasized by New Labour. Tony Blair has promoted the idea of a stakeholder economy as part of the 'Third Way' and this is mirrored in many of the points made below.

Activity 3.1

Draw up a 'stakeholder map' for yourself as an individual. Who has a legitimate stake in you and your objectives? What are their interests and what is the nature of the relationship between you? How do you have an impact on these stakeholders? How could they potentially have an impact on you?

Knowing your own personal stakeholders provides an insight into the importance of such knowledge to an organization. It also may help you assess your current position in both work and life in general. How do you cope with the pressures these stakeholders may seek to put on you? Do you try to play one off against another? Do you know how they are likely to respond to any major initiative you are considering? Can their response affect the intended outcome?

(**See** Activity debrief at the end of this unit.)

The seven steps in stakeholder analysis

1 Which publics are important to the firm's operations?
2 Are they increasing or decreasing in importance?
3 How strong are company–stakeholders relationships?
4 What is the impact of corporate actions and operations on these publics?
5 What actual or potential impact could they have on the business?
6 What are the interests of each relevant public?
7 Which groups pose a threat and which an opportunity?

Which publics?

Each business should map out its own unique set of stakeholder publics. Not all of the general categories we identified in Unit 2 will be relevant to all businesses. This is particularly the case with the indirect categories. The 'set' will vary according to whether the business is small or multinational, in manufacturing or services, commercial or public sector. The weight and significance of each stakeholder will vary as will the strength of the relationship.

Question 3.1

Compare and contrast the stakeholder relationships for a large national company and a small local business.

Are the direct stakeholders (customers, suppliers, employees, owners/creditors) the same? Is the relationship different, and if so, why does the smaller concern have the advantage in developing a sound basis to them?

What about indirect stakeholder publics – government, consumer and environmental groups, unions, other businesses, community groups, the media and analysts?

Can you list all of the publics/groups in each of the above categories who are relevant to an organization of your choice? This should not be too difficult, but it is the important first step in analysing their potential impact on the organization you have selected.

Within each main stakeholder-public group there will be subcategories that need to be identified and appraised. The local community, for example, may break down into a number of subgroups, each with their own specific interests or causes which might impact on the business:

Residents – central, suburban and outlying, permanent and transient, e.g. students
Other businesses – utilities, manufacturing, transport/services
Council taxpayers – different band categories
Schools and colleges – primary, secondary, tertiary level concerns
Farmers and horticulturalists
Civic associations
Churches, charities and good causes
Heritage groups
Environmental groups – subdivide into groups concerned with noise, congestion, emissions and effluents
Visitors and transit road users

When subgroups are listed under the other main stakeholder headings it becomes clear that a medium-sized or large nationally based organization will be confronted with a diversity of publics. Resource constraints of time, management and finance mean that these must be screened and prioritized on a regular basis not least because their strength and potential impact will change over time. Company decisions involving such matters as closures, new processes, redeployments, logistical changes and expansion of facilities will also raise its profile with particular publics at particular times.

What are the stakeholder interests?

One possible way of classifying stakeholder publics would be to divide them into those supporting the objectives of your business and those opposed to them. This is too simplistic, however, since business strategies can be deployed to form alliances or understandings with groups such as Friends of the Earth to achieve mutual objectives. This may allow a competitive edge to be achieved in the marketing of such joint initiatives to interested publics.

| Exam Tip | You must be prepared for exam questions that adopt a non-standard format. The examiner will be particularly concerned to see if you can apply some of the different formats for communicating information you will have dealt with in your Business Communications syllabus. |

Exam Tip

You must be prepared for exam questions that adopt a non-standard format. The examiner will be particularly concerned to see if you can apply some of the different formats for communicating information you will have dealt with in your Business Communications syllabus.

You should therefore practise communicating information in a number of forms (for example, lists, summaries, presentation slides, reports, briefs or structured prompts).

Business must therefore understand the interests and objectives of its key publics and seek to satisfy these within the framework of its own goals. Stakeholder public interests may be classified as:

Single-cause group	*Multiple-interest group*
Simpler to deal with	Need breadth and expertise
Less concern for other	Room for compromise / negotiation
stakeholder interests	(e.g. Local authority)

Social cause	*Economic vested interest*
Benefit accrues to society	Benefit accrues to the group
Qualitative / relate to values	Can quantify costs and benefits
Often intangible benefits	Language business can understand

While it is very difficult to measure such aspects as visual amenity, wildlife protection, equal opportunities for minority groups and comprehensive product information they are often as, or even more, important than clear-cut economic self-interest issues.

Local interests	*National/international interests*
Focus on a specific operation	Focus on industry operations
Train local management to handle	One company may be used as a
Be aware of possible escalation	'demonstration effect'

Activity 3.2

- List the key stakeholder publics for your organization.
- Classify their current demands on your organization under the following headings:

  Legitimate demand *Debatable demand* *Doubtful legitimacy*

- Rank each demand on a scale of 1–5 according to how strongly the stakeholder group holds it. Add a + or a – if the strength is expected to increase or decrease over the next 12 months.
- Rank each demand in terms of its probable impact on the organization's image. This should range from 5– for a severe impact on key publics to 5+ for a large positive impact.

This exercise analyses the relationship between each stakeholder and organization of your choice. For each you should assess the *direction of effect* (are company operations impacting on the group or vice versa?), the *strength of the impact* (if unaddressed how might goodwill, sales, shareholder relations, etc. be affected?) and the *likely time scale of the impact* (is immediate management action required?).

How should management and the marketer respond?

The marketing response will be considered in more detail at the end of this unit, but it is appropriate at this point to consider some of the general issues in dealing with this complex of publics.

We saw when considering social responsibility in Unit 2 that where a business is sensitive to the interests of its publics it is more likely to react effectively to change in its marketing environment. Issues are more complicated than internal operations and more long term in their impact.

Conflicts of interests between its stakeholders as well as with company objectives are also more frequent. Returns on efforts to manage these consistently are increasing, however, and trust built up through a record of 'public' service is an asset and an investment to protect. Customers are discouraged from consuming brands where *negative publicity* arises and insensitivity in one area can cancel positive efforts elsewhere.

Question 3.2	Can you think of some recent 'negative publicity' for your or any high-profile company? If not, scan the newspapers until you have a number of relevant examples on file. **Hint:** Shell, Microsoft, M&S, Prudential, rail franchisers.

The stakeholder planning and policy-making process should involve:

- A framework of stakeholder analysis outlined above
- Review of current policies towards stakeholder groups
- Establishment of a stakeholder monitoring system
- Identify scope for competitive advantage through 'reputation'
- Implement mechanisms for achieving change
- Measure and review progress.

The organization must decide its fundamental responsibilities and develop a policy towards each stakeholder based on the values it considers important. Priorities must be established to ensure that limited resources are not spread too thinly. It should logically focus first on current and prospective legal obligations towards stakeholders.

Due to the slow working of the legislative process and political manifestos, companies have advance warning of such developments. Organizations, or their trade associations, must therefore monitor proposed developments, both in the UK and in the European Union, very carefully, since they may wish to influence its detailed formulation in their own interests.

Second, the organization will wish to consider its moral responsibilities and where it stands on these (and relative to its competitors). In these, as well as with projected legislation, it will wish to concentrate its attention where the likely impacts on its business are greatest. Investment, in other words, should be in respect to publics which are most important to the company and achievement of its objectives. Is the action to be taken going to help both the company and the stakeholder group concerned?

Exam Tip	There is always a strong temptation in a time-constrained examination to start writing as soon as possible, especially when those about you seem to have done so already. It is more than likely, however, that such candidates will be writing unstructured answers which do not address what the question requires, and certainly not in a logical sequence. As any effective marketer will tell you, it is the planning that goes into a campaign that is the secret of its success. The same is the case with exam questions. Understanding what the customer (i.e. the examiner) wants and then spending four or five minutes to plan how best to effectively satisfy these

wants is what produces the excellent pass. Writing it out in a form the examiner can comprehend is merely the mechanics of the process.

You should develop the habit of jotting down *trigger word plans* for all the sample exam questions in this workbook. Each 'word' represents an idea or factor you will introduce into the essay. Just one word will remind you of the idea and it ensures that you will not omit to include it at the appropriate point in your answer.

As Figure 3.1 suggests, any organization (let us say a grocery retailer) is confronted by a seemingly endless procession of stakeholder issues in whose crossfire it threatens to be caught. It is important that the organization does not over-react to these issues since they can be double-edged. Politically correct behaviour, not least in the area of sexual harassment and the promotion of women into senior managerial positions, may also rebound if the result is a steep rise in the turnover of company trained male managers. Performance against intended objectives must be measured and assessed. Every effort should be made to frame objectives in such a way that progress towards them can be estimated.

Animal testing	Minority recruitment	Solvent abuse
Women managers	Sunday opening	Sponsorship
Passive smoking	Part-time contracts	Organic foods
Employee share-ownership		Political donations
Alcohol sales	MARKS & SPENCER	Rain forests
Environmentally friendly supply sourcing		City-centre decline
Use of recycled material	Diet and health	Product labelling
Third World sourcing	Irradiated food	Land use/parking

Figure 3.1
Real-world stakeholders issues

The methodology of marketing has a role in many of the stages discussed above. Understanding the needs of the various publics and their legitimate demands on the organization requires the equivalent of a segmentation analysis. Each group can be evaluated in terms of its needs and wants, expectations and concerns. Market research methods can be used to gain understanding of their interests and objectives.

The effectiveness of company policies towards stakeholders may also be assessed using surveys and panels. Marketing communication and persuasion is required to target representative 'influencers' or champions among these publics and secure their ongoing contribution to the organization. Just as the marketer must reach both the target market and the individual consumer within it, so account must be made for the individual employee, shareholder and member of the community as well as the stakeholder groups as a whole.

Question 3.3

What is your own personal role in maintaining the good reputation of your business? Think about this question in terms of your behaviour both at work and outside work.

Refer back to Activity 3.1 above where you identified your own personal stakeholders. Are there similarities to your behaviour in building your own personal reputation?

Do your own ethical standards match those of your organization? What options do you have if there is a mismatch?

(**See** Activity debrief at the end of this unit.)

Pressure groups

Characteristics of pressure groups are as follows:

- They are subsections of the population organized on the basis of *specific common interests or attitudes*.
- They exert pressure on people, organizations or government for their *own special purpose*.
- They seek to *influence* the context of government decisions.
- They do not seek election to government office and *are not political parties* (e.g. Green Party).
- They exercise pressure both for the purpose of securing favourable decisions and for preventing undesirable ones.

We have already made the distinction between a *sectional or interest group*, whose membership is based on the performance of a specific economic role, and a *promotional or cause group*, who are bound by shared values or attitudes and seek to promote a particular issue or prevent an adverse outcome. The latter may be formed to fight a specific issue and then disband when it is won or lost.

Activity 3.3

List the pressure groups you have belonged to and classify them into the two groups above. Do the same for the following: Chambers of Commerce, the Mothers' Union, Campaign for Real Ale, British Medical Association.

(**See** Activity debrief at the end of this unit.)

Examples of sectional pressure groups include trade unions, the Consumers Association, trade associations and businesses themselves. The Trades Union Congress (TUC) and Confederation of British Industry (CBI) are representative organizations. Promotional groups are very numerous and have expanded rapidly in recent years. They fall into several groups:

Welfare	Age Concern, RSPCA, Action on Smoking & Health (ASH)
Recreation	National Cyclists' Union, Ramblers Association
Cultural	Citizens' Advice Bureau, Lord's Day Observance Society
Environmental	Conservation Society, Noise Abatement Society, AA
Political	Tenants associations, Campaign against Racial Discrimination
International	Oxfam, Anti-Apartheid movement, Save the Children Fund.

Pressure groups are the activists of the stakeholder publics considered so far. They are the means through which the individual can be heard on important issues by joining forces with like-minded people whether locally or nationally. Groups can arise to fight factory or hospital closures, unacceptable business practices and motorway proposals (e.g. A30 tunnellers). They will usually use all means at their disposal to achieve their objectives:

- *Complain* (e.g. to the local media)
- *Inform and persuade* those likely to be affected
- *Debate and challenge* at local meetings
- *Lobby and petition* local MPs and Parliament
- *Canvass and opinion form* among stakeholder groups
- *March and demonstrate* outside the factory gates
- *Demand and negotiate* action and concessions from the company
- *Take legal action*

Identify an issue of importance to business, such as congestion, the route of the high-speed rail link, genetically modified foods, the nuclear fuel reprocessing plant at Sellafield or a topical/local equivalent (e.g. banning hunting with hounds).

Map out the protagonists in the issue and classify them according to whether they are sectional or cause groups, where they stand on the issue, their respective interests and what they stand to gain or lose.

Monitor their activities and strategies under the headings mentioned above and try to identify others (e.g. alliances, leaks, infiltration, bribery, opinion forming, misinforming and blackmailing).

The formal channels through which pressure groups function are:

- *Pressure through government* Formal pressure may be applied when the group is invited to give evidence to, for example, Royal Commissions, Committees of Inquiry, Select Committees and other quasi-non-government organizations such as the Competition Commission (formerly the Monopolies and Mergers Commission) or the Office of Fair Trading. Government departments will also consult directly with recognized and responsible pressure groups to sound out views on proposed legislation. Input at the initial drafting stage is an important advantage, although all may comment once a 'Green Paper' has been issued for discussion. Governments cannot legislate effectively without consultation with interested parties, and these are part of the routine relationships it maintains.

- *Pressure through parliament* Pressure groups will seek to recruit sympathetic MPs to their cause. MPs will be concerned with any matters affecting their constituencies and re-election prospects and are therefore susceptible to particular issues and causes. Businesses often employ professional lobbyists to identify and mobilize such support for their interests. MPs can introduce private members' bills and ask parliamentary questions to publicize a cause, but this is normally much less effective than pressure exerted through government ministers and departments. The need to disclose earnings arising out of representation may also constrain such pressures.

- *Pressure through public campaign* Educational and propaganda campaigns can be mounted to move public opinion in the longer term. Attention in the short term will tend to focus on raising public and stakeholder awareness and seeking to mobilize them against a specific threat. The typical means here include public meetings, demonstrations, petitions, newspaper advertisements and exposure in the media in general. This has been relatively successful in the case of drink-driving, for example, but less certain in the current campaign developing against fast urban driving.

The consumerist movement

The consumer movement had its origins in America during the late 1950s when commentators like Vance Packard and Ralph Nader began to alert consumers to the fact that businesses were concerned more for their own profits than customer or environmental welfare. Nader's book, *Unsafe at any Speed* successfully challenged the might of one of the world's largest multinationals, General Motors, and signalled the birth of consumerism.

In Britain, its development was slower. The publication and interest in the Consumers Association's *Which?* reports, comparing the relative performance and merits of rival brands from the users point of view, served notice on the ancient maxim 'caveat emptor' (let the buyer beware), replacing it with 'caveat vendictor' (let the seller beware). There is little wonder that the reduced willingness of customers to suffer in silence coincided with more proactive companies adopting a marketing orientation towards these increasingly aware stakeholders.

Activity 3.5

Visit your local reference library and request back copies of recent *Which?* reports or their equivalents in your own country. They should be conveniently bound into yearly volumes. Using these as your reference data, report on the main areas of current interest to the consumer movement.

There is no one accepted meaning of the term 'consumerism'. Some of the suggested definitions are as follows:

- The search for getting better value for money
- A social movement seeking to augment the rights and powers of buyers in relation to sellers
- Anything consumers say it is.

Consumerism is clearly a force within the environment designed to aid and protect the consumer by exerting legal, moral and economic pressure on business. It has evolved over time and as the following chart suggests it means different things to different consumer groups:

Early causes	*Later causes*	*Future causes?*
Unfair pricing tactics	High credit costs	
Fraud and deceit	Promotion of superficial values	
Lack of competition	Designed obsolescence	
Deceptive advertising	Deceptive packaging	
Unsafe/junk products	Product labelling – GM foods	
Lack of product information	Price/quantity/value for money	
Poor service	Ecolabelling and claims	
Pressure selling tactics	'Free' goods offers	
Misleading warranties	Junk promotional literature	
Poor-quality products	Complex technology products	
Exploiting the poor/young	User-unfriendly instructions	
Limited means of redress	Poor value extended warranties	
Refusal of refunds	Easy credit-card availability	
Unsolicited marketing	Tied holiday insurance/promotions	

Question 3.4

In the light of the above lists and your survey of recent *Which?* reports, what do you consider will be the future 'causes' of the consumerist movement?

How might a marketing-orientated organization exploit your perceptions and obtain a competitive advantage over its rivals?

(See Activity debrief at the end of this unit.)

In 1962 US President John Kennedy laid the foundation to consumerism by proposing the four basic rights set out in Figure 3.2.

Right of safety	Right to be informed
Right to be heard	Right to choose

Figure 3.2
Consumer rights

- *Safety* The right to protection against the marketing of any products which are hazardous to life, especially where hidden dangers may be involved. Products such as pharmaceuticals, cars, household appliances, insecticides and foods have been the source of many customer-related accidents and a major spur to consumerism. Current targets for legal actions include the tobacco and drinks industries. Mobile phones constitute a future target due to microwave emissions, interference and in-car usage.

  The long-term implications of food additives, irradiated and genetically modified foods, E-coli bacteria and the transfer of BSE from cattle to humans are four further examples of such concern. Safe alternatives do not always cost more and may provide an edge for companies in the marketplace. However, where extra cost is involved, as in fire-retardant furniture foam, or fully effective air bags and ABS (electronic vehicle braking systems), competition often prevents concerted action in the interests of greater safety. However, note the marketing consequences of the Transport Research Laboratory impact tests on seven popular European 'super-minis'. Though the methods were disputed, those vehicles warranting 3 stars benefited significantly in media terms. European car-makers claim they must undertake 450 tests to comply with 47 EU design directives applying to each vehicle. Similarly, rollover during tests of the small A class Mercedes forced expensive re-engineering on the company to resolve the problem. The marketing consequences of a vehicle initially nicknamed 'the flipper' appear to have been overcome by the heavy investment to restore the quality and safety assurance normally associated with this brand.

- *Information* The right to protection from fraudulent, deceitful and grossly misleading information and to be given the necessary facts to enable an informed decision to be taken. This is an important role for consumerists and an area which impacts directly on the ethics of marketing departments. The consumer is a generalist lacking the expertise, the time and often the inclination to acquire the product knowledge necessary to make an informed purchase.

  Reliance for comprehensive and comprehensible information is therefore placed on the marketer in respect of advertising, promotional copy, personal selling, packaging, guarantees and service contracts. Time share, insurance and packaged holiday companies, for example, still seem to inhabit the lower reaches of the pressure sell and 'small print' jungle!

Exam Tip

Remember you are a consumer as far as the CIM and your college are concerned. You have a 'right' to expect a relevant syllabus, an applied approach, comprehensive information on examination requirements and feedback on performance.

Make sure you take advantage of your consumer rights and do not forget to read and carefully file each copy of *Marketing Success*. There is no better source of up-to-date customer information.

- *Choice* The right to variety and a competitive service at a fair price. The customer should have the information and opportunity to make an objective selection and be able to distinguish between me-too and 'real' competition in promotional offerings.
- *A hearing* The right to express dissatisfaction over poor service and sub-standard product performance. Consumers should have easy-to-navigate channels for airing their grievances and receive full and sympathetic consideration. The need for legal process and an external policing mechanism will be examined in Unit 6, when fair trading principles are considered.

Consumerist responses to those businesses which sought to exploit them have included individual refusal to buy, collective boycotts, lobbying and media campaigns through 'Watch-dog' television programmes. Consumer power has always suffered from diffusion arising from the variety of calls on available buyer purchasing power. Agitating over dissatisfaction with a low value or infrequently purchased good or service is often judged a waste of time and effort. This probably explains the resort to legislation rather than place reliance on voluntary codes of practice. A prime example of 'power diffusion' arises in the Common Agricultural Policy where half of the total EU budget subsidizes farmers. They form a small but concentrated and vociferous pressure group while unorganized households pay higher prices and taxes thought to average £1500 per household.

Business initially viewed the consumer movement as a threat which created extra costs of compliance and inhibited their freedom of operation. Marketing-orientated organizations, however, soon learnt to listen to what consumers really required and found acceptable in terms of good business practice.

Consumers vote with their money and, given acceptable choices, will shop elsewhere. Better to accept the challenge of consumerism and take constructive steps to address the problems before the competition does it for you!

Question 3.5

The impact of customer power and green marketing

Read the following extracts from the *Financial Times* and consider the questions posed:

Green consumerism has the briefest of histories in Britain, but there are signs that it is entering a new phase, one in which businesses will have to take greater care to substantiate their claims before wrapping their products in a green label.

The government too has signalled that it is losing patience with manufactures who plaster their wares with unjustifiable claims of eco-virtue in an attempt to cash in on the environmental bandwagon. They support a European Union labelling scheme that would require products to be independently vetted before they could carry an eco-label.

Pressure from environmental groups like Friends of the Earth and consumer organisations such as the Consumers Association, has already forced many companies to review their marketing approach:

- Rover cars quickly withdrew its mistaken claim that an unleaded model was 'ozone friendly'.
- BP contravened Advertising Standards when they claimed their Supergreen petrol offered 'no pollution of the environment' simply because it was lead free.
- General claims to be environmentally friendly misleadingly applied to specific products which are not neutral in impact have been challenged by Consumer groups, e.g. Sainsbury's own green label.
- Varta cadium free battery labels were revised, after criticism, to 'environmentally friendlier', recognising that an absolute standard for such a product was currently impossible. Market share rose from 4 to 15 per cent.

Such efforts by companies at self-regulated labelling is a half-way house to a statutory scheme. This will take time, however, since the Environment Department will only introduce an eco-label after agreement on an EC-wide system.

News reports also claim responsibility for the algae blooming in the Adriatic lies partly with the phosphate residues from detergents. The Soap and Detergent Industry Association, however, points out that Italian detergents do not even contain phosphate! They are concerned about confusion in the consumer's mind over the relative merits of 'allegedly green' labels. The rapid emergence of phosphate-free brands like Ecover, Ark and Bright White has challenged the market domination of Unilever and Procter & Gamble. Their market is threatened by the rising tide of consumer belief that products which make no overt claims to be 'green' are to be deemed harmful.

New product labels claiming 'no chlorine bleach', for example, are misleading since such ingredients are used in *no* fabric washing powders in Britain. Biodegradable is another term much used for marketing advantage yet this is also a legal requirement for all domestic detergents. However, as the market leaders are well aware, once a simple, apparently reasonable proposition is implanted in the mind of the consumer, it can be almost impossible to uproot.

1 In what sense can green consumerism be both a threat and a potential opportunity for the marketer?
2 How would you advise companies such as Procter & Gamble and Unilever to counter the threat to their 80 per cent combined market share, posed by these allegedly eco-friendly detergents?
3 Visit two competing major supermarkets and compare and contrast their policies on eco-labelling. Are their claims responsible, or misleading to the consumer?

(**See** Activity debrief at the end of this unit.)

Exam Tip

You must get as much practice as possible at answering case questions based on extracts and articles. The compulsory question worth 40 per cent of the marks will typically follow this format. You must remember, however, that the examiner is testing not your specific knowledge of the article in question but your ability to relate it to your overall knowledge of the marketing environment.

A typical question is reproduced at the end of this unit, but you will see that the questions only use the article as a *context*. They ask you to relate concepts or terms mentioned in the article to your broader knowledge and understanding of the syllabus.

Summary

Consumerism has provided many customer-orientated businesses with an opportunity to make product strengths and socially responsible marketing a source of competitive advantage. It is a well-established feature of the marketplace and will remain so while ever there is scope for opportunist sellers to mislead and confuse the consumers. Its concerns now extend far beyond consumer protection to issues such as pricing, design obsolescence and, increasingly, the environment. Marketers must therefore respond positively to the interests of this fundamental stakeholder group.

Environmentalism

There are an estimated 1400 environmental pressure groups in Britain alone. Demands they are making range over the following:

- Conservation of resources
- Re-use, redesign and recycling of products
- Energy saving
- Elimination of non-eco-friendly products
- A slowing of economic growth
- Protection of the natural environment and endangered species
- Animal rights

Question 3.6

How many environmental pressure groups can you list? How would you classify these different groups?

(**See** Activity debrief at the end of this unit.)

Clearly such demands imply economic and financial costs for business, potential redundancies and higher consumer prices. Despite a cyclical pattern to such pressures and some decline recently they are likely to increase rather than diminish with time. Some industries are more likely to be targeted than others but none are immune. Those most recently in the firing line include aerosols, agriculture, airlines, animal testing, chemicals, fertilizers, motorways, oil tankers, plastics, pulp and paper, refrigeration, tobacco, tourism, toxic waste and water.

Question 3.7

1 Take each of the industries listed above and suggest the environmental issue that has placed them in the firing line.
2 What responses have businesses in these industries made that you are aware of?
3 What other industries, not mentioned above, would you include as high-profile targets for environmentalists?

(**See** Activity debrief at the end of this unit.)

A number of possible threats arise if a business ignores its environment:

- The corporate image deteriorates in the eyes of stakeholders
- Customers may prefer alternatives they perceive as less harmful
- Shareholders may prefer to invest in ethically sound companies
- Recruitment and retention of quality staff becomes more difficult
- Unnecessarily strict legislation enacted due to failure to act
- Loss of community support, harder attitude from authorities
- Increasing competitive disadvantage to proactive rivals
- Cost penalties – higher energy bill, insurance, legal claims

Activity 3.6

In the light of the potential threats outlined above, make a case to your board of directors stating the potential benefits of becoming a more environmentally aware company.

Suppose the board is persuaded by the force of your arguments but asks you for guidelines to ensure that this new philosophy is adopted throughout the company. What would you suggest?

(**See** Activity debrief at the end of this unit.)

We will return to the natural environment as an issue in Unit 10 of this workbook, but before concluding this section on environmentalism, two final aspects should be mentioned: first, the importance of legal form and second, the business response required to such pressure groups.

Sole traders and small limited companies normally face more intense competition and are less likely to have the resources to commit to achieving environmental standards in excess of those required by legislation. On the other hand, they will be owner-managed and do business in localities where they live. Such business people have traditionally filled many civic posts in the local community and may sacrifice profit to maintain their reputation and standing in this and other respects. Plcs, in comparison, will be well resourced and have a higher national profile. They will be more aware of developments with regard to the industry and its environment and are more likely to participate in government and other initiatives to bring about improvements.

On the other hand, they are often in a position to relocate production activities to other parts of the world where legislation is less stringent. Small firms will find it less easy to justify the cost of meeting new environmental management standards such as BS 7750, although there are increasing pressures on suppliers to adopt these, irrespective of legal form.

The compulsory question counts for 40 per cent of the total marks on the paper. Given that the paper is 3 hours long, this means you should spend 40 per cent of the time on it, i.e. 1 hour 12 minutes. If this compulsory question has four parts to it, then you should be allocating just 18 minutes per part. The question paper will tell you if the parts are worth different mark values, but typically they will be the same.

At 18 minutes per part it is very important that you keep to the time allowed. What examiners find, all too frequently, is candidates who spend too long on parts they happen to know a lot about at the expense of one or two of the others on which they have time to write very little at all. Do not be tempted to fall into this trap. Spend roughly the same amount of time on each and give the examiner something to mark even in those parts where you are less confident.

The response

The final question is, how should the business respond to pressure from environmentalists, or any of the other publics, for that matter? We have already seen that the organization must prioritize since it has insufficient resources to deal with all pressures. It must assess which pressures are significant and offer the greatest likelihood of impact on the business. The response may be framed in very simple terms, but each option requires considerable management effort and time to make it effective:

- Listen to them
- Consult with them
- Liaise with them
- Work with them
- Support them to work for you
- Oppose them

Extending Activity 3.1

Take your own organization (if appropriate) or one of your choice which is in the environmental firing line. Select an environmental pressure group currently concerned with the consequences of this company's operations and think through all the above options in practical terms. How would you go about listening, consulting, liaising, etc. and why might their support provide the marketing department with a competitive advantage?

As you scan both the newspapers and promotional packaging look for examples of cooperation between companies and pressure groups (e.g. Tidy Britain Group on cans of soft drinks, Automobile Association recommendation of car safety products).

Conclusions on pressure groups

Pressure groups and their relationship with governments will be dealt with in Unit 7. At this point we can conclude that pressure group activity and influence is increasing and becoming better organized and more professional in their approach to both government and target companies. They are now much more adept at marketing their causes and highlighting the deficiencies of companies towards their stakeholder groups.

Green consumers guides and the Friends of the Earth green 'con' awards are just two examples of potentially damaging copy for a business's reputation. To minimize such risks a company must establish and apply values and beliefs conducive to a sustainable business. It must be aware of threats as well as the considerable opportunities of enhancing its reputation in the eyes of stakeholders through effective and well-managed policies towards the environment. Unilever and the World Wildlife Fund for Nature, for example, recently agreed a sustainable standard for fish products with a special logo if the product was from accredited fishing grounds.

Communicating with its publics: the role of marketing

The organization has a number of communication channels available to relay messages to its publics:

The promotional mix
- Advertising
- Sales promotion
- Publicity – public relations
- Personal selling

to which may be added:

- Internal marketing
- Relationship marketing

Communication is the process of establishing a oneness of thought between the sender and the receiver. A business wishing to communicate effectively with its publics must tune its channels to operate on the same wavelength. The marketer is competing for the attention of stakeholders who are being blasted with rival messages from all sides. The communication must be encoded into a visual, printed or spoken message and transmitted through a TV commercial, newspaper advertisement, poster or letter to the receiver who then decodes it. To check the message has been received and the intended meaning understood, the marketer must monitor the outcome and act on the feedback obtained.

Marketing communication using the promotional mix is well understood by the marketer as a means of establishing links with the buying public. It is also recognized that the total product offering, or bundle of satisfactions within the augmented good or service, are the means of retaining the contribution of the consumer and securing the mutual achievement of one another's goals.

Activity 3.7

Consider the appropriate promotional mix to communicate most effectively with the following stakeholders:

- Shareholders
- Local community
- Environment group

Will this vary according to the size of the business concerned?

Find examples of companies using price, product and place to communicate the company's social responsibility stance and values on stakeholder issues (e.g. incentives to re-use/recycle packaging; purchase secures company contribution to a worthy cause; product features – use of recycled materials).

The characteristics of the product or service itself provides numerous cues to the various publics and represents the litmus test of an organization's real commitment to its stated ethical values. The design, fuel economy, inherent safety, recyclability, packaging economy, durability and so on are revealing indicators of a company's focus on its publics. The promotional mix raises awareness and reinforces perceptions of a good business image or, alternatively, seeks to ensure that it is not undermined.

Ensuring that your organization is one that stakeholders want to do business with involves some obvious and basic steps:

- Ensure systems are in place to listen to the publics
- Ensure systems are in place to respond to them and make the necessary things happen.

With customers, for example, most organizations have three points of direct contact:

- The point of sale
- Servicing or repair
- Complaints

The key at each stage is to demonstrate that the company really cares about the customer. This will only be convincing if the company and its employees actually do care. Smile training is not therefore sufficient and the product supplied must, first and foremost, be fit for the customer's purpose. Showing that the company cares might also be effectively signalled by:

- A director responsible for customer service and requiring that performance is regularly monitored
- Staff who are fully trained with expertise always available to handle customer queries
- Decisions to resolve customer problems being taken closest to where they originate by staff with the power to resolve them
- Complaints being treated as an opportunity, providing focus for locating where performance can be improved and competitive advantage gained
- A published customer service policy, and any code of practice adhered to is indepen-dently audited
- Customer involvement in direct feedback, through panels and suggestion schemes, for example.

The Citizen's Charter initiative launched in Britain in early 1991 is an example of seeking such improvements in public services. Progressively improving published standards will lead to customer compensation when the organization fails to achieve them, as in the case of rail services.

Exam Tip

Questions on this part of the syllabus are most likely to require some explanation of a concept such as stakeholders, publics, social responsibility and then some evidence that you can apply it in a marketing context. It is therefore important that:

- You prepare outline marketing responses to deal with stakeholder groups such as described above.
- You find examples to illustrate the ideas you suggest.

Public relations

'Public relations practice is the deliberate, planned and sustained effort to establish and maintain mutual understanding between an organization and its publics.' This definition by the Institute of Public Relations clearly recognizes the plurality of publics to be addressed. Its central objective is to establish meaningful communication between the organization and its stakeholders with a view to building mutually beneficial relationships and resolving any conflicts of interest. The intention is to establish a consistent and clearly defined corporate identity that its publics can relate to. The term 'corporate image', however, seems to be at odds with a responsible business of substance.

To be effective, all aspects of the business must be in tune with this identity. Its policies, management style, staff behaviour and operational activities must all consistently reflect it, if public perceptions are to respond positively.

Internal marketing

This is an area which can contribute to the achievement of consistency in corporate identity although its main aim is to improve service quality within the organization. Internal marketing seeks to apply the principles of marketing to the internal transactions between members of the same organization.

The key is to encourage staff to view themselves both as suppliers to certain members of the organization and as customers to others. In this they are trained and rewarded to respond to a common set of goals and objectives. Any organization with a mission to serve its various publics will then achieve a comprehensive customer orientation coordinated throughout all functions and departments.

Activity 3.8	Apply this idea, of each department being the customer or supplier of the other, to your own organization.

- How would this customer orientation affect the activities of:
  Research and development
  Production departments
  Finance functions
  Training department
  Building services
- Compare your suggestions with what happens now.
- What must the organization do to implement internal marketing?

(**See** Activity debrief at the end of this unit.)

You may already have seen a similarity between this approach and relationship marketing. The achievement of quality improvement and effective customer service requires that staff are all pulling together in the same direction. Communication is clearly critical to success and to the reduction of conflict between functional departments. It also requires commitment from the highest level and an open management style if staff are to be mobilized to cooperate across defined boundaries.

The role and importance of intermediaries and suppliers

The final section of this unit is concerned with relationships and partnerships in the supply chain. The focus here is not with internal marketing of an organization's publics but with primary stakeholders and the increasing importance of *relationship or partnership marketing*. Any business, unless it is vertically integrated throughout its entire operations (e.g. tobacco from plantations to sales kiosks), is part of a supply chain (Figure 3.3). Each deals with independently owned and operated channel members, each with their own mission, strategy and goals. Profit maximization might be pursued at the expense of others in the chain leading to potential for conflict.

There is, however, clear interdependence in this chain since none can prosper without the input or output of the other. Each benefits from the advantages of specialization in focusing on their own core business in order to gain from trade and exchange with the others in the chain. They all form part of the others' micro-environments and each can be viewed as a stakeholder.

Porter's analysis, which is discussed in Unit 4, suggests that profitability partly depends on the relative bargaining power of the parties. Where suppliers are small or fragmented their power is slight compared to monop-

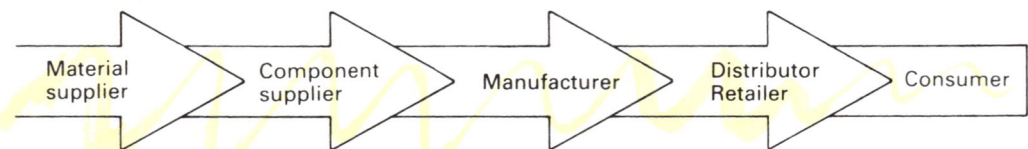

Figure 3.3 A business supply chain

sonists who hold a dominant position. This might lead to the natural conclusion that it is in the best interests of buyers and suppliers to use their bargaining power to the full to secure the best possible price.

The emphasis here is on the *transaction* rather than on the *relationship* with the supplier or customer concerned. Attention is focused on the single contract and the short run rather than the prospects for repeat business in the long run. There is, therefore, very limited contact or commitment on behalf of the supplier or the intermediary.

The relationship is *competitive* and suppliers and distributors would change frequently in what is known as a zero-sum game, i.e. if one side wins the other, by definition, loses. The firm will play one supplier off against another to achieve lower prices, but this would frequently be at the expense of assured quality, delivery and service.

In recent years, however, many companies have moved towards much more *cooperative* relationships, forging ever stronger links between otherwise independently owned businesses in the supply chain. The aim is to achieve a win–win outcome based on partnership, cooperation, involvement and agreement: as in the case of Marks & Spencer and its dedicated suppliers. The key elements involved were:

- Partnerships in logistical solutions.
- Partnerships in productivity, improvement and price control.
- Partnerships in quality control.
- Partnerships in product development and innovation.
- Partnerships in information systems.

The impetus came partly from academic writers such as Peters and Waterman, who suggested in their book, *In Search of Excellence*, that the best-managed companies got close to their customers, and partly from the demonstration effect of Japanese companies in their single-minded drive for *total quality*.

Exam Tip

A quality answer earns an 'excellent' mark. Jot down what you consider to be the ingredients of a quality answer and compare them with the points made in the final unit.

Japanese companies such as Toyota and Sony are at the summit of a complex hierarchy of primary suppliers who in turn contract to second-tier suppliers and so on down the pyramid. Relationships are long term, secure and mutually beneficial often being cemented by cross-shareholdings. Any changes to specifications are by negotiation rather than unilateral action or a move to a rival substitute.

Pursuit of concepts like zero defects and just-in-time (JIT) stock control has made closer relationships essential. This may take the form of electronic data interchange (EDI) between members of the chain, where each can interrogate the other's internal information systems. The supplier may maintain staff permanently on the customer's site to ensure co-ordination, service and the required performance standards. In the extreme, a plant may be purposely located adjacent to the customer to guarantee alignment of quality, service and JIT delivery. The satellite plants that have formed around the Nissan and Toyota assembly operations in Britain are good examples of this tendency.

Businesses have then been able to sharply reduce the number of suppliers with whom they deal. This process has perhaps gone furthest in motor components, where single-sourcing has become the norm in some areas. Partnership marketing with intermediaries is conducted with equivalent cooperation in mind. Jointly funded market research and promotional activity is undertaken, customer service standards are monitored and new initiatives are jointly developed.

The growing importance of relationship marketing

Relationship marketing can be considered in the context of the micro-environment and stakeholders. Kotler has defined it as the process of creating, maintaining and enhancing strong value-laden relationships with customers and other stakeholders. It represents the impact that marketing has on relationships not only with customers and suppliers but also on actual and potential employees, government agencies, financial and other groups. It also seeks to integrate customer-orientated marketing with total quality across all the functional areas of the business and customer service.

IKEA, one of the world's most successful multinational retailers, operates as a global organization using subcontracted manufacturers from all over the world. Close relationships allow the company to keep costs between manufacturers and customers as low as possible and fulfil their vision of creating a better everyday life for the majority of people. The Cooperative Bank has recently linked up with the Post Office, enabling its one million account holders to make cash transactions at 15 500 outlets.

Extending Activity 3.2	Relationship marketing could be the key development of the decade according to Christopher, Payne and Ballantyne in a book of the same name published by Butterworth-Heinemann. It covers the concept in much greater depth than can be considered here and includes a number of highly relevant case studies. Use these as the background for considering whether your organization is 'transactions based' and the steps required to secure competitive advantage from building relationships based on quality and service.

Instead of concentrating on trying to recruit new customers this approach stresses 'keeping' the customers and suppliers you already have by building strong relationships with them, making them, in effect, trading partners. By successfully conforming to customer perceptions of required product quality and service they will effectively become part of the sales force by generating new customer business through referrals. The Insurance Service, for example, a company providing direct car insurance, offers discount bonuses to formally recognize those customers who refer friends and acquaintances.

In an environment of widening choice and maturing markets the loyalty of the customer or supplier cannot be taken for granted. The marketer must calculate the costs and benefits of action to improve customer retention. The lifetime value of a customer is the excess over time of revenues over the cost of attracting, selling to and servicing them. This may be substantial for the regular customer of a public house spending, say, £10 a night, six nights a week and amounting to around £3000 per year. It certainly repays the efforts of the proprietor to retain the custom. This accounts for the actions of supermarkets like Tesco and Sainsbury's to convert from basic to relationship retailers. Long-term value is provided through the product range, quality and pricing structure but this is supplemented by:

- Financial inducements – loyalty points making it costly to switch.
- Targeted promotions using customer sales data and personalized communications.
- Treating customers as individual clients at checkout.
- Providing carrying baskets that only fit into company trolleys.

• Providing banking services.

Question 3.8

Taking your own organization or one you have dealings with as a customer/supplier, consider the following:

1 Use Kotler's framework to assess the quality of its customer/supplier relationships:

   (a) *Basic* – product is purchased/sold without any effort or intention to communicate, follow-up or generate future business.
   (b) *Reactive* – the organization will respond to customer/supplier problems or complaints.
   (c) *Accountable* – the organization positively seeks feedback on problems/potential improvements.
   (d) *Proactive* – on-going communication with the customer/supplier.
   (e) *Partnership* – joint activities undertaken for mutual benefit now and in the future.

2 Which businesses are most suited to (a) basic marketing, (b) partnership marketing, and why?
3 What is the real value of a loyal customer or supplier and how do you create one?

(See Activity debrief at the end of this unit.)

Christopher, Payne and Ballantyne see the following factors as central to relationship marketing:

• A focus on customer retention
• An orientation towards product benefits rather than product features
• A long-term view
• Maximum emphasis on customer service
• High customer commitment and contact
• Total quality philosophy throughout the organization

They see the marketer's role as one of achieving the *best match* between the controllable internal marketing mix and the largely uncontrollable external environment. As can be seen in Figure 3.4, success will be a function of the degree of match obtained.

Activity 3.9

Based on what you have read about relationship marketing, draw up a contract of mutual responsibilities between a company of your choice and a representative supplier and distributor.

Think about new product development and product specification, quality-improvement initiatives, information systems, training and coordination, exchange of ideas, flexibility, cost reduction and mutual obligations (e.g. scheduled orders and scheduled deliveries).

Note that the philosophy is one of continuous cooperation, partnership and coalition between otherwise separate businesses. Mutual trust is the basis for mutual profitability in designing, developing, producing and delivering the product or service.

The clear message from this analysis is the importance of monitoring change in this turbulent environment, adjusting the mix to exploit opportunities and closing any gaps between customer expectations and actual provision. This is particularly important in industrial and service markets, where building interactive relationships between all the stakeholders should be seen as critical. Also, for businesses with products in maturity or

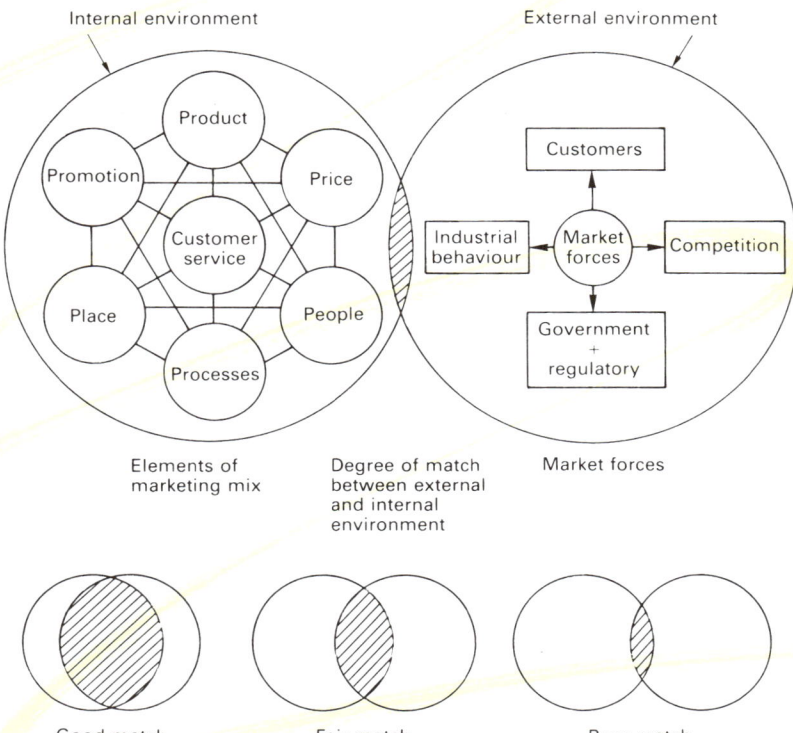

Figure 3.4
The marketing programme as a matching process. (From Christopher, Payne and Ballantyne, *Relationship Marketing*, Butterworth-Heinemann)

late maturity stages of the product life cycle customer service may be the only means of achieving an edge over rivals. The scope for manipulation of the elements of the marketing mix are very limited in this situation.

Under the pressure of two intense recessions and the demonstration effects of foreign multinationals, expectations have been changing. Businesses cannot afford to be anything but professional and demanding of their suppliers. Equally, they must seek a competitive advantage with customers/distributors by building a close relationship with those they judge will be future industry winners. This has even created a need in some high-technology sectors for network marketing, where a web of interdependence between suppliers of a complex aerospace product, for example, necessitates intense relationships.

We can conclude that if the organization is to communicate effectively with its publics it must pursue the unity of purpose required through both internal and relationship marketing. This will, if successful, enable a consistent customer orientation and a coherence between its internal and external marketing efforts.

Summary

In this unit we have seen that:

- The organization must understand its stakeholders and the pressures they seek to apply.
- In a resource-constrained business, stakeholder interests and pressures must be analysed and prioritized before action is taken.
- Action by the organization involves a number of steps, including establishing its own values and giving priority to legal obligations.
- Pressure groups are increasing in importance and can be classified as interest or cause groups.
- Pressure groups can employ a number of means and channels through which their pressure may be brought to bear.
- Consumerism has become a force for companies to reckon with, especially as the causes pursued have broadened out from just narrow consumer protection issues.
- One of the important current issues for consumers relates to the claims and counter-claims of marketers regarding the eco-friendliness of their offerings.
- The scope of environmental concerns and the specific threats posed to businesses are potentially serious (e.g. Perrier water – benzene traces; *Exxon Valdez/Sea*

Empress – tanker spillage; meat products and BSE; genetically modified foods).

- The constructive response is not necessarily to confront and oppose pressure groups but, where possible, to understand their interests, listen to their point of view and work toward a common solution.
- The organization must coordinate and focus the deployment of all its resources and expertise to achieve the necessary orientation towards its customers and publics. All aspects of the marketing and promotional mix must be mobilized to maximum effect supported by an evolving philosophy built on internal marketing.
- The developing importance of relationship marketing was considered in the context of suppliers and customers. The need to build mutual trust and support in the supply chain is increasingly vital in the context of rising quality expectations among customers and the need to share and make effective expensive research and development resourcing.

Activity debrief

Question 3.3 You are an ambassador for your company and your appearance, attitude and views will colour the perceptions of others to it. Whenever you come into contact with customers or other stakeholders your behaviour will positively or negatively affect their preconceptions.

If your ethical standards (i.e. regarding how people treat one another, what you believe in and think is right) conflict with your organization's view of acceptable behaviour then you may:

- Move to a more sympathetic organization
- Try to change organizational ethics
- Adapt your beliefs and conform to the organization's
- Try to avoid situations where conflict arises

Question 3.4 Most topical would be millennium overcharging and internet fraud. Product labelling is also to the fore of GM foods.

Question 3.5 Environmental consumerism is a threat where it allows your market to be penetrated by allegedly eco-friendly alternatives. Consumers may perceive your own product as unfriendly merely because it does not make claims to the contrary. It is an opportunity for new entrants or smaller firms since it sidesteps product-proliferation strategies based around traditional product values.

To counter this threat, the companies must either try to communicate to correct the misinformation associated with the so-called eco-friendly labels *or* press for tighter legislation on labelling *or* develop and promote own brand alternatives.

Question 3.6 Environmental groups could be classified as local, national and international; by type of impact (e.g. Noise Abatement Society or National Society for Clean Air).

Question 3.7 Aerosols – CFCs/ozone layer; agriculture – fertilizer runoff; airlines – energy, noise, ozone; chemicals – effluent, spillage; paper – energy, greenhouse effect; refrigeration – CFCs and disposal; tobacco – health, passive smoking; tourism – areas of natural beauty; toxic waste – leaks, accidents, health.

Other industries coming into the firing line might include biotechnology – genetic implications; transport – congestion, safety and accidents; pharmaceuticals – dependency and ethical considerations.

Question 3.8 (2) In commodity markets (where price is the key) or high volume organizations with low margins, customers will favour basic marketing, e.g. crisp manufacturer, whereas high margin, low volume suppliers to customers with high switching costs will favour partnership. Similarly the computer manufacturer is likely to work closely with the memory chip and software supplier. The 'why' aspect comes down to economic calculation. Customer defection means a possible lifetime stream of lost revenues and profits. If the causes of defection are avoidable (e.g. poor customer service/quality) then the costs of reducing them must be set against any resulting improvement in profit. If you run a hotel or sell a subscription magazine the pay-off may be large.

(3) Think about lifetime revenue flows/recommendation/ assurance/ support in hard times. Creating one may require financial inducement (e.g. loyalty points/upgrades; regular payment/schedules); social relationships and bonds (treat as individual clients); and possibly physical ties (e.g. Walls supply freezers to retailers/National Lottery supplies terminals).

Activity 3.1 Your map should have included some of the following: parents, lecturers, boss, colleagues, religious leaders, neighbours, peers, friends, spouse, etc. You impact on these in any number of ways, but notably how you allocate your time, your activities, attitudes, values and reactions. They may impact on you in terms of financial and time pressures, various social demands and requirements.

In considering the second part of this activity think of an issue or objective and map their likely responses and your responses to them.

Activity 3.3 Sectional interest – Chambers of Commerce, British Medical Association.

Cause/promotional – CAMRA and the Mothers' Union.

Activity 3.6 Potential benefits include enhanced reputation for companies at the leading edge (e.g. Body Shop or Norsk Hydro – the Norwegian chemicals, paper and energy company which was first to use independent environmental auditing); attracting a new market segment of environmentally concerned consumers; cost savings through recycling or improved energy efficiency.

Guidelines for implementation might include:

- Apply from product conception through to final disposal
- Responsibility of staff at all levels
- Build achievement of environmental objectives into the reward structure of the business
- The business should not knowingly do harm to the environment
- The business should behave as a custodian of resources for future generations.

Activity 3.8 Implementation implies heavy investment in employee quality and performance; teamworking among support staff; a change of culture; and modified incentives.

Examination hints and specimen questions

The first question below is an example of a *compulsory* question of which there is one on every CIM paper. Your tutor has already been advised of the importance of this type of question, reflecting as it does the breadth of the syllabus. This means that you will normally have to draw material from different elements of the course in order to answer all parts of the question successfully.

It has been suggested that you practise interpreting news clippings of this type and relating them to relevant parts of the syllabus. I suggest that you read quickly through the clipping once and then read the questions very carefully. Underline key words and remember that you only have, say, 15 minutes for each part after reading time so *stick closely to what the question asks for*!

Now reread the clipping more slowly using a coloured marker pen to highlight sections relating specifically to the questions posed.

This particular case has already been referred to in Unit 1 and, as the last one to be examined prior to publication of this workbook, is comprehensively answered in Unit 11. It provides the context for the questions that follow but only a limited amount of the necessary content. This must always be drawn from your knowledge of the syllabus itself. Merely repeating sections of text from the case will not earn marks unless you process, supplement and apply them first.

One final warning: are you watching the time? With 10 minutes to study the clipping and plan your structure and just an hour to answer three or four parts you will have to get on with it. You might even consider doing the three optional essays first to avoid the danger of spending too long on this question.

The importance of the marketing environment

The CIM defines marketing as '… the management process which identifies, anticipates and supplies customer requirements efficiently and profitably.

This focuses attention on the importance of the marketing environment for practitioners and students alike. Identifying and anticipating customer requirements is impossible unless the organization looks outward from itself, to understand its external environment and the implications of changes taking place on its current and future profitability.

No organization, whether small or large, public or private, profit or non-profit making can afford to ignore its environment. As the strategist H. I. Ansoff observed.

> … the firm is a creature of its environment. Its resources, its income, its problems, its opportunities and its very survival are generated and conditioned by the environment.

It is the generally uncontrollable forces in the macro-environment that create a succession of potential threats and opportunities for the business. These broad trends and changes are extremely important in shaping the competitive situation and the actions and perceptions of relevant stakeholder publics.

Societal concerns are often translated through the legislative process to impact on the freedom of business to manage. The marketer must always be aware that the environment reflects the pressures from a range of interested groups to which a positive response may be called for. It is also the domain of actual or potential competitors, and is consequently ignored at the organization's peril.

> But to tomorrow always arrives, it is different and then even the mightiest company is in trouble if it has not worked on its future.

Large firms, particularly multinationals, may be able to exert greater influence over their business situation, but small firms may have the advantage in responding to the need for change more flexibly. Both must recognize they are on the equivalent of a moving conveyor, they must move fast just to stand still as tastes, technology and competitive forces alter. (Extracts from *The Sales and Marketing Environment*, Butterworth-Heinemann.)

1 '… the firm is a creature of its environment. Its resources, its income, its problems, its opportunities and its very survival are generated and conditioned by the environment.'

   (a) Using examples, fully explain your understanding of this quotation.
   (15 marks)
   (b) What can organizations do to effectively keep abreast of environmental changes? (15 marks)
   (c) Explain the term **relevant stakeholder publics**. Use an example to show how stakeholder perceptions may impact on the marketer.
   (10 marks)
   (CIM Marketing Environment paper, December 1998)

2 (a) Explain the terms:
       (i) Partnership sourcing. (4 marks)
       (ii) Partnership marketing. (4 marks)
   (b) Draft a short report for consideration by your Marketing Manager on: 'The partnership approach – the value of long-term relationships'. (12 marks)
   (CIM Marketing Environment paper, December 1997)

3 Prepare **two** slides representing the impact of 'green' environmental groups in respect of:

(a) The means and the channels by which they can bring pressure to bear on a company like Unilever.

(b) The main areas of concern and the possible threats they pose for Unilever. (10 marks)

(CIM Marketing Environment paper, June 1996)

Note: Questions on concepts like relationship marketing or pressure groups often appear in 'choice' questions, or as one part of a two- or three-part question. Examples include:

4 (a) Write a brief memorandum on the growing importance of relationship marketing with one of these primary stakeholder groups.

(CIM Marketing Environment paper, June 1998)

5 (b) Discuss the importance of 'relationships' to the marketer and briefly comment on how good relationships might best be achieved with consumers.

(CIM Marketing Environment paper, June 1996)

6 Discuss the impact of sharp increases in the membership of pressure groups on the marketing operations of a large retailer.

(CIM Marketing Environment paper, June 1996 – adapted)

Question 1(a)   see end of Unit 1

Question 1(b)

- Attempt this here but refer to Unit 10 and the end of Unit 5 for inspiration if you need it.
- Provide suggestions in an examiner-friendly bullet point form.
- Focus immediately on how to keep abreast, don't worry about why.
- Think about scanning the environment, information sources, help from stakeholders and techniques.

Question 1(c)

- Expect a mark breakdown of up to 6 for the first part due to the use of 'explain'.
- Explain stakeholders, publics and the term relevant.
- Use just one example and relate the perception of two or three stakeholders to it.
- Be sure to link the positive or negative perception to the impact on the marketer.

Question 2(a)/(b)

- Explain implied definition of the terms plus a brief outline of their significance.
- Relate sourcing to suppliers and partnership marketing to intermediaries.
- Provide a report format in (b) but keep it brief and to the point.
- Focus on the 'value' of the relationships.

Question 3

- This was part of a case question which concerned the marketing of detergents.
- Note the requirement to provide slides – make these as realistic as possible but don't use elaborate colours or graphics – it is the information content that is important.

SLIDE 1
THE MEANS AND THE CHANNELS

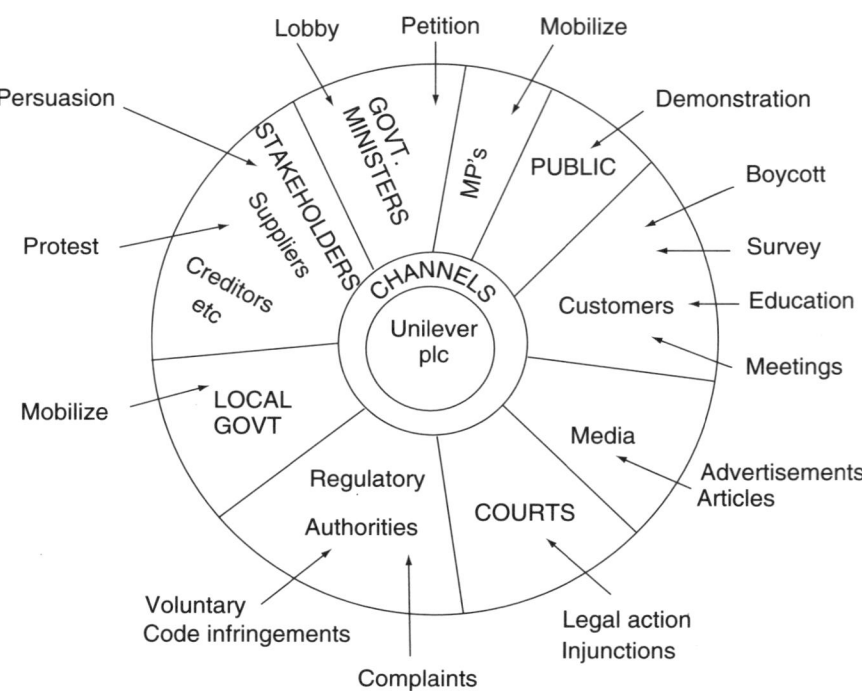

SLIDE 2

MAIN AREAS OF CONTROL

1. Pollution through discharge of wastes

2. Consumer and product safety – harmful additives

3. Heavy use of packaging – non biodegradable

4. Animal testing – product side effects

5. Consumer exploitation – excessive promotion costs

POSSIBLE THREATS TO UNILEVER

1. Falling sales and loss of market share

2. Expensive outlays to limit environmental impacts

3. Damage to corporate image among key stakeholders

4. Possible regulatory inquiry and subsequent conditions imposed

5. Longer research and development lead times/higher costs

6. Loss of staff on ethical grounds

7. Promotional costs of restoring brand loyalty

Analysis of the competitive environment

In this critically important core unit you will:

❏ Examine the importance of monitoring competitors.

❏ Undertake a five-force structural analysis of an industry.

❏ Consider the impact of competition policies on the organization and its marketing environment.

❏ Recognize the key sources of information on the micro-environment.

By the end of this unit you will be able to:

❏ Understand the importance of competitor analysis.

❏ Appreciate the workings of the competitive environment.

❏ Assess the long-run profitability of industry structures.

❏ Identify strategies to improve profitability.

❏ Weigh the significance of polices and legislation as it impacts on the market environment.

❏ Access information relevant to understanding the micro-environment.

Study Guide

This unit is the most analytical one in the book. It is concerned with the market environment of the organization and deals with the aspect which impacts continuously on most businesses – *the competition*. It is the aspect that the marketer is most concerned with on a day-to-day basis and therefore has most experience of. You must remember, however, that you will be examined primarily on your understanding of the competitive market environment. The application of marketing to alter or respond to changes in this environment is normally the secondary part of any question posed or is more effectively dealt with in *Marketing Fundamentals*.

Much of the content in this unit is economic, or legal, but the examiner will be looking only for an appreciation of the competitive environment and its impact on organizations and the marketer.

This unit accounts for 10 per cent of the syllabus, but it represents a very important segment of the external environment. Subsequent units, which consider other environments, have most of their effects on competitive relationships. You will find that you will spend more time working through this unit since you will have to read and reread some of the sections. The activities should take less time since you will be able to readily relate the material to your organization and work experience. Together they should take around 8 hours.

It is suggested that you:

- Open a new file under the heading Competitive Environment.
- Subdivide this into six sections: industry competitors, potential new entrants, suppliers, intermediaries/distributors, substitutes and legislation and policies.
- Add a further section on micro-environment information sources.
- Ask your marketing director if you can scan the executive summary and conclusions of a recent industry analysis consultancy report. Alternatively, use inter-library loans to obtain a copy of a report on an industry that interests you (e.g. Economist Intelligence Report on the car industry).
- Study the annual reports for references to competitors.
- Search for reports by the Office of Fair Trading (OFT) or the Monopolies and Mergers Commission (MMC).

Monitoring competitors

Competitors have already been referred to in the micro-environment section of Unit 2. You should reread both this section and the one on customers before commencing this section. It was made clear that a two-way relationship exists between the marketing function and its actual or potential competitors and customers. To be fully effective, however, the marketer must fully understand the dynamics of markets, the behaviour of its rivals and the realities of customer preferences and their execution.

The need to monitor competitors varies according to the structure of the industry.

Fragmented industries

In fragmented industries the number of participants is very large while average size is relatively small. There is little to be gained by monitoring the competitive behaviour of rivals other than those that represent their closest competitors in terms perhaps of location or product characteristics. Such industries are characterized by businesses competing for market share based on meeting buyer preferences rather than random selection amongst identical providers. The market is underlain by a diversity of incomes, attitudes, tastes and preferences so that sellers must discover the qualitative mix which best satisfies the needs of the target customer base. Firms must make the most of their product's unique selling points before the competition arrives, as it inevitably will. Market leaders do not tend to dominate because the scope for cost advantages from greater scale of operation is comparatively small. Advantage goes to those who are flexible and adaptable and such firms will seek to establish a competitive edge over their immediate rivals through innovation or successful differentiation of the marketing mix. Unfortunately barriers to entry tend to be low into such industries making new entry into the market likely if high profits are being made by existing firms. The extra supply this represents, combined with imitation of successful trading formulas, drives down margins and profitability over time. Any improvement in general demand conditions due, say, to changing tastes, rising incomes or unfortunate circumstances affecting substitute products will lead to initial improvement in sales and margins. However, subsequent erosion of profitability is characteristic of fragmented industries.

Question 4.1

Which of the following would you identify as fragmented industries?

- Health and fitness centres
- Restaurants
- Fast food outlets
- Hotels

What factors account for the fragmentation?

Are there forces leading to consolidation in the fast food sector?

(**See** Activity debrief at the end of this unit.)

There are markets where competition is intense but this is due to special conditions. One situation, which is familiar to marketers, is where the product has become a so-called 'commodity' as it enters the late maturity stage of the product life cycle. A saturated market dependent on repeat buyers, who are particularly knowledgeable as regards desirable product and service characteristics, will make successful differentiation extremely difficult or costly to sustain. This produces a price taker situation where the forces of market supply and demand determine the going price, rather than the individual firm. Potential customers will view product offerings as identical and rationally purchase the cheapest. Any attempt to set prices above what the market will bear will lead to drastic loss of sales and market share.

Activity 4.1

You have been appointed as consultant to a small concern currently operating in a fragmented and highly competitive market environment. Based on your knowledge of the competitive process and observations of more profitable firms and industries, suggest possible courses of action which could help to improve profitability. Which approach offers the best prospect of improved profit over time?

(**See** Activity debrief at the end of this unit.)

One course of action you may have recommended is to monitor close competitors. As we will see in the section on concentrated industries, competitors who supply close substitutes are in a strong position to win customers by offering better value for money. Such firms, and particularly new entrants, will strive to win your established customer base by making it attractive to switch allegiance. The marketer, in such circumstances, must firstly recognize the threat and then respond by making switching more difficult for existing customers.

Possibilities include:

- Invest in relationship marketing to build long-term mutual benefits.
- Build other barriers to protect the market.
- Create the equivalent of an habitual or 'monopoly' good by niche marketing, product differentiation or effective branding.
- Buy out the competitor.
- Cut unnecessary costs in order to offer keener prices.
- Innovate to continuously distance your product or service offering from rivals.

Exam Tip

Have you considered the advantages of 'differentiation' for your own examination script? An examiner is faced with marking scripts, literally into hundreds, all answering the same questions. How are you going to make yours stand out?

What you require is a premium product which catches the examiner's eye at the outset. See the final section of this unit for some hints in achieving this effect.

Product differentiation is the marketer's natural response to competition. If this is forcing down profit levels they respond by mobilizing the marketing mix to differentiate the product either by specification or in the minds of the consumer. The dimensions of possible differentiation are, of course, immense:

- *Product* Permutations of the *core, tangible* (e.g. design, quality, packaging) and *augmented* product (e.g. brand name, delivery, after-sales service).
- *Price* Credit and payment terms may vary, as could allowances and trade-in values.
- *Promotion* To support the differentiation (e.g. sales force, advertising).
- *Place* Offers opportunities through location adopted, coverage and, most importantly, service provided.

Businesses will therefore segment the market in the search for a profitable niche which they will then service with a product combining the optimum blend of characteristics that are clearly differentiated from those of close competitors. Those that satisfy customer needs and wants most effectively will earn *excess profits*. The seller, in effect, obtains a monopoly of the branded product and, due to the successful differentiation, is able to charge a higher price and still retain customers who 'prefer' the product. But what will happen next, given this situation?

Question 4.2	Can you think of local examples where small firms innovated product or service offerings which were quickly imitated by rivals or new entrants? (**See** Activity debrief at the end of this unit.)

As we saw above the returns associated with successful differentiation will attract imitation from both existing firms, wishing to expand sales, and new entrants, seeking profitable opportunities. The customer benefits as the imitation enables rapid diffusion of superior product and service ideas. In addition, the new entrants provide extra choice although there is a tendency to excess capacity in such industries as available customer demand is spread across the increased number of suppliers. There comes a point where attempting to fully utilize available capacity through extra promotion or discounting adds more to cost than to revenue. Hairdressers and restaurants are therefore seldom full.

Concentrated industries
Here the number of competing firms is generally small but their economic size is large. In economic terms this is known as high seller concentration and is typical in so-called oligopolies.

Activity 4.2	*Seller concentration* is defined as the degree to which production or sales for a particular market is concentrated into the hands of a few large firms. With this definition in mind calculate a *five-firm concentration ratio* for your own industry (i.e. add up the market shares of the five largest firms). Alternatively, look up a Mintel report on an industry of your choice.

Oligopoly means *competition among the few* and is the typical market structure in economies such as the UK. It arises where the largest four or five firms account for perhaps 70 per cent or more of total sales to the market. Monitoring competitors is of critical importance in this situation because the marketing actions and decisions of any one oligopolist depends crucially on the reactions of its competitors. Their relative strengths and weaknesses must be evaluated and every facet of their marketing behaviour identified and assessed.

Since each firm accounts for a large slice of the market any substantial change in the market share of one firm, whether achieved by lower prices, product innovation or successful advertising, will adversely affect the shares of competitors. The activities of 'popular' national newspapers often provide an interesting case study of such a market. Firms will watch each other very closely, producing a tension in the market between the *desire to compete* and gain sales at the expense of competitors, on the one hand, and the *desire to collude* in order to limit mutually damaging competitive activity, on the other.

The key features of this market may be summarized as:

- Economies of scale and entry barriers tend to be significant, e.g. car manufactuers
- Customer needs are standardized and integrated through mass distribution systems, e.g. petrol
- Dominant market leaders may emerge, e.g. Microsoft
- High concentration with the balance often held by a tail of small firms, e.g. grocery retailing
- Demand is uncertain because it is dependent on how rivals react
- The market outcome is not predictable when oligopolists have multiple competitive options available to them.

For example, if one of the oligopolists cuts its prices, another may follow suit, or it may cut its prices by more or less than the first firm. Alternatively, it may choose to do nothing, or respond with a large promotional campaign, or launch a new brand.

Extending Activity 4.1

Economists argue that oligopolists must make assumptions about rivals and play competitive games if they are to succeed. They suggest each oligopolist may be faced by a kinked demand curve. This is formed partly by the demand which faces the industry (DD) and partly by the demand situation that would result for the oligopolist (dd) if rivals leave their prices unchanged. Demand curves show how much would be sold at different prices. Figure 4.1 suggests that because rivals would match a price cut, but not follow a price increase, the pay-off from either action is probably negative. Now consider the following tactics and suggest how they would affect the demand curve shown:

- Price leadership
- New product development
- Collusion
- Promoted expenditure

(**See** Activity debrief at the end of this unit.)

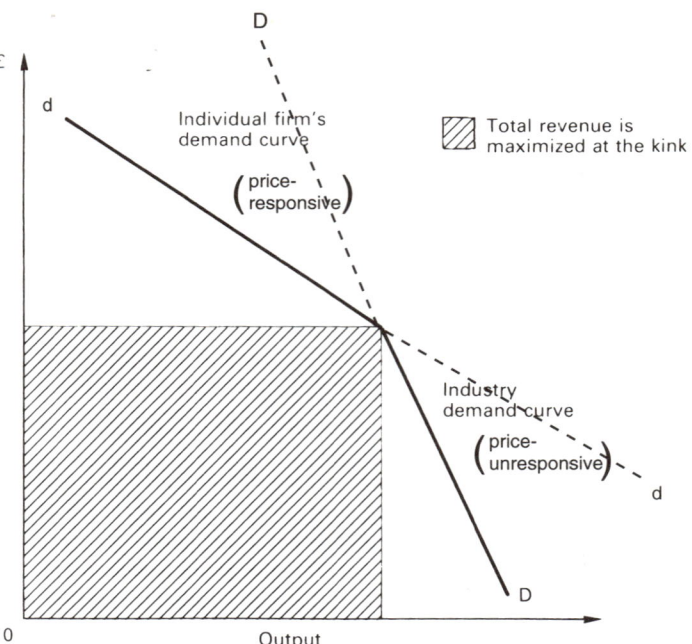

Figure 4.1
The kinked demand curve of the oligopolist

However, a number of generalizations are possible:

1. Oligopolists tend to avoid the use of price as a competitive weapon. They are termed 'sticky' because:
    -   If price is cut relative to competitors it is assumed that they will follow suit to avoid loss of market share. Sales volume therefore rises less than proportionately and total revenue falls.
    -   If price is raised, rivals will not follow suit, leading to a large loss of market share and sales revenue.
2. Non-price competition, promoting carefully differentiated branded products, is preferred.
3. There is a tendency to occasional price war when a restructuring of market shares is in progress.
4. Collusion is an attractive option but normally illegal (e.g. sixteen European steel producers were fined heavily in 1994 (£79 million) for price fixing in steel beams. British Steel alone was fined £24 million. British Sugar was also fined £28 million in 1998 for operating a cartel with three other UK companies. Note also the collapse of the Net Book Agreement and pressure being applied by Asda supermarkets on over-the-counter medicines and perfumes.
5. Price leadership often occurs to reflect underlying cost changes (e.g. retail petrol, tobacco, car and beer prices). Watch the press for large firms announcing price changes, e.g. interest rates, and then look for their competitors reactions. Do they follow suit or not, and if so, how quickly?

✳Summary

We have seen that competitive activity involves more than the price variable. Choice between alternatives is the key as firms compete on service, innovation and non-price variables. Large firms predomnate in concentrated industries due to the importance of barriers to entry in which economies of scale figure importantly. Smaller firms are the product of more fragmented structures although profitable niches can be found in most markets.

The need to monitor competitors, while providing some predictions of competitive response, only accounts for other firms within the market. More complete analysis requires consideration of certain other groups in the micro-environment.

Exam Tip	An examination question in this area will often state 'in the context of an industry example, explain ...'. Make sure you know an industry example inside out, and preferably your own.

Five-force analysis of competitive structures

Any organization which seeks growth and profitability in its existing market or perhaps is considering diversification into an emerging industry must carefully weigh future prospects and the shape of evolving competitive forces at least in general terms. A competitive strategy must then be determined which will provide achievement of its objectives within a defendable market position.

Businesses earn profit by being more successful than competitors in creating and delivering value to the customer over time. Real success demands that the business:

- creates value for money
- achieves a competitive edge in delivering that value
- operates efficiently.

The profit potential of the industry will be determined by the balance of supply and demand for the product in the short run and industry structure in the long run. Long-run profitibility will vary according to the strength of five basic competetive forces which governs the distribution of the added value created by the firm.

Michael Porter, in his books *Competitive Strategy* (1980) and *Competitive Advantage* (1985), provided the five-forces model of industry structure. This is summarized in Figure 4.2.

All marketers must seek to understand the nature of their competitive environment if they are to exploit and profit by it. They must assess what is driving the competition in the industry and recognize that the collective strength of these five forces will set the present and future degree of market rivalry. This will determine the profit potential of the industry although each firm within it will seek to position itself so as to exploit maximum competitive advantage.

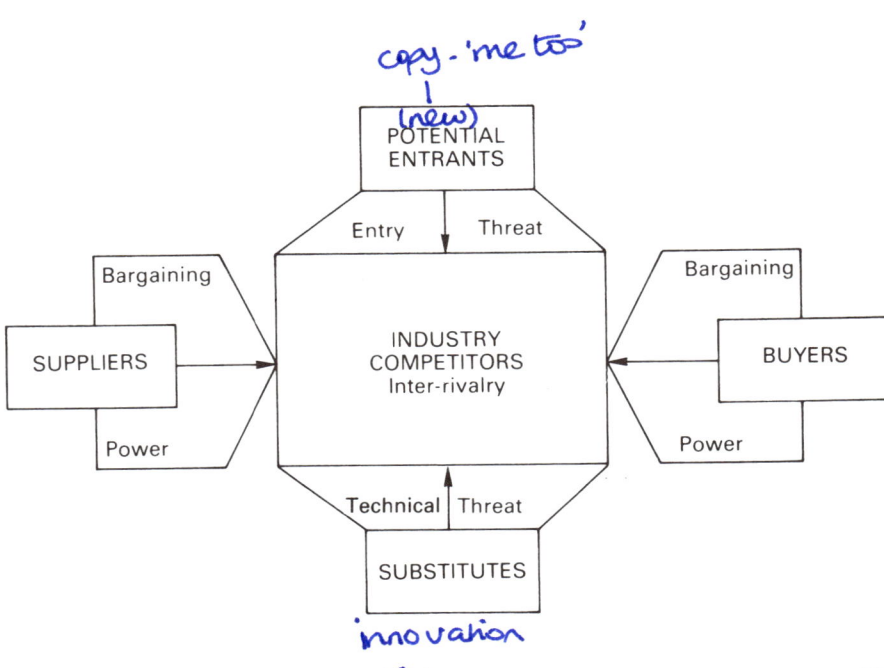

Figure 4.2
The five forces model. (Adapted from M. E. Porter, *Competitive Strategy*, The Free Press, 1980: © The Free Press/Macmillian)

Use five-force analysis to match fragmented and concentrated industry structures to two of the following combinations:

1 Intense inter-rivalry, high threat of entry, high buyer and supplier bargaining power, strong threat from substitutes.
2 Limited inter-rivalry, high threat of entry, low buyer and supplier bargaining power, weak threat of substitutes.
3 No inter-rivalry, no threat from substitutes or entry, no buyer or supplier bargaining power.
4 Intense inter-rivalry, weak threat from substitutes and entry, low buyer bargaining power, high supplier bargaining power.

(**See** Activity debrief at the end of this unit.)

Unlike market structure models, this approach provides marketers with a framework for analysing the complexity of their own industry situation. The approach is less rigorous but perhaps more useful in understanding the effect of structural and environmental change over time.

The intensity of inter-rivalry
We have considered the degree of competitive rivalry in the sections on fragmented and concentrated industries. Rivalry can range along a spectrum from non-existent at one end (designated by a powerful monopoly position protected by high entry barriers) to a cut-throat price war at the other. In between are found gentlemanly understandings (found in collusive oligopoly) and normal marketing based cut and thrust typically involving advertising and promotion, new product development and improvements to customer service. Rivalry may succeed in expanding the overall market and its profitability by drawing in new customers or increasing the volumes purchased or it may undermine it by reducing margins or increasing marketing costs while merely redistributing overall static sales amongst the combatants. Porter provides additional insight by identifying the variables which determine the degree of rivalry now and in the future:

- *The rate of industry growth* Rapid growth reduces rivalry over market shares and favours emerging industries in the early stages of their life cycles. Saturation produces conflict as mature firms battle over stagnant sales.
- *Use of specialized equipment and high fixed costs* Overheads must be covered and specialized equipment must be fully utilized to justify the cost. Any threat to sales levels will be vigorously resisted leading to a strong possibility of price war.
- *The extent volatility of supply and demand produces intermittent over-capacity* If an industry is subject to severe amplitude in orders over the business cycle or a new hotel opens in a locality then rivalry will, in all probability, sharpen.
- *The degree of product differentiation and brand loyalty* Effectiveness tends to dull the impact of competitive activity on sales and margins.
- *The significance of switching costs for buyers* If strong bonds have been established with the customer then transfer to competing products is less likely so reducing rivalry. This clearly links with the degree of brand loyalty outlined above.
- *The number of firms and their relative size* This affects the prospects for collusive activity since the more concentrated and balanced the industry the less the potential for rivalry. Dominant firms often tend to suppress vigorous competition.
- *The diversity of corporate cultures* As mentioned above, if only one firm seeks market dominance or increased share at the expense of the others then rivalry will be intense. Japanese firms, for example, pursue such goals at the expense of short-run profit. Take-over or a new generation of management out to impress can disturb existing equilibrium and unleash unexpected competition.

- *What is at stake* If a firm is a specialist dependent on a single product or market, or has made a considerable commitment to an industry in terms of investment, or staked corporate reputations and the future success of the business on the outcome, then defence of that position will be vigorous. Japanese companies, until recently, have not been taken over or allowed to fail. Fear of such failure provides real impetus to rivalry.
- *Understanding of competitor's intentions* Misinterpretation of competitive actions can lead to damaging mistrust and recurrent price wars. Clearly it is in the interests of all that firms deploy a marketing intelligence system to monitor competitor behaviour.
- *The cost of leaving the industry* High costs are the result of exit barriers which deter weaker rivals from sensibly re-deploying their resources elsewhere. Excess capacity and depressed margins often result. Examples include the costs of honouring contractual obligations such as redundancy payments, industry specific assets with weak resale values and loss of face.

Activity 4.3

Take each determinant outlined above and relate them to your own industry or one you are familiar with. Create a grid, as in the example shown, and rate each factor in turn on its contribution to overall rivalry on a scale from low to high. Make an overall conclusion and consider if anything might be done to reduce overall rivalry in the industry concerned.

Chemical feedstock production

Determinant	Low rivalry . . . . .High rivalry
Industry growth	*
Fixed/storage costs	*
Intermittent over-capacity	*
Product differences	*
Brand identity	*
Switching costs for consumers	*
Concentration/balance	*
Diversity of competitors	*
Corporate stakes	*
Exit barriers	*

Overall judgment on the intensity of rivalry: *Very intense but market leadership acts as a stabilizing factor*

The threat of substitutes

An industry is a group of firms producing goods or services which are close substitutes for each other. In practice, the nature of substitutability is complex and a galaxy of widely differing offerings compete for limited discretionary purchasing power which can only be spent once at any point in time. Package holidays compete with conservatories and new computer systems with upgrading the transport fleet.

The threat may materialize in many forms; for example, different materials, an alternative technology or a new distribution channel. Vinyl records, for example, have been partly replaced by cassettes, which in turn have been substituted by compact discs which are now threatened by digital mini discs and even the internet. Factors affecting this threat are:

- The relative *price–performance* ratio of the substitute (e.g. glass compared to metal or plastic containers) – this places a ceiling on the prices an industry can charge. Long-run profitability is seriously threatened the better this ratio becomes.
- *Switching costs* for customers to the substitute (e.g. switching from coal- to gas-fired equipment or from branch to home banking)
- Buyer willingness to search out substitutes.

The rule of thumb to apply here is the higher the price and excess profitability, the greater the incentive to search for and develop substitutes.

Question 4.5

You have been asked to make the travel arrangements from London to Paris for your marketing director, who has an important morning meeting to attend, and a small group of friends who want a weekend of sightseeing. In each case:

1 What substitutes would you consider?
2 How close is their current relative price–performance ratio?
3 Why might the ratios be changing?

(**See** Activity debrief at the end of this unit.)

The threat of new entry

Long-run profitability and market share will be damaged if significant entry occurs. Supply capacity will tend to increase sharply, putting downward pressure on margins, while extra competition for inputs will bid up costs. Any profitable industry is susceptible to this threat, particularly where a recent improvement in returns has occurred. The dynamics of the competitive process ensures that forces are set in motion to eventually return profitability to levels that no longer attract further entry.

However, as Porter recognized, there are factors that may delay or even prevent this outcome known collectively as barriers to entry. Their strength will vary from industry to industry. Where barriers are substantial the threat of entry will be weak (e.g. chemical feedstocks, nuclear reprocessing), whereas if they are virtually non-existent the threat will be ever-present. The factors to be considered include:

- *Economies of scale* These increase the initial set-up costs and therefore the costs and risks associated with entry. The minimum economic scale or break-even point at which an entrant must establish and operate will be high due either to capital costs (e.g. a modern microprocessor plant costs $1 billion), research and development expenditure (e.g. drugs) or promotional spending (e.g. branding in detergents). Marketing economies include bulk discounts, spreading fixed costs (e.g. advertising) over large sales volumes and the employment of specialists.

Activity 4.4

Examine the grid below and insert in each box an indication of the probable size and stability of returns to be earned, i.e. you may designate one box *high and stable returns*, while another you decide on *low and risky returns*.

	Exit barriers	
	Low	*High*
Entry barriers *Low*	1.	2.
Entry barriers *High*	3.	4.

(**See** Activity debrief at the end of this unit.)

- *Brand loyalty and product differentiation* Promotional expenditure over time builds goodwill and customer loyalty for incumbent firms. Available product space may also be filled by a proliferation of products. Positioning of a new entrant's brand becomes difficult and heavy spending would be required to establish a new brand image.
- *Capital requirements* These differ widely across industries and despite the huge resources available to the likes of Microsoft, there are many high

technology and resource intensive sectors that would attract few entrants despite superior prospective rewards.

- *Switching costs for buyers* These determine the likely pulling power of a new entrant's package. If by purchasing an alternative computer operating system the customer is faced with retraining costs, redundancy of equipment and knowledge, inconvenience, time lags as well as the risks inherent in adopting an untried product and supplier relationship, then considerable cost savings and guarantees must be on offer.
- *Distribution channel access* Existing firms may dominate existing channels. Long-term contracts may be in place and working partnerships established.
- *Absolute cost advantages* Existing firms may gain absolute cost advantages which are difficult for entrants to match. Entrenched firms may control prime sites, patents and critical labour skills. Accumulated knowledge of the market and experience with the technology will provide an important advantage.
- *Expected retaliation* Potential entrants will weigh the possible responses of existing firms very carefully. An extended price war could quickly remove the attractions of entry into the industry. The financial reserves of profitable incumbents may finance price cuts, particularly through the use of 'fighting' brands. Easyjet and Ryanair reacted to the entry of Go, a British Airways subsidiary by resorting to the courts. Manufacturing firms may expand capacity to pre-empt entry or illegally seek to enforce exclusive dealing on intermediaries, so denying access to entrants.
- *Government policies and regulation* As we will see in the next section, the degree of government vigour applied to maintaining fair competition is an important factor. The American courts are currently pursuing Microsoft for seeking to deny access to the operating systems software market. Equally governments may provide subsidies to aid incumbents to protect their market, e.g. Air France or Rover.

It is clear from the above factors that potential entrants will carefully weigh what is a high risk strategy in many cases and particularly where start-up losses are high and reactions uncertain.

Activity 4.5

Refer back to the section on barriers to entry and under each heading (e.g. economies, access to inputs and channels, switching costs, learning effects, cost advantages, etc.) rate your industry on threat of entry. The same approach may be applied to remaining forces.

When was the last time a new competitor entered your industry? How did existing firms react? Was it successful and if so, why? What was the origin of the entrant?

New entry into concentrated markets is not as frequent as you might think due to the high barriers. The main threat comes from *cross-entry* by a well-financed business in an adjacent industry or one using similar processes and distribution channels. Takeover by a foreign company of an existing firm, to provide a base for future growth in market share, is another possibility.

The bargaining power of suppliers

Where the relative power of suppliers is considerable and their behaviour aggressive, the rate of profit in an industry will be squeezed. However, an ability to establish some corresponding control over supplies will strengthen the hand of businesses in the industry. The main factors determining relative power are as follows:

- The degree of supplier concentration relative to the industry
- The degree of substitutability between the products of rival suppliers determines whether the buyer can switch to alternatives
- The switching costs involved in doing this
- The dependence of suppliers on maintaining large volumes of sales

- The importance of being unimportant – the lower the cost of the supplies as a proportion of total cost, the higher the bargaining power
- The threat of forward integration by suppliers (i.e. they may establish their own production facilities in the industry).

The bargaining power of buyers

Buyer power will tend to reduce profitability although the ability of individual firms to develop specific arrangements with distributors and/or customers may prevent this. Buyer power depends on two main factors:

1 *Price responsiveness* The responsiveness of the buyer's purchases to a change in the relative price is, in effect, price elasticity of demand. This is determined by such things as:
   - The importance of the product as a proportion of the total purchases of the buyer
   - The emphasis given by the buyer to product differentiation and branding
   - The profitability of the buyer, which may dull price sensitivity if substantial. Alternatively, buyers may be under pressure to cherry-pick for best value for money, while others give precedence to availability, delivery and quality.
2 *Buyer leverage* A number of factors also affect this:
   - *Buyer concentration and size*. The five largest grocery multiples provide an excellent example of this with nearly 65 per cent of total sales.
   - *Volume and the importance of purchases* to the seller
   - *Practicality and costs of switching to alternative suppliers* for the buyer
   - *Knowledge of the market and information available to buyers*
   - *Existence of substitutes*
   - *Threat of backward vertical integration*

Extending Activity 4.2

A useful group activity to reinforce your grasp of Porter's five-forces model is to consolidate the activities above into a full industry analysis. Select your own or a representative industry and go through all the factors listed above under the five headings and evaluate them in turn. You will find it useful to interview key people within your organization (e.g. purchasing manager, sales and marketing executives). Other sources could include trade associations, the trade press, market intelligence reports, the business press and company sources.

It is very important that you apply this model and not just content yourself with 'learning' the factors. It is a much more challenging and useful exercise to 'really understand' what drives the profitability within an industry.

Strategic and marketing implications

Five force analysis is useful to the marketer as:

- A means of determining the attractiveness of an industry and its ultimate profit potential.
- A framework for examining relationships in their micro-environment.
- An evaluation of the probable degree of rivalry, now and in the future.

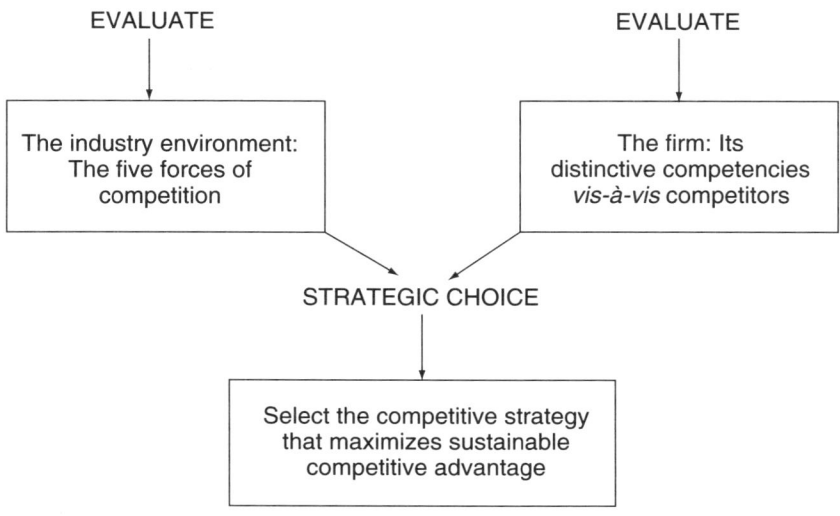

Figure 4.3
Strategic choice

- A justification for continuous monitoring of the micro-environment.
- The basis for formulating strategy.

Strategy is the match an organization makes between its own resources and the risks and opportunities created by its external environment. Competitive strategy is a search for sustainable advantage through a favourable market positioning which achieves above average profitability over time. The process of strategic choice is seen in Figure 4.3.

Porter saw a choice of generic strategies between the following:

- *Broad cost leadership* but with parity or proximity in product features. Such a strategy would emphasize efficient scale of operations and tight control of costs and margins. Entry barriers are therefore created together with defences against powerful buyers and suppliers.
- *Broad differentiation* with proximity in cost terms. This creates a product or service perceived as unique and desirable by customers in terms of design (e.g. Gucci), brand image (e.g. Coca-Cola) and/or customer service (e.g. Virgin airlines). High marketing costs are offset by insulation from rivalry and mitigation of buyer power, while high margins cushion supplier power.
- *Cost or differentiation focus* on a narrow segment which is least vulnerable to competition. This strategy is vulnerable to imitation or structural decline in demand. Broader based competitors may overwhelm the segment, e.g. in-store specialists within multiple grocers.

Question 4.6

Study the grid in Figure 4.4 and suggest companies which would fit into the strategy boxes for the following industries:

- multiple groceries;
- travel agents;
- cars

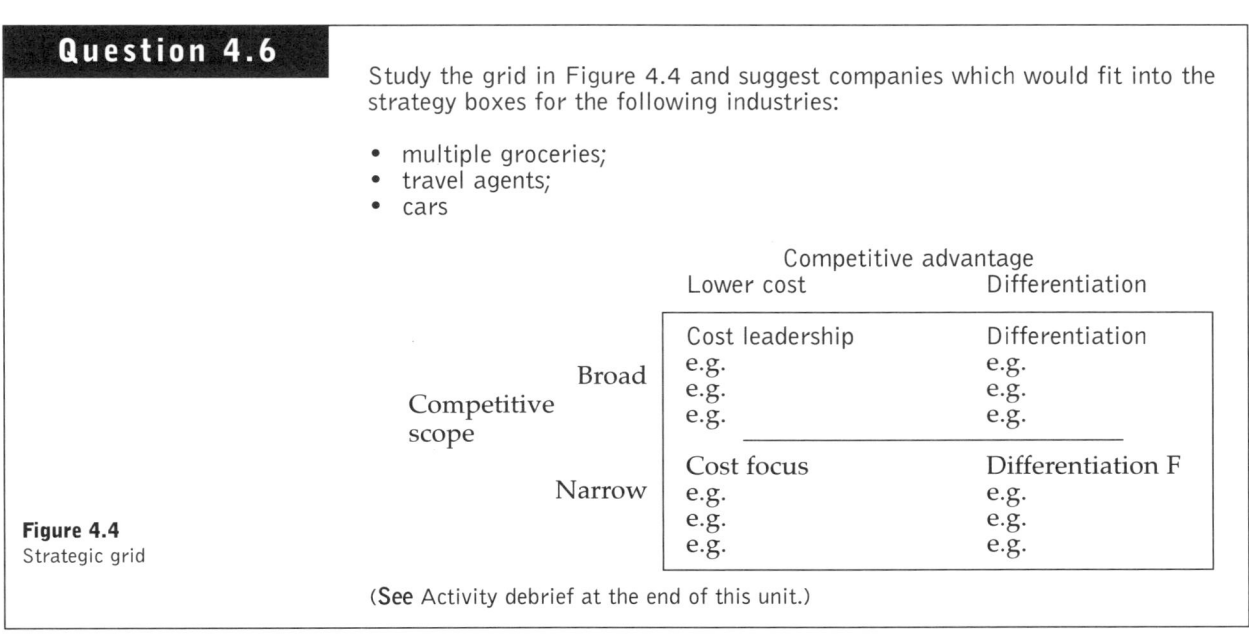

Figure 4.4
Strategic grid

(See Activity debrief at the end of this unit.)

One weakness in the above strategies is that they all imply hostile options. In reality and as we saw in Unit 3, there are massive changes taking place in industry as businesses collaborate in alliances (e.g. British Airways, Quantas, American Airlines and others to provide a global network) and joint ventures (e.g. mobile phones). Another aspect of horizontal collaboration, that we will consider in the next section, is forming cartels. This is an attractive form of collaboration since if successful it would become the sole supplier to the market. Output could be restricted and market price and overall profitability would rise. The existence of restrictive practices legislation (see later) has ruled most forms of collective agreement illegal but cartels still appear to operate clandestinely in some industries (e.g. sugar/concrete/PVC) and internationally (e.g. OPEC (oil), IATA (airlines) and De Beers (diamonds)).

All cartels, however, are subject to instability in the longer term:

- Internal dissension over the allocation of quotas necessary to restrict supply and justify the higher cartel prices
- Incentive for any cartel member to exceed quota for higher profits. This raises supply, making it harder to sustain the price
- Internal policing is essential plus control over market entry
- New producers operate outside the cartel at slightly lower prices, forcing increasing excess capacity on cartel members.

Activity 4.6

Consider the gondoliers of Venice. What enables them to charge such high prices for a glorified boat-ride? How do you think they manage to maintain these prices over time? Is clever marketing the explanation?

A collaborative approach to five-force analysis is shown in Figure 4.5.

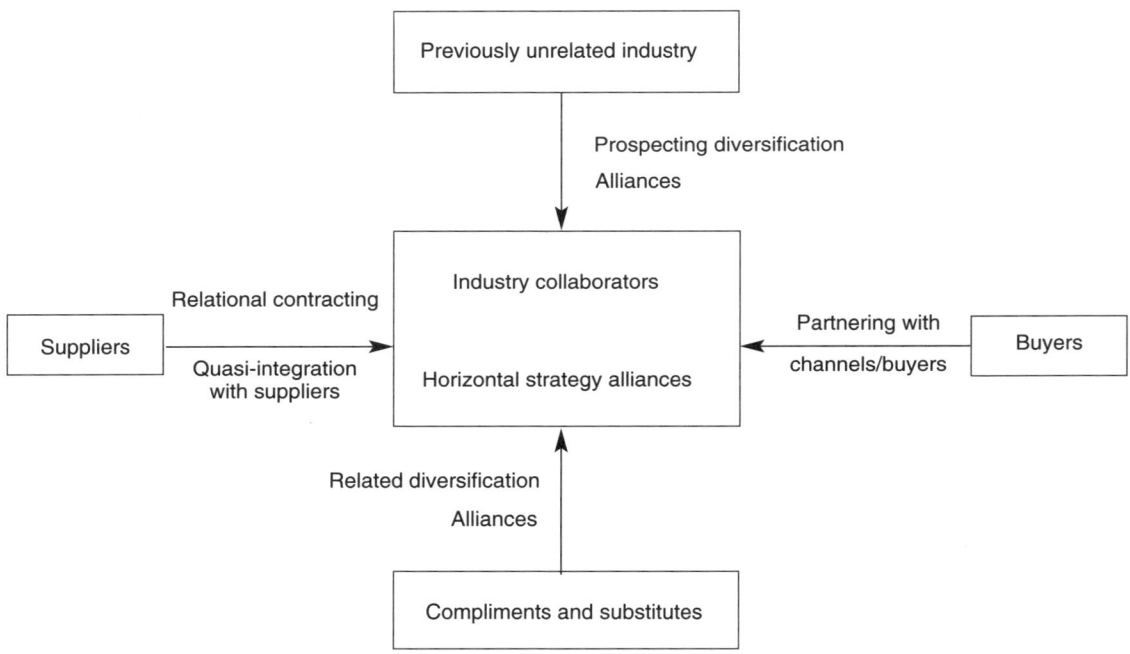

Figure 4.5 Analysing collaboration – the five forces framework

In this approach, the organization makes its strategic choice by evaluating the five forces of collaboration, as shown in the figure, alongside its distinctive competencies relative to collaborators. The aim would be to maximize collaborative advantage. In reality the business should combine both approaches as seen in Figure 4.6.

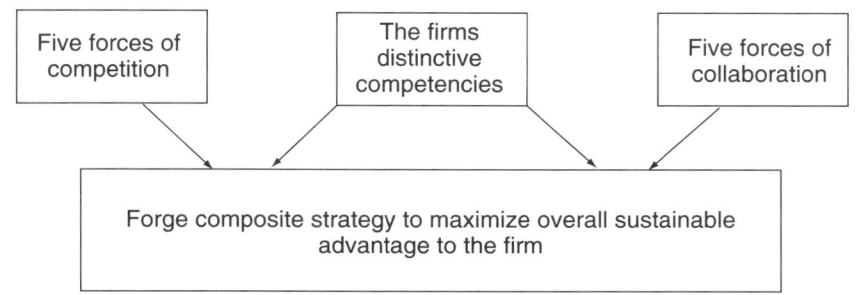

Figure 4.6 The two faces of business strategy – formulating composite strategy

The nature of competition policies

Governments formulate competition polices for a number of reasons:

- They fear that market forces may be insufficient to prevent anti-competitive behaviour.
- They see a level playing field as fair and just.
- They desire efficient and effective use of scare resources.
- Monopoly is seen as the natural outcome of the competitive process and must be controlled.
- They don't wish to see economic power abused at the expense of the consumer / taxpayer.

Making markets more competitive means creating the conditions associated with it. Policies have therefore attempted to achieve the following:

- Resist mergers and acquisitions which threaten to reduce the number of sellers to the point where consumer choice is restricted.
- Keep entry barriers into markets as low as possible so that supply, through new entrants, can respond.
- Deregulation of markets (e.g. domestic energy market).
- Encouragement of small and medium enterprises.
- Appointment of regulators in natural monopoly sectors.
- Improve the knowledge of the consumer through prevention of misleading advertising / promotion.
- Legislative action against anti-competitive behaviour.

Legislation and competition

Understanding the industry environment in terms of competition and collaboration alone ignores the role of government and the law. Firms facing intense competition may seek to form cartels and associations as a means of restricting output to raise prices and profitability. Equally firms in concentrated industries may find collaboration and collusion more rewarding than rivalry. Large firms, including those that monopolized their industry, might also abuse their power and position to discourage potential entrants.

While all these actions would be to the disadvantage of the customer, legislation governing such restraint of trade has been introduced more with a view to promoting more effective use of resources and to support a belief in the virtues of workable competition.

1 *Restraint of trade* Most agreements in English law must not involve terms that restrict or prevent a person from doing business. Exceptions include where the seller of a business or an employee agrees not to set up in competition within a given area or period of time. Another example is where a business agrees to restrict its suppliers in exchange for an advantageous supply contract.

Example In the USA the Justice Department barred Microsoft, the world's largest software firm, from forcing its Web browser on buyers of its Windows 95 software. This did not avert the $85 million fourth quarter loss announced in 1997 by Netscape, who previously led the internet market for such products.

2 *Restrictive practices* Legislation to curb monopolies and agreements between companies, which had grown up in the adverse trading conditions of the 1930s, was introduced soon after the Second World War. It was consolidated by legislation introduced in the 1970s and covered any form of agreement between the majority of firms in an industry which affects their freedom of action in disposing of their output.

Question 4.7

The spectrum of restrictive linkages between firms

Can you fill in the gaps?

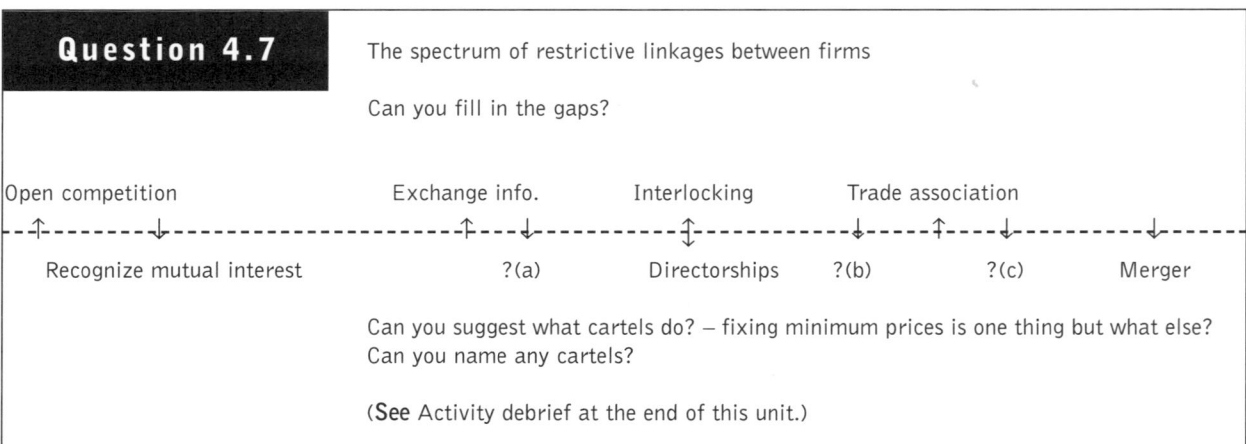

Open competition		Exchange info.	Interlocking	Trade association		
Recognize mutual interest		?(a)	Directorships	?(b)	?(c)	Merger

Can you suggest what cartels do? – fixing minimum prices is one thing but what else? Can you name any cartels?

(**See** Activity debrief at the end of this unit.)

Fair Trading Act 1973
- Extended coverage to restrictive agreements in services and those involving the exchange of information
- Monopolies and Mergers Commission (MMC)
- Director-General of Fair Trading (DGFT) took overall control

Resale Prices Act/Restrictive Trade Practices Act 1976 Competition Act, 1980
- Cover agreements on prices, recommended prices, terms, areas/businesses supplied and so on
  Example The MMC may outlaw the practice of 'recommended retail prices' following investigation of the retail consumer electronics market. This found that the prices of products such as TVs and videorecorders varied little between competing stores. Discount retailers also claimed they experienced difficulty in obtaining supplies. Manufacturers such as Sony and Panasonic protested that the similar prices were evidence of the high degree of competition
- Agreements must be registered
- Agreements are presumed to be against the public interest unless the parties can justify it to the Restrictive Practices Court
- Eight gateways can be used including protection of or benefits to the public, protecting jobs or export earnings or to countervail competition or monopoly
  Example Medicines but not books, following the withdrawal of major publishers from the Net Book Agreement in 1995. The attempt by Asda supermarkets to cut the price of vitamin products, however, was met with legal action by manufacturers. However, the supermarket is to continue its campaign against this agreement
- Must not 'on balance' be detrimental to the public

- Enforcement of minimum retail prices on distributors was also out-lawed in the Resale Prices Act. Withholding supplies with a view to coerce was also prohibited
  Example Withholding supplies of perfumes to cut-price multiples like Superdrug was allowed by the MMC
- 1980 Act empowers the DGFT to investigate anti-competitive practices by firms with over £5 million turnover. Defined as a course of conduct which restrict, distorts or prevents competition in the production, acquisition or supply of goods and service. It includes discriminatory and predatory pricing (to force out a rival), vertical price squeezing (e.g. raising prices of controlled inputs to competitors), tie-in sales/full line forcing (buy one item – must buy range) and discriminatory supply.

Extending Activity 4.3

Research suggests there are many uncompetitive parts of the economy. The OFT is about to report on enquiries into the cost of new cars ($40 billion market) and supermarket profitability while an OECD study shows Britons paying 55 per cent more than Americans for furniture/carpets/hotels and 30 per cent more for sports goods. A European Commission report suggests car prices are up to 50 per cent more expensive as Figure 4.7(b) confirms. The market is unusually profitable with over half of Peugot's total profits being made in the UK. Government concern has now led to the setting up of an official price monitoring unit to advise customers with possible reference to the newly formed Competition Commission. However these differentials have existed for over fifteen years with little being done.

lowest price in EU 15=100, June 1998

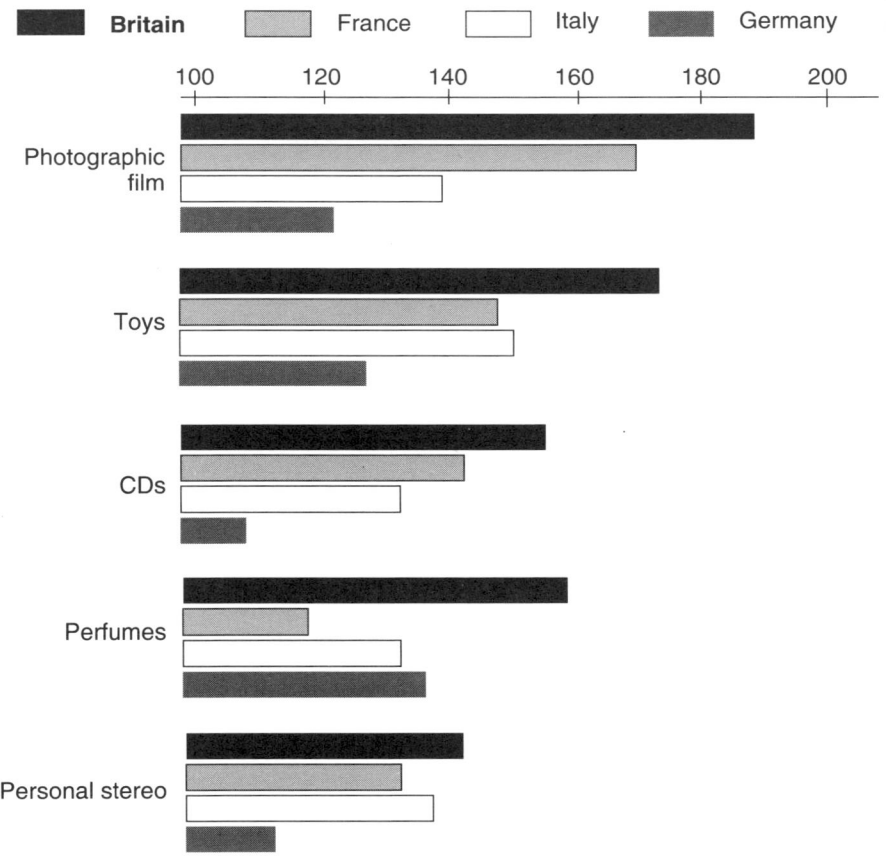

Source: Bureau Européen des Unions de Consommateurs

Figure 4.7(a) Cost of consumer goods – June 1998

Conduct some research into why UK prices for identical models of car are 30–50 per cent or more expensive compared to Eire or the Netherlands. Consider the influence of the following during your studies:

- Price discrimination
- Red tape
- Buying economies of scale
- Collusion on discounts/refusal to supply
- Exchange rates
- Weak competition laws
- Variable specifications and right hand drive
- Heavily discounted company cars
- European Commission renewal of exclusive dealerships block exemption till 2002

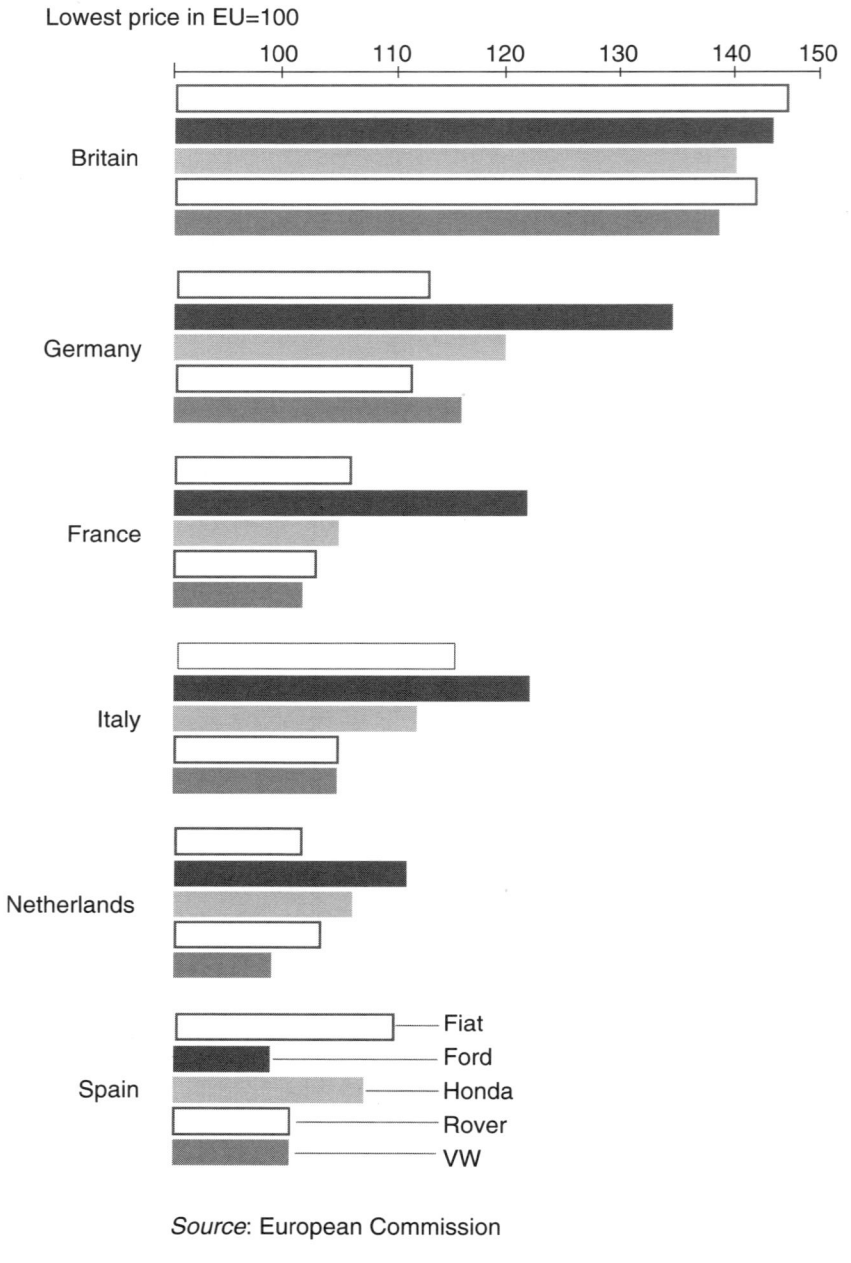

Lowest price in EU=100

Source: European Commission

Figure 4.7(b) Average car price by marque – 1997

Monopolies and merger legislation

The methods adopted in Britain involve:

- A case by case judgmental approach.
- A cost benefit framework to compare good and bad effects.
- A loose presumption that monopolies are against the public interest.
- A recognition that market dominance might reflect superior efficiency.
- Removing barriers to entry is seen as more appropriate than preventing firms getting larger.
- Investigating horizontal mergers as these are more likely to be motivated by the desire for monopoly.

Both the Secretary of State and the DGFT (but not mergers) have powers to refer a case to the Competition Commission. The legal definition of a referable monopoly is a 25 per cent market share while proposed mergers involving assets in excess of £30 million, or where they would create a legal monopoly or add to it, may be referred.

With Vodafone buying America's Airtouch Communications for $62 billion and Exxon's $76 billion takeover of Mobil to create the world's biggest company in revenue terms ($250 billion) these qualifying sums are easily achieved. Despite the apparent scope for cost savings and extra market power, recent research by J. P. Morgan suggests that only 56 per cent of large European merger deals since 1985 have created value for the acquiring company. Many mergers that appear to offer a 2 + 2 = 5 synergy opportunity end up as 2 + 2 = 3! Horizontal mergers of companies in the same line of business, however, tend to achieve better returns, but this may well be at the expense of reduced competition and the consumer.

In practice, only a very small proportion of qualifying monopolies or mergers are referred and then the MMC may just report or will make recommendations. The final decision, however, rests with the Secretary of State, who has been known to overrule MMC recommendations. This is particularly likely when the benefits of greater size are thought to offer increased international competitiveness.

The government appears to be adopting a more aggressive approach to competition policy with reviews into high profile sectors like airports and water currently underway. These might turn into MMC references in due course.

If the Secretary of State decides to act, he or she may ask the DGFT to obtain appropriate undertakings or lay an order before Parliament prohibiting continuation of the practice. Orders are enforced through trading standards officers and offences are punished under criminal law.

Other powers range from regulation of maximum prices to forced sale of controlling interests (e.g. BA had to give up some landing slots if they wished to merge with American Airlines). However, as a recent MMC report into the electrical appliance industry indicated, covert price fixing is not uncommon yet the relative lack of powers means that offending companies usually get away with an assurance of good behaviour in future. The new 1998 Competition Act, provides no excuse for the authorities not to act and will see much stiffer penalties, with fines of up to 10 per cent of turnover and permission for civil actions to be brought. The OFT has been given extra resources and an enhanced role to root out cartels, with attempts at obstruction made a criminal offence. This may please companies such as Intel, Compaq and Fujitsu who have criticized dominant distributors like Dixons, with 45 per cent of the market, of stunting the market through high prices.

Question 4.8

State five ways in which the DGFT is active in the protection of consumers.

(**See** Activity debrief at the end of this unit.)

The promotion of free competiton between member states of the European Union is fundamental to the success of the Single Market and its legislation therefore overrides national legislation. Relevant sections include:

- Article 85: prohibits all restrictive agreements affecting trade between member states which prevents or distorts competition.
- Article 86: relates to abuse of a dominant market position.
- Articles 92–94: forbid government subsidies to firms or industries which distort or threaten to distort competition.
- Cooperative agreements which share facilities, market research and consultancy are acceptable.

Directives have also been introduced governing such matters as ingredients in food and the introduction of sell-by dates. UK law is only now coming into line with EU law and its tough fines of up to 10 per cent of domestic turnover for illegal anti-competitive agreements.

Activity 4.7

Monitor the quality press for examples of decisions by the Secretary of State as to whether to refer a monopoly or merger proposal to the MMC or not. Note the reasons that are given for the decision in question. Recent examples include:

- BSkyB and Manchester United FC – to refer
- Bass and Carlsberg Tetley – to refer
- Independent and Mirror Group Newspapers – not to refer
- Lyonnaise des Eaux and Northumbrian Water – to refer
- Lloyds Bank and TSB – not to refer
- British Airways and American Airlines – not to refer
- GEC and VSEL – to refer but DTI overturned MMC decision against merger

---

Other areas of legislation and the marketer

1 *Patents* This is a right given to the inventor to reap all the rewards accruing over a specified period, normally 20 years. Application must be made to the Patents Office and be covered by the Patents Act 1977. To qualify, the invention must be novel and go beyond the current state of the art. A European Patent Office has also been established as a cost-effective means of achieving coverage across member states.
2 *Trade marks* Of considerable importance to the marketer who has invested heavily in a particular brand name, the Trade Marks Act provides exclusive rights to registered marks (words or symbols). Infringement may lead to an injunction and damages.

Monitoring the micro-environment

Systems thinking, you will recall from Unit 1, helps to provide an integrated view of the world. Organizations may be viewed as interrelated parts of a wider marketing environment with which they interact. We have seen in the first four units of this workbook how the organization is part of a wider micro-environment in which it competes and collaborates with a variety of primary stakeholders. This environment is subject to continuous change but organizations are also adaptive causing them to seek greater understanding of the environment in order to plan or react more effectively. To be effective the business organization must possess the following sub-systems:

- A *sensing system* – to access sources of information and appraise developments.
- An *information classification system* – to convert data into potentially usable information.
- An *information processing system* – involving feedback and two-way exchanges.
- An *information database and retrieval system*.
- A *control system* – to establish any deviations from established objectives.
- A *planning and policy making system*.

The characteristics of a sensing system will be fully explored in the next unit in conjunction with information needs of the macro-environment. As regards the micro-environment it should be clear that many different types of information are required depending on the decisions to be taken. Examples of the more important types include:

Competitors
- Prices, discounts, credit terms, etc.
- Sales volumes by segment, product, region, distribution channel
- Market shares and key objectives
- Promotional activities, catalogues, distributor incentives
- New product development, expansion plans, changes in personnel
- Financial strength and relationships with key stakeholders

Similar information is required on suppliers, distributors and potential entrants into the market.

Industry
- Sales volumes by product, segment, region and country
- Sales growth and seasonal/cyclical patterns
- Production capacities, levels, plans and stock positions
- Technical change and investment plans

Information gathered through marketing intelligence and market research needs to be combined with that gathered internally before being classified, processed and analysed. Information databases are central to modern marketing. Collecting information on customers is one thing, but processing and utilizing the massive amounts of data captured by computers is another. This can provide a critical element in the process of:

- Forming or deepening customer relationships and loyalty, e.g. one cruise line sends a 'best table' photograph award in a New Year's card to remind recipients of happy times spent on a recent cruise.
- Spotting emerging patterns and trends to provide focus for marketing campaigns.
- Segmenting customers for receipt of tailored offers.

Main sources of information

A framework of sources will be dealt with at the end of the next unit. To complete this unit it would be useful to briefly examine the nature and requirements of an information system for effective competitor analysis. Attempt the following extended activity before reading on.

Extending Activity 4.4

You have been delegated the responsibility of undertaking a 'competitor and collaborator analysis' of your industry (or one of your own choice). At the initial stage of this analysis you are required to identify the sources of information that will prove useful in understanding and assessing the relevant stakeholders. List at least four relevant sources under each of the following headings:

- **Internal sources** – e.g. sales force records

- **Company sources** – e.g. company reports
- **Industry/market sources** – trade association information
- **Government sources** – business monitors/census of production
- **Commercial sources** – e.g. A C Nielsen
- **Academic sources** – e.g. *Journal of Marketing*
- **General sources** – e.g. quality press reports

Select one source under each heading and explain how it would contribute to the analysis.

Competitor analysis involves the gathering and interpretation of intelligence from a range of sources, regarding key rivals, with the intention of achieving a competitive edge over them by:

- Identifying and exploiting competitor weaknesses.
- Avoiding actions that provoke aggressive and possibly damaging responses.
- Discovering moves that competitors are unable/unwilling to respond to.
- Avoiding any surprises that may give rivals the advantage.

Actual and potential threats must be accounted, e.g. firms that could overcome entry barriers, customers or suppliers that could integrate backwards or forwards, possible take-overs of existing rivals or foreign firms benefiting from tariff or regulatory changes.

There are literally hundreds of potential intelligence sources but these are useless unless meaningful information can be extracted. To understand potential rivals you must understand their goals, capabilities, strategies and view of the future. This drives the spectrum of information needs which includes the following:

- *Financial information* Successive company annual accounts reveal information on performance and direction of growth. Future borrowing capability can also be ascertained. These may be accessed through websites or the Companies Registration Office. Business reference services and commercial databases, such as Dun and Bradstreet, Lotus and Datastream provide detailed reports and comparative analyses on hundreds of companies in the form of graphs and ratios. Credit reference agencies and your own company's treasury department may provide insight on bill payment habits and credit worthiness.

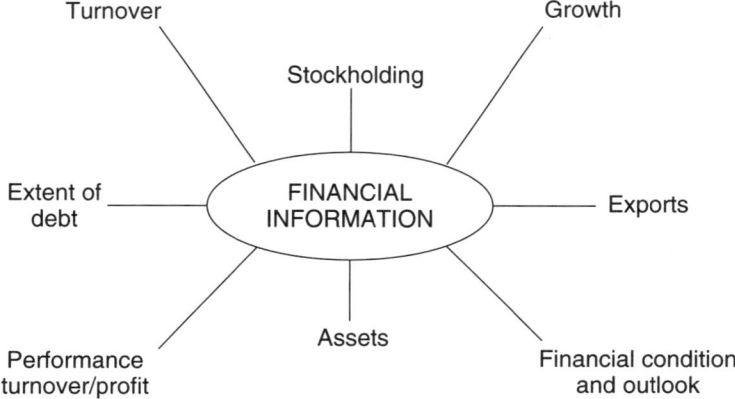

Figure 4.8 Financial information on rivals

- *Organizational information* The trade and quality press are up-to-date sources of such information. A variety of business periodicals often provide in-depth coverage of specific companies. Access is often eased through electronic databases. Monitoring the comments of the chairman and chief executive in consecutive annual reports and responses to questions at AGMs provide strategic background on goals, activities and corporate values. More detailed knowledge may be provided through the salesforce of common suppliers or purchasing staff of mutual intermediaries. Stakeholder information networks are of general importance as are local papers and planning application records.

Figure 4.9 Organizational information on rivals

- *Production and product information* Patent application records provide clues to future plans, a rival's research capability as well as technical information. Research networks and the scanning of technical papers give warning of breakthroughs. Consumers association provide independent product comparisons and reverse engineering can provide information on attributes and costs. Local chambers of commerce will be a useful source on facilities and employment. Intermediaries are in a good position to contribute product knowledge.

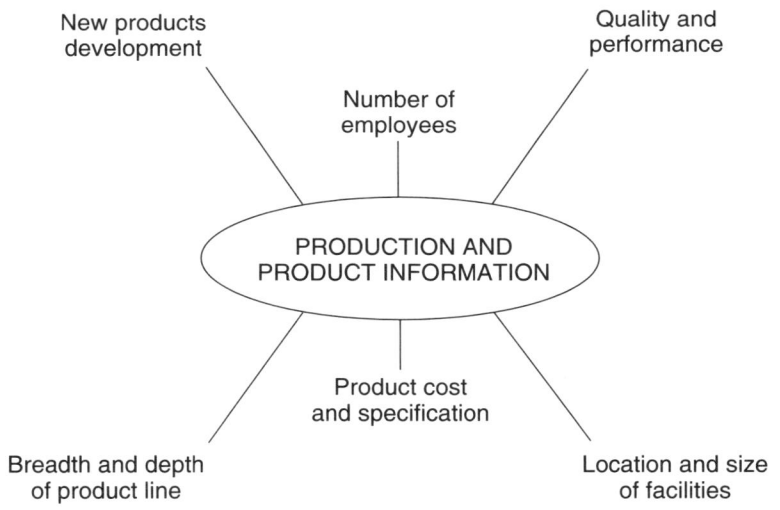

Figure 4.10 Production and product information on rivals

Question 4.9

The darker side of competitor analysis

How would you like to know everything there is to know about your competitors? Wouldn't it make your life as a marketer a lot easier? No, you don't necessarily have to break any laws to get it! There are many ways to find out useful information on troublesome rivals:

- *Milk job applicants* for inside information – they will be keen to impress and probably won't have been warned about divulging secrets.
- *Go on plant tours/monitor aerial maps/monitor staff and transport movements.*
- *Recruit staff from competitors.*
- *Quiz staff at trade shows/conferences/exhibitions* – informal atmosphere and easy conversation.
- *Commission 'academic' research among relevant suppliers and intermediaries.*
- *Undertake reverse engineering* on competitor products to determine performance/costs.
- *What about: examine rubbish, apply pressure, act under false pretences, offer bribes or outright espionage?*

Is the marketer failing in their duty if they don't fully exploit publicly available information?

Some of these practices seem acceptable, some unsavoury – where would (a) you, (b) your organization draw the line that defines ethical behaviour?

Does the line move if corporate survival is threatened?

- *Marketing information* The field salesforce is a key source of marketing intelligence. Properly trained and with an effective recording and retrieval system they can generate vast amounts of information on new products, comparative prices and discounts, promotions and packaging. They are at the daily interface with customers who are in the business of comparing product and seller capabilities. Other sources include the Marketing Surveys Index and product research organizations such as Mintel.
- With markets often changing so quickly and dramatically, a formalized information system is required. It must incorporate procedures for the coordination and communication of intelligence to relevant decision makers without delay. The existence of a system should encourage participation in the information gathering process by all organization members. This important need for environmental intelligence will be developed further in the following unit.

Figure 4.11 Marketing information on rivals

Summary

In this unit we have dealt with the following important aspects:

- The nature and implications of competition in fragmented and concentrated industries.
- The importance of monitoring the actions and reactions of competitors.
- An appreciation of the five forces required to undertake a structural analysis of industry profitability.
- A practical framework for assessing the intensity of competition within a market and changes over time.
- Adaption of the five-force framework to allow consideration of collaboration.
- The regulatory framework relating to competition.
- Recognition of the need for an information system and the important sources of information required for a competitor analysis.

Activity debrief

Question 4.1 Health/fitness, restaurants and large sections of fast food, increasing concentration at top/city end and travel lodges on main routes. Factors include need for close personal attention (restaurants), early growth stage (health/fitness), easy entry (fast food).

Question 4.2 Examples could include longer opening hours for convenience stores, fast-food deliveries, store-interior formats.

Question 4.4 Fragmentation is best described by 3, concentrated by number 4.

Question 4.5 Substitutes include charter/scheduled flights/Ryanair/Easyjet/Eurostar/car and ferry/hovercraft. Price performance ratios are relatively close with the exception of charter and some scheduled flights. If opportunity cost, duration and timing are of the essence the director will justify the latter. Change is taking place due to the entry of new airlines, e.g. Go (a BA subsidiary) and the curtailment of duty-free sales.

Question 4.6 Aldi – Airtours – Toyota (cost leadership); Sainsbury's – Thompson's – Ford (diff.); Lidl – Wallace Arnold's – Hyundai (cost focus); Iceland/M&S – Kuoni – BMW/Land Rover.

Question 4.8

1 He or she receives information on potentially harmful business activities from various sources and can refer them for investigation by the MMC or the Consumer Protection Advisory Committee (CPAC) as appropriate.
2 He publicizes consumer rights.
3 He actively encourages industry associations to introduce and progressively improve codes of practice.
4 He can obtain assurances from or injunctions against persistent offenders or publishers of misleading advertisements.
5 He can propose new laws to the independent CPAC who then reports to the Secretary of State.

Activity 4.1 Getting bigger brings cost advantages, build barriers in a defendable niche, innovate to provide continuous differentiation/edge over rivals.

Activity 4.4

1 has low/stable returns.
2 has low/risky returns – liable to entry in upturns and periods of windfall profit but firms don't exit as conditions deteriorate.
3 has high/stable returns – very attractive as the unsuccessful leave the industry.
4 has high/risky returns – unsuccessful stay and fight.

Extended activity 4.1 Price leadership avoids the kink allowing movement along the DD industry curve; new product development makes the dd curve less responsive for price rises (i.e. now more differentiated) and more responsive for price cuts (customers will prefer); collusion converts kink to DD; promotion shifts the demand curve to the right.

The importance of this section of the syllabus has already been emphasized. It is a critical environment that confronts virtually all organizations in some way or another. It is also the bread-and-butter concern of the marketer. The examiner has a variety of question options available. These range, as the specimen shows, from Porter's analysis, to the competitive/cooperative relationships between a business and its suppliers or distributors, to assessment of the impact of policies relating to competition.

You must demonstrate not just an understanding of theories and analysis discussed in the unit but also an ability to relate to your own or a representative industry. You must be very clear as to the contribution of the marketer to shaping marketing forces and sustaining better than normal profitability over time.

1 You have been asked to provide a summary report to your product managers on the subject of Michael Porter's five-force structural analysis.

   (a) Explain to them the relationship between the five forces and long-run profitability in the market concerned.
   (b) Recommend one strategy that could help maintain profitability in the face of these five forces.   (20 marks)
                     (CIM Marketing Environment paper, June 1998)

2 (a) What determines the degree of competitiveness within a market?
                                                                  (6 marks)
   (b) Provide a brief to your marketing director on the strategies available to a firm facing intense competition to improve its profitability.
                                                                 (14 marks)
                     (CIM Marketing Environment paper, June 1997)

3 Using a country of your own choice:

   (a) Explain what you understand by the legislative environment.
                                                                  (6 marks)
   (b) Supply your marketing manager with a summary of how legislation contributes to fair trading between businesses and:
       (i)   consumers
       (ii) other businesses.   (14 marks)
                     (CIM Marketing Environment paper, June 1997)

4 (a) Explain the main ways in which competition polices may impact on the marketing environment.   (10 marks)
   (b) Comment on the view that competition policies exist to maintain a balance between competition and collusion.   (10 marks)
                                    (Specimen examination question)

Hints: Indicative content and approach

Question 1(a)/(b)

- This is a fairly typical question on five-force analysis.
- Note the provision of a summary report means headings, bullet points and a concise approach.
- Don't be tempted to put down all you know about Porter. The question wants this knowledge relating to its effect on long-run profit.
- Provide a market/industry setting – the question implicitly requires one.
- Provide just *one* strategy as directed but then demonstrate its effectiveness in neutralizing the negative effects on profit of *each* of the five forces.

Question 2(a)/(b)

- This is testing your understanding of the competitive environment.

- You could answer part (a) by referring to the number of firms/nature of the product/size of barriers or you could amend five-force analysis.
- Notice the format requirement of a brief – provide a heading and be concise.
- Focus on strategies rather than marketing tactics.
- Link each strategy to how it alleviates competition and contributes to profitability.

Question 3(a)/(b)

- This is a fairly typical breadth question on the legal environment (see Unit 7).
- It also requires more depth of understanding on the legislation providing for fair trading between firms. As such it is a question which cuts across two parts of the new syllabus.
- Note the format requirement for a summary rather than detail.
- No detailed knowledge of legislation is now required but recognition of key acts and a summary of their main provisions is expected.

Question 4(a)/(b)

- This is a specimen question to provide illustration of the possible form of future questions.

The macro-environment

This unit introduces the important macro-environment of the business. Subsequent units consider the economic, legislative social, technical and natural environments in more depth while in this one you will:

❏ Recognize the critical importance to an organization of monitoring change in its macro-environment.

❏ Understand the nature of the PEST environments and their potential impacts or influences on the marketer.

❏ Appreciate the concept of the environmental set and its relevance to corporate strategy.

❏ Become aware of the main sources of data on the macro- and micro-environment.

By the end of this unit you will be able to:

❏ Appreciate the breadth and significance of the external environment.

❏ Undertake an identification and assessment of environmental threats and opportunities facing an organization of your choice.

❏ Review your understanding of the organization as an open system.

❏ Access and assess relevant data on the environment of business in a time- and cost-effective manner.

Study Guide

This unit relatively provides the framework for a section of the syllabus accounting for 45 per cent of the total. It is primarily concerned with the importance of monitoring and understanding changes in the wider environment. The main elements of the macro-environment were briefly defined in the second part of Unit 1 and you should refresh your memory of this before reading on.

Although this is, in a sense, an introductory unit to the ones that follow, it is also a fertile source of possible questions on the examination paper. Questions may be posed on your general understanding of the macro-environment not least because of its importance in the development of marketing strategy. Another area is that of information sources, which, given their importance to the marketer's ability to monitor a changing environment, will form the basis of questions from time to time. As you will see from the sample questions, these may be related to any particular aspect of the macro-environment.

The June 1998 paper contains a broad question on the macro-environment, with a focus on threats and opportunities, while the June 1997 paper explicitly questions your knowledge of sources of information and assistance. So despite this unit being relatively short, do not underestimate its potential importance in examination terms.

I would expect you to work through the unit material in 2–3 hours but the activities could take more than double this, depending on whether you are able to cooperate with a group to spread the work. As was stressed in Unit 1, it is vital that you seek to relate your work to up-to-date and relevant examples and applications. I hope by now you *have* acquired the habit of scanning the quality press for these, since the examiner will expect and give credit for your knowledge of *current* developments as befits a student of the marketing environment!

Your file on the micro-environment should be fairly substantial by now and still expanding as you add relevant clippings and cases. It is therefore time to open a new file devoted to the macro-environment:

- Divide this file into six sections; Introductory concepts and information needs, Political/legal, Economic, International, Social, Technical and Natural.
- Determine what environmental information is currently gathered by your organization.
- Scan the quality news media on a regular basis.

Understanding the macro-environment

Marketing, as we have already learned, is actively concerned with anticipating and then responding positively to changes occurring in the external environment. It is these generally uncontrollable forces in the macro-environment that create a succession of potential threats and opportunities for the business.

In Unit 1 we considered the business as an open system interacting with its external environment. Figure 5.1 provides an appreciation of the link-

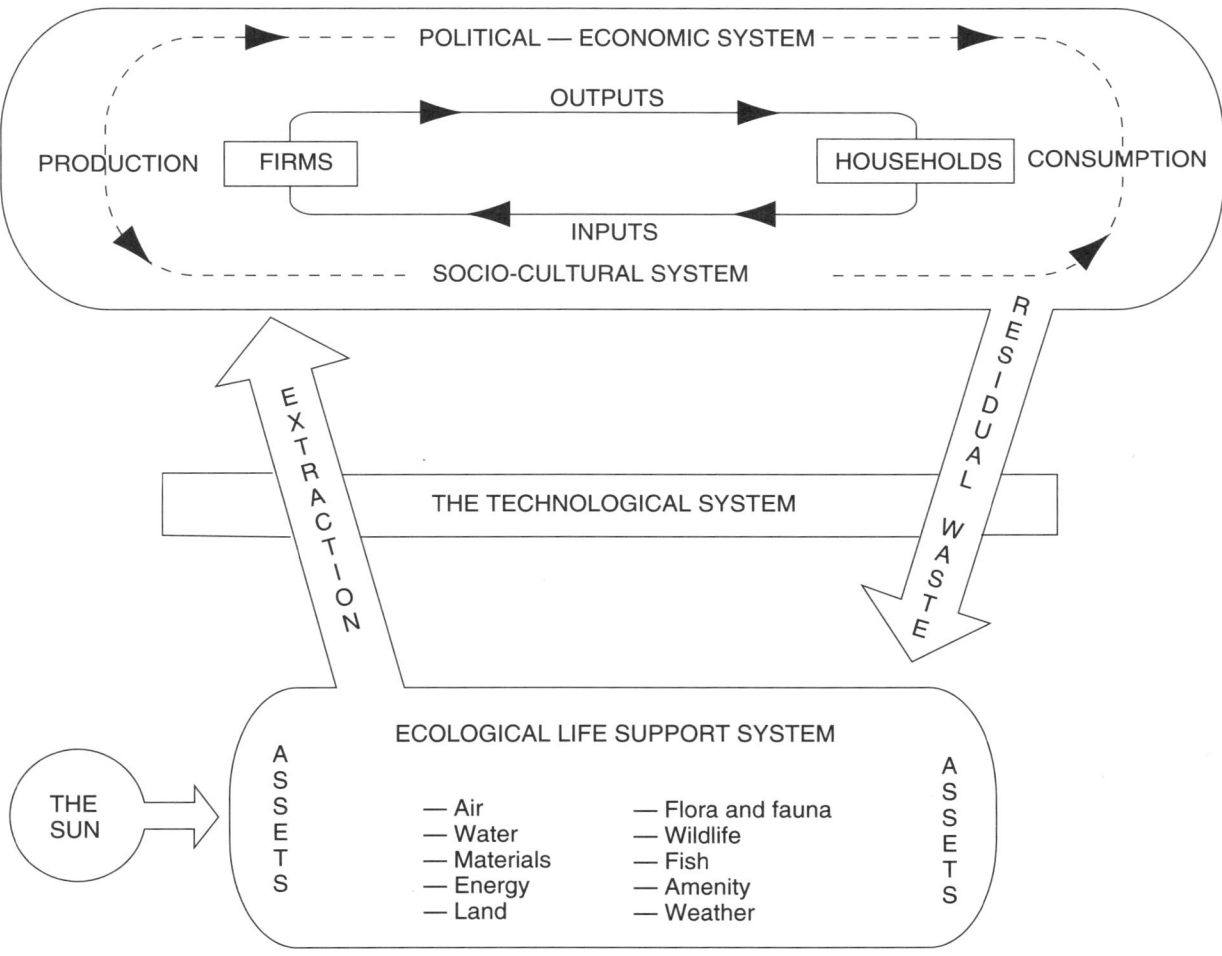

Figure 5.1 Business as open systems within the macro-environment

ages involved (you may also refer to case 4 in Unit 10). The business, as an open system, competes for inputs which are privately owned by households. These inputs are converted into outputs of goods and services which are desired and purchased by households using incomes received from selling factor services to the firm. These transactions are not only conducted in the micro-environment of any given business, but also within the wider political, social and economic systems.

The political system, as we will see in Unit 7, provides for the election of a government on the basis of a declared manifesto. Broad policy objectives are set and legislation is enacted to implement it. One important political objective is to secure re-election and this has enhanced the attractiveness of economic growth as the main driving force in the economic system. Households in relative poverty want improved living standards while the rich seem inclined to get richer. If forced to choose they will both opt for the political party that offers sustainable growth. Firms also operate within a social and cultural system. The number and structure of households are changing as populations alter. The attitudes and values of those households also change over time and the influence of education and the media. Patterns of consumption reflect evolving lifestyles, and societal expectations impact on what is deemed to be acceptable behaviour within businesses.

Figure 5.1 also shows the SLEPT factors as part of a much larger system upon which they depend. This is the natural environment that forms the backdrop to our social and economic lives. A growing economy must draw part of its necessary inputs from this life-supporting system. Some inputs are renewable, as in the case of softwoods, while others, like oil, are effectively non-renewable assets accumulated through natural processes over very long time periods. Resources do renew, but due to an input of energy from another system, the sun. Similarly, the environment receives discharges from the economic system in the form of residual waste. Waste in excess of the natural assimilative powers of the environment is pollution, which impacts on air, water and land quality as well as the weather. The technological system can be double edged. It can open up the natural world to the ravages of uncontrolled tourism or exploitative cultivation of the rain forests but also facilitate recycling and substitution. Reconciling the demand for economic growth with the protection of our natural life support systems may be the primary challenge of the new century.

| Activity 5.1 | In his books such as *The New Industrial State* and *Economics and the Public Purpose* J. K. Galbraith suggests that firms pursue growth in size to protect themselves from hostile takeovers and to secure some control over their environments. The costs and risks involved in developing new products today are so high that firms attempt to control their inputs, the market and even the consumer. He even went so far as to suggest that big business was attempting to *create dissatisfaction in the minds of consumers* by bombarding them with broadly based promotional activity which encouraged them to replace existing products with successive generations of 'new and allegedly better products'. Can you think of any examples which may support Galbraith's thesis? Can you provide a positive defence against what is clearly an attack on the contribution, values and social responsibility of modern marketing methods? |

Unlike the micro-environment, these broad natural, political, economic, social and technical trends and changes do not directly impact on day-to-day operations. They are, however, extremely important in shaping the competitive situation and the actions and perceptions of relevant stakeholders.

How many businesses do you know that can afford to be purely production orientated as we enter the new century? Ever since the dawn of the industrial era, *change* has been the predominant and enduring feature in both industry and wider society. The marketer is actively involved in the shaping and changing of consumer tastes but such effects are nothing compared to the evolving influences of educational expectations, the media, peer groups and travel.

It is also likely that the twentieth century will be best remembered for technological achievements that have put astronauts on the moon, transformed communication and automated industrial processes. Satellites, computers and supersonic aircraft have produced a 'global village' where events on the other side of the world are known earlier than those in a nearby town or village. Business must therefore be constantly alert to new processes and technology, to possible substitutes and, increasingly, competitive threats.

Question 5.1	Can you think of any businesses that face *static* market conditions? This implies no change in both consumer tastes and the state of technical knowledge. (**See** Activity debrief at the end of this unit.)

'But tomorrow always arrives, it is different and then even the mightiest company is in trouble if it has not worked on its future.' This quotation by Peter Drucker underlines the reality of continuous change in modern societies. Size is no automatic defence against the forces of change, indeed, of the companies listed in the *Financial Times Top 100* twenty-five years ago, only half still remain there today. Those missing have fallen victim to a number of misfortunes such as:

- Acquisition by another firm
- Spectacular failure
- Poor relative performance
- The state forced to take ownership

Clearly, the larger business must stay on its toes to survive changing circumstances, although the weight of its bureaucracy may make this difficult. Smaller businesses may have the flexibility to adapt more effectively, but only if given access to sufficient resources. Both must recognize that they are on the equivalent of a moving conveyor, they must move fast just to stand still as tastes, technology and competitive forces alter.

Activity 5.2	It was mentioned above that since 1975 half of the largest firms operating then no longer exist. Conduct some research among relevant groups and individuals to build up a picture of what life was like twenty-five years ago. You may be surprised at the differences! Try to find out as many dimensions as possible regarding life at work, at home, leisure activities, living standards, type of goods and services. What kind of things that we take for granted today were not available? What product or process technologies were not in use or even thought of? (**See** Activity debrief at the end of this unit.)

Although *change* is the characteristic feature of industrialized societies, its pace and complexity also appears to have increased. The 1950s and 1960s, for example, while still experiencing change, were relatively stable and predictable. In Britain, economic growth was continuous and fluctuated within narrow limits. Unemployment and inflation were relatively low and steady and a high degree of social consensus prevailed. Political parties had similar agendas and both technological and market changes were manageable. The oil crises of the 1970s replaced this comparative calm with turbulent, complex and often dynamic interactive change which has continued ever since. This was even more the case in Asian economies such as Hong Kong or China, where rapid growth was compounded by critical political uncertainties.

In Britain such change exposed previously sleepy market sectors to considerable threats since familiarity with previously established conditions had led to complacency. Similar effects have been felt more recently with privatization and deregulation, the Single European Market, the GATT agreement, European Monetary Union, and so the list goes on. As we will see in Unit 10 dynamic and complex market environments demand that the marketer aims to understand the future rather than rely on the patterns of the past. Any organization wishing to be consistently successful in the future must:

- Scan their environment
- Identify those forces relevant to the organization/its industry
- Respond to threats and opportunities by implementing strategies
- Monitor the outcome of planned action
- Continue to scan their environment

The scope for scanning relevant forces may be seen in Figure 5.2.

Each of the elements highlighted for scanning will be examined over the next four units while identification of specific external forces relevant to a business is the subject of the following section on the environmental set. The response to what have been defined as 'uncontrollable forces' in terms of strategies requires more explanation. 'Standing still is the fastest way of moving backwards in a rapidly changing world', is a quotation attributed to Anita Roddick, founder of Body Shop International. Businesses cannot afford to passively accept change in the macro-environment but must

Figure 5.2 The scope for forecasting

110

adapt or suffer the consequences. This requires the marketer to not only scan and analyse threats and opportunities but also develop positive strategic responses.

This might involve lobbying for political change or managing the media in order to influence critical publics. Being proactive, even where scope for direct influence on events is limited, will always have more effect on the outcome of the 'game' than the pure spectator role.

The environmental set

Every organization faces a set of environmental factors over which it may have some influence but seldom any direct control. Small or large, public or private, manufacturer or service organization, they all operate in the context of a shifting set of what are, in effect, potential threats or opportunities. The set that concerns any specific business will, however, be individual to its own particular circumstances and situation. It will also change over time as the elements in the set shift in relative importance and actual impact upon the business.

The board of directors must ensure that they monitor changes in their set and rank the elements in terms of likely impact on the business. The set is a vital stating point for environmental assessment and SWOT analysis providing the basis for formulating a strategic response.

Activity 5.3

Obtain the three most recent annual reports of a public limited company of your choice by writing to/or phoning the company secretary or visiting a main reference or college library with a strong business section. Paying particular attention to the chairman's and managing director's reports, identify the main opportunities and threats for the company. Observe any change in importance attached to these set factors over the period covered.

The set of the business in Figure 5.3 changed significantly even in one year.

- As with 1998–99, the continuing strength of the pound relative to the Euro is the most important set element for this manufacturer. Although it serves to reduce the cost of imported raw materials and components, helping to hold down factory prices in domestic currency terms, the damaging effect on export volumes continues to be felt. Foreign competition is advantaged, with not only European manufacturers eyeing the British market but also the recession-hit Asian dragons. As the fifth item in the 1998–99 set signalled, currency destabilization and sharp stock

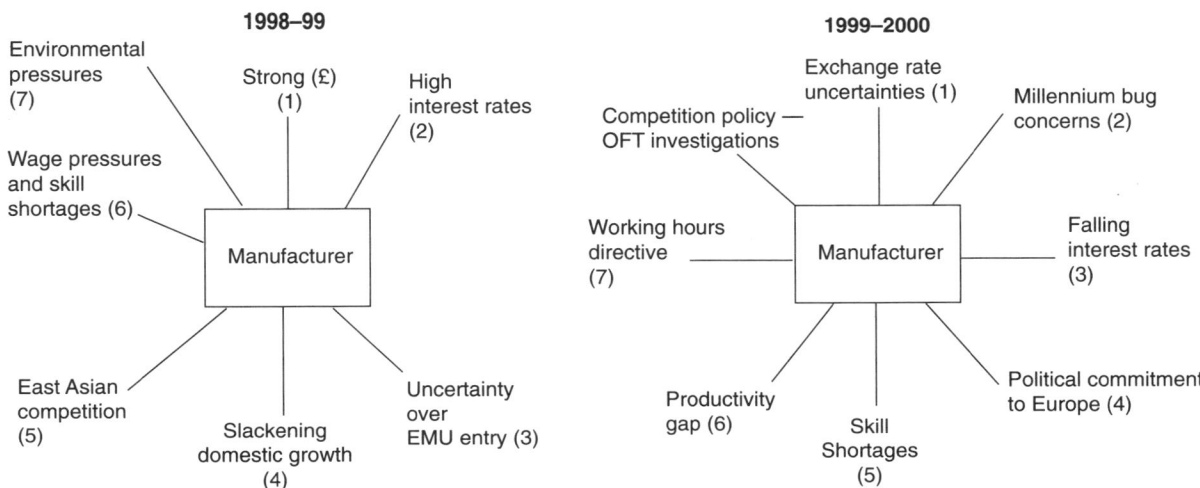

Figure 5.3 Environmental set for a large UK manufacturer, 1998–99 and 1999–2000

111

market falls in Malaysia, Hong Kong, South Korea, Japan and elsewhere were bound to provide a competitive advantage to these already productive economies.

UK textiles have been particularly hard hit, forcing rationalization and/or relocation overseas. Also, with the onset of the Euro, the whole manufacturing sector fears disadvantage through uncertain currency fluctuations or market exclusion.

- The millennium bug is causing concern in many boardrooms not least because insurers are inserting exclusions, and customers for manufactured finished goods and components are demanding compliance. Legal claims may arise if computer controlled equipment fails. This theme will be further explored in Unit 10 (Case 3).
- Interest rates have fallen into third ranking due mainly to the cuts that have occurred through 1999. This has not only narrowed the gap with the rates paid by competitors in the EU but also served to encourage aggregate spending and halt the output fall in a manufacturing sector that had previously been sliding towards recession. Some ex-factory prices for products such as cars and computers had been falling leading to fears of a spiralling deflation. The downward trend in rates should progressively feed through over the next two years to avert this.
- Uncertainties over European Monetary Union (EMU) have given way to a delayed reality. Many multinational manufacturers have been voicing concerns over Britain's current wait-and-see policy. The Prime Minister's strong statement on industry's need to invest in the changeover for entry provided a positive set factor. It suggests interest rates will fall further in preparation for entry and the £ will shadow the Euro. Manufacturing firms need to make the structural changes necessary to meet the challenges of transparent Euro pricing. This sign of political commitment removes a degree of uncertainty surrounding the future.
- Despite a slowing economy, some high-profile closures and threatened redundancies, the rate of unemployment in the economy continued to fall in 1999. This caused skill shortages in some key areas affecting manufacturer's supplying electronic and digital equipment.
- East Asian economies, particularly Japan, continued to suffer recession, dampening the global economy. However the US economy continued to expand strongly. However, manufacturers were concerned over a reported productivity gap with American and Japanese companies of around 40 per cent.
- Manufacturer's were also concerned at the ramifications of EU directives concerning working hours and the minimum wage. These regulations provide potential limitations on the flexibility of operations and the ability to respond effectively to changing demand conditions. The minimum wage might affect the ability of some labour intensive businesses to compete with imports. The government also proposes a 'Fairness at Work' bill which could add to business costs by giving new powers to unions and new rights for time off to workers.
- While environmental pressures are ever present, given concerns over climate change and conservation, this set factor has been displaced in the 1999–2000 set by the threat of tightening competition policy. Concerns in the car and consumer electronics sectors, in particular, are drawing attention from the Office of Fair Trading. Any downward pressure applied to final prices in these product groups would clearly be communicated through the ranks of manufacturers in the supply chain.

Activity 5.4

Produce a current environmental set either for your own organization or the one you chose in Activity 5.3 above.
Rank the elements you identify and consider their significance:

- 12 months ago
- In 12 months' time

The set for a public sector organization reflects very different managerial concerns (Figure 5.4). Factors affecting the income of the authority are clearly important although their nature has changed between the two years.

Labour dominance in government is reflected at local level with many authorities, such as Hull, being wholly Labour controlled. New labour policies therefore exert a significant influence on local authorities. The government also plans to change their relationship with local authorities by giving ministers wide powers to intervene. The main intention is to ensure that services provide good value for money but could be exerted to secure significant control. For example, already one failing school has been transferred to private sector management. Local authorities will also be watching the formation of the Greater London Authority with interest.

- The size of the central government grant was a critical issue in local authority finances. With the government determined to pursue a policy of financial rectitude in its early years the prospect for relaxation was not good. Many authorities faced the prospect of either increasing debt, sharp rises in council tax levels or further redundancies.
- The state of the local economy provided a continued opportunity, not only for revenue growth from the tax base and service charges, but also from joint capital projects with the private sector. For example, Kirklees Council in West Yorkshire has participated with Henry Boot in the construction of housing estates and with McAlpine plc in the development of a state-of-the-art multi-purpose stadium with multiplex, swimming and golf facilities. The Private Finance Initiative will continue and expand under the new government.
- With responsibility for funding local schooling, educational issues have become prominent in the set due to the priority being accorded to them by the government. Local authorities will be expected to contribute actively to the improvement in standards demanded. Government use of the windfall tax on privatized utilities to fund education and training for long-term youth unemployment will also require initiatives from them.
- A new element in the set involves inner city congestion. Traffic densities are forcing local authorities to consider further urgent action to deal with the problem. Authorities must balance a diversity of competing interest groups ranging from local retailers, concerned at trade being

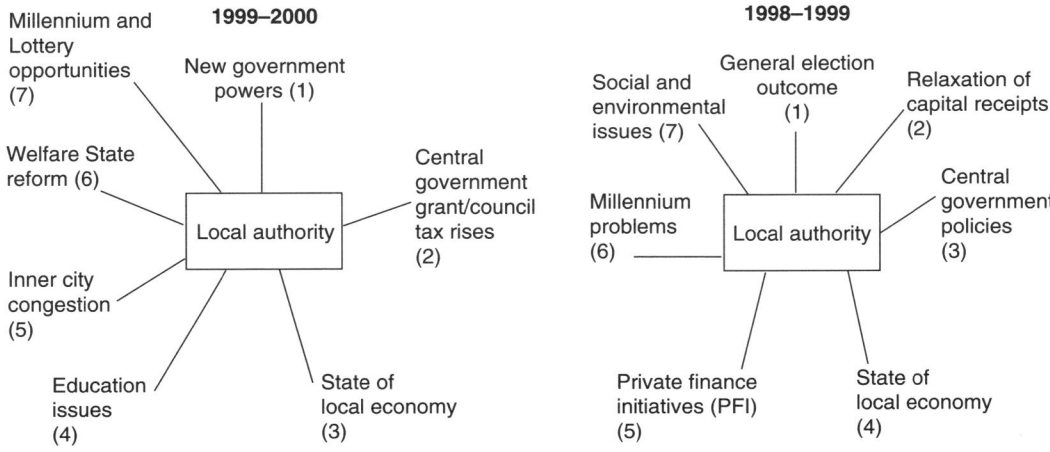

Figure 5.4 Environmental set for a local authority, 1998–1999 and 1999–2000

lost to other towns, to residents affected by traffic growth. Kirklees have introduced a charge on residents who park vehicles outside their residences.

- Welfare state reforms are at the top of the Blair government agenda but it will be at local authority level that many of the administrative consequences will be felt. Local authorities ultimately have a duty and responsibility to those residing within their boundaries. If welfare support is lost then people will turn to the authority for support and protection. The Welfare to Work initiative in the budget will have a major impact.
- Authorities continue to face the impending deadline of the year 2000 as they struggle to meet the cost and technical difficulties of re-programming their often aged computers to recognize the new century. On the other hand, the continuing flow of funds for Lottery projects provides welcome opportunities. The millennium dome in Greenwich promises considerable local benefits.
- Environmental issues have disappeared from the set this year but are still significant. The demand for new homes to meet a changing household structure will not diminish, with 4.5 million new homes required over the next 20 years. Authorities have the responsibility for identifying and approving suitable land for development. Pressure groups, such as the Council for the Protection of Rural England, are already mobilizing to block proposed greenfield development plans.
- The establishment of Scottish and Welsh Assemblies may also introduce the issue of more devolved powers to English regions.

Further sets could be developed to represent the major influences to be accounted for by businesses in financial services (e.g. a unified financial authority raising concerns over accountablility and right of appeal), import–export, retailing, construction and so forth. As seen above, though, the elements will vary and a threat for one organization may be an opportunity for another. Private security firms (Group 4, for example), are seizing the opportunity provided by the government in privatizing low-security prison facilities. CIM, who are potentially threatened by a Malaysian policy to reverse its large services deficit by encouraging foreign universities to set up campuses, have taken the opportunity of setting up a branch there as well as in Singapore.

Question 5.2	Which functional areas of the business will be most affected by environmental set factors and which will be least affected?
	   How will the research and development function be affected?
	   What can the business do to influence elements in its set?
	(**See** Activity debrief at the end of this unit.)

The main sources of environmental data

Organizations that have the ability to sense environmental change and be proactive in their response to it tend to perform better than those that lack it. It often signals the need for organizational change and reformulation of marketing strategy, but there is no guarantee of the appropriate response taking place in time. This vitally depends on the quality of the information systems available to the business and the extent of management's understanding of the complex and often-interacting changes taking place in the external environment.

'To manage a business well is to manage its future, and to manage its future is to manage information' (M. Harper, Jr).

As Figure 5.5 shows, any business needs an integrated internal and external information system to provide the means for dovetailing organizational and marketing developments with environmental change.

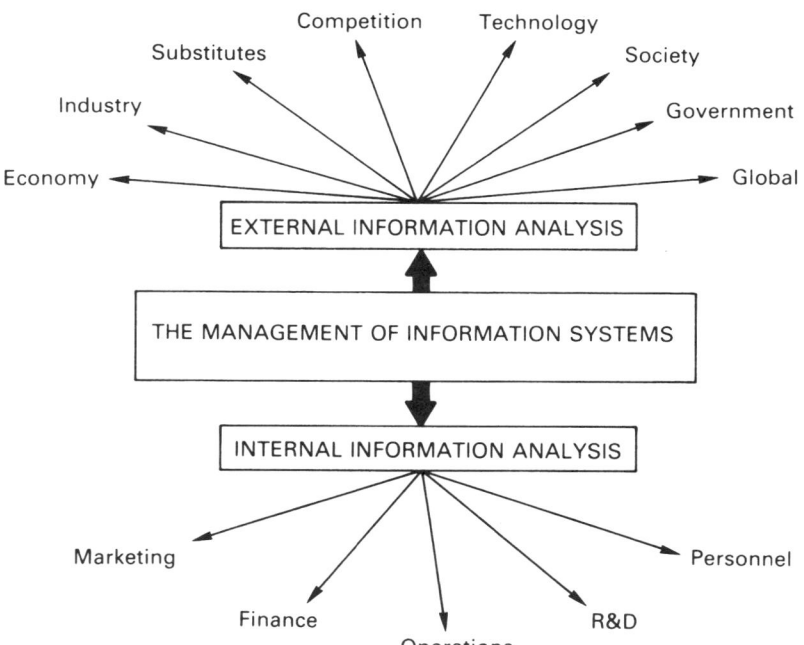

Figure 5.5
An integrated internal and external information system

Internal and external information systems

There are two main categories of existing information:

- *Internal data* gathered in-company as a result of operational activities (e.g. employment, cost and sales figures)
- *Secondary data* gathered from external sources (e.g. government statistics, published surveys, etc., see Figure 5.6).

A third source of information is *primary data* commissioned specifically to fill knowledge gaps left by the much cheaper alternatives above.

Figure 5.6
Secondary data for a business

115

What kind of information is required?

Many different types of information are required, depending on the decisions to be taken. Examples of the more important types include:

Economy
- Main economic indicators – inflation, interest rates, vacancies
- Business confidence indicators – capacity utilization, investment
- Labour market changes
- National income, output and expenditure patterns
- Government taxation and spending plans

Society

- Demographic indicators – birth/death rates, inter-regional migration patterns
- Household and working patterns
- Leisure activities – indoor/outdoor
- Changes in cultural norms
- Ownership ratios for homes, cars, mobile phones, etc.

Similar factors could be identified in other areas of the SLEPT environment underlining the diverse nature of information requirements in modern business today. In an environment of rapid change, where time and delay can cost a company dearly, the ability to obtain a clear and accurate picture of developments can provide the firm with a distinct competitive advantage. Information is power, but to achieve this requires a knowledge not just of key sources of information but also of how to access them quickly and resource effectively.

Exam Tip

News analysis is one means of assessing the importance of current environmental issues. Since editors only have limited space they must make critical choices as to what and what not to include. They will therefore tend to include subjects that are of current and future concern but exclude those they identify as 'yesterday's news'.

One method of defining whether an economy is coming out of recession, for example, is to track the number of references to it in the quality press over time. As this index declines so the economy must be picking up, since writers and editors no longer see articles on it as 'news'.

The conclusion must therefore be to keep your finger on the pulse of environmental change by scanning the news media regularly.

Internal sources
Many questions can only be answered by reference to internal records. The strengths and weaknesses of the business may be identified in this way, although this must be assessed relative to competitors. To be useful, however, this must be gathered in a form that is accessible, accurate and relevant to the forecast or evaluation required. The flow of information through a business should be analysed systematically to achieve these objectives.

Question 5.3

The marketing department is the primary interface between the business and its customers. What information should it generate? Suggest three key pieces of information from each of the following:

- Management accountant
- Purchasing department
- Operations

(**See** Activity debrief at the end of this unit.)

Published material

Such sources are seldom used regularly or systematically by business decision makers. The diffuse nature of many of the sources shown in Figure 5.6 makes collection, classification and distribution to interested managers an expensive and time-consuming process. The government is one of the main producers of primary data, published through the re-named Office of National Statistics (formerly CSO).

Published business information sources

Some larger organizations delegate a junior executive to undertake this task and circulate a regular summary to appropriate staff. Organizations such as McCarthy and Extel also grew by providing information on specific companies in a readily referenced format. However, while the value of such information in informing decisions has been recognized by perceptive marketing executives and planners, their use has been haphazard and on a need-to-know basis only.

Activity 5.5

The key skill for a marketer to develop is to know *what information is available* on a particular issue and, most importantly, *where to find it*. Published material is available on most topics and is far cheaper than undertaking primary research.

You *must* familiarize yourself with the operations and opportunities within a modern business library. Visit the best one in your locality and familiarize yourself with the following:

- The index system – usually a computerized database enabling you to interrogate by subject, author, class number, etc.
- The inter-library loans system allowing you to access material not held in the library itself. All you require is the title, author, publisher and date.
- Electronic databases – these are often based on CD-ROM systems for easy use and linked to printers so that you can obtain a hard copy.

Trade sources

The usual means by which managers keeps informed of both internal and external developments, in many cases, is through the grapevine. They establish and build *networks* of information sources which can be drawn on when the need arises. Regular conversations with colleagues, customers and other stakeholder contacts provide a moving tapestry of events supplemented with such things as sales records and consultancy reports. Much of the material gathered from the sources in Figure 5.7 will be sifted, cross-referenced and assimilated on a day-to-day basis.

Figure 5.7
Trade sources and networks

Summary of sources of information and assistance in the macro-environments

Social-cultural environment

- *Guide to Official Statistics* – provides an overview of statistics available on the macro environment.
- *Annual Abstract of Statistics* – statistical series on all major aspects of government responsibility.

- Office of National Statistics (ONS) Census – size, distribution and structural changes in population.
- *Social Trends* – annual survey of key societal indicators.
- *Family Expenditure Survey* – annual statistical analysis of spending/lifestyle patterns.
- ACORN/Mosaic – classification of local neighbourhoods for segmentation purposes.
- Journals/Quality press society sections, e.g. *New Society* – changing social patterns.
- British Market Research Bureaux – research cases on lifestyle change.

Political-legislative environment

- Select Committee reports – monitor and report on political issues of the day.
- JUSTIS on-line legal database – current legislative developments.
- Legal digests – recent case law.
- European Commission – EU directives and implementation timetables.
- Mainstream media and news databases.

Exam Tip

Don't be tempted to use report format for every answer you provide. This undifferentiated approach of producing reports when none are required wastes time, annoys the examiner and deflects attention away from the actual answer content which earns the majority of the marks. Where no specific format is required just break up your answer, where appropriate, with headings and bullet points to make it examiner friendly.

Economic environment

- ONS National Income and Expenditure/the *Blue Book* – comprehensive macro-economic analysis.
- *Monthly Digest* – most recent figures on the economy, industry and labour market.
- *Economic Trends* – changing economic structure and activity patterns.
- *Bank of England Quarterly Review* – monitors changes in the monetary system and exchange rates.
- *Regional Trends* – detailed annual data on social and economic change in the planning regions.
- *Employment Gazette* – monthly publication covering wage and price movements.
- *CBI Quarterly Survey* – measuring industry confidence and intentions.
- *National Institute Economic Review* – quarterly commentary on the current and future state of the economy together with country comparisons.
- Journals and quality newspapers, e.g. *Economist, Financial Times*, various databases.
- Bank reviews – articles and economic analysis.

International environment

- Department of Trade and Industry – export credits/advice.
- Chambers of commerce – advice/trade missions/contact networks.
- Professional bodies, e.g. CIM, Institute of Exporters – networks of contacts.
- Embassies and trade missions – on-the-spot advice/promotion/contacts.
- Banks, e.g. HKSB, foreign banks based in London – credit rating/market analysis.
- International organizations, e.g. OECD/IMF/WTO/UN World Economic Survey – country studies.
- Trade blocs, e.g. EU/ASEAN/NAFTA – research studies/comparisons/trade patterns.
- Government departments, e.g. customs and excise/planning – specific sectoral data.
- World wide web.

- Quality press, journals and directories, e.g. *Kompass*, EIU Country Reports/Asia Week – current developments.
- Research journals and conference papers
- Trade press reports
- Channel intermediaries and ultimate customer-need surveys
- Technical abstracts and databases
- Professional associations and industry networks.

Technical environment

- Research journals and conference papers
- Trade press reports
- Channel intermediaries and ultimate customer need surveys
- Technical abstracts and databases
- Professional associations and industry networks

Information at your fingertips

Keeping an ear to the ground (or, more likely, to the phone or the internet!) in this informal way may not always be effective in times of rapid change. The information may either come too late or not become available to the decision maker who requires it. The volume of potentially useful data appears boundless, and as it expands from year to year, the need to manage it more effectively becomes more pressing. Excellent companies must work more smartly if they are to survive, and this raises demand for better-quality information to support decisions.

Marketers need information at their fingertips to manipulate and add value to. This implies that we should all invest, not only in the development of a personal information system, but also in a network of business contacts. Building a matrix of stakeholder and organizational contacts is one of the keys to working effectiveness. Figure 5.8 reflects some of the critical linkages in a professional's personal information system.

A changing economic structure has shifted the emphasis in favour of knowledge-intensive sectors such as financial services, retailing and high-technology industries. Small firms similarly add to the demand for value-added information services from government and consultancies.

Mass markets are also fragmenting into specialist niches as tastes become less standardized and predictable. Sophisticated marketing information and analysis is, however, required if businesses are to take advantage of the opportunities presented.

The explosion in business-focused information is a reflection of these forces. Sources range from new national newspapers such as *Sunday Business* to more than 3500 business-to-business magazines. Collectively, such sources are termed the 'business press'.

Extending Activity 5.1	If you are part of a wider college group then a useful exercise to extend your knowledge of available information sources is to compile an *information booklet*. If you divide up the task and each cover a handful of references this should be manageable. The objective is to identify key sources of information on the environment classified under various headings and summarize in a short statement their location, ease of access, content, application, ease of use and 'star rating'. The categories might include, sources on companies; on industries; on the economy; on wider society; on international markets and developments; on trade media; business environment texts, etc.

The internet and on-line business information

An efficient information system must be able to programme information into the 'corporate memory' of organization members in much the same way as a computer. The objective is to make the information accessible and usable by the relevant decision maker when required. The power and flexibility of networked computer database systems now offer this capability and can support the more 'human' networks mentioned above.

Figure 5.8
Personal information system

Databases are revolutionizing management information systems. A database is simply a file of information in electronic form providing ease and speed of access and manipulation. On-line means that the database is stored on a remote computer but can be accessed directly by business users through phone lines. Real-time systems mean that they are constantly being updated with new inputs of information while CD-ROM systems are millions of pieces of information stored on compact discs, updated on a regular basis (e.g. monthly) and accessed flexibly by the computer. The rapid development and take-up by business of fax machines and intelligent printers is also expanding the potential of such information sources by providing hard copies to remote locations when required.

Some of the main types of databases currently available include those shown in Figure 5.9. Computers can therefore offer the solution to many of the marketer's problems. By keying in a competitor's name, for example, such systems can search out all available published material.

Question 5.4

List the types of information on competitors which will *not* be available in published sources. What other methods are available for obtaining information in the areas you have identified?
(**See** Activity debrief at the end of this unit.)

Computers combined with communications technologies are generating a wealth of readily transmitted business information available at rapidly falling costs. Global knowledge brings global competition as Asian and other emerging economy companies assess the competitiveness of Western markets as a prelude to exports or direct entry.

The benefits of on-line searching compared to traditional methods may be summarized as follows:

On-line features	*Benefits*
Speed in searching	Time-saving
Selectivity in searching	Quality data
Flexibility in searching	Comparative data
Interactive searching	Flexible scope
Data manipulation	Usable statistics
Up to data	Best available data
User-friendly	Will be used
Charge on actual use	Economic access
Professional methodology	Competitive edge

With information of particular importance to the marketer, areas of business database application should include:

- Market research
- Marketing plans

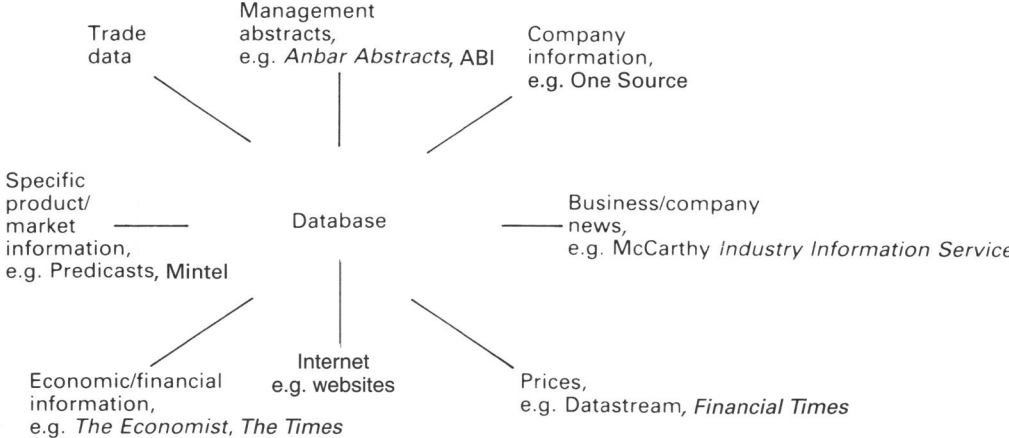

Figure 5.9   Relevant database source

- Marketing presentations
- Sales force coordination
- Market analysis
- Sales analysis
- Customer communications

The explosion in computer, information and communications technologies, demonstrated most dramatically by the global web of computer networks known to all as the internet, provides the ultimate information source for marketers. It links anyone in the world with a PC and a modem and has seen a dramatic expansion both in terms of websites to access and the spiralling number of users. Dixon's introduction of the Freeserve internet connection in Autumn 1998, for example, had generated an additional million UK subscribers by early 1999. This expansion is set to continue as other suppliers, such as BT, remove subscription charges or digital services are provided through televisions and set-top boxes linked to telephone lines. Given appropriate software the user can browse the net, obtaining or exchanging information with others.

New websites open daily including that of The Chartered Institute of Marketing (http://www.cim.co.uk) offering access to new syllabus information, examiner reports, specimen answers, but unfortunately not forthcoming examination questions! Having said this, the CIM has had to take steps to counter the transmission of such questions from one time zone to another. Most organization's now have such a site and while sensitive information may be withheld there is much that may be inferred in intelligence terms from what remains. The technology also means that more research can be desk-based and up to date.

The interactiveness of the internet means that the marketer can readily build information networks and relationships with stakeholders. Information can be both gathered from and distributed to stakeholders, including employees and customers more quickly, and at a fraction of previous cost levels.

One final word of warning in regard to computer databases as a panacea for marketing solutions. There is a considerable *learning curve* involved in the effective use of such systems and many commercially available databases are expensive to subscribe to for any but the largest company. It is also the case that the most important information, namely that relating to future plans and developments, is not available even on real-time systems.

Extending Activity 5.2	As a final exercise in this area of information sources and their interpretation by the sales executive and marketer you should undertake a *competitor analysis*. Taking your own company or a selected plc, choose one of the main markets it competes in and identify its main local, national and international competitors using directories such as *Kompass*. Gather and summarize information on these companies using sources such as the Companies Registration Office, Extel and Datastream. Trade sources should also be used for 'insider' assessment of competitor strengths and weaknesses. Trade association statistics and an interview with the research officer would be particularly useful. You need to establish a framework of criteria by which to compare and contrast the companies – think of what aspects are most important here. You will certainly want to assess their product and its positioning, pricing, promotional mix, unique selling propositions and distribution channels. Present your report to the marketing director or your college tutor for their assessment.

Summary	In this unit we have seen: • Why it is crucially important for the organization to monitor change. • That the marketer should recognize the implications for business being part of larger social, economic and ecological systems. • The importance of identifying the environmental set of an organization so that scarce management time can be focused on these threats and opportunities. • Why and how the marketer should draw on internal and external sources of information. • The potential of the internet and electronic databases in accessing information.

Activity debrief

Question 5.1 Few examples. Craft industries, personal services (e.g. funerals and nursing homes).

Question 5.2 Marketing and sales most affected, perhaps administration and after-sales least affected. R/D affected by the technical and competitive set factors. It can use the marketing mix.

Question 5.3 Sales volume by product, product group, region, channel and market segment. Intelligence reports on competitor prices and promotion, strengths and weaknesses. Assessment of own promotional mix effectiveness. Accounts provide data on cost of sales, debtors, overall sales analysis by customer, variances. Purchasing provides assessment of supplier reliability, stock control and availability, service levels. Operations provide order status, completion dates, production capacity.

Question 5.4 Information on strategies, product developments planned promotions, future intentions, likely reactions. Methods range from industrial espionage to debriefing former employees to questioning associated stakeholders.

Activity 5.2 No calculators, personal computers, colour TVs, unemployment, or equal status for women.

Examination hints and specimen questions

The importance of this area of the syllabus has been outlined earlier. The first specimen question is a challenging one and you must *read it very carefully* to ensure that you understand what the examiner requires. As you will see, it combines a knowledge of elements in this unit and Unit 1, since it offers a choice of macro- or micro-environment factors. The macro aspect is, in effect, a question on the environmental set of a chosen business. This question broadens out your choice to the micro-environment and puts the onus on you to select relevant threats and opportunities as well as an appropriate business context. You must prepare for such eventualities as these in this examination paper. Notice however, that while it allows you to draw on knowledge-area strengths by providing open-ended selection, it also means you must exercise great care to ensure that what you select is appropriate and relevant to the precise wording of the question. Question 2 is a much more specific 'choice' question leaving you in little doubt as to what information is required. Both questions require a business context and you clearly need to prepare a case company exemplar for all aspects of the syllabus. Questions 3 and 4 are part questions on sources of information. This has been a familiar format in the past, but there is no reason why a full question could not be set on this area in future. It is certainly advisable to know four or five key information sources for each environment and be able to summarize their value to the marketer.

1   As the year 2000 approaches, your Marketing Manager has asked you to identify relevant threats and opportunities in both the macro- and micro-environment of the business.
    (a) Draft an outline of three threats and three opportunities for a business of your choice. (12 marks)
    (b) Select one threat and one opportunity and provide a bullet point summary of the impacts or implications arising for the marketing department. (8 marks)
                            (CIM Marketing Environment paper, June 1998)
2   (a) What do you understand by **two** of the following terms:
        • Secondary stakeholders
        • The macro-environment
        • Social responsibility
        • The environmental set (10 marks)
    (b) Using any company of your choice, produce and justify an environmental set. You should include and rank at least five factors in your set. (10 marks)
                            (CIM Marketing Environment paper, June 1995)
3   Suggest **two** useful information sources to consult on the social aspect of the environment. Comment on the content of **one** of these sources. (5 marks)
                            (CIM Marketing Environment paper, June 1998 – adapted)

4   Statestrong is also setting its sights on the rapidly growing East Asian economies. Write a memorandum to the Marketing Director outlining sources of information and assistance available to small firms in assessing the potential of markets such as these. (10 marks)
                            (CIM Marketing Environment compulsory, December 1997)

Hints: Indicative content and approach
Question 1(a)/(b)
• This is a potential gift question since threats and opportunities could be drawn from all areas of the syllabus.
• The question refers to the year 2000 so try to relate some factors to this.
• Don't overlook the format requirements in *both* parts: a draft/outline in (a) and bullet points in (b).
• The business context is there to test whether you can relate your understanding to your/an organization, e.g. a bank.

- Macro threats could include the millennium bug or viruses and possible economic downturn.
- Macro opportunities could include provision of millennium service expertise, the Euro, upgrades.
- You could explore the impact of an IT systems failure on stakeholders, contingency plans, etc.
- You could explore the opportunity for competitive advantage from making systems compliant.

Question 2(a)
- Make sure you only attempt two parts.
- Avoid attempting such a question if you know the answer to the first part but can only guess at the second (as many candidates who had not studied this workbook did!)
- Don't spend too much time on the first part – only a concise summary is possible and required for 5 marks. Define them, produce one or two examples and briefly explain their role, function and importance.

Question 2(b)
- Be sure to use a company context – your own or a high profile one from a sector you are familiar with.
- Include five factors (5 × 2 marks) but for full marks you must rank them in terms of actual/potential impact on the company.
- Rising interest rates, for example, could be justified if the company is highly geared or dependent on credit sales.

Question 3/4
- Be sure to provide 'sources' such as the ONS Census of Population or *Social Trends*.
- Provide a brief commentary on the content, accuracy and usefulness to marketers.
- Provide the memo format and an outline of sources in 4.
- Distinguish between information (EIU Country Studies, UN World Economic Survey) and assistance (DTI, chambers of commerce, embassies, banks, professional bodies, e.g. CIM).

The economic and international environment

Objectives

In this fundamental unit you will:

❑ Consider the nature and significance of macro-economic objectives.

❑ Understand, in basic terms, the workings of the economy and the role and objectives of government in influencing it.

❑ Identify the nature of the business cycle and its significance for business decision making.

❑ Appreciate the policy issues of current importance in macro-economics.

❑ Asess the implications of the international environment.

By the end of this unit you will be able to:

❑ Evaluate measures of economic activity and living standards.

❑ Understand the conflicts in achieving macro-economic objectives.

❑ Recognize the use and limitations of economic indicators.

❑ Assess the likely effects of alternative economic and trade policies.

❑ Evaluate the varying impacts and implications for marketers in different types of organization.

Study Guide

The economic environment is one area where we all have first-hand experience. Not only do we read the newspapers and listen to items on television or radio, we also feel the direct impact of economic events such as rising taxes at budget time, a falling interest rate or a pay freeze. However, a little knowledge is said to be a dangerous thing, and we need to set our day-to-day experience within a framework of understanding as to how the economy works.

Macro-economics is about the *aggregate* behaviour of consumers, businesses and governments. Concern is with the general or average price level rather than the prices of individual products, and interest focuses on the output, income and spending of society in total. The rate of economic growth is also of central importance as are cyclical fluctuations around this trend.

Despite the wide focus on aggregates and a very limited ability to influence them, all businesses must take very careful account of this environment. Decisions on capital investment, the timing of a new product launch or hiring and firing, for example, will need to be set against the general economic background. Unanticipated movements in interest or exchange rates can quite literally convert expected profit into loss.

The economy is a complex system and the marketer who can master the diagnosis of current economic problems and anticipate the direction of policy changes will possess a considerable edge over rivals. An 'economic way of thinking' as regards this aspect of the environment is therefore a useful attribute for you to develop!

The international environment is also increasingly familiar to us, not only through our travels, but also by membership of trade blocs such as the EU.

Civilizations throughout the mists of time have grown and prospered as a result of trade. Recognition of the gains to be made from exchanging surpluses, with a relatively low value in the domestic market, for scarce and desirable products from foreign lands, led in the seventeenth century to the development of international trading companies and then colonial empires. International trading networks now form a tightening web of linkages between virtually all corners of the globe with multinational subsidiaries the nearest modern equivalent of a colonial outpost.

Trade as we enter the new century is therefore more complex with multilateral exchanges facilitated by international finance. It is also the case that participating nations and businesses are increasingly vulnerable to global political and economic influences.

The international environment therefore presents the marketer not only with considerable opportunities but also with greater challenges than the domestic market.

CIM is a qualification undertaken by students from at least thirty-six countries from around the world. The global environment forms a context common to all and may provide more than its fair share of questions as a result.

As with your own economy, it is therefore vital that you have a clear appreciation of your country's international trade position. Is its balance of payments in surplus or deficit? What is its pattern of trade with other countries and the composition of its imports and exports? Does it belong to a trading bloc and, if so, what regulations govern its internal and external relationships?

Due to syllabus changes this workbook can provide only an outline of such factors and you must take steps to fill in the gaps by monitoring press reports.

This unit requires careful reading since you must understand rather than memorize the subject matter. Allow yourself at least 3 hours to read and reread its contents.

Subdivide your economic and international environment file into subsections on: Measurement of economic performance; Macro-economic objectives; The business cycle; Economic policy and relevant indicators (divide this into Fiscal, Monetary, Physical and Supply side policies); Impacts of trade; Trade and payment policies and marketing implications.

This is an area where there is no shortage of information so you will have to be selective in what you file. Your goal is to be able to provide an outline economic assessment of your own country, assess and give examples of economic policy impacts on business and marketers, understand the implications of being an open economy and finally to evaluate how a business should respond in varying economic circumstances.

Unit 10 will consider the concept of globalization and its implications.

Government economic objectives

Governments, like businesses, have a number of objectives. They range from social concerns to national security and political aims. In the economic realm it has been traditional to identify four main objectives together with a variety of subsidiary goals. However, it is now more useful to recognize that there is one overriding goal:

- Faster and more sustainable economic growth

plus three other objectives which might otherwise limit or constrain achievement of the overriding goal.

- Maintaining higher levels of employment or 'real' jobs.
- Controlling inflation at very low levels and avoiding deflation.
- A favourable balance of payments averaged over a period.

Subsidiary goals might include:

- Keeping the aggregate tax burden below 40 per cent of GDP.

- A balanced regional development.
- Resource conservation and concern for the environment.
- Distribution of income reflecting equity, economic contribution, etc.
- A competitive exchange rate.

Exam Tip

To help focus your mind on the syllabus and the pattern of questions posed, it is always helpful to draw up a matrix of syllabus elements against which you place a tick or number if a question was included. This is done for each occasion there is an available and relevant examination set. The resulting grid enables you to identify patterns, trends and possible bankers at a glance. Remember that your examiner will be using one to ensure coverage of the syllabus content over a run of papers. Refer to Unit 11 and study the patterns in the current grid.

Economic growth

This is the fundamental objective, since a growing economy allows a government to achieve other goals requiring resources, to resolve allocational conflicts and, most importantly, to win re-election. An electorate that experiences real improvements in purchasing power, job opportunities and increased spending on health, education, defence and pensions is more likely to vote for the return of the party in office. They say that oppositions do not win elections, governments lose them, and failing to deliver improvements in living standards is often the main cause.

Real growth in Britain has averaged around 2.25 per cent since 1945. The current Chancellor's objectives are to raise this overall trend performance on the one hand and to minimize fluctuations around the trend on the other. Sustaining continuous growth by better economic management, and so avoiding recessions, should create an atmosphere of investment confidence and more positive expectations for the future. This will be reinforced by working on the other factors that determine growth such as encouraging entrepreneurship and innovation through tax incentives.

Growth does not always mean rising consumption, of course, even though this accounts for two-thirds of aggregate demand. An export or investment-led rise in output will be much healthier for the longer-run competitiveness of the economy but does nothing to raise domestic consumption in the short term. A distinction has also to be drawn between an increase in GDP, which is achieved by employing spare or unemployed resources and *real* growth, sustained by rising productivity in resource use through investment in skills, infrastructure, capital and new technology or products.

The *production possibility curve* (Figure 6.1) illustrates these ideas and is

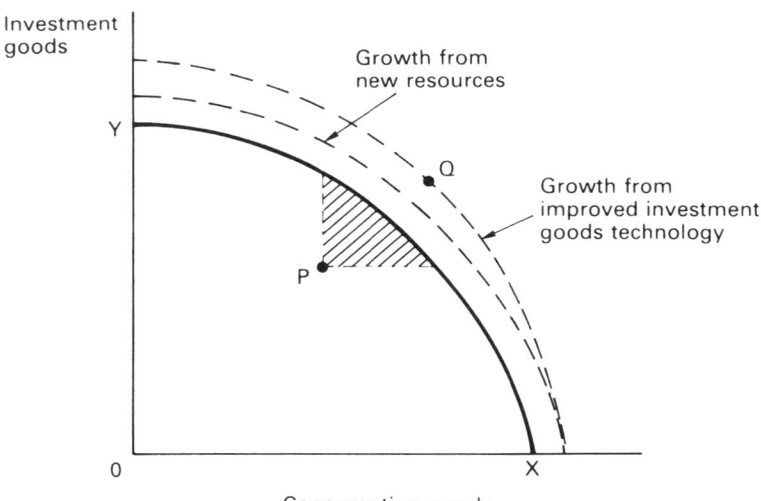

Figure 6.1
The production possibility curve

drawn on the assumption that scarce resources can be used to produce just two types of good. If available resources are fully and efficiently used they could produce 0X of consumption goods *or* 0Y of investment goods or a combination of both at any point along the curve. If the economy is operating at Point P then it is below capacity and inefficient. It could produce more of both goods, shown by the shaded area, if resources are better utilized. Point Q is currently unattainable and real economic growth would be required to push the curve out. This could take the form of either new or more productive resources through investment in skills, for example, or improved methods and technology making existing resources more productive. Investment in research and technology would be required in this case. None of this is costless, and more investment today, to increase production possibilities tomorrow, will require resources to be diverted from current consumption.

Activity 6.1

Use the above framework to list the factors you consider account for the different rates of economic growth between your own country and another that you know is significantly more or less successful in this respect (e.g. a European and Asian economy).

Once you have identified economic explanations, brainstorm other dynamic contributing factors from the macro-environment.

(**See** Activity debrief at the end of this unit and Question 5 in the sample examination paper (Unit 11).)

Economic growth as an objective has attracted growing criticism because of externalities associated with it. Concern has focused on non-renewable resource depletion and greenhouse effects arising from the combustion of carbon fuels in power stations and vehicles. Projected growth, particularly in developing countries, is expected to expand greenhouse gases and raise the temperature of the planet. Melting polar icecaps will raise sea levels and disrupt climatic conditions with potentially damaging side effects on living standards. Acid rain, ozone depletion, oil and chemical spillages, industrial pollution and rising congestion are just some of the other 'bads' associated with economic growth.

Question 6.1

Referring to Figure 5.1 is there a solution to the quandary outlined above? If so, what are the marketing implications?

(**See** Activity debrief at the end of this unit and Case 3 in Unit 10.)

Key concepts

We will consider the other three macro-economic objectives once concepts have been defined and basic understanding has been established.

Concept 1 – The circular flow of income

This is a simple model of the workings of the economy.

To understand how the macro-economy works you must think in terms of 'flows' between households and businesses, banks, foreigners and governments. These flows which we first examined in Figure 5.1 are composed of either incomes or expenditures, and circulate around the economic system. Taking households and firms, we can see in Figure 6.2 that households, as the *owners* of productive resources, receive a flow of income from firms who employ them to produce goods and services.

The households use this income (i.e. wages, salaries, rents, interest and distributed profit) to purchase goods and services from firms. This flow of expenditure is demand for the products of the firms and the revenue received meets the cost of inputs for the next round of production. In this

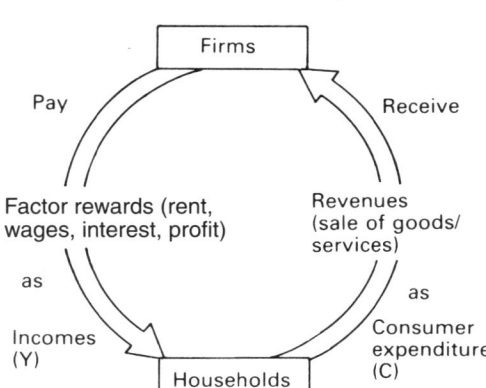

Figure 6.2   The circular flow of economic activity

simple model all income is spent and the flow continues period after period.

In reality, of course, many households would save a portion of their income. Consider the effect of this on the circular flow. Imagine it as a circulating flow of 'liquid' spending power for which an equivalent flow of real goods and services is produced and which in turn provides employment for available resources. As we can see in Figure 6.3, savings are a *leakage* and the level of the flow will continue to fall as savings are made out of any additional income received.

You will probably argue that since a fall in household spending forces firms to cut back production and because of lower revenues hire fewer resources and pay out less income, so the newly unemployed will spend their savings, channelling demand back into the flow.

Question 6.2

What will the households still in employment save as they see unemployment rise and fear that perhaps they may be made redundant next?

Can you now explain what economists call 'the paradox of thrift'?

* Think about your younger days and what you were encouraged to do with presents of money.
* Think also about the opportunity cost of consumption today compared with investment and more consumption tomorrow.

(See Activity debrief at the end of this unit.)

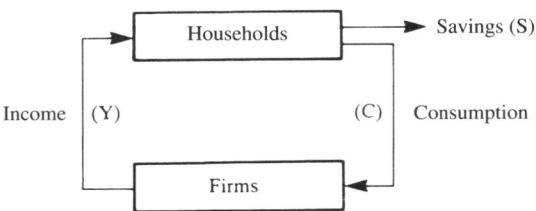

Figure 6.3
The effect of savings

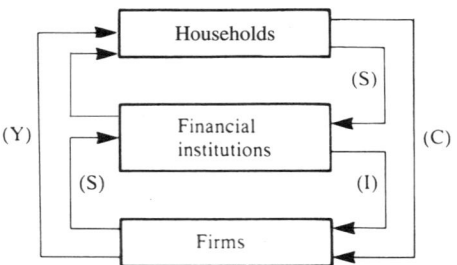

Figure 6.4
The effect of investment

Of course, the above situation is simplistic, since savings are normally not just withdrawn from the flow and hoarded but are deposited in financial institutions where interest may be earned. These funds are normally then either borrowed for investment purposes (I) by firms or loaned to other households (Y) and re-spent in the circular flow restoring equilibrium as seen in Figure 6.4.

Investment is known as an *injection* into the flow and creates demand for the producers of plant, equipment and supplies. However, is there any guarantee that sufficient aggregate demand will be forthcoming to sustain production at the desired level? Those who decide to invest are often different people from those who save, i.e. the savings leakage may not be exactly balanced by the investment injection.

Question 6.3

Can you think of a mechanism that might bring savings and investment to equality at the equilibrium level? Do you think this mechanism will work quickly and effectively?
What is the condition for equilibrium or stability in the flow?
(**See** Activity debrief at the end of this unit.)

To complete our circular flow and make it fully realistic we introduce flows to the government and the rest of the world (Figure 6.5). Households pay taxes on income and expenditure (e.g. VAT) and these are leakages from the flow. Similarly, spending on imported goods and services creates demand for the output of foreign firms. Government spending and exports, on the other hand, are injections of purchasing power into the flow.

To summarize:

● Savings, all taxes and imports are leakages from the flow.

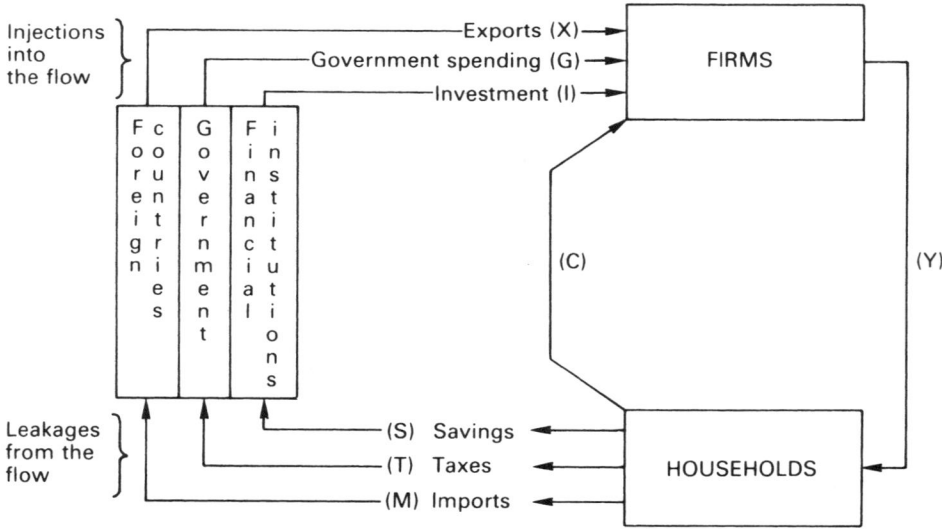

Figure 6.5 The full-economy model of injections and leakages

- Investment, government spending and exports are injections.
- The flow is in equilibrium when leakages = injections, i.e. $S + T + M = I + G + X$.
- If injections exceed leakages and there are unemployed resources in the economy then incomes, output and expenditure should rise as firms respond to increased demand.
- If leakages exceed injections, the process reverses.
- *Aggregate demand* is the sum of:
  Consumption + Investment + Government + Exports – Imports (i.e. $C + I + G + X - M$). **Note**: There is import content in C, I, G and X.

$C + I + G + X - M$ is the *pressure of demand on domestic businesses* to produce goods and services and is of critical importance in determining levels of activity and employment.

Activity 6.2

Draw a diagram linking the income and expenditure flows between households, firms, government and overseas and trace the effects of the following:

- An increase in domestic consumption even though total spending on consumption remains unchanged.
- The government agrees to fund a high-speed rail link.

Use newspaper or bank review reports to calculate the pressure of demand in your economy relative to capacity. Is it rising or falling? What is the leading aggregate in the total?

(**See** Activity debrief at the end of this unit.)

Concept 2 – The multiplier effect

An extra injection of government or investment spending may actually increase the level of income in the flow by more than the initial expenditure. This *multiplier effect* arises due to the circular nature of the flow. The injection creates demand for extra output which requires businesses to employ more resources, given they are available. If so, this generates new incomes which are paid to households. Households receiving this income pay taxes, buy imports and save but the rest is spent on domestic consumer goods and services at the second round of the process.

Affected businesses produce more output to meet this demand, more resources are brought into employment and incomes are paid out to households and the process repeats. Leakages determine the ultimate size of the multiplier. The higher these are as a proportion of the circular flow, the lower the multiplier value and vice versa.

Employment is affected in a similar way in that construction jobs are created directly by, say, a Millennium Dome type project. As these workers receive incomes they spend them in the local economy on goods and services, creating further jobs in these sectors. Do note, however, that the multiplier also works in reverse, as falling injections (e.g. reduced exports or a contracting road spending programme) cause a cumulative fall in income, output and jobs down the supply chain.

Question 6.4

The multiplier may be defined as:

$$\frac{\text{Change in national income}}{\text{Change in injection}}$$

It may also be expressed as:

$$\frac{1}{\text{Leakage ratios}}$$

131

If an industrial economy has the following leakage ratios calculate the value of the *realistic multiplier* for a $5 billion project:

Taxes 0.4 ; imports 0.2 ; savings 0.1

If your government decided to cut the tax bill by $5 billion would the size of the tax multiplier effect be smaller or larger than the investment multiplier?
(**See** Activity debrief at the end of this unit.)

Concept 3 – The accelerator effect

The *accelerator* reinforces the effect of the multiplier. It arises from the fact that the value of the capital stock (i.e. the equipment required to produce an annual output) is, on average, four or five times as great. For example, if capital has a useful life of ten years and total car production of 2 million units is supplied by ten similar-sized plants then average replacement investment, equivalent to one plant, is required each year. Suppose that household demand rises 10 per cent to 2.2 million units. By how much will investment rise?

You may well be surprised at the answer, since a 100 per cent rise in investment spending is substantial and will trigger further multiplier expansions in income. In practice, of course, the effect is not usually this dramatic. The car firms will wish to be sure that the increase in demand will be sustained before expanding capacity. They may also utilize existing plants more intensively or repair plant rather than scrap it. In any case, the capital goods sector will find it difficult to cope with a doubling of investment demand.

Question 6.5	What would happen if investment doubled but sales then stabilized at 2.2 million in the following year? What would happen if sales then fell back to 2 million units?

Given that multipler–accelerator effects do operate in an economy, what kind of economic activity pattern would you expect over time?

(**See** Activity debrief at the end of this unit.)

Concept 4 – Inflationary and deflationary gaps

If there is insufficient aggregate demand to enable businesses to operate profitably utilizing all available resources in an economy, a *deflationary gap* exists. This means the circular flow will be in dis-equilibrium with downward pressure on average prices. Alternatively, if aggregate demand exceeds the amount necessary to secure employment of all available resources, an *inflationary gap* would exist. General prices would tend to rise to ration out the available supply of goods given sufficient money was available to fuel the process.

Study Tip	Whether economic news is 'good' or 'bad' depends on the recipient. A rise in interest rates, for example, might trigger a media headline: *interest rate gloom* and yet savers will be very pleased indeed. The same applies to trade statistics. A rise in the trade surplus is normally viewed as good and yet the recent increases in Japan and East Asia were associated with depressed economies.

While underlying inflation in Britain has been around the target level of 2.5 per cent, headline rates have been falling, prompting fears of deflation. While this would be counter to post-war trends, deflation was a common phenomena prior to this. Indeed, average inflation in the G7 countries is just 1 per cent due primarily to falls in producer prices. Commodity prices have fallen sharply along with some manufactured goods like cars and computers. Deflation that arises from better technology or increased competition is beneficial. As higher productivity reduces prices, it increases real income and spending, causing overall activity levels to rise. Deflation caused by a contraction of money supply and demand is the real worry, prompting fears that monetary authorities may have their guns facing the wrong enemy. Japan and parts of East Asia have been in the grip of deflation where expectations of falling prices reinforce a downward spiral as customers hold off purchasing. A widening gap between actual and potential output is the result. Hopefully lessons have been learnt since the last big deflation in the 1930s when prices and output both fell around 30 per cent between 1929–33. Try Question 6.6 and see if you have the solution.

Question 6.6

If your economy, along with other trading partners, is stuck in a deep recession with activity levels falling and unemployment climbing to disturbingly high rates:

* Which of the aggregate demand components would you expect to rise, fall or stay unchanged, and why?
* Which component(s) could be altered?
* Would falling interest rates, exchange rates and wage rates:
  Increase activity levels in the short run?
  Increase activity rates in the long term?

(**See** Activity debrief at the end of this unit.)

Neither gap is desirable, so you may have concluded that the solution is to remove both, i.e. broadly stable prices should be the key objective of the authorities. This would involve injecting extra spending power into the flow for deflationary gaps and withdrawing it for inflationary gaps. This clearly involves government action which we will return to later in the unit.

The importance of gross domestic product

The circular flow represents the value of goods and services produced in an economy. This can be measured in three ways:

* *National income* incomes created from producing the output, e.g. wages, rent, profit
* *National output* sum of final output or the value added by each domestic firm
* *National expenditure* aggregate spending $(C + I + G + X - M)$ on national output

Annual gross domestic product or GDP is what is being measured and is the terminology used in government reports and the quality press. It differs from gross national product (GNP) in that this includes 'net income from abroad', although in Britain's case this only represents about 1–2 per cent of GDP despite an accumulation of net overseas assets second only to the USA.

GDP, as the term implies, is not adjusted for capital used up in the process of producing annual wealth due to difficulties in agreeing its value. Great care is taken, however, to avoid double-counting output or incomes. Only final output is accounted and transfer incomes such as pensions and student grants are ignored. The three measures are so defined as to be conceptually equal to each other, although in practice a balancing item is required to ensure equality. Errors and omissions in the collection of the data on income, output and spending make this necessary. If capital consumption is removed from GNP it is then termed net national income.

The uses of national accounting data

In Britain the Office for National Statistics collects this data and publishes it in the so-called *Blue Book*. The information provides the basis for forecasts and analysis of the health of an economy. The Treasury has developed a sophisticated computer-based model to predict the future path of the economy and upon which the government will partly base its policy judgments. The financial markets, on the other hand, will respond immediately to any unexpected deviation.

The marketer must therefore understand the significance and potential weaknesses of these figures if decisions affecting the business environment are to be anticipated.

GDP figures can provide a measure of the following:

- Gross physical output of goods and services of domestic firms
- Annual percentage increase or growth in the economy
- Productivity or GDP per head/capita by dividing GDP by working population
- Average standard of living by dividing GDP by the general population.
- Comparison of performance between different economies.

Question 6.7

If Britain's GDP is growing by 3 per cent per annum, and its population is growing by 0.5 per cent while China is growing by 9 per cent and its population by 1.5 per cent, which country is better off?

- What is the GDP of your economy in local currency terms?
- Does an increase in GDP automatically mean that you are better off?
- How has your country's GDP fared over time?

(See Activity debrief at the end of this unit.)

Care must be taken by the marketer when assessing the potential of overseas markets using national income data. Different countries have different values, tastes and needs and the proportions spent on armed forces will affect the amount of available disposable income. Asian economies tend to have higher savings ratios than Europeans, while America's high energy-consuming life style is more than double that of other countries.

The efficiency of governmental statistical agencies also varies widely and exchange rate fluctuations often make comparisons very difficult. Some economies may even understate their GDP to attract aid from international agencies while others have very wide disparities in income, making figures on average living standards very misleading. Less-developed economies also tend to have large barter economies, making many transactions difficult to record.

Activity 6.3	Select an overseas country which may represent a possible market for your company's product. Use sources like the OECD, IMF, WTO and World Bank to gather national income data. Critically appraise its likely degree of accuracy in the light of the points made above and report on your assessment of prospects.

Limitations of the data: are we really better off?

We have already seen that there are a number of reasons for caution over the accuracy of the statistics. One further vital factor to note is that GDP data are normally expressed in nominal or current prices terms. If the inflation in China in Question 6.7 was 8 per cent while only 2 per cent in Britain then the overall position is 0.5 per cent *real* growth for the latter and −0.5 per cent *real* decline in the former!

Always check if the figures are expressed in nominal or real terms to avoid being misled, i.e. GDP at constant prices adjusts for inflation by expressing GDP in terms of prices prevailing in a base year (e.g. at 1997 prices).

Even if all the calculations and estimates were entirely accurate, some problems of interpretation would still remain:

- An increase in exports or investment will not increase *current* living standards.
- An increase in GDP may be due to either the workforce working much longer hours or increased female participation rates. This might involve unaccounted costs in terms of stress, reduced health or less leisure time.
- No account is taken of *externalities* associated with growth such as emissions, effluents and waste. Economic activity to remedy environmental damage (known as defensive expenditures) is actually counted as part of GDP. Measurement of *sustainable* income would also have to take resource depletion into account.
- GDP increases when people pay to have services undertaken they would have previously performed themselves. Child-minding, garden maintenance, laundry and so forth are all examples. If someone married a person they previously employed to provide services, GDP would actually fall (this is known as the Pigou effect)!
- No attempt is made to value leisure time or unrecorded activities occurring in the informal economy (see Unit 1).

GDP is no longer the undisputed measure of economic progress. Although never intended as a measure of welfare its primacy with economists as a tool of analysis tends to obscure its limitations. It does not allow for 'consumption' of non-renewable natural assets or subtract the impact of untreated pollution causing some interest groups to call for an environmentally adjusted measure. Others call for a single *measure of welfare* that reflects indicators besides income. These might include distribution of income, voluntary leisure time, environmental quality, the standard of health and education, crime levels, employment and informal activities.

The business cycle

This refers to the periodic fluctuations in economic activity that occur in industrialized economies. Left to themselves economies tend to oscillate between periods of high activity, growth in employment and booming confidence, and opposite conditions of falling output, rising unemployment and relative despondency.

The underlying trend of real GDP growth for the world economy has been firmly upward since the Second World War, particularly in Japan and subsequently in other parts of East Asia. However, these strongly export-orientated economies have not avoided irregular oscillations particularly during the regions recent crisis. In a global economy part of the fluctuation is due to their interdependence with the main markets they supply. High specialization and focus on a narrow band of products and market segments exposes countries to risks identical to those confronting companies. A downturn in Asian markets or new US trade rules might severely affect German electronic exports or British textiles.

The business cycle represents the *average* of a multitude of individual industry cycles. Any one business may therefore be in advance or lag the main cycle. The marketer must locate their relative position since published data always refer to the average. The duration of the cycle up to the First World War was 8–9 years while a 4–5 year pattern prevailed from 1945 to 1979 in Britain. Since then, the two deepest and longest recessionary shocks since the great depression of the 1930s has produced a 9–10-year cycle. Figure 6.6 shows the typical stages of the cycle.

Activity 6.4

A useful activity for any salesperson or marketer is to track the business cycle. Statistics are published monthly showing trends of output and expenditure.

You can also track your own industry cycle by plotting orders received. For comparison you may wish to smooth this information by using a 12-month moving average. This involves dropping the order value of 12 months ago, adding the current one and dividing by 12.

(See Unit 10 for further discussion of forecasting).

Businesses in the capital good sector will exhibit much greater fluctuation and follow (lag) the business cycle. Can you think why?

(See Activity debrief at the end of this unit.)

Recession is defined as at least two successive quarters of *falling* GDP. Unemployment will be rising alongside spare capacity and a widening output gap. Wage and price rises will be difficult to achieve, so inflation will moderate, as will labour militancy. These are difficult times for the marketer since as consumption spending falls, competitive forces will mount while budgets come under increasing pressure. Profitability will be declining, business confidence will be low and investment spending depressed.

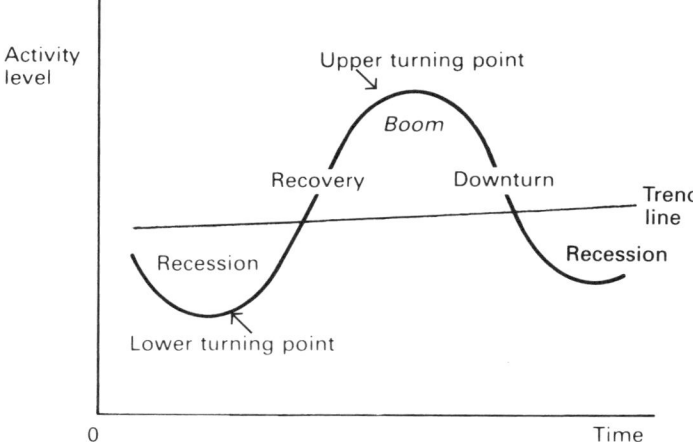

Figure 6.6
The stages of the business cycle

Question 6.8

Now identify the key features of the following phases:

- Recovery
- Boom
- Downturn

(**See** Activity debrief at the end of this unit.)

The severity and duration of these phases vary from cycle to cycle. The 4–5-year cycle, which characterized Britain up to the mid-1970s, had short phases and limited amplitude. It was known as *stop-go* since business experienced fast growth, often as elections approached, followed by no growth at all as the economic brakes were applied. The long-term trend growth rate of 2.25 per cent per annum compared poorly with most other developed economies.

In contrast, Britain has experienced two serious and long-lasting recessions in 1979–1982 and 1990–1992 interspersed with a boom between 1986 and 1989 when 3 million new jobs were created and the economy grew by 15 per cent in real terms. However, as is often the case, the bigger the boom, the bigger the bust, and much of the benefit was reversed as GDP fell for more than two years and unemployment climbed to over 3 million. Despite recession conditions in early 1999 the limited scope of the preceding 'boom' is predicted to lead to recovery as the uncertainty of the new millennium dawns. These patterns may be seen in Figure 6.7.

The marketer must clearly anticipate fluctuating economic conditions of this nature. The upper and lower turning points are the key moments in time to identify since they signal a significant change in economic conditions to which the business must actively respond. The upper turning point often occurs more quickly than the lower one. Falling sales and confidence can be contagious in the downturn but slow to ignite in recovery. Once the turning point is passed, the multiplier-accelerator mechanism should progressively move the economy to boom or recession conditions.

Activity 6.5

The previous activity asked you to plot the cycle for your firm or industry using order data and a moving average. Using historical data, you will be able to plot the course of the cycle and divide it into phases. The point of doing this, however, is to provide a framework within which the cycle can be *managed*.

For each phase of the cycle, set out the kind of policies the business should be pursuing. For example, in the *boom* phase, the rate of growth of sales level out as demand bumps along a peak. The firm must remain in stock but all expansion plans should be frozen. Any surplus plant should be sold at this time to realize top prices. New markets may be explored but emphasis should be on controlling costs to meet the gloomier times just around the corner.

(See Activity debrief at the end of this unit.)

If the marketer expects cycles they will not come as a surprise. View them as positive opportunities which can assist new product launch and market penetration if introduced at the right time. The key to success is in timing and the rule of thumb is that the higher and longer the period above the growth trend line, the lower and the longer the subsequent period below and vice versa.

Predicting the turning points is not easy as demonstrated by the poor performance of highly respected forecasting groups, including the UK Treasury, who failed to predict the 1990 recession, or its length and then overestimated the speed of recovery! Businesses may, however, be able to judge developments more effectively using two monitoring techniques:

- *Leading indicators* These foreshadow change in the pace of the economy by identifying indicators that consistently give advance warning of upward or downward movement. A composite index is used, including the FT 100 share index, total dwellings started, the rate of interest and the aggregate financial surplus or deficit of all companies. In early 1999 interest rates were falling, housing starts were up, the stock market was near all time highs and the corporate surplus was rising. Can you predict real GDP growth in 2000 (external shocks allowing)?
- *Confederation of British Industry Trends survey* A large representative cross-section of domestic companies is surveyed in depth to measure changes in *business confidence*. Psychology is important and the famous British economist John Maynard Keynes suggested that the *animal spirits* of capitalism produced alternating phases of optimism and pessimism, both of which tend to feed on themselves! The marketer must always beware of being carried away by such 'herd instincts' which may cause capital spending to fluctuate from over- to under-investment.

Investment takes time and is an act of faith in the future. The penalties of a wrong decision are considerable since if the firm commits resources and the market then fails to materialize, or if it does not but demand booms, then market share will be lost to competitors. Environmental changes will often influence expectations and competitive decisions which may be *self-fulfilling* in the short term. If a critical mass of households and businesses

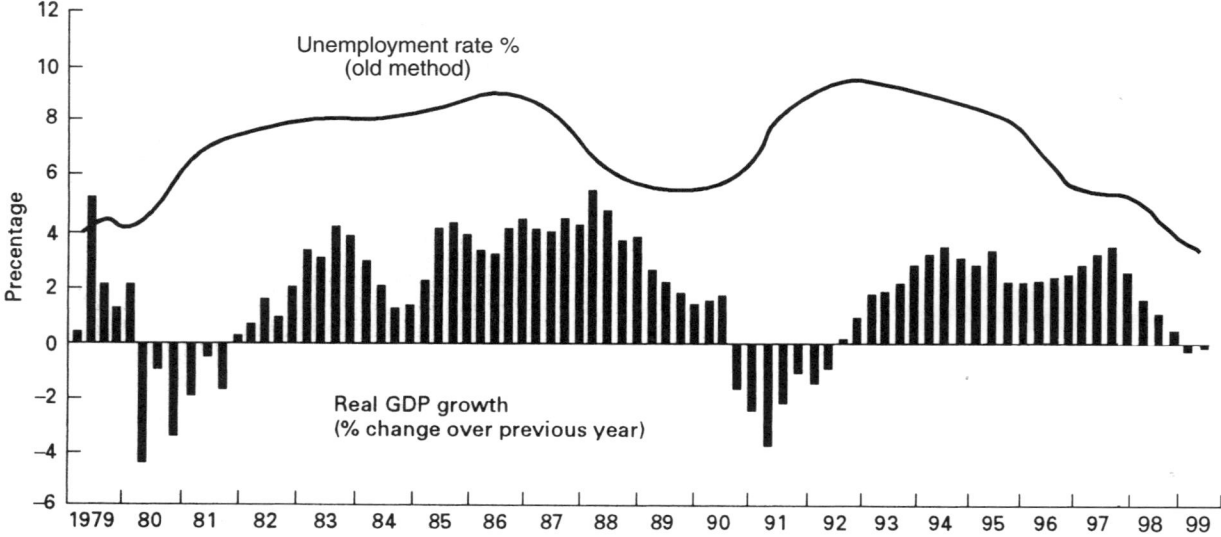

Figure 6.7 The British business cycle – real GDP and unemployment 1979–1999

138

believe things will improve, and invest and spend on that assumption, then things will, in general, improve, *feeding back* into even more positive expectations. A 'feel good factor' is the expression of such considerations, easy to visualize but economically less easy to achieve. The process can also lead to enormous over investment, as, for example, in Asia up to its crisis. The world is now awash with excess capacity in computer chips, steel, ships, textiles and chemicals. There is thought to be 30 per cent unused global car capacity as yet more factories come on stream.

Question 6.9

Review your grasp of this important aspect of the macro-economic environment by working through the effects of the following on the business cycle:

1 Multipler – accelerator
2 Adjustment in stock levels
3 Business confidence
4 Openness of the economy
5 Elections
6 A shift towards services
7 Random and erratic shocks (e.g. trade war)

(**See** Activity debrief at the end of this unit.)

Having studied the importance of GDP and its tendency to fluctuate around a rising trend, we can now consider the other three major macro objectives. We will then assess the government polices intended to achieve them and their implications for the marketer.

Objectives: higher employment

Full employment was the primary goal of post-war governments up to the mid-1970s. The existence of 18 million unemployed in the European Union in 1998 suggests that it no longer has priority. Even at the height of the Lawson boom (1989–90) in Britain, unemployment failed to fall below 1.5 million and within three years had doubled. However with sustained recovery through the rest of the decade, unemployment fell to below 1.3 million while full and part-time employment rose to a peak of 27.3 million. This contrasts with the larger EU economies where jobless rates are over double those in Britain. However, while the labour market is tight in certain service sectors, manufacturing employment in the North and Midlands was suffering from the effects of a strong pound and the Asian crisis. Predictions, using the Treasury economic model, suggest half a million job losses in this sector by 2001, reducing its share of employment to just 17.5 per cent (21.5 per cent of output).

Unemployment is often referred to as a social and economic evil which can and does impact negatively on businesses:

Economic evil	*Social evil*
Scarce resources not utilized	Loss of income
Tax burden of benefits reduces incentives to work/invest	Relative poverty compared to those in work with affluent life styles
Reduces mobility of labour	Alienation from society leading to
Reduces purchasing power	crime, vandalism and other social
Depresses confidence	ills
Discourages risk taking	Dual society of haves/have-nots
	Young entrants to labour market particularly hit in finding work

Unemployment is a personal tragedy since work binds us to society and gives meaning to our lives. Not only is our income lost, but also our status, esteem and self-respect. Long-term unemployment affects specific groups such as the young, as employers cease recruitment; the unskilled; ethnic groups and the over-50s; the disabled and those living in inner cities or areas of structural decline (e.g. mining communities). The young are forced to move away from such areas, condemning the latter to unemployment rates double the national average and a downward spiral of decay and producing a marketer's nightmare.

<table>
<tr><td>**Question 6.10**</td><td>Is unemployment an 'evil' as far as business managers are concerned? Think carefully about this question from the view of your own company. Think about wage levels, recruitment, discipline and ease of achieving change.

(**See** Activity debrief at the end of this unit.)</td></tr>
</table>

The seeming inability of many governments to achieve permanently lower unemployment and their 'acceptance' of a certain rate as unavoidable is a reflection of a number of factors:

- A more rapid rate of technological change
- Customer orientation, changing tastes and shortening life cycles
- Inflow onto the job market exceeding outflow as married women's participation rises
- The idea of a 'natural' unemployment rate that is consistent with low and stable inflation
- A more turbulent environment making business focus on job flexibility rather than long-term security and commitment.

These factors can be best understood in the context of different types of unemployment arising from the three main causes:

1 *Insufficient aggregate demand* This gives rise to *cyclical* unemployment due to a so-called deflationary gap in total spending. The downturn and recession phases of the cycle imply activity rates well below capacity. Businesses will respond to a downturn in orders by cutting overtime, halting recruitment and curtailing its use of contractual labour. Only then will they be forced into redundancies and these will be voluntary where possible. Unfortunately, as an economy begins to recover there is normally a lag before employment responds. Employers who have suffered the costs of redundancy and restructuring will seek to avoid new full-time recruits until they are reassured that the recovery is firmly based and all flexible alternatives are exhausted (i.e. the existing workforce will be used more intensively and part-timers employed where possible).

<table>
<tr><td>**Activity 6.6**</td><td>For each of the types of unemployment being considered, brainstorm possible policies to minimize its occurrence. Once you have generated a list of possibilities go through each one and ensure that they meet the following requirements:

- The policy *will not* lead to increased inflation.
- The policy *will not* lead to inefficiency/uncompetitiveness.
- The policy is consistent with people's needs and wants.

(**See** Activity debrief at the end of this unit.)</td></tr>
</table>

2 *Imperfect market forces* These prevent labour markets clearing at wage levels where no *involuntary* unemployment exists. Many factors prevent a matching of the supply and demand for different types of labour skill such as lack of knowledge, immobility, discrimination, employment

legislation and poor management. *Frictional* unemployment arises due to a mismatch between the end of one job and the start of the next for many of the millions of job changers each year. Its duration is short and reflects the mobility of labour in response to vacancies in expanding sectors of the economy. *Structural* unemployment is the longer-term variety of resource reallocation. It is caused by shifting tastes, technologies and competition, and is reflected in changing patterns of consumption and production. Certain industries and employments contract while others expand. Skills are often so specialized and industry-specific that redeployment is only possible if completely new ones are acquired. If job opportunities also involve moving, then housing cost and availability may preclude this.

3 *Relative wages are too high* If the wage is set too high to clear the market due to minimum wage levels or union bargaining power then unemployment will result. The productivity associated with the wage paid is also part of this equation. If European wage-for-productivity levels are too high then business will respond by:

Moving operations to lower-wage countries
Investing in technology as a substitute for relatively expensive labour.

Technological unemployment arises from *new process innovations* which have typically displaced the tasks performed by semi- and unskilled manual and clerical workers. Increasing sophistication of computers and information systems is now threatening the jobs of middle managers (known as downsizing) and other knowledge worker groups.

This type of unemployment tends to emerge in the following downturn as obsolete factories and technology are closed. Ever since the Luddites in the early nineteenth century, technology has been viewed by workers as an enemy in the short term even though over time it has created clusters of *new product innovations* which until recently have allowed jobs to grow in line with the working population. So long as wants exceed our ability to satisfy them, human resources will be demanded. Machines will specialize in doing what they do best, as will humans.

However, there is now a clear mismatch between those with unwanted skills and abilities in declining industries, or where machines have a comparative cost advantage, and skill shortages in high-technology and creative knowledge-based employments. Considerable investment in education and flexible skills will be required if a permanent 'underclass' of the hard-to-employ is not to emerge. Little wonder that education policy was a key issue in the last election campaign and the top spending priority of the Labour government. The alternative of large falls in the relative wages of unskilled will be resisted by unions or prevented by minimum wage legislation as enshrined in the European Union's social chapter.

Extending Activity 6.1

Research the meaning of the term 'de-industrialization' and examine its implications for the supply and demand for marketing services.

Control of inflation

Inflation is a general increase in the average price level that is sustained over a period of time and is usually calculated by changes in the retail price index (RPI). This is measured by a 'basket' of around 600 goods and services typically consumed by the average household and weighted by their importance in total spending. You should distinguish between the so-called 'headline rate' and the 'underlying rate'. The latter excludes mortgage interest which tends to inflate the index in times of rising rates.

Inflation has been a persistent problem in many countries for most of the post-war period. Governments were happy to trade off a little more inflation for a little less unemployment. However, from the late 1970s both tended to rise together to politically and societally unacceptable levels. Known as *stagflation*, this is the worst of both possible economic worlds!

Conservative governments under Margaret Thatcher pledged themselves to control inflation as the central priority even at the expense of sharply rising unemployment. The battle to conquer inflation became a constraint on the government's ability to achieve more growth and jobs. Politically acceptable unemployment became the level that was sustainable without inflation increasing, or rising significantly above levels in the major economies with whom we compete internationally. The policy was a 'success' with inflation falling to 30-year lows by early 1999. Although above major competitors like Japan, France and Germany, it is around the government's 2.5 per cent target.

Activity 6.7

The retail price index (RPI) or your national equivalent is normally published monthly. Watch the quality press for the publication date and analyse the news report. Identify which categories in the index are rising more than the average and which are rising less.

Can you explain the price trends you observe? Are they supply or demand driven? Are they the result of government policies? What is the effect on prices of imported goods and services?

Is inflation a problem from the marketer's point of view?

The answer to this question depends on the rate of inflation involved. If this is slow and predictable then it can be a good thing. *Creeping inflation*, when associated with buoyant high demand, can generate buyer confidence and business investment. Since borrowings are repaid in gently depreciating currency and the value of stocks appreciate, it tends to enhance profitability. Households experience 'money illusion', whereby they feel better off than they really are as nominal incomes rise. They fail to notice or account the real value eroding through cost of living rises. This eases the process of change and is preferable to the continuously depressed economic conditions that may be necessary to keep prices from rising at all.

However, once inflation exceeds a critical rate the costs outweigh any possible benefits as:

- A rapid fall in the value of money hits confidence.
- Uncertainty over future price levels deters firms from entering long-term contractual commitments and makes future planning very difficult.
- Arbitrary and unintended redistribution of income occurs:
    Debtors gain and creditors/savers lose;
    Fixed income groups like pensioners suffer;
    Weak bargaining groups are unable to keep pace.
- Taxation rises as allowances are eroded and rising nominal income moves consumers into higher tax brackets.
- Domestic marketers suffer competition from more competitive imports while rising export prices hits overseas sales.
- Frequent price changes means continuous adjustment to lists, packaging, etc. which upsets customers.
- Prices no longer accurately reflect 'relative' values, confusing the consumer but making them more price-sensitive and less responsive to other marketing-mix elements.
- Investment funds move into unproductive inflationary hedges such as gold, antiques and property.
- Wage groups fight for income shares, disrupting business activity with strikes.

- It may trigger price wars due to misinterpretation of rival intentions.

Finally, the marketer must remember that what goes up must come down! As inflation accelerates so governments will be forced to drastically reduce demand pressures to restore stability. Curing inflation, with the attendant squeeze on spending, is often worse in its effects than the disease itself!

The causes of inflation

The marketer needs to appreciate the causes of inflation so that an assessment may be made as to the likely future path of general prices and to avoid being damagingly surprised by sharp changes in their pace or direction. The sources of inflationary pressure originate on both the supply and demand side of an economy:

- *Demand-pull inflation* Too much spending relative to available productive capacity results in an inflationary gap which bids up prices of both inputs and outputs. As wage costs rise these feed into higher prices, prompting further wage demands and creating a wage–price spiral. Research by A. W. Phillips showed that as the pressure of demand increases, wages rise more than proportionately, accelerating this process.
- *Monetarist inflation* Money is the fuel that sustains inflation. If the money supply is not expanded to provide extra cash for higher wages and prices, then interest rates rise, real aggregate demand in the circular flow declines, goods are left unsold and businesses reduce their employment of factors of production. Inflation can only continue at the cost of rising unemployment.
- *Cost-push inflation* This occurs when a cost element causes prices to rise but in the absence of any excess demand to justify it. Stakeholders such as employees may push up wages through militant action to increase their real income at the expense of profits. If businesses then raise prices to restore profit margins this reduces the purchasing power of wages and the process repeats, producing a wage–price spiral. Competition between different wage groups to maintain *wage differentials* can also lead to a *wage–wage spiral*.

We have seen that when inflation becomes rapid and uncertain it creates net costs for business and society. It poses difficult marketing-mix problems for the marketer, especially those serving segments most seriously affected. In the extreme, *hyper-inflation*, defined as price rises in excess of over 50 per cent per month, causes all confidence to be lost in paper money and barter re-emerges.

Consider the recent situation in Russia or the customer service problems of German café-owners in 1923, forced to raise coffee prices while customers sat waiting for their bills. At one stage during the German hyper-inflation prices were rising by 5 per cent per hour!

Governments have also learnt that *expectations* adjust as actual inflation is experienced. Any attempt to run an economy at less than the natural or non-accelerating inflation rate of unemployment would cause prices to rise more than expected and compensating wage demands to occur. No permanent trade-off of a little less unemployment for a little more inflation is possible. Inflation would accelerate instead.

Balance of payments

The balance of payments is the systematic annual record of all exchange transactions between the residents of one country and the rest of the world. It is made up of a current account comprising:

- a *visible* balance of trade – foods/fuels/materials/semi-manufactured/finished goods plus
- an *invisible* balance of trade – financial/travel/other services; government transfers; net earnings *plus* a capital account composed of net short- and long-term capital movements. A balancing item is also included to adjust for the often sizeable errors and inaccuracies in the accounts. Since the balance of payments must balance (although parts may be in imbalance) there is a final balance for official financing which either adds to, or draws from, official currency reserves and borrowing depending on whether a net surplus or deficit arises.

The current account is the best indicator of the long-run health of an economy since it reflects whether an economy is trading successfully. No country can run a persistent current deficit since its reserves would eventually run out, together with the confidence of its foreign creditors. Action would have to be taken well before this point, or, alternatively, be forced on it as condition for a loan from the International Monetary Fund. However, since the balance of payments of all countries must logically sum to zero, some countries cannot avoid being in deficit at times. What is more important is the cause, whether it is manageable through overseas borrowing or reserves, and the direction of change. If a developing country, such as Nigeria, incurs a deficit in order to import investment goods to develop its oil and gas deposits, this will increase productive potential (and exports) in the future, a very different case from one importing conspicuous consumption goods and living beyond its means. In any case all countries rely to some degree on international trade. The benefits of specialization and trade have made most economies dependent on the import of certain materials, fuels, manufacturers or services. Japan and East Asia, for example, have few indigenous resources other than their skills, but have succeeded in creating large payment surpluses with the rest of the world.

Britain's current balance has deteriorated sharply in 1999. Invisible's are in healthy surplus, but exports of oil and manufactures have been badly affected by a stronger pound and East Asian devaluations. The balance of payments is not a desirable objective in itself, but rather, as a deficit worsens it will become a tightening constraint on the government's ability to achieve other macro objectives.

In the short term the deficit can be financed from foreign currency reserves or by raising interest rates in order to attract foreign capital flows. The latter will only succeed if creditors believe an offsetting fall in the exchange rate is not imminent. Higher rates will also tend to depress consumer and investment spending, reducing aggregate demand and therefore sales.

A short-term deficit need not necessarily give rise to concern. It may reflect capital imports to promote economic development which subsequently generate extra export revenues. Loans are often forthcoming from the IMF or World Bank to support such a rise in productive potential. If, however, the deficit derives from excess consumption it is a different matter. Sources include:

1 *Excess demand* Imports are sucked in to reduce inflationary pressures
2 *Import prices rise faster than export prices* An adverse movement in the terms of trade
3 *Economic weakness* This may arise for many reasons, such as:
  - World demand is declining for the country's main exports
  - A failure in supply (e.g. internal conflict)
  - Tastes develop for imported goods
  - Business structure favours declining industries
  - Business culture, regulations or vested interests are preventing improvement.

<table>
<tr><td>

Activity 6.8

</td><td>

You should familiarize yourself with the trade and payments position of your economy, the direction of change and the possible implications of policy changes: Obtain an annual or monthly copy of your government's *Annual Abstract* or *Digest of Statistics*. On graph paper plot the following, against time, over a ten-year period. You will need positive and negative values graduated on the vertical axis.

- Visible trade balance (food, materials, fuels, semi-manufactured and manufactured goods)
- Invisible trade balance (services)
- Current balance (visible + invisible)
- Volume of exports (in real terms – exclude price changes)
- Volume of imports (use the same base year for both).

Assess the balance of payments position in the light of the above.

</td></tr>
</table>

Economic indicators

Governments use a wide range of economic indicators to decide on policy changes and monitor their effectiveness as will the independent Bank of England before deciding interest rate policy. Stock markets may react quite strongly to publication of such figures when they diverge from expectations and cause a fundamental reassessment of the underlying health of the economy. Such indices are equally important for businesses in determining their future marketing plans and policies. We have seen that governments have a number of objectives and may be faced with the problem that achievement of one goal may conflict with realizing the others. It is therefore necessary to have as many policies as objectives if they are to be mutually accomplished.

<table>
<tr><td>

Exam Tip

</td><td>

Make sure that you know and memorize the current values of the main economic indicators in your own country. Macro-economic questions frequently ask you to discuss the current or future situations.

</td></tr>
</table>

Key indicators to monitor include the following:

Activity and growth rates
- Volume of retail sales
- Volume of output
- Output and income per head
- Industry surveys (e.g. CBI) of investment intentions/confidence
- The rate relative to main competitors (gaps may prompt action!)
- The public sector borrowing requirement (see below)

Inflation rates
- Cost of living index (e.g. RPI) *Retail Price Index*
- Rate of change in earnings
- The growth in the money supply (e.g. £M0 – basically notes/coins)
- Underlying rate of inflation

[handwritten margin note: Gross national product / Gross domestic product]

- Tax changes in the pipeline
- Rates of main competitors (implication for balance of payments)

Unemployment rates
- The rate of change is more important than the level
- Vacancies partially reflect strength of demand
- Unemployment rates elsewhere (beware comparability problems)
- Regional spread of unemployment
- Rates among key groups: skilled, young, male, female

Trade figures
- A potent symbol of international 'competitiveness' and success
- Relate to phase of cycle: should improve in recession
- Figures are often unreliable and subject to revision
- Share of world trade in manufactures reflects longer term performance

Exchange rates
- Rate at which one currency exchanges for another
- May be fixed by government or be free to reflect supply and demand
- Rise reflects strengthening in future prospects and vice versa
- Terms of trade reflects relative movement of import/export prices
- Exchange rates tend to fall if deficit on trade payments occurs

Interest rates
- The price of borrowed money
- A fall encourages consumer spending and investment, reduces costs but discourages savings and overseas funds inflow
- A rise reflects the need to choke off demand or attract overseas funds to finance a balance of payments deficit.

Extending Activity 6.2	Using the material in this unit so far and the results of the various activities, undertake a SWOT analysis of your economy.
	Draw up a balance sheet of it strengths and weaknesses and then identify opportunities and threats. Such an approach has formed the basis of a past exam question since it requires an overall appreciation of your country's macro-economy.

Economic policies

The main types of policy available for use by a government are:

- Fiscal and budgetary
- Money and credit control
- Physical policies – wage and price controls
- Supply side
- Trade and exchange rate

The syllabus requires an appreciation not an in-depth understanding of these polices. Our main concern will therefore be with their influence on business and the implications for marketing.

Exam Tip	At this stage of the workbook you will be giving serious thought to revision for the forthcoming examination. One important key to planning a revision schedule is to try to determine possible topics. Bear in mind that your paper will have been set up to a year previously due to the administration required in approving it and ensuring efficient distribution to centres around the world.
	What questions would you choose if you were setting an exam paper based on the syllabus and relating it to a dynamic environment? Why don't you brainstorm some possibilities with your tutor? Look at previous papers and think about 'topical' issues at the time the paper was prepared, which would still be relevant 12 months or so later.

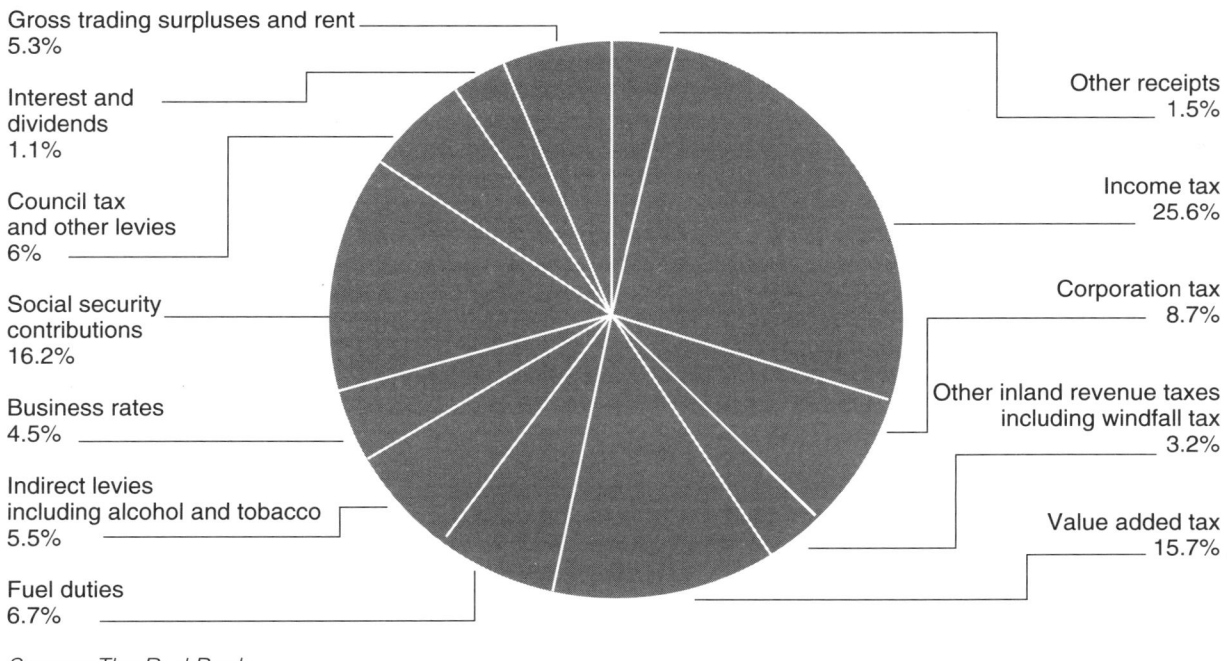

Gross trading surpluses and rent
5.3%

Interest and
dividends
1.1%

Council tax
and other levies
6%

Social security
contributions
16.2%

Business rates
4.5%

Indirect levies
including alcohol and tobacco
5.5%

Fuel duties
6.7%

Other receipts
1.5%

Income tax
25.6%

Corporation tax
8.7%

Other inland revenue taxes
including windfall tax
3.2%

Value added tax
15.7%

Source: The Red Book

Figure 6.8 General government receipts 1999–2000 (total receipts excluding North Sea revenues: £344.3bn)

Fiscal and budgetary

Taxation is the main source of revenue for government to finance its desired expenditures. Both are important policy instruments as we saw when we considered injections and leakages in the circular flow. Accounting for around 40 per cent (i.e. £350 billion) of total spending, the government has an important impact, although with revenues at similar levels (see Figure 6.8) the overall effect is broadly neutral. Indeed the current budget surplus is helping to reduce net public debt below 40 per cent of GDP, well within the entry requirement to the Euro. Revenue and expenditure are now decided together in a unified annual budget in early March. The marketer should monitor this event closely, together with the pre-budget report in the Autumn.

Government spending and taxation offers a relatively quick and effective means of changing the pressure of demand and therefore activity levels. Extra spending on health and education, for example, impact on demand for a whole range of goods and services including medicines, textbooks and computers. Marketers should carefully consider the implications of Treasury plans as well as actual policy changes because:

- They review performance and set out the government's economic forecasts/objectives/plans, e.g. GDP is forecast to increase 1–1.5 per cent in 1999; 2.25–2.75 per cent in 2000 and 2.75–3.25 per cent in 2001.
- Policy actions may be inferred from the objectives set.
- Tax and spending changes impact on the circular flow at different points in time, e.g. the fiscal boost of the 1999 budget was a modest £1.2 billion in 1999–2000 but £3.6 billion by 2001–2002.
- Tax changes on specific groups/classes will affect income/spending in specific segments, e.g. mortgage rate cuts may benefit middle income groups but not abolition of mortgage relief, whereas low income/pensioner households have fared relatively well recently.
- Tax on specific product groups can have serious and selective consequences, e.g. tobacco duties on retailers; up-market estate agents hit by stamp duty; sales of 1198cc and 1200cc vehicles.
- The scope for lobbying activity by special interests, e.g. last-ditch efforts to retain duty-free.

147

- Measures have ramifications for trends in other environment, e.g. employment credit for the over 50s is designed to help reverse the sharp decline in labour force participation of this group.

The key requirement of fiscal policy is that it produces sound public finances and so avoids any danger of the government sector being a source of adverse shocks in the economy. It can also support monetary policy in containing inflationary pressures or providing the scope for interest rates to fall. The marketer must appreciate the broad intention of these polices while recognizing that projections involve considerable uncertainty. Outcomes rely heavily on assumptions regarding economic growth and the position of the economy relative to its long-run sustainable trend.

Money and credit
This involves control of the supply of money and the credit-creating power of the retail banks. The central bank may seek to control this capability, if it fears that its target for inflation will not be met, by means of:

- Controlling the supply of new money.
- Changing base rates of interest.
- Controlling existing money supply by open market operations – selling/buying government securities injects/withdraws money from the banking system.
- Cash/liquidity ratio requirements – limit the size of the credit multiplier effect.
- Quantitative controls to ration credit (seldom used now).
- Lender of the last resort power to enforce base rate.

Such measures can be used to expand or contract money and credit as required, but with a long lag, in terms of full effects, of up to two years. The marketer must therefore calculate the full impact of successive interest rate cuts in early 1999 as actually stimulating sales in late 2000. It takes time for consumers to react in terms of demand for housing and other durables and the strength of the reaction is often unpredictable.

Anything that might affect the stability of money needs to be carefully monitored. As Milton Friedman observed, following a massive research study, 'inflation is always and everywhere a monetary phenomena'. Success in reducing inflation to very low levels in recent years suggests that monetary stability has now been achieved in major economies. The key is to set intermediate targets for money supply growth, government borrowing and exchange rates which are consistent with the growth desired in nominal GDP and inflation, and then stick to them. The marketer must take account of the direction of monetary policy and learn to interpret signals. So what do you make of the following?:

- Why are base rates reduced on fears of recession or negative shocks like stock market crashes?
- Why are UK interest rates higher than those in the EU but similar to those in the USA?
- Are UK rates now tending to converge towards the average of 3 per cent in the EU?
- If so, why are they and what are the implications?
- What, then, is the link between interest rate changes and the exchange rate?

Question 6.13

Which type of firms are most affected by a credit squeeze?

(**See** Activity debrief at the end of this unit.)

Prices and incomes policy
Such policies were much used in the UK during the 1960s and 1970s in an attempt to achieve lower unemployment without incurring higher inflation

and consequent balance of payments problems. If wage groups could be forced or persuaded to moderate their pay settlements and firms their price increases, despite demand pressure to justify them, then employment and output would rise. More recently the Conservatives introduced a 1.5 per cent public sector pay restraint as a means of controlling public spending and as a demonstration effect to the private sector.

Government's are still prone, particularly in boom times, to introduce public sector pay restraint as a means of controlling public spending and to set a 'good example' for the private sector to follow. In practice, such policies normally prove counter-productive or short-lived due to shortages or pay explosions. The appropriate analogy was a boiling pot with the heat (demand pressure) turned up and the lid tightly on.

<table>
<tr><td>**Question 6.14**</td><td>Are you clear as to the difference between a slowdown, a soft landing, a recession, a deflation, a slump and a depression in an economy – or is it just 'economist jargon' to keep us guessing?</td></tr>
</table>

Supply side policies

These grew out of disillusion with UK government policies to manage aggregate demand to achieve the four objectives. The standard response to low growth and rising unemployment had been to stimulate consumer, government and investment spending on the assumption that domestic firms would raise production and resource use. Multiplier and accelerator reactions would then stimulate businesses to invest in extra capacity and productivity improvements. The business response in practice was:

- To improve margins and profits instead of raising output
- A reluctance to invest due to stop-go patterns of demand
- An inability to respond quickly enough led to import penetration
- Inflation and payments deficits quickly forced policy reversal.

Supply side policies aimed to promote higher growth and employment without triggering inflation by relaxing constraints on productive capacity and efficiency. The policies involved:

- Reform of trade unions to ensure that their reduced power was used responsibly and democratically (UK strikes at a record low in 1999)
- Removal of tax distortions and disincentives to work and invest
- Measures to improve the quality, quantity and relevance of training
- Improved job, career and training information
- Measures to encourage mobility and flexibility
- Encouraging employee share-ownership and self-employment
- Reducing red tape and regulations inhibiting business
- Greater competition and removal of minimum wages
- Privatization and the opening up of state services to private competition or internal markets, as in the National Health Service.

<table>
<tr><td>**Extending Activity 6.3**</td><td>Supply side policies such as deregulation, tax reform and privatization, have been taken up by governments around the world. Others, like Hong Kong and Singapore, have always encouraged enterprise through free-port status, etc.

By scanning newspapers and databases, approaching government departments and so on, summarize the specific supply side policies currently applying in your own country and any new ones in the pipeline.

Think carefully how these developments affect marketers in various businesses.

Consider the implications of reversals such as the 48-hour week, £3.60 minimum wage and the abolition of the internal market in the NHS by the Labour government.</td></tr>
</table>

Trade and exchange rate policies

Britain currently operates a flexible exchange rate system which acts as an automatic two-way adjustment mechanism to keep the balance of payments in approximate balance. Should the payments position worsen then the exchange rate should fall relative to trading rivals making British exports cheaper in foreign currency terms and therefore more competitive. Imports become relatively more expensive so favouring home produced products. Export receipts rise, import payments fall and the balance of payments position is restored. Unfortunately, this process is just a little too good to be true and the marketer should recognize one or two qualifications:

- Short-term and speculative capital movements can occur on a massive scale in the global economy and this can drive exchange rates rather than fundamentals like supply/demand for products.
- The full effects of a falling exchange rate take time to work through. Initially the deficit worsens before it improves. Imported materials and semi-manufactures are now more expensive, but must be paid for before extra exports can be produced and shipped.
- The strength of reaction to a falling exchange rate may be uncertain. This is an important marketing decision but important questions must be answered. How big will the demand increase be in foreign markets? How will foreign competitors react? Can we meet the extra demand? Won't costs rise due to higher import prices? Will businesses gear up for extra production or merely raise export prices and make higher profit?
- Unplanned exchange rate movements creates risk. A transaction negotiated at one exchange rate may become unprofitable by the time it is fulfilled. Foreign assets purchased at one point in time may later become a balance sheet liability due to currency appreciation.
- Currency appreciation is a serious threat to foreign sales (and domestic markets), as many export marketers have found to their cost in Britain recently. Is the solution to cut export prices in foreign currency terms, reinforce product and promotional policies to reduce price sensitivity, or source overseas? For example, is the Marks & Spencer sourcing policy the right one?

Of course, the government may prefer to aim for exchange rate stability given the uncertainties and costs associated with exchange rate fluctuations. This may cause it to manage its exchange rate or shadow the value of a critical currency such as the Euro or the $. Another alternative is to join that currency block and accept the disciplines of an exchange rate set by the EU. The danger in this approach is that the economy must be managed with this sole objective in mind. Any tendency towards a persistently expanding deficit or surplus would be unsustainable. The latter would draw criticism from trading partners, while the former leads to a progressive drain on reserves and national economic confidence. A lasting policy response would be required but correction of the problem may be painful because only two policy options exist:

1. *Expenditure reduction* – higher taxes reduce household incomes causing consumer demand, including demand for imports, to fall. Falling domestic sales encourages firms to export more as well as putting downward pressure on wages and prices, so improving general competitiveness.
2. *Expenditure switching* – switch resources and expenditure away from imports to domestically produced goods. Policies include various types of protectionism and incentives for exporters. The other means is devaluation which implies sacrificing the stable exchange rate (or leaving the Euro!). The first two policies deal with symptoms of a deficit at the expense of trading partners, rather than with the basic cause. International trade agreements also limit their scope. All governments seek to promote exports by providing information, advice, assistance and often insurance against bad debts. Aggressive use of hidden subsidies to obtain unfair trade advantage, however, are not internationally acceptable.

Question 6.15

Expenditure reduction policies appear to be an effective solution for a persistent deficit. Can you explain why:

- This might not be a wholly effective solution?
- Why governments are reluctant to use them?

(**See** Activity debrief at the end of this unit.)

The impact of international trade

All countries are open systems and must deal with the realities of the international environment. Some economies, such as the USA, are so large that the domestic economy is the dominant influence. Most, however, are like the UK, which accounting for just 5–6 per cent of global output and being export orientated, is always susceptible to outside shocks. Falling world oil prices seriously damage its export revenues while a slowdown in global growth force cuts in its interest rates. Why then are countries like Britain so eager to expand their international exposure? A number of reasons can be noted:

- World trade brings a consistent diversity of choice – as seen in any sizeable supermarket at any season.
- National differences in culture, human skills, resource availability, ingenuity and technology lead to product, cost and price differences.
- A global market rewards specialization and allows exploitation of comparative advantage.
- International trade curbs monopoly power, increases competition and lowers prices for consumers
- World markets offer scope for economies of scale and significantly reduced costs.
- Access to world markets spreads risks, balances domestic activity and irons out imbalances
- Trade and distribution networks encourages and enables rapid diffusion of new ideas/inventions.
- Trade brings contact, mutual interest, cultural understanding, interdependence and cooperation.
- The fact there is Coca-Cola in Beijing and a McDonald's in Moscow fosters peace and security.
- Collapse or liberalization of former planned economies and their integration into the world trading system.
- Growth in world trade has been continuous offering expanding opportunities.
- Trade liberalization agreements by GATT encouraged emerging economies to open their markets. (A millennium round may be proposed by the USA.)
- The World Trade Organization (WTO) was established in 1994 with a mandate to enforce world trade laws.
- Unimpeded development of internet, travel and trade links are producing a global culture.
- Continued expansion of multinational enterprises and development of global companies.

Exam Tip

By now you should know the meaning of the many acronyms used in this subject. These might arise in the examination paper, so make sure you revise the meaning of GATT, WTO, GDP, Plc, SWOT and SLEPT.

The basis for trade: at the micro level

Although the principle of comparative advantage holds across a range of commodities, in practice, equivalent consumer and industrial goods are imported and exported by many countries. Trade in such goods as cars and computers is partially explained by the fact these are differentiated products and the consumer desires a wide choice. Households do not want identical telephones or saloon cars and, in addition, each manufacturer gains economies by producing one main brand for an international market rather than lots of brands in low volumes for a purely domestic one. Gains from trade in this case do not necessarily derive from relative cost differences but rather from brand diversity and effective marketing.

Although large numbers of small and medium companies either do not participate in international trade or engage in only a peripheral way, the advantages for them can be substantial:

1 Providing a wider market for specialist niche producers
2 Additional volume to reduce the cost base and secure economies
3 Escape from a saturated or threatened domestic market
4 One possible means of extending the product life cycle
5 As a source of volume growth to support expensive R&D
6 To counter a depressed home market and maintain capacity
7 As a competitive strategy to counter and deter foreign rival entry into the home market
8 As a means of spreading risks.

If a business is to become an international marketing company then it must make a serious commitment to enter foreign markets. It is a long-term strategic decision, and not to be taken lightly, since the implications of subsequent withdrawal due to lack of preparation would be substantial and expensive in terms of finance, image and credibility.

Activity 6.9

Examine government statistics on international trade and the balance of payments to determine in what goods and services your country has a comparative advantage. What are the factors that account for the comparative advantage? Are there any factors that appear to be eroding this advantage (especially if trade is deteriorating)?

Frictions in the international environment

Notwithstanding the powerful forces encouraging ever greater participation in the emergent global market-place, there are numerous reasons for sparks to fly in international trade. These can appear arbitrary to the marketer and yet be extremely damaging. Take the threat of 100 per cent duties to the marketers of Scottish cashmere and even whoopee cushions caused by the threatened trade war over bananas. The WTO has ruled that EU import rules discriminate in favour of Caribbean producers and against US distributors such as Chiquita. Despite modifications the USA considered the EU was dragging its feet. Similar pressure was applied to steel imports from East Asia and can only grow as the US balance of payments deficit widens and its economy slows down. Producers threatened by imports are organized, concentrated, supported by their unions and very vocal compared to the exporters or consumers who stand to lose from such controls. China, Russia and Taiwan are especially vulnerable to US trade sanctions because they are not members of the WTO.

Match the following terms with the appropriate definition:

- Tariff
- Quota
- Embargo
- Non-tariff barrier
- Terms of Trade
- Customs duty

1 Taxes imposed on imported goods with the intention of reducing their competitiveness with domestic equivalents.
2 Various standards and regulations to which imports must conform.
3 A tax imposed on imports in order to raise revenue.
4 The index of average export prices compared to average import prices.
5 A quantitative limit on the volume of imports per time period.
6 A prohibition on the export of a particular good or classes of goods to certain countries, usually for political reasons.

(**See** Activity debrief at the end of this unit.)

Both the USA and the EU are pursuing anti-dumping duties and 'illegal' industry subsidies are in the pipeline. Dumping involves goods sold in foreign markets at below cost of production and are viewed as an unfair trading practice under WTO rules. However, interpretation is difficult and lower prices might reflect superior efficiency. Given these developments what are the implications for marketers?

It is important that you not only recognize the basis for international trade and factors encouraging and inhibiting its growth, but also that you are aware of the *sources of turbulence*. Even though the trend in recent years has been upward a number of developments could: (a) Cause the trend to reverse or (b) cause fluctuation about the trend.

Sources of turbulence is a section of the CIM syllabus and you should be able to think through the possible explanations by reflecting on the content of this unit and other ones in the macro-environment.

Prepare a report for your college tutor or work superior summarizing these sources.

(**See** Activity debrief at the end of this unit.)

- Marketers must monitor the international environment for advance warning of impending threats.
- A deflationary scenario encourages protectionist instincts and threatens global prosperity.
- A tension exists between free trade advantages to the world as a whole and self interest – one country can always gain from controls if all others continue to trade freely.
- Fear of international retaliation is often the main force against protectionism.
- Protection of infant industries is frequently used as a defence in developing nations.
- International marketers must still contend with tariffs and quotas imposed for a variety of reasons, such as, raising revenue, protecting domestic interests and avoiding foreign dependence.
- Non-tariff barriers add even more to cost and prices since they involve compliance with specific environmental, quality, health or safety standards and so require expensive product modification.
- The marketer may also find a far from level playing field as domestic

producers receive preferential assistance, e.g. tax breaks, supports and patriotic attitudes.

Exam Tip

As mentioned in the 'Study guide', the international environment has global candidate appeal. Since the papers are set with at least a one-year lead time it always pays to see if anything significant was happening at exam time minus 12/18 months. Remember, the examiner will be influenced by current events as well as syllabus content and its coverage over a run of papers.

So check it out: was anything of major global importance happening then? If so it *could* be the basis of a question in *your* examination.

We may conclude that governments are continuing to grapple with the problems of achieving its objectives simultaneously. Supply side policies are directed towards making markets work more effectively and altering the structure of incentives. However, unemployment of 1.3 million and high general taxation makes this appear to be a long-term solution, and experience has already shown that when demand rises strongly, inflationary forces tend to reassert themselves.

It is hard to escape the conclusion that any sustained improvement in economic conditions will quickly produce profit and wage-push forces. Marketers must make their own assessment based on circumstances in their own country and act accordingly.

Summary

In this important unit we have analysed important aspects of the macro-economic and international environment and focused on the need for marketers to appreciate the meaning of economic indicators. A grasp of future economic conditions will provide an important edge over rivals. To achieve this we have:

* Assessed each of the main macro-economic objectives.
* Investigated the workings of the circular flow to understand how changes in income, output and expenditure occur.
* Examined concepts such as the multiplier, the accelerator and deflationary gaps.
* Looked at the meaning and measurement of GDP.
* Identified the phases of the business cycle and considered how it might be managed to advantage.
* Focused on the key indicators for marketers to monitor.
* Outlined the impact of the main policy weapons on business and the marketer.
* Examined the benefits and implications of expanding world trade.
* Considered frictions in the international trade process.

Activity debrief

Definition 6.1 1, 5, 6, 2, 4, 3.

Question 6.1 The only viable solution to this conflict between growth and a pollution-free environment is to pursue *sustainable growth*. Zero growth is not a real option due to concern over rising unemployment in industrial economies and rising populations in less-developed ones. Continued progress towards industrialization is required but using cleaner technologies, renewable energy and recyclable products.

Question 6.2
* They will save more as a precaution (currently over half the work force feel insecure in their jobs, which adversely affects the 'feel good' factor and willingness to spend).
* We are taught that thrift is a good thing and happiness cannot be achieved by spending more than income. Yet saving without corresponding investment leads to lower income and employment and therefore unhappiness.

154

Question 6.3
- The rate of interest. As the rate of interest falls, less is saved and more is invested and vice versa. It will not work quickly because other factors also affect the decision to save (e.g. income, expectations and preferences) and invest (e.g. expected returns, competitive pressures).
- Where injections = leakages.

Question 6.4
- Multiplier $= \dfrac{1}{t(=0.4)+m(=0.2)+s(=0.1)} = \dfrac{1}{0.7} = 1.43$
- The tax multiplier is smaller because households who receive £5 billion of new disposable income save 0.1 before any spending occurs.

Question 6.5
- One plant if stabilized and no investment at all if demand falls back to 2 million.
- A cyclical pattern between ceilings and floors.

Question 6.6
- *Consumption* will remain unchanged due to uncertainty and savings as a precaution against unemployment. *Investment* will be unchanged or falling due to idle capacity and 'wait and see' attitudes. *Exports* will be unchanged or falling due to depression in overseas markets. Only *government* can be increased to stimulate activity. This was Keynes' main policy recommendation.
- No significant effects in the short run due to stickiness in the response. In the longer run costs would fall and business would become more competitive leading to higher activity rates. However, Keynes observed that 'in the long run we are dead' and people want jobs and incomes today.

Question 6.7
- China 7.5 per cent to Britain 2.5 per cent.
- No, not automatically – see 'limitations of the data'.
-

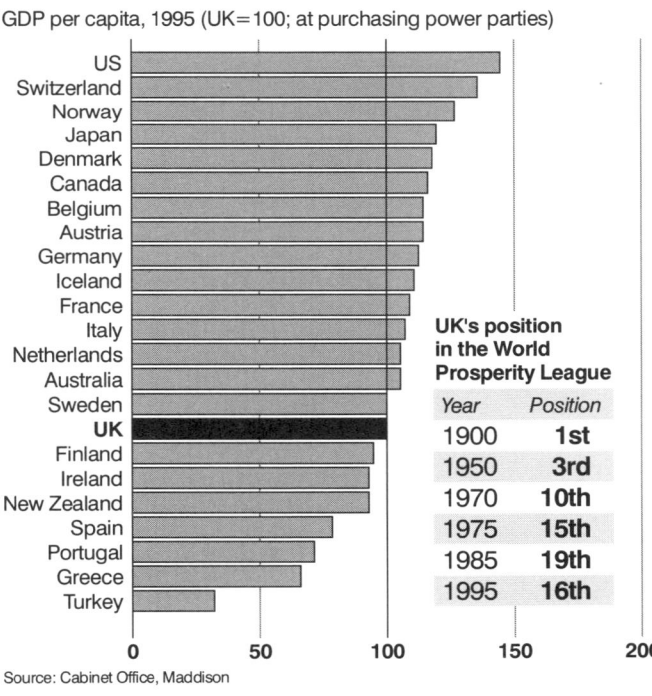

A century of relative decline. GDP per capita, 1995 (UK=100; at purchasing power parties)

Question 6.8
- *Recovery* starts from lower turning point; income, output and expenditure rise at an increasing rate; employment rises/unemployment levels off; caution at employing full-timers; new investment planned as confidence recovers ; inflation remains low as increased utilization occurs.
- *Boom* bottlenecks in faster growth sectors; resource prices bid up; passed on in higher prices; fully utilized resources; productivity is the

only source of higher output; profit, investment and confidence high; interest rates rising sharply, imports sucked in.

- *Downturn* starts from upper turning point; momentum through multiplier–accelerator; confidence and spending falls; precautionary savings rise; investment becomes unprofitable; business failures rise and cutbacks multiply.

Question 6.9

1 Cumulative expansion/contraction.
2 As 1, since retailers faced with unsold stock will cut back orders and sell from stock. This forces a bigger cut in output by the manufacturer. However, once desired stock level reached, reorder occurs providing stimulus.
3 As 1.
4 More vulnerable to imported fluctuations.
5 Cycle tied to duration of elections.
6 Services are less sensitive to income changes than manufactures.
7 May trigger turning point.

Question 6.10 High and rising unemployment means downward pressure on wages. Businesses can recruit without raising wages to attract labour. With many people chasing each vacancy in Britain managers can pick from the top of the barrel. Workers are likely to work harder to preserve their jobs and also accept technical and other change.

Question 6.11 Think in terms of technology transfer, value added (wages + demand for local components + local taxes), balance of payments (initial investment + exports), demonstration effect for positives. Competition, remitted profits, power (e.g. avoid taxes) for negatives.

Question 6.12

- If the government puts a higher priority on growth and high employment or if an election was close and it feared the effects of cutting spending on voting decisions.
- *Profit-push inflation* may occur in the recovery phase of the cycle as firms widen margins to restore profitability.
- *Import-push inflation* is often important in open economies when primary product prices rise sharply in a boom or a depreciating currency value raises import prices. Since commodity and energy prices are currently falling this is no threat.
- *Tax-push inflation* occurs when wage groups seek to compensate for tax erosion of their real earnings. The steep rise in British taxes after April 1994 might have triggered such a reaction, for example, but failed to.

Question 6.13

- Small firms who tend to rely on bank credit for cash flow
- Small firms who suffer when large customers delay payment
- Fast-growing firms
- Manufacturing firms with higher working capital requirements
- Such firms suffer in three ways – higher interest costs, limited credit and reduced consumer spending power (e.g. small builders).

Question 6.15 What happens as the expenditure rises again? Will not wage and price inflation resume? What if other economies are in recession? Will this mean that the economy will have to be kept in a state of low demand for a long period? What of the cost in terms of unemployment and lost economic growth?

Activity 6.1 Economic growth is primarily determined by the quantity, quality and distribution of resources; the proportion of resources invested; growth in the workforce; efficiency in resource use, and ability to shift resources from low- to high-productivity sectors. Non-economic factors are known as the 'substantial residual' since they often account for much of the differences in growth rates: flexibility and mobility of resources, incentive structures, quality of management, power of trade unions, social and political stability, deficiencies in education, regulations and so on.

Activity 6.2

- Increased domestic consumption means less is spent on imports. Leakages fall and demand for domestic output rises.
- Increased government spending is an injection of aggregate demand and income, output and expenditure rises.

Activity 6.4 This is the accelerator effect and consumer demand has to increase in other sectors before investment orders pickup.

Activity 6.5

- *Downturn* = control stock in line with order slowdown. The psychology is still one of growth with orders up on a year ago. This is the right time to conduct a Pareto analysis to weed out weak products and channel outlets. Recruitment should be halted and no further long-term commitments taken on.
- *Recession* = sit tight and wait for upturn. Be aware of brighter times ahead so retain skilled core and upgrade. Order capital equipment for installation 18 months hence since prices are at the lowest for all resource contracts.
- *Recovery* = Talk is still of recession but the rate of change in orders is upward. Start building stock and encourage distributors to do likewise. Start hiring and prepare new products for launch.

Activity 6.6 Policies fall into six groups:

- *Stimulate demand for labour directly* (e.g. government spending) – higher prices?
- *Reduce the number of job seekers* (e.g. more in higher education) – inefficient?
- *Improve the matching of unemployed to vacancies* (e.g. job centres)
- *Reduce the real wage* (e.g. pay restraint)
- *Share out the available work* (e.g. part-time, early retirement) – do workers want to?
- *Increase domestic at expense of overseas* (e.g. tariff barriers) – inefficient?

For jobs to be *sustainable* they must not be subsidized. Unemployment can only fall if the growth of GDP exceeds the net growth of the working population and its productivity.

Activity 6.10 Sources include *political*: war, terrorism, breakdown in relationships, even elections in a major trade economy; *economic*: coordinated recessions, multiplier – accelerator effects, major trade disputes, movement toward protectionism, failure to coordinate economic policies; *confidence*, and *technical* factors also figure. Turbulence will vary in different parts of the world and affect different industries to different degrees. Natural factors can also disrupt trade.

Examination hints and specimen questions

The economy is always going to be an important part of the macro-environment and the origin of major impacts on the business. It is the aspect that the marketer is primarily concerned with on a day-to-day basis and it would therefore be surprising if questions based on the content of this unit did not occur with some frequency.

As we saw in the specimen question at the end of Unit 5, a sound knowledge of your own economic environment is very important. The economic situation in your own country might be summarized under headings such as: inflation, unemployment, balance of payments, economic growth, phase of the cycle, investment activity and the economic policy stance, in brief. The use of a variety of *broad* statistics drawn from some of the mentioned sources would be expected by the examiner.

The specimen compulsory question in Unit 3 also had questions relating to the meaning of the business cycle.

1. The collection and assessment of macro-economic data is the key to successful management of the business cycle.

   (a) Provide a checklist of key economic indicators you would include in your data collection and detail the sources of information you would use. (8 marks)
   (b) Use these indicators to analyse the current economic situation facing your country. (12 marks)

   (CIM Marketing Environment paper, June 1997)

2. (a) Explain what you mean by the term sustainable growth:
   either (i) As an objective of economic policy;
   or (ii) As a concern for environmental pressure groups. (10 marks)
   (b) Briefly describe monetary and fiscal policies. (10 marks)

(c) Brief a marketing trainee on the impact of a cyclical downturn and suggest how a marketing department might respond. (10 marks)
(CIM Marketing Environment compulsory question, June 1998)

3 You have been asked to write a short article, suitable for inclusion in a marketing newsletter, on the issue of: 'Potential turbulence arising from the balance of payments.' The text should address the potential impact of government corrective actions on the marketing environment and not exceed 700 words. (20 marks)
(CIM Marketing Environment paper, June 1996)

Hints: Indicative content and approach

Question 1(a)

- Format is important here – provide a checklist, i.e. a box to put tick into once checked.
- Given the marks available provide 6 or 7 indicators/sources.
- Try and provide a variety of sources, e.g. ONS *Blue Book*, bank quarterly, CBI survey.
- No further information is required apart from the list.

Question 1(b)

- This is a stock question on the economy.
- Prepare in advance and be sure to know key indicators like GDP and inflation.
- Provide an analysis/explanation of what the indicators/their direction may mean.
- Use the indicators from Question 1(a) to provide structure to your answer.

Question 2(a)

- Define the concept in terms of positive and continuous growth.
- Central policy objective – stable framework to allow its achievement.
- Implies control of inflation and preventing balance of payments becoming a constraint.
- Optimal growth path avoiding cyclical excesses.

Question 2(b)

- Primary means by which the government seeks to achieve its objectives.
- Monetary policy undertaken by independent Bank of England.
- Fiscal policy mainly by the budget and includes spending.
- Both aim to control the level of aggregate demand.

Question 2(c)

- Relate to the section of the business cycle following the upper turning point.
- Present in a brief format with bullet points and headings.
- Emphasize the sea-change nature of this phase.
- Look at response in a 4P's framework, e.g. trim margins, more promotional focus and economy, seek overseas markets, introduce budget brands, rationalize stocks.

Question 3

- The emphasis on short article and space limits is not window dressing.
- Target audience is marketers so focus accordingly.
- Explain the nature of the turbulence.
- Focus on expenditure switching and reducing policies.
- Specify the potential impacts on sales volumes and margins.

The political and legislative environment

In this important unit, we will explore the interface between two significant and closely inter-linked aspects of the macro-environment. The societal agenda is set within the political environment and enacted and applied within the legislative environment. In this unit you will:

❑ Explore the relevant dimensions of the political environment.

❑ Consider the political processes of policy making and the influences brought to bear on it.

❑ Examine how the legal environment impacts on the organization.

❑ Appreciate the essential features of a complex legislative environment.

❑ Define the significance of legislation and regulation for marketers and their relationships with key stakeholders.

By the end of this challenging unit you will have:

❑ Consolidated your knowledge of the political system.

❑ Reinforced your grasp of the points of political pressure and influence.

❑ Distinguished between different forms of regulation.

❑ A raised awareness of legal issues as they apply to the marketer.

❑ Assessed legislation as a legitimate means of achieving society's objectives.

❑ Identified when to seek legal advice.

This unit considers a political environment which embraces institutions, agencies, laws and pressure groups. These elements may influence and constrain both organizations and individuals in society. They also define freedom in terms of what can not, and, by definition, what legally can be done in business today. We have already considered pressure groups in Unit 3 and this can be combined with consideration of lobbyists and the media in this unit. If marketers are influenced by the political environment in general, they are most certainly influenced by the legislative dimension in particular.

It first considers general issues concerning the legal framework within which the organization must work. This will involve such matters as the role and objectives of law and regulation; the methods available; an outline of the legal system; the costs and benefits of compliance as well as the impacts involved on business and society.

An appreciation of relevant areas of the law will be provided using British statutes as examples. Students from Asia, Africa, Europe and the Caribbean should understand that they may refer to their own legal system when examples are cited in examinations. Different countries have different legal traditions and systems. Even in Britain the law applying to England and Wales is different in many respects from that applying in Scotland.

You should note that the examiner will definitely not expect a detailed or definitive knowledge of the law. An appreciation of general principles and their application in the business context is what is important. Legal issues are, however, becoming increasingly important in business, not least in the area of marketing. A marketer must know when to seek legal advice and understand it sufficiently to ensure that the right questions are posed. Remember, lawyers are primarily concerned with the finer points of the law and are in an advisory capacity. Final decisions balancing commercial as well as legal considerations rest with the marketing and other directors.

This second micro-environment unit accounts for just under 10 per cent of the weighting. It represents a part of the syllabus that will be relatively unfamiliar to you. While it is shorter than previous units and should take only 2 to 3 hours to read and reread thoroughly, it is very important that you put the required effort into the activities to reinforce your understanding. These will take another 3 to 4 hours and it is suggested that you:

- Open a new 'political file' with a sub-section for 'legislation'.
- Remember that the law relating to competition has been considered in Unit 4.
- Refresh your understanding of pressure groups in Unit 3.
- Consult your legal department (if your company has one) for information on current legal issues.
- Scan the media for examples or implications of changes arising in these environments.
- Summarize what you read to no more than a short paragraph so that it is usable in the examination.

The political environment

The political environment might produce a variety of emotions ranging from apathy to outright cynicism, but it is one that marketers ignore at their peril, since its impacts on business activity are both numerous and potentially damaging.

As we have partly seen in Unit 6, the role and significance of government in a market economy is considerable:

- The government has full political power and executive authority to pursue the policies of its choice.
- The public sector, including executive agencies, accounts for around 30 per cent of jobs, over 20 per cent of direct spending and 40 per cent of total expenditure when transfer payments are accounted for.
- It is a 'swing sector' in terms of policies available to it to influence economic activity levels.
- It influences most key decisions – to work, save, spend, invest, etc. – by setting tax and interest rates.
- It enacts legal and regulatory frameworks that limit business freedom in the wider interests of society – well conceived regulation is accepted as a key role of the state and most aspects of marketing activity are covered by some form of control.
- Governments are democratically elected and must present their executive and legislative record for electoral scrutiny at prescribed intervals. This exposes government to external influence.
- The day-to-day practice of government relies on gathering feedback from interest groups within the environment and as such is susceptible to pressure and influence.
- Present-day governments operate in an open global system which may constrain its freedom of action. Governments must recognize the power of the markets; the need to keep national performance in line with com-

petitor benchmarks; the influence of trading partners and the rules of club membership, e.g. the EU.

National and European legislation and the decisions of public authorities clearly have an increasing influence on business activities and must be monitored carefully to:

- Alert management to impending legislation
- Mobilize efforts to represent stakeholder interests to the legislators
- Develop awareness of the intentions of those public bodies that can make decisions affecting business operations
- Identify likely changes arising out of electoral shifts
- Assess the implications of political manifestos and the evolving convictions and philosophies of the party and ministers in power.

As we have seen, the government also controls the macro-economic framework and its decisions affect both its position as a major customer of the private sector and the political distribution of the tax burden. Business has a collective interest in the relative burden of business taxes and rates as well as trends in the size and composition of government spending on goods and services. It was recognized in Unit 6 that governments now seek to create overall stability and this is reflected in spending despite the pressures exerted by the demands of social security, health and education.

The public sector itself has undergone a fundamental transformation in recent years with policies of privatization, deregulation and the contracting-out to private tender of more and more local authority and civil service functions. The conviction politics of Margaret Thatcher based on the values of private ownership and an enterprise culture have, however, been modified in the 1990s by the 'responsible' capitalism of John Major and its attendant social charters. Blairism seeks a partnership of private initiative and responsible public enterprise to promote the welfare of all members of society.

Definition 7.1

Match up the following terms with their definitions:

- Privatization
- Deregulation
- Enterprise culture
- Social charter
- Party manifesto
- First past the post
- Electoral cycle

1. The candidate with the most votes cast in an election is the winner, irrespective of the distribution of votes to other contenders.
2. Removal of rules and requirements restricting competition.
3. A programme of intended policies if successfully elected.
4. A 4–5 year pattern of stop–go economic activity.
5. A climate that encourages and approves self-reliance, entrepreneurship and individual wealth creation.
6. Transfer of 50 per cent or more of the voting shares to private hands.
7. Published performance standards for customer service in public sector organizations.

(**See** Activity debrief at the end of this unit.)

The political framework

Political systems are located along a spectrum ranging from totalitarianism to popular democracy. The main features of these two systems are outlined below:

Totalitarianism	Democracy
Power concentrated in single leader of the ruling party	Universal suffrage
Official ideology rules	Periodic free elections
Repression of opposition parties	Freedom of speech/media
Central direction/command	Open political competition
Government controls media	Pluralistic – power spread
Minorities persecuted	Majority rule/minorities are protected and equal under the law
	Pressure groups free to lobby between elections

Political power is the ability to bring about change through influencing the behaviour of others. All organizations are affected by politics because people have different views, ideals and interests. Disagreements naturally arise over such matters as objectives to be pursued, decisions to be made and, perhaps most importantly, resources to be allocated. These must be resolved, otherwise conflict would result and organizations and indeed society would cease to function effectively. Political stability arises out of the identification and effective resolution of disputes through a mixture of authority, enforcement and compromise.

Political stability is important, not least to investors who wish to minimize their risks. Multi-nationals, for example, were reluctant to invest in Britain during the labour unrest of the late 1970s and early 1980s, while the Tiananmen Square incident in Beijing in 1989 had serious repercussions not only in China itself but also in Hong Kong and the wider East Asia region.

Question 7.1

What are the areas and issues where 'politics' are involved in:

- The marketing department?
- Relationships between marketing and finance?

What sources of information should the marketer consult to keep a finger on the political environment pulse? Are there more cost-effective means of keeping abreast of national and supra-national legislative developments?
(**See** Activity debrief at the end of this unit.)

The political process is outlined in Figure 7.1 and is based on the British system. It is, however, applicable in general terms to most democratic market economies.

The main features of this process will be explained in turn together with

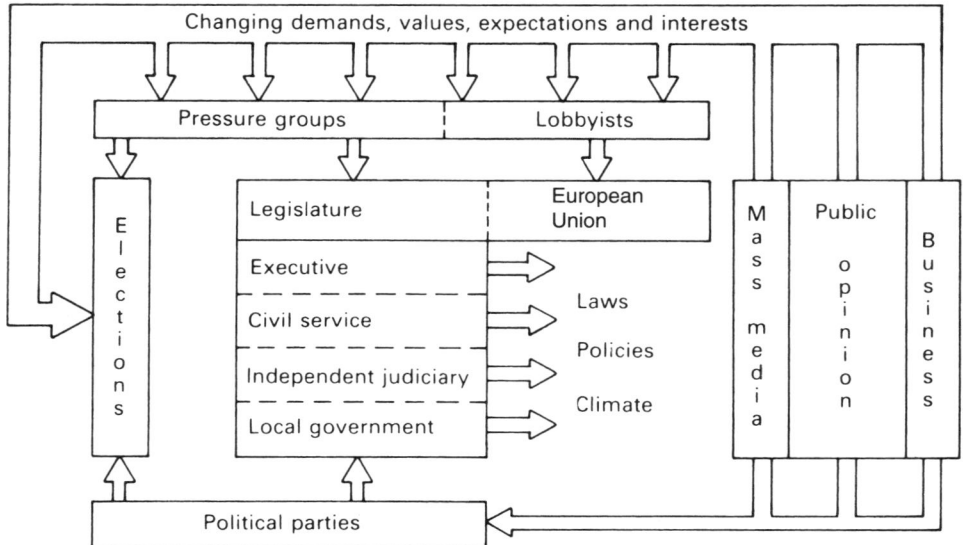

Figure 7.1 An outline of the British political system

the implications for business and the marketer. The inputs into the political system originate in wider society and arise out of their changing attitudes, perceptions and demands. These will be diverse and conflicting and tend to coalesce around support for alternative party manifestos at election time, e.g. lower taxes, devolution of power to the regions, more education spending, etc. Political parties seek to differentiate themselves from their rivals, but also appeal to a sufficiently wide constituency as to gain election to government.

Elections are the ultimate democratic control over government and provides the electorate with an opportunity to pass judgement on performance. It is also an opportunity to judge the 'promises and proposals' of the opposition. Fear of defeat at the next general election, or a very strong wish to preside over a second term, should encourage account of the public wishes.

Question 7.2

Since voters are very much like customers as far as political parties are concerned, what advice would the marketer offer to the election campaign manager of:

- The party currently in office?
- The main opposition party?
- A Green party looking to establish a base in Parliament?

(**See** Activity debrief at the end of this unit.)

Britain has a first-past-the-post electoral system which produces a number of characteristics:

- A simple majority of seats contested gives one party the power to form the government.
- Governments seldom win a 'majority' of votes cast.
- Smaller parties do not see their proportion of the vote reflected in seats won.
- A majority of the electorate may vote against the government but split the opposition vote.

This appears unfair but elections are held to produce governments. There has also been considerable resistance in Parliament to a more proportional voting system, despite the fact that Britain is out of step with the rest of Europe. The key question is whether a strong and effective government is what is wanted or a more representative one.

Question 7.3

Summarize from a business point of view the case for and against electoral reform.

(See Activity debrief at the end of this unit.)

The main concern of business is for a minimum of instability arising out of political decision making, a dependable planning horizon and a positive climate in which to operate. The landslide election of a Labour government following four consecutive terms with the Conservatives may have caused discontinuity. Some policies may be reversed (e.g. the Social Chapter), institutions abolished (e.g. the House of Lords) and legislation amended to reflect New Labour political philosophies despite any assurances to the contrary. Business must ponder the implications of Tony Blair's cabinet implementing their pledges, or not, as the case may be. 'New Labour's Ten Pledges' are:

- To increase the proportion of national income spent on education.
- To reduce the proportion spent on the welfare bills of social failure.

- To cut spending on NHS bureaucracy and increase it on patient care.
- To reduce the number of long-term unemployed and cut the number of jobless youngsters by more than half.
- To halve the time it takes young offenders to get to court.
- To keep government borrowing and inflation within low targets.
- To keep the promises Labour makes on tax.
- To reduce class sizes in primary schools and raise school standards.
- To devolve power to Scotland, Wales and the regions of England.
- To build a new and constructive relationship in Europe.

This discontinuity can create uncertainty for business, especially if the party in power is changed frequently. Similar discontinuity faced the people of Hong Kong after June 1997 although much political energy had been invested in assuring smooth transference of power, so limiting adverse business and popular reaction.

Activity 7.1

With New Labour over halfway through its term of office why not check out how it is doing with its pledges. Take each one in turn and compare current progress to the original intention. Assess the marketing implications, arising from both achievement/non-achievement, as appropriate.

The electoral cycle

The other source of political instability is the tendency for elections to 'influence' business cycles. Governments know that reducing taxes and increasing spending as an election approaches will create a temporary sense of well-being. Disposable income rises, as does employment and business activity. This will be short-lived if prices and imports also tend to rise, since action will have to be taken to reverse the resulting inflation and trade deficit. However, since there will be a lag before such effects are felt, the government may well win re-election and be in a position to apply the economic brakes. These can then be released as the next general election approaches. This may explain the Chancellor's budget measures having their full impact in election year.

One final point to note is that an adversarial two- or three-party system does tend to widen the credibility gap between politically nurtured expectations, on the one hand, and actual performance of the economy, on the other. It is as well that the marketer takes with a pinch of salt the ideals and objectives advertised and promoted by the various parties in general and the government in particular. Politics is said to be the 'art of the possible' but this sometimes has a habit of being less than expected!

Extending Activity 7.1

The marketer should always be aware of the political agenda. Governments issue their plans annually in the Queen's speech (or your national equivalent) while party manifestos are published in the run-up to an election.

You should scan the contents of these when they become available to assess their implications either directly through proposed legislation or indirectly on stakeholder groups.

Central and local government

Parliament is the supreme legislative authority in Britain. Although private members (of Parliament) can propose bills the vast majority that become law are government sponsored or supported. The marketer should understand the origins of new laws and how businesses might influence their form and content:

Stages	Influence
1 *Origin* Popular issue, committee of inquiry recommendation, election pledge, pressure group, government initiative, to close loopholes.	Trade association may press for legislation

2 *Green Paper* Government puts ideas on paper for discussion — Monitor and contribute if industry interests are to be affected

3 *White paper* Government sets out definite proposals — Comments from parties affected will be accounted/included

Note: It is vitally important that business views on proposed laws are made clearly and persuasively at this time. If legislation is inevitable, then business must ensure that it is workable and no unintended disadvantageous side-effects result. Emotional legislation in response to a public outcry is to be avoided through active lobbying.

4 *Draft bill – first reading*

5 *Main debate – second reading* — MPs can be lobbied to speak in support

6 *Committee stage*

7 *Report stage — to full House of Commons*

8 *Final debate and amendments – third reading* — Last opportunity to lobby support

9 *To House of Lords – process repeated*

10 *Possible reference back to Commons*

11 *Royal Assent – the law is enacted*

The process is long and complicated, placing a limit on how much legislative business can be completed. Virtually all government-sponsored bills become law although the opposition can use delaying tactics. Case law, in contrast, evolves through independent judicial decisions and is not susceptible to influence by business, although the right of appeal exists.

Activity 7.2

The ability of business lobbies to influence legislation which affects them is considerable. The drinks industry in 1999, for example, was able to persuade the Chancellor to freeze duty for a year but was previously unable to prevent concerns over the attractions of alcopops to underage drinkers forcing a 40 per cent rise in duty. The travel lobby persuaded the government to push for a last minute reprieve for duty-free goods within the EU. The motor industry lobby campaigned successfully to remove special taxes on new cars. The farm and defence lobbies are other notable examples.

Select either a current Green or White Paper, or a recently enacted piece of legislation affecting a strong business lobby and compare the original proposals with the final legal form. Try to identify why and how the lobby was effective. Draw up a list of groups for and against the legislation.

Pressure groups were discussed in some detail in Unit 3, where it was concluded that from a pluralistic view they are a good thing. They represent a channel through which individuals and groups can make their views known to governments between elections. They are much more important than political parties in terms of membership and represent numerous, overlapping and competing influences within society.

Pressure group effectiveness requires *commitment, cohesion, organization, resources and strategic positioning*. Ministers who decide government policies need pressure groups. They often have a statutory duty to consult and require advice, information and feedback of views and reactions from those affected. They favour those groups with the ability to deliver on bargains and compromises made and who provide support in return. They also need cooperation in the implementation and administration of new laws.

Exam Tip

The marketing environment is still a large syllabus containing diverse subjects on which to keep abreast. So, on the principle that two heads are better than one, why don't you pool resources with a fellow student and actively compare notes and ideas? Your combined strengths will produce synergy $(1 + 1 = 3)$ and help to reduce the overall workload.

Businesses are strategically well positioned to obtain political support when Conservatives are in office but not always as successful when Labour rules. It should be noted, however, that effective pressure group activity tends to stimulate the development of counter-pressure. Countervailing action between rival groups and coalitions limits the influence of any one grouping. Ministers will also be in a position to play one group off against another!

Government through devolved powers

Brief mention should be made of other dimensions of government with which the marketer might interact. Very close to home are local authorities to whom businesses, both large and small, will have to make representations from time to time. If a problem area is within local government jurisdiction it is usually politically inappropriate to seek redress centrally. Local politicians are protective of their independence and often represent opposition parties and policies. The appropriate decision-making authority has therefore to be identified and lobbied, as in the case of central government.

Local government in Britain has undergone radical change in the last ten years. Their powers to set business rates, raise taxes independently and decide expenditure totals have all been constrained by central government actions such as spending caps. Setting of national standards in education and other social services have also limited local autonomy. In previous units we have learnt that local government officers are now service facilitators rather than direct providers because of the requirement on them to also offer contracts out to competitive bidding.

This has made local authorities much more marketing orientated in pursuing value for money services for their ratepayers. Formerly 'free' services, such as libraries and leisure centres, are now run on a more commercial basis. Consumer needs are identified and services provided priced and promoted in order to cover costs and make a contribution to council funds.

Apart from bidding for council contracts in street cleaning, parks maintenance, refuse disposal, etc., there are also opportunities for working jointly on projects combining civic improvement and commercial development. Local authorities are important stakeholders since they undertake town planning and re-development, decide planning applications, control the supply of school leavers, maintain local roads and infrastructure and provide a variety of inspectorates that impact on local business. It is an aspect of the environment, therefore, where the business should build positive and mutually beneficial relationships.

Extending Activity 7.2

Local authorities produce Economic Development Plans. Contact your local planning office and arrange to view one. Consider whether any of the proposed developments represent threats of opportunities for your business.

List the ways in which your business could get its views heard locally.

(**See** Activity debrief at the end of this unit.)

While local authorities have suffered from centralizing tendencies and a reduction of powers delegated by central government, New Labour has pursued the devolution of powers to Scotland and Wales. Marketers serving these populations must in future recognize the implications of the transfer of legislative authority although the Chancellor's budget will continue to dictate the agenda. Similar significance attaches to an elected mayor for London.

One final area to note is that of government agencies and other quasi-government bodies. The intention of the current government is to transform much of the civil service into executive agencies. These will be free from day-to-day control by ministers and therefore able to focus on the achievement of long-term performance objectives. Some will also be privatized. If the experience of previous privatizations is a guide then this will underpin a significant rise in both marketing and competitiveness in the areas concerned. Such agencies are un-elected, however, and this has raised questions over their independence and accountability. This has led to a Code of Practice for making such public appointments and the appointment of auditors to seek out malpractice. Examples, such as the National Rivers Authority and NHS hospital trusts, give some idea of potential spending power or influence some of these organizations command.

Supra-national bodies – the European Union (EU)

The EU is the most integrated and economically powerful bloc of countries in the world. Its members represent a combined market of over 350 million affluent consumers. As such, it is a magnet for marketers from around the world.

The Single European Market (SEM) initiative originated over concern with Europe's declining competitiveness relative to America and the emerging nations of the Pacific Rim. Despite the Common Market, Europe remained fragmented into culturally differentiated markets protected by an array of non-tariff barriers to trade. A common desire for increased competitiveness and employment opportunities was the driving force behind the idea of a truly free market, which, it was hoped, would release a dynamic and revived spirit of enterprise within European businesses.

In marketing terms, much of European industry appeared to be in the late maturity stage of both product and industry life cycles. Unless a new innovativeness emerged, or the life cycle was extended, it would enter the delcine stage as the centre of gravity of world economic power shifted permanently from the Atlantic to the Pacific. Deregulation was seen as the means of releasing competitive forces which would revitalize its mature industrial base.

Activity 7.3	Use CD-ROM databases or newspaper summaries to locate any surveys assessing progress to date in implementation of the SEM. Identify any evidence either for or against the hypothesis that European industry is becoming more competitive as a result.

Membership of the EU and the SEM have created economic and legal obligations that have meant the loss of a degree of national sovereignty. Entry into the European Monetary System with its single currency would potentially accelerate this transfer of legislative authority as we will see in Unit 10. The institutions relevant to the exercise of this authority include:

- *The European Parliament* is an elected body (MEPs) with widening powers. Originally it was primarily consultative, supplying advice through the workings of various standing committees. More recently it has acquired powers to reject proposals and even veto the budget.
- *The Council of Ministers* is where the real decision making power lies. It is composed of representative ministers, according to the issue under discussion. More and more of the voting is on a 'qualified majority' basis implying that marketers wishing to influence outcomes must broaden their lobbying base and/or cooperate with other sympathetic interest groups.
- *The European Commission* as the executive body of the Union, has drafted regulations and directives to promote the SEM and achieve a level competitive playing field. Its membership is decided by the member governments and its role is to coordinate national policies and secure adoption and execution of the EU policies. We saw, in Unit 4, the power of the Commission to impose punitive fines on British companies for contravening competition rules.

The outcome has been a large number of measures and directives to facilitate the evolution of an integrated market. Compliance costs have arisen for business in the process, but so too have the opportunities for greater trade.

Before we turn to the scope for influencing the legislative environment, we may note the jurisdictional power of the European Court of Justice. This deals with any actions a business may wish to bring against EU institutions. It also provides a means of individual redress where member states are not fully complying with their legal obligations. Both national governments and organizations have often learnt to their cost the consequences of referral to this final court of appeal.

Lobbyists and the media

Lobbying may be defined as influencing members of a relevant legislature and soliciting their votes. This important activity has attracted recent adverse publicity arising out of scandals such as 'cash for questions', Formula 1 tobacco sponsorship and Olympic Committee decisions. Such examples may represent the extreme tip of a very big iceberg but most lobbying activity comes within accepted definitions of ethical behaviour. To be effective it must be exerted *where and when the decisions are being made.*

The value of professional lobbyists to a business are as follows:

- *Monitoring*   an early-warning service on forthcoming legislation
- *Interpreting*   the implications of draft bills
- *Identify*   MEPs/MPs/ministers with a special interest in your issue
- *Inform*   MEPs/MPs/decision makers about (your) industry developments
- *Prepare*   background briefs and cases for busy MPs/MEPs
- *Coordinate*   constituency 'protest' letters to MPs/MEPs
- *Advise*   the business on strategy and tactics to adopt.

While there is little likelihood of stopping proposed legislation, the lobbyist will be seeking to persuade ministers and senior civil servants to *think again on details, clarify ambiguity, gain assurances and secure legislation the industry can live with!*

The pre-budget period is a busy one for lobby groups. The industry lobby, for example, are pleased with the outcome of their representations, not least the cut in corporation tax and introduction of a 10p starting rate to encourage small businesses. The transport and farming lobbies are less pleased with the rise in diesel duties. Business, union, consumer, heritage, environment and an array of other interest groups wish to make their presence felt. However, public perceptions and public opinion are also clearly important inputs into the political process. The climate the government seeks to create through its policies and laws is an equally important output intended to positively influence these opinions. Putting a positive 'spin' on events will, if successful, make the public more likely to re-elect the government concerned.

The mass media, including press, radio and television, are important influences on these perceptions and opinions. They supply awareness of political issues and scrutiny of government behaviour and performance. As with pressure groups, they can influence decision makers and their policies through their campaigns. Investigative journalism in particular can have serious impacts on business as well as politicians. Exposure of malpractice can lead to loss of sales, resignations and policy changes. For example, the Malaysian embargo on British exports in 1994 was a direct reaction to press reports in *The Times* and the cash-for-questions exposé prompted a radical overhaul of Parliamentary privilege.

Public relations is an equally important aspect of marketing management and special skills are required to create and maintain mutually beneficial relationships with the media. It is a two-way relationship based on principles similar to those between a minister and a pressure group. PR aims to influence both the media agenda as well as the tenor of any debate that results. Issues and outcomes must be monitored through market research to assess shifts in public opinion.

Question 7.4

If you were contacted by the local media requesting an interview regarding an issue arising over the marketing of a new product how would you respond and what would you say?

(**See** Activity debrief at the end of this unit.)

Conclusions

The marketer should continuously reassess the political landscape surrounding the business. Inertia ensures that much of the political environment remains constant but pressure to set and implement a policy agenda means there will always be shifts in direction and corresponding impacts, particularly in the medium to long term.

A pluralistic society ensures that political change is often the product of compromise and consensus. Business interest groups can influence decisions but only if they understand the real nature of the political agenda. This may be driven by considerations of tactical or party advantage especially approaching election time.

The legal framework

Legal issues and cases involving businesses are regularly in the news. Seldom a week goes by without mention of such things as a copyright infringement, an advert being withdrawn, an out-of-court settlement for negligence, a new law governing video nasties, a case of insider dealing or a fine imposed by a government inspectorate. Law was initially based on a concept of natural justice and parties to a transaction were treated as equals. Each party looked to their own best interest and suffered the consequences of their own poor judgement. Consumers were faced with the reality of 'caveat emptor' (let the buyer beware). The growing power and size of businesses relative to individual consumers, however, made this untenable, and pressure grew for legal protection which tilted the scales by increasing the rights of buyers and the duties of sellers. As mentioned in Unit 3, 'caveat vendictor' (let the seller beware) became the operating principle.

Question 7.5

How does the law influence or affect you during a typical working day? This may not be directly, unless you get a speeding ticket! But how does it affect your day indirectly?

(**See** Activity debrief at the end of this unit.)

The framework of law is the product of both legal and political influences. An independent judiciary are responsible for the interpretation of common law. These are broad, comprehensive principles based on ideals of justice, fairness and common sense. The term 'common' means that it applies to all subjects. The way that common law is interpreted and applied changes over time through the effect of legal judgments. When made by the High Court, the Appeal Court or the Law Lords they become precedents which must be applied by lower courts such as Crown or Magistrates' Courts. Such judgments adapt the law to reflect current attitudes and values within society. One recent judgment awarded damages to asbestosis sufferers who had grown up in close proximity to the plant manufacturing the product. This exposed the company to substantial liabilities arising from potential claims from other victims.

Governments introduce new laws in the form of statutes in order to implement their political manifestos. These Acts of Parliament reflect political philosophy as well as a growing pressure from society on government to regulate undesired activity or behaviour. This arises partly out of need, but also from the various stakeholders in the form of pressure group activity and vested interests.

The resulting increase in parliamentary workload has forced governments to concentrate on 'enabling Acts', delegating authority to government departments, agencies or local authorities to fill in and administer the details. These are issued in the form of statutory instruments, regulations and bye-laws.

These authorities are normally responsible for the following roles:

- Rule making and their interpretation (i.e. regulations)
- Standards setting (e.g. emissions, food and hygiene)
- Inspections – usually unannounced spot checks due to complaints
- Enforcement – various sanctions from fines to closure.

As we saw earlier, entry into the European Economic Community in 1973 made Britain subject to the legal provisions of the Treaty of Rome. These laws and regulations apply throughout the European Union. Directives require implementation by member states superseding national laws. They affect business, particularly in the area of competition policy, where fines of up to 10 per cent of turnover may be levied. The European Court of Justice is now the final court of appeal in legal cases.

Role and objectives of legislation

Legislation involves a delicate process of balancing the diverse and often conflicting interests of the the various stakeholders involved. Some of these may be summarized as follows:

- Governs exchanges between parties – the foundation stone of the market economy.
- Ensures a level playing field between individuals and companies.
- Counterbalances the economic power of business.
- Settles disputes between stakeholders.
- Denies market access to certain groups (e.g. alcohol to children).
- Balances the rights of the individual company with the collective rights of wider society.
- Prohibits certain goods or activities (e.g. hard drugs/pornography).
- Seeks to prevent abuse without imposing excessive regulation.
- Governs what business can and cannot do.

Unfortunately the law is a relatively blunt weapon in the achievement of such objectives, not least because society's attitudes and concerns can often change rapidly whereas the law tends to lag behind. There is a limit to what Parliament can amend or enact each year and many worthy legal bills fail to become law because of lack of parliamentary time. The activities of the media and pressure groups such as the Consumers Association and Citizens' Advice Bureaux have, however, made consumers more aware of their rights and more willing to initiate action to seek redress. Attitudes have changed dramatically in recent years with much more demanding expectations of the 'service' consumers believe they have a right to expect from business. Not all this pressure on business to deliver the 'proper' goods comes from the law alone as Figure 7.2 shows.

1 Let the seller beware
2 The process of making laws
3 Voluntary guidelines to encourage desirable modes of behaviour
4 Let the buyer beware – no legal obligation to notify defects
5 A quango established to set product safety/quality standards
6 An official appointed to investigate individual complaints of maladministration (e.g. as in banking)
7 Law laid down by government legislation
8 A mark, given by an expert, to confirm or guarantee a product.

(**See** Activity debrief at the end of this unit.)

The government then has primary responsibility for the establishment, updating and operation of the legal framework. The law provides a means by which it can constrain business activities by defining the powers and responsibilities of owners and management. Recent governments in Britain, however, have sought to curtail the amount of regulation in recent years. They have launched successive campaigns to reduce bureaucracy and red tape especially where it impacts on smaller businesses. They have also deregulated a number of industries, such as telecommunications and coach services, in order to increase competition and release the latent potential for productivity improvements where slack and inefficiency had accumulated. On the other hand, they have had to establish a large number of quangos to regulate and oversee these operations. For examples of these extra legal bodies let us take an aspect important to advertising and promotion, the regulation of broadcasting:

ADVERTISING STANDARDS AUTHORITY (ASA)
Origins: Set up in 1962 by the UK advertising industry to keep its own house in order and counter the need for legislation.
What does it do? Ensures that everyone who commissions, prepares and publishes advertisements complies with the industry's British Codes of Advertising and Sales Promotion. Carries out research, issues advice to the industry, and handles complaints from members of the public.
Members: The ASA is made up of the Committee of Advertising Practice, comprising representatives from various trade associations, and the ASA Council. This council comprises 12 people from differing academic backgrounds to adjudicate on complaints.

INDEPENDENT TELEVISION COMMISSION (ITC)
Origins: Set up with the passing of the Broadcasting Act in 1990, replacing the IBA and Cable Authority.
What does it do? Licenses commercial television services in the UK, terrestrial and cable/satellite. Regulates services with a code of practice on programme content, advertising, sponsorship and technical standards, and has a range of penalties for failure to comply. Has a duty to ensure a wide range of services is available, that they are high quality and appeal to a variety of tastes and interests. Also ensures fair competition. Reports on complaints about programmes and adverts, dealing with issues of content and scheduling, are published monthly.

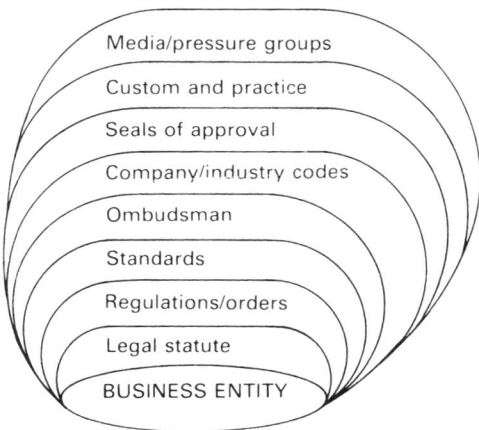

Figure 7.2
Regulatory pressures on business – a broader view

BROADCASTING STANDARDS COUNCIL

Origins: Established in 1988, and became a statutory organisation under the 1990 Broadcasting Act.

What does it do? Although it has statutory powers in the handling of complaints, its role is advisory, not regulatory. Its remit extends to the portrayal on television and radio of violence, sexual conduct and matters of taste and decency, including bad language, treatment of disasters and issues of stereotyping. Also conducts audience research to determine attitudes.

Source: The *Sunday Times* (adapted)

Question 7.6

What do you understand by the term 'red tape'? Survey different departments of your business for examples of this phenomenon but try to distinguish between that created directly by the government from that arising due to business procedures designed to ensure compliance.

(**See** Activity debrief at the end of this unit.)

Impacts and influences on business

There is something of a pendulum effect operating with regulation since fresh societal concerns regarding certain business activities will bring calls for the government *to do something about it!* The costs of regulation and ensuring compliance must be balanced with the benefits to stakeholders and society of the legislation in question. Some of the drawbacks of legislation and regulation include:

- The extra costs of purchasing and installing required equipment; training staff to conform to standards; recording, reporting and taking action where deviations arise.
- Conforming to legal requirements (e.g. tighter emission standards) adds to business costs and reduces competitiveness with overseas rivals.
- Conforming to safety standards (e.g. testing required on new pharmaceutical products) delays introduction and returns so deterring investment and innovation.
- Complicated regulatory procedures may form a barrier to entry against smaller companies.
- Employment or environmental legislation may drive businesses to locate in Third World countries, taking jobs, investment and potential exports with them.
- Legal and insurance costs – fines and adverse publicity.
- Reduced consumer choice – loss of the right to buy as we wish.

Note: Small companies are much harder hit by regulations. Compliance costs will be a much higher proportion of total cost, they lack form-filling expertise and the time involved is a diversion from the sole trader's real business. Since small firms tend to be single-product or single-market operations, regulation is more likely to affect the whole business than in a large multi-product concern.

Exam Tip

Questions on the legislative environment may be concerned with the effects of particular aspects of the law (e.g. fair trading) but often they will focus at least in part on the impact of the law on the activities of the marketer. Examples of recent legislation demonstrate your awareness of this environment.

It would be advisable therefore to have thought through these impacts and find appropriate examples from your own country's legislation. Figure 7.3 provides an outline of the relevant areas.

While many businesses complain that they cannot compete fairly or profitably with current or proposed legislation, others cannot seem to compete without it, pressing the government for tariffs and quotas or longer periods of patent protection for the products they develop. Suppliers of branded goods, such as Coca-Cola and Nescafé for example, are seeking stricter regulations to stop retailers using 'me-too' packaging for their own-label products.

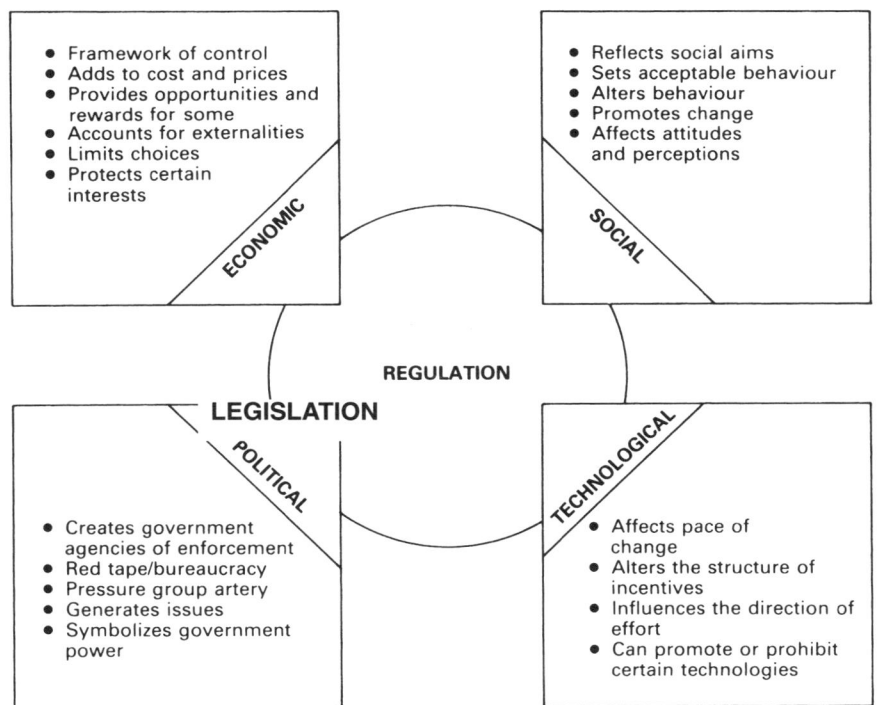

Figure 7.3 Macro-environment impacts on the legislative framework

Clearly, legislation can be double-edged, in some cases making markets more competitive while in others creating new entry barriers. Industry will be well advised therefore to actively lobby for workable legislation when the government proposes change.

Some of the positive impacts on the marketing environment

- *Facilitates desirable social change* Legislation in the areas of equal pay, equal opportunities and sex discrimination have underpinned increasing female participation rates in the labour force and rising proportions in higher managerial positions.
- *Corrects market failures* Legislation to deter restrictive practices and the exercise of monopoly power produces workable competition to the benefit of consumers in the form of lower prices and wider choice.
- *Encourages further knowledge* New environmental standards encourages research into problems like the greenhouse and ozone effects.
- *Reassurance of the public at large* The introduction of more stringent vehicle tests, for example, reduces safety concerns and improves emission standards.

It should be noted that the beneficial impacts of regulation are both difficult to measure and more likely to be understated. Business will also be more inclined to measure the costs of compliance and to a much greater degree than society will be inclined to calculate the benefits.

Question 7.7

How are different areas and functions of the business affected by the law? Use the following chart to think about this question, the factors to the right are stakeholder groups while the ones on the left are functional aspects of the business. Think of legislation that applies to each function.

Product design — Customers
New product development — General public
Promotion — BUSINESS — Other businesses
Information systems — ENTITY — Employees
Operations — Local authority
Transportation — Shareholders

(**See** Activity debrief at the end of this unit.)

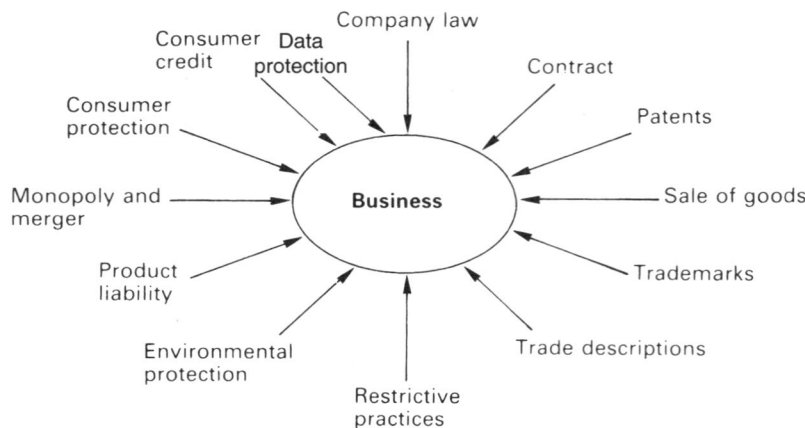

Figure 7.4
The potential impact of legislation on a business

Appropriate action

The relevant legislation which impact on the business in general and the marketer in particular may be seen in Figure 7.4.

Management needs to formulate a coherent policy in respect of legal matters. Primarily it must seek to avoid liability under the various laws and regulations that affect it. This means establishing policy guidelines to ensure that at least minimum standards are attained. It also requires a policy regarding whether to take legal action against others and if so in what circumstances. This may involve competitors infringing patents, for example, or bad debts, or even a libel action against environmental activists maligning the company product, as in the case of McDonald's.

In all but the simplest of cases a business should hire professional legal advice and representation. The law is extremely complex, not least where precedents are involved. Solicitors may deal with out-of-court advice and small claims, such as recovery of bad debts in the Small Claims Court. Barristers may be required for higher courts and specialists will probably be retained where highly technical matters are concerned. Larger companies will tend to have legal departments who will be well versed in the interests and affairs of the business. Smaller concerns will normally use an independent firm of solicitors as and when needed.

Exam Tip	We are now on Unit 7, which means that on its completion you will have undertaken nearly three-quarters of the syllabus.

We are now on Unit 7, which means that on its completion you will have undertaken nearly three-quarters of the syllabus.

Have you attempted any of the sample examination questions yet, including those at the end of the workbook? *Or* did you think you could safely leave it until later? If the latter is the case, think again and attempt the questions set while the material is fresh in your mind. This also means you can come back and review your effort later in the light of further knowledge, ideas and, most importantly, confidence in the subject.

A number of considerations will need to be accounted here:

- The expensive nature of legal actions
- The effect of actions on the company image
- Longer-run interest in ongoing business relationships may incline companies to live and let live rather than resort to law
- Business contracts may therefore be deliberately drawn up to include means of resolving any disputes that arise between the parties: the use of mediators or arbitrators to resolve disputes is an example of this
- Regulatory agencies may be content with assurances from an offending company that standards will be met in future
- Voluntary codes may be preferred to regulation and legal processes. These are standards of practice all businesses in the industry are

expected to follow. They are difficult to enforce and may be replaced by law if widely ignored or flouted. Reporting standards in the British press are governed by such a code and yet have been much criticized. UK retailers have recently agreed on a code to promote Internet retailing.

- Industrial Tribunals are semi-judicial bodies used for cases of unfair dismissal, discrimination and related matters. To avoid liability in such cases a business must ensure that it meets all its obligations by establishing the required internal policies and procedures and monitor their operating effectiveness (e.g. verbal and written warnings prior to dismissal of employees)
- Smaller companies are often exempted from certain legislation because of the high costs of compliance (e.g. employee protection).

Activity 7.5

Use your local reference or college library to research and assess the operations of the Advertising Standards Authority or its equivalent in your own country. List the advantages and drawbacks of voluntary codes. What sanctions does the authority possess? Where and why have they taken action recently? What does this tell you about their ethical position? Can you find examples of other codes of practice?

(**See** Activity debrief at the end of this unit.)

Fair trading and the consumer

The syllabus wants you to achieve a general understanding of the influence of legislation on marketing. Detailed and specific knowledge of statutes or cases is not required, but a broad grasp of implications for marketing is expected. There will not be specific questions on, say, the finer points of contract law, but there may be general questions on the current legal position of the consumer and the possible scope for future legislation. The remaining section of this unit therefore provides a broad appreciation of the main areas of law which impact on the marketer.

Contractual relationships
Contract law is the legal cornerstone regulating exchanges between buyers and sellers. Without a contract there is no direct relationship between the parties and hence no rights and obligations. A contract, in effect, exchanges promises. The buyer may promise to pay a certain sum of money in exchange for a specified product or service.

The basic legal assumptions originally involved here were freedom and equality of contract. Buyers had the right not to buy the products on offer, but in the spirit of fair competition it was their responsibility to negotiate the best deal possible for themselves when deciding to buy.

A contract comprises a number of elements, including:

- *Offer* Unlike an invitation to make offers, this is a definite offer by word or deed to be legally bound on the stated terms. It can be withdrawn before acceptance and may be terminated, but only in circumstances such as rejection by the intended buyer, lapse of time or death.

Activity 7.6

Try to make some time to study the 'terms and conditions' attached to goods or services supplied by your company and compare them to the elements outlined here. Alternatively, study those you have to sign when making a major purchase.

- *Acceptance* This must be unconditional, involving no new terms and must occur within a reasonable time period. Acceptance by the person or company to whom the offer was made must normally be communicated by word or conduct. For the contract to be valid, agreement between the parties must be voluntary and genuine.
- *Intent to create a legally binding contract* Most commercial contracts make this assumption.
- *Consideration* English law normally requires that something of value is exchanged for a contract to be enforceable. In commercial terms this would normally involve cash or other goods. The seller is then legally obligated to fulfil the contract.
- *Capacity* Parties to a contract must have the capacity to make one for it to be binding. Possible exceptions include minors, intoxicated adults and those claiming to be of unsound mind. Certain contracts are unenforceable against minors by statute, as in the case of non-essential goods supplied on credit.
- *Legality* Contracts are deemed illegal if they contravene existing statute or common law (e.g. are in restraint of trade).

The main remedies include injunctions and award of damages. Companies must, however, weigh the desirability of such actions very carefully. Any award made will be to compensate the injured party for damages but no more than that. If no actual loss has occurred, only nominal damages are likely and all reasonable steps must be taken to mitigate (minimize) the extent of the damage sustained.

A small painting and decorating company, for example, is confronted by difficult judgements where a customer challenges an invoice by claiming that the work done was not performed as specified or agreed. If the sums involved are small, is it worth the time and effort involved to take the case to court? Given the highly technical issues in judging whether a contract has been satisfactorily completed, is the risk of an adverse judgment worth the considerable legal costs involved? Finally, what of the impact on the image of the company if it is seen to be taking its customers to court over relatively trifling amounts, not to mention the need to retain the goodwill of large customers in the longer run?

Protecting the consumer

This area of the law has grown incrementally in recent decades. The pressures, bringing a move away from the legal presumption that the consumer was king, and assumed equal to enter contracts with suppliers on the basis of independent judgements of product quality or description, included:

1 The increase in the size and power of businesses and the sophistication of the marketing techniques they could deploy provided them with an unfair advantage relative to consumers.
2 The inability of consumers to make objective purchasing judgements in the context of increasingly complex and technical products.
3 Mainly passive consumers meant that prices and products were set on the supplier's terms. Consumers, in any case, did not have the knowledge, expertise or inclination to bargain effectively.
4 Available civil law remedies were not widely known to consumers and implied potential risks and high legal costs.
5 The activism of interest groups such as the Consumers Association.

Question 7.8

Consider the above set of pressures which led to legal protection for the consumer. Go through each one and decide whether the pressures have increased, decreased or stayed the same. In the light of your assessment, is more protection required in future?

(**See** Activity debrief at the end of this unit.)

The factors influencing the ability of the consumer to make informed judgements may be seen in Figure 7.5.

Since the Fair Trading Act 1973 the British consumer has enjoyed the protection afforded by the Director-General of Fair Trading (DGFT), in effect a 'consumer watchdog'. His or her role is to gather information on the activities of suppliers, identify those detrimental to consumers and recommend action to be taken. This covers terms and conditions of sale, selling and promotional methods, packaging and supply as well as payment methods.

A permanent Office of Fair Trading (OFT) provides a pool of expertise

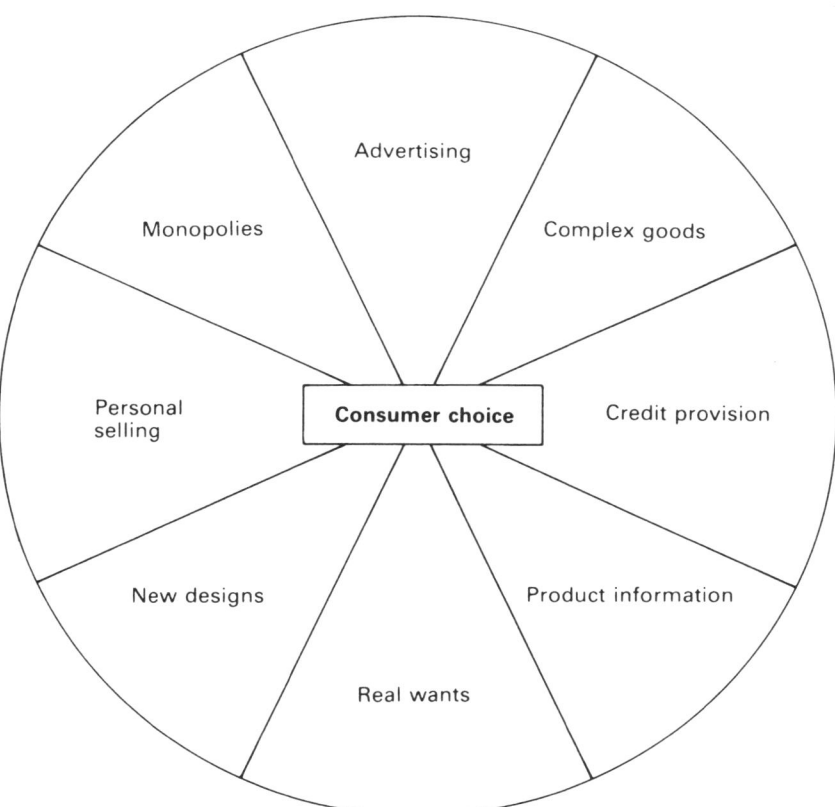

Figure 7.5 Factors influencing the consumer's judgement

and experience in consumer affairs and represents a considerable deterrent to dishonest traders. As a statutory body it can deal with suspected abuses as they arise and prosecute actions against persistent offenders on behalf of the public. Local authorities are responsible for most of the day-to-day enforcement of consumer protection legislation and their knowledge in areas such as weights and measures, trade descriptions and trading standards are complementary.

The areas where consumers require positive assurance of the good faith of suppliers are outlined below with the main corresponding legislation relating to it:

Assurance on labelling and description of goods
{ Trade Descriptions Act 1968
Weights and Measures Act 1985
Food Safety Act 1990

It is a criminal offence to falsely describe goods or services offered for sale. This applies to physical features and fitness for purpose. Similarly, prices must not be misleadingly stated.

For suppliers to defend themselves against such actions they must show that they have taken all reasonable steps to prevent the occurrence of such an offence and that it arose due to a mistake, accident, third party, information supplied or some other cause beyond the firm's control.

The other Acts govern how food can be stored, described and sold. Quantities and contents in prepackaged foods must comply with the stated amount (a current issue in this area is the labelling of genetically modified foods – see Unit 10):

Assurance on quality and expected performance
{ Sale of Goods Act 1979
Supply of Goods and Services Act 1982

Goods supplied must be as described by the vendor and of merchantable quality. This means fit for the purpose bought for with due regard to price, description and any other factor (e.g. a second-hand good could not be reasonably expected to conform to the same standards as a new one). Any consumer contract clauses intended to limit liability in this respect are void.

Similar protection is extended to services whereby consumers have a right to expect that these will be carried out with reasonable care and skill, within a reasonable time and at the agreed price, or at a reasonable charge where none was previously agreed. A recent example concerns PC manufacturers who have knowingly sold computers with 'millennium' bug (year 2000) defects. Cases are already pending in California. Compliant real time clocks have been available since 1992.

Assurance of safety
{ Consumer Protection Act 1987
Medicines Act 1968

Various Acts regulate the sale of dangerous goods in terms of availability, packaging and labelling. Retail chemists, for example, must be under the supervision of a registered pharmacist.

Product liability also comes under this heading. This is where a manufacturer can be shown to be under a duty of care to the customer, i.e. to avoid acts or omissions that could reasonably be expected to harm.

A 1985 EU directive makes producers, including importers into the European Union, liable for product defects. A defect exists if the safety of the product 'is not such as persons generally are entitled to expect'. Damage to property as well as death and personal injury are covered although each case is considered on its merits and not with hindsight.

Factors considered include the product purposes that are marketed, any warnings or instructions and what constitutes reasonable usage. The courts will also seek to balance the benefits of use of the product against the risk(s) involved.

One important defence is where the state of scientific and technical knowledge at the time was not such that the producer might have been expected to have discovered the defect.

| *Restraint of objectionable sales promotion* | { | Broadcasting Act 1990 |
| | | Food Safety Act 1990 |

Controls on advertising are to be found in a number of laws. False statements in adverts are an offence under the Trade Descriptions Act while the Broadcasting Act devolves executive power to the ITC (see page 171) whose 'voluntary' code evolves to reflect changes in public attitudes towards issues such as drink and tobacco advertising. Health warnings on cigarettes are the result of voluntary agreements between the government and the industry concerned, while the ban on poster cigarette adverts within a mile of schools is the work of the ASA. Similar bodies exist for commercial radio and cable advertisements.

Furthermore, the DGFT may seek an injunction (i.e. court order) from the High Court to prohibit false or misleading advertisements. Such systems are intended as a 'backstop', used only when other methods have either failed or are not swift enough in effect.

Extending Activity 7.4

Contact your local office of the Citizens' Advice Bureau and ask for leaflets published by the Office of Fair Trading giving information on industry codes of practice.

Assess the provision of these codes in the light of President Kennedy's consumer rights of safety/information/choice and being heard as discussed in Unit 3.

Relaxations in the ITC Code has led to previously restricted products such as condoms and sanitary products being advertised at adult viewing times. Conduct a small survey on the views of both sexes among your peer group on this issue and report on changing social attitudes and values. Consider what has been the impact on competition in these markets.

Assurance on fair payment Terms   Consumer Credit Act 1974

This Act provides comprehensive protection and enforcement on consumer credit and hire agreements. As with much of this legislation, it does not apply to corporate transactions. The main provisions include:

- The DGFT is responsible for overall supervision and enforcement.
- Disclosure of the real interest rate (the %APR) and total to be paid plus full awareness of transaction rights and liabilities (e.g. the right to repay debt early)
- A 'cooling-off' or cancellation period will apply if the credit agreement is drawn up away from the business (e.g. at home) so reducing the effectiveness of high pressure sales techniques

Question 7.9

In the light of recent scandals over misleading selling of pension policies and endowments, up-front commissions and so on, what is the appropriate response to recent surveys suggesting that 30 per cent of life insurance policies are *terminated within 2 years* at considerable financial loss to the consumer?

(**See** Activity debrief at the end of this unit.)

While consumers' awareness of their rights has increased as a result of the above legislation, considerable ignorance and lethargy still remains. Consumers often have neither the time nor the inclination fully to exercise their existing rights, especially where small-value purchases are concerned. On the other hand, suppliers are more likely to implement the letter of the law rather than risk their reputation or the wrath of the enforcement agencies. The legislation has successfully removed outright dangerous products from the market (although concerns were raised recently over firework accidents) and out-lawed dubious methods such as pyramid selling and mail order trading of unsolicited goods.

Implications for the marketer

Since the customer now has the option of settling a dispute directly with the supplier concerned or going directly to the authorities, it has forced even reputable companies to review and formalize their trading standards. Companies like Marks & Spencer who have prospered by guaranteeing quality, no-quibble exchanges and refunds, must now codify their excellence in practice. They may also be forced to resort to law to counter adverse media coverage, as in the allegation in early 1996 of the use of under-age labour by one of their Taiwanese suppliers. Individuals, often supported by pressure groups, are now bringing more civil suits on a no win–no fee basis. Recent landmark cases in the USA have seen a record $50 million settlement against Phillip Morris. The plaintiff argued that she had taken assurances from the company that there was no proven link between smoking and cancer at face value. In a similar vein, a gun manufacturer has had to pay out $4 million to a gunshot victim.

One way forward for businesses are voluntary industry codes. These are both encouraged and monitored by the authorities. Tailor-made to the needs of the industry concerned, they can be effective if membership is conditional on compliance. Normally, such codes include a means of resolving disputes with customers through a process of arbitration. They also may provide a marketing edge to participating companies where the customer looks for a mark of service or quality assurance.

Activity 7.8

Use the information you obtained on codes of practice to draw up a model for one of the following sectors:

* Estate agents
* Holiday companies
* Legal services

We can summarize some of the more important implications of this legislative environment as follows:

* Failing to comply with at least the minimum legal requirements is bad business.
* As in the case of individuals, prosecution leads to a bad public image and damage to credibility.

- Being forced to resort to law is potentially costly and time consuming.
- Systems must be in place, and staff suitably trained, to ensure compliance with existing legislation.
- Proposed legislation should be monitored and a proactive approach to implementation adopted.
- Employee legislation must also reduce the marketers' flexibility and freedom of action.
- Voluntary codes, if perceived as equitable to stakeholders, can be cost effective alternatives.
- The marketer can use superior legal standards as a source of potential competitive advantage. Compliance with exacting consumer legislation may put foreign competitors at a disadvantage in home markets, and enable successful differentiation abroad via an image of 'best practice'.

One final question to consider is whether the consumer is now overprotected. Certainly from the marketer's point of view there has been a marked increase in legal and pressure group constraints on what can and cannot be done. The legislation is unlikely to be reversed but it can be viewed *positively* in defining the areas within the boundaries of the law and voluntary good practice where the firm has *'freedom to market'*:

- It has the right to market any good or service given compliance with health and safety requirements.
- It has the freedom to price products provided it does not conspire or discriminate.
- It has discretion in the marketing and promotional mix adopted providing it does not mislead or misrepresent.

Laws therefore represent freedoms as well as constraints; rights as well as obligations.

Question 7.10

The tobacco industry has been under considerable pressure in recent years arising out of the habitual nature of consumption and its links to cancer, heart and respiratory diseases:

- If there is a proven link to these diseases why, given a rising trend of consumption among younger age groups, has not smoking been made illegal?
- Why do major retailers, who profess to be socially responsible, continue to sell such products?
- What is the legal position regarding smoking in public places? Why does the prevalence of no-smoking areas vary between public buildings, offices, shops and restaurants?

Summary

In this unit we have dealt with important aspects of the closely linked political and legal environments for marketers. They have included recognition that:

- The political process is complex but pressure points are available to business lobbies at central and local level.
- The political environment is a source of potential instability for business particularly when elections are approaching and outcomes are uncertain.
- The authority of supra-national bodies, like the EU, must now be accounted and monitored.
- The media plays an important part in setting the political agenda. The influence of lobbyists is less readily detected but of greater potential importance to business interests.
- The law represents an evolving framework to reflect societal concerns and enable commercial activities to take place in a fair but effective manner.
- There is an underlying tension between the needs of business to innovate and deploy resources efficiently over time, and the health, safety and equitable treatment of various stakeholders.

- Quasi-legal means of regulation, such as codes of practice, serve an important function.
- There are many considerations to weigh before an organization initiates legal proceedings.

Activity debrief

Definition 7.1 6, 2, 5, 7, 3, 1, 4.
Definition 7.2 4, 1, 5, 3, 2, 7, 6, 8.
Question 7.1 Think about office politics and positioning for promotions and perks. Departmental conflicts arise over resources and priorities. The quality press and periodicals like *The Economist* and *Newsweek*. Trade associations and lobbyists.
Question 7.2 Think in terms of product positioning, 'value for voting' and differentiation (of manifestos and policies, i.e. clear blue water between the parties).
Question 7.3

Case for	*Case against*
Coalition government produces continuity of policies	Allows a strong government to take bold initiatives
Avoids short-term focus on the next election	Coalitions lead to compromise Too many small parties
Moderate consensus policies avoids the extremes	Government more susceptible to pressure groups
Avoidance of extreme swings in government enables planning	Strong link MP – constituency

Question 7.4
- Don't be rushed – no obligation to give interview there and then!
- Don't start an interview until you know why, why *you*, who is calling, which paper, how long, what's wanted
- Don't do it there and then – phone back
- Gather your thoughts – take advice
- Prepare a statement if you are suspicious of their motives
- Don't answer leading or hypothetical questions
- Keep it short and to the point. Be polite and positive
- Don't make off-the-record comments.

Question 7.5 This might include the requirement for public liability insurance, laws governing the use of public transport, road traffic laws, health and safety at work, employment protection law including discrimination, unfair dismissal, sexual harassment and equal pay. If you go shopping then a whole battery of legislation will apply if you feel unreasonably treated.

Question 7.6 Excessive, unnecessary and often complicated formalities involved in government regulations.

Question 7.7 Design (environmental standards), development (patents), promotion (trade descriptions), information systems (Data Protection Act), operations (health and safety), transportation (lorry sizes/tachographs), customers (sale of goods), public (public liability), businesses (agency agreements), employees (employment protection), local authorities (planning) and shareholders (Companies Act).

Question 7.8 In Britain it could be argued that:
1 has increased subject to increased regulation;
2 little improved although the internet might assist;
3 decreased as consumers more educated/aware of rights but companies have more information to underpin bargaining;
4 remedies might be better known but legal risks remain;
5 increased with more media coverage. Legislation is increasingly EU driven and aims to raise standards to those practised by the best companies.

Question 7.9 With such a high rate of terminations it begs the question that many policies were sold to people for whom they were not suitable or really wanted. You might therefore consider that much more and clearer information should be given to potential customers, including the likelihood and cost of early cancellation. Consultation with the industry to ensure workability would probably be advisable.

Extending Activity 7.2 A business person could stand for the council, cooperate with initiatives, be a member of a Training and Education Council, establish relationships with local schools and colleges, etc.

Activity 7.5 Virtues include: flexibility – adapt to changing needs; quicker response; balance of interests likely; less red tape; association with accreditation/trustworthiness; participation in formulation – more likely to adhere; less costly procedures; members have a say; exclusion/expulsion are credible threats for compliance; self-policing so saves taxpayer funds; threat of legislation if not effective. Drawbacks include: no legal recourse; expensive redress for the consumer; observance only as good as weakest member – may drive down standards; expulsion often a very last resort; favours self-interest of the association; may use as a protection device against entrants; it may slow innovation.

Examination hints and specimen questions

Given the number of questions on the paper as a whole, you cannot guarantee that a full question will always come up on this environment. There is a strong likelihood, however, that it would form at least part of a question should this be the case. The examiner will be aware that candidates come from different national backgrounds and will set questions accordingly. The focus is much more likely to be on the impact of this environment on marketing than on political or legal specifics. The examiner has the option of setting a question which asks candidates to relate to their own country's position, so care must be taken to become knowledgeable in this area.

1 'There should be freedom to advertise anything which it is legal to market.'
   (a) Debate this statement **either** for tobacco products **or** for any alternative product currently subject to challenge by socially concerned pressure groups. (11 marks)
   (b) Briefly compare the merits of the following methods of regulating tobacco sales:
     (i) voluntary codes
     (ii) taxation
     (iii) legislation (9 marks)
           (CIM Marketing Environment paper, December 1997)

2 Using a country of your own choice:

   (a) Explain what you mean by the legislative environment. (6 marks)
   (b) Supply your Marketing Manager with a summary of how legislation contributes to fair trading between businesses and:
     (i) consumers
     (ii) other businesses (14 marks)
           (CIM Marketing Environment paper, June 1997)

3 Produce a series of slides for a Trade Association presentation, describing the current effects of **four** of the following macro-environment influences on the transport and distribution industry:

   (a) social and demographic trends
   (b) environmental pressures
   (c) new technology
   (d) market forces
   (e) political and legislative trends (20 marks)
           (CIM Marketing Environment paper, December 1996)

Note how this question embraces not only the main macro-environments, but also the market environment in the shape of market forces. It is a good example of a question set at the very general appreciation level. With four environments to cover you clearly only have time for an outline of points.

Question 1(a)

- This is a challenging but topical question using a quotation which sets the rights of business and the individual against those of society as a whole.
- Be careful to provide a debate format, i.e objective debating of points for or against the proposition.
- Beware of personalizing or making unsupported assertions.
- Make clear at the outset whether you are dealing with a tobacco context.
- The debate should combine political, legal and socially responsible points.

Question 1(b)

- This is a straight forward comparison of *merits*.
- With only 9 marks available focus on bullet points – brief format!
- Use the word 'compare' – legislation removes freedom of choice compared to paying more tax.
- Relate your points to the tobacco context.

Question 2(a)

- With 6 marks available only an outline of salient points is possible.
- Define the legal framework, state the purpose/objectives and relate to environmental impacts.

Question 2(b)

- There will be marks available for implementing the summary format.
- The question provides a choice between discussing fair trade in terms of competition law (Unit 4) and consumer law.
- Refer to some of the relevant statutes but concentrate on assessing contribution to fair trading.

Question 3

- The format is very important in this question – provide the content within a slide format which could be used in such a presentation.
- Remember that the content earns most of the marks and focus on *effects*.
- Examples could involve devolution/effects of Scottish tax-raising powers; impact of new Food Agency; Challenge of Europe initiative; new competition act/OFT powers effects on prices.
- Refer to Unit 3 for environmental pressures; Unit 8 for social/demographic and Unit 9 for technical.

The demographic, social and cultural environment

In this important and challenging unit you will:

❏ Appreciate the fundamental importance of population trends to market analysis.

❏ Consider the implications of change in the structure of the population.

❏ Review the shifting patterns of employment and identify those with particular significance for marketing.

❏ Briefly examine the emerging role of women in work.

❏ Assess the cause and effects of social changes.

❏ Relate specific social influences to segmentation.

❏ Examine the meaning and importance of cultural change.

By the end of this unit you will:

❏ Have acquired an insight into key demographic changes and their marketing implications.

❏ Recognized the inter-relatedness of the socio-cultural environments.

❏ Appreciate the processes leading to the development of social and cultural values.

❏ Understand and apply concepts such as lifestyle, reference groups and social class.

❏ Have considered emerging trends and their potential impact on the marketer.

Study Guide

A knowledge and understanding of demography and socio-cultural change is vital if the marketer is to truly appreciate the origins of buyer behaviour. Both evolve very slowly but their cumulative impact on market realities over time is considerable. Real living standards in the longer term are more likely to be determined by population changes, for example, than the economic policy making of governments.

Change in this environment is the most difficult to assess, yet the opportunities presented must be grasped and exploited by the marketer. The relevant variables are interrelated, thereby making it difficult to understand the contribution of any one element. As we will see, much that is important in this environment is often unspoken and unwritten, making it one of the greatest challenges to the marketing practitioner.

As a member of society you will be able to identify with much of the content of this unit. It is shorter than the previous two units but no less important as far as examination content is concerned. Accounting for just under 10 per cent of the total syllabus, this should normally be a reliable source of a part or whole examination question.

Spend 2–3 hours studying this unit and 3–4 hours addressing the various questions and activities. You should sub-section your file into demographic, social and cultural segments. There is less continuous coverage of this environment than the economic but what there is tends to be very business related. Just as *The Economist* is a useful weekly periodical for the economic, so *New Society* is the equivalent for the social. The Office of National Statistics (ONS) also publishes *Social Trends* (useful articles on current population trends) and the census is available on CD-ROM.

Trends in population

Demography is the study of population trends and is important to the marketer because of its concern with the size, structure, composition and characteristics of the population. Segmentation and the assessment of market potential is clearly related to the analysis of such factors but for a specific target population. The ONS publishes detailed population statistics derived from full censuses every ten years, and updating sample surveys every five years. The last full census was in 1991 and businesses may supplement the data obtained with targeted surveys of their own.

The important trends to appreciate include changes in:

- The context of world population
- Developed as against less-developed country growth rates
- The future size of a population
- The age and gender structure of a population
- Its distribution by region and locality
- Migration within and between national borders
- The impact on world resources and the physical environment

Activity 8.1

You must become familiar with both the structure of, and the change in, your national population. Use the resources of your local or college library to prepare a revision brief on the following:

- Total population, current and trend rate of change
- Age, gender, marital status and location of population
- Occupational structure and ethnic mix
- Significant trends in structure (e.g. ageing, urbanization, etc.)

(Hint: Browse through the charts and tables in *Social Trends* or its equivalent)

The implications of population trends to the marketer are felt:

- On the aggregate demand for goods and services
- On the demand side, in the size of different market segments
- On the supply side, in the availability of labour
- On the mix of public services required
- On the taxation impact of the dependent population
- On living standards – GDP divided by the total population
- On the distribution of demand – by region/locality

One of the most significant trends in mature industrial economies, for example, is the ageing of the population structure. Japan, Europe and, to a lesser extent, the USA are facing a sharp increase in the proportion of pensioners in the new millennium. Falling birth rates, greater longevity and the ageing of earlier baby booms are combining to 'grey' the population and shift the centre of gravity of spending power in the economies affected.

Old, but still fit, healthy and relatively *affluent* pensioners will become the norm in future rather than the old-age pensioner (OAP) image still prevalent today. Better educated, better off and better informed than their forebears, they will command considerable purchasing power. Given current trends by 2050 there will be some 70 million West Europeans aged 65+, representing over 20 per cent of the population. In Britain there are forecast to be more over 65s than under 16s by the year 2016. Only greater longevity is preventing declining populations in many parts of Europe.

Question 8.1

Taking a local company such as Saga Holidays in Britain (specializing in holidays for the over-60s) or McCarthy & Stone (building retirement complexes), suggest how and why their marketing mix may have to be modified to meet the needs of those in the next century.

(**See** Activity debrief at the end of this unit.)

The dependency ratio

This is the ratio of the number of dependents in the population relative to the working population. It is the latter who create the nation's material wealth and so support the non-working population either directly or through tax transfers. Figure 8.1 shows an improvement in the ratio until around 2010, when lower birth rates will combine with retirement of the post-war baby boomers.

This will be good news on the unemployment and career advancement fronts with opportunities for promotion, but bad news on taxation since real resources will need to be diverted to support those no longer contributing productively to society. (Labour market entrants face the burden of personal pension contributions and higher education fees and loan re-payments.) Health services will need to expand continuously in real terms especially as life expectancies keep on rising. Health expenditure for the over-65s is already 4 times the average for the under-65s, while for the over-75s it is 8 times. Life expectancy has risen to over 75 for men and 79 for women, but the 'healthy life expectancy', before a limiting long-term illness is suffered, is stable at 59 and 62 respectively. The proportion of over-75s has already increased from 4 per cent to 7 per cent since the mid-1960s.

Question 8.2

What is the dependency ratio in your economy? In Singapore, for example, how is it affected by the ethnic mix?

What are the implications of dependency ratios for

- Your own marketing career?
- Sectors offering the greatest marketing opportunities?
- Your company?
- Recruiting marketing personnel?

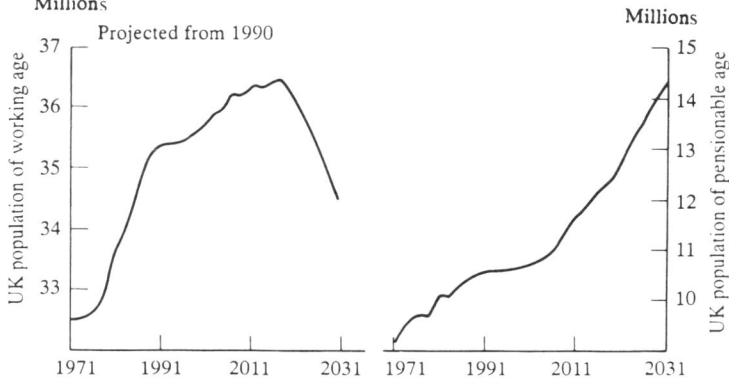

Figure 8.1
UK population of working age and pensionable age in millions (projected from 1990). (*Source*: OPCS)

187

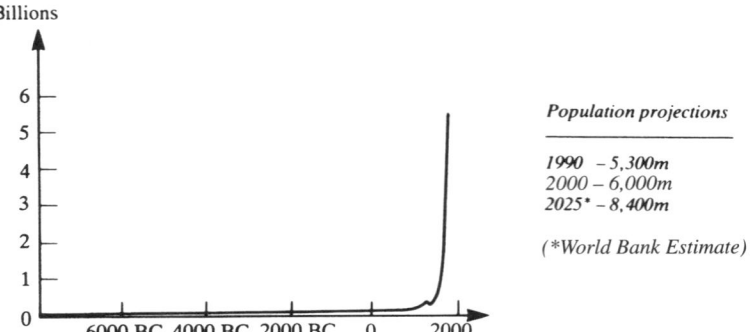

Figure 8.2
World population growth

Billions

Population projections
1990 – 5,300m
2000 – 6,000m
2025* – 8,400m

(*World Bank Estimate)

Before moving on to consider other demographic aspects you must note that the age, gender and location of a target population is only one of the factors relevant to marketers. The fall in the number of births would seem to be a serious development for manufacturers dependent on this segment. Silver Cross, for example, makers of quality prams, might have been expected to lose sales volume. In practice, married couples, who were now delaying births were more likely to spend more on their fewer offspring, and with established careers, could afford to do so. On the other hand, rising car ownership was shifting preferences towards a dual-purpose carrycot/pram, probably causing the demise of the company in 1999. The marketer must therefore take nothing for granted in this complex area.

World population

Global population has grown exponentially over the last two or three centuries, as Figure 8.2 shows. Stability up to around AD 1000 was replaced with progressively rising rates, especially with industrialization and advances in health care and hygiene.

As industrial economies matured, however, they enjoyed a *demographic transition* whereby customarily high birth rates fell to levels closer to already-reduced death rates. This process has yet to be completed in many less-developed countries, especially in Africa, meaning that world population will continue to rise, at a reducing rate, at least until the middle of the next century. On the other hand, the Aids epidemic is reducing life expectancy thereby neutralizing some of this growth.

Less-developed countries therefore account for a steadily increasing proportion of total population while the already industrialized will shrink from 25 per cent to 17 per cent by 2025. Such trends have raised the spectre of T. R. Malthus, who predicted a 'dismal' outcome some 200 years ago. He suggested that if food production grows arithmetically (i.e. 1–2–3–4) while population grows geometrically (i.e. 2–4–8–16) then crisis was inevitable. In the absence of voluntary preventative measures to restrict population (e.g. China's one child policy) then equilibrium could only be restored by positive checks such as war, disease, pestilence and famine.

Question 8.3

How did developed economies avoid Malthus's dismal predictions? Think about factors that shift out the production possibility curve when trying to answer this.

Do the same arguments apply to less-developed economies today and what are the implications for the international marketer? Is there such a thing as an optimum level of population?

(**See** Activity debrief at the end of this unit.)

Aggregate population

The record in population forecasting has been remarkably inaccurate, especially as regards births which tend to fluctuate quite considerably. As can be seen in Figure 8.3, births vary significantly compared to deaths. The

United Kingdom

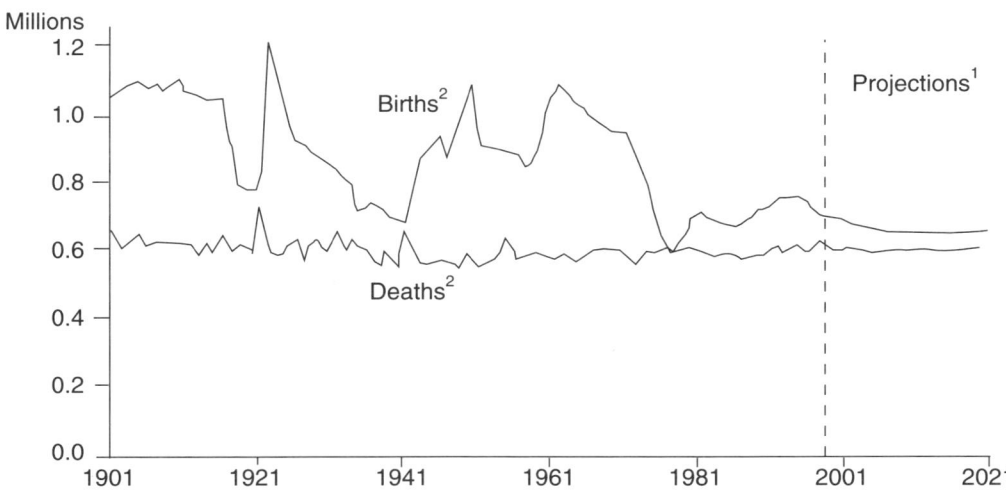

1 1996-based projections
2 Data for 1901 to 1921 exclude the Irish Republic which was constitutionally a part of the United Kingdom
during this period

Figure 8.3 Births and deaths. (*Source*: Office for National Statistics; Government Actuary's Department; General Register Office for Scotland; Northern Ireland Statistics and Research Agency

recent rise in the 1990s could be projected based on a peak occurring about 28 years previously. This means more women of childbearing age since the average age when giving birth to a first child in Britain is currently 28 and rising. On this basis, the steady rise in births from 1997 is set to continue falling back to a low in around 2005.

Population growth = birth rate – death rate + net migration

Total population is currently around 58.8 million but with a rate of increase now of under 0.3 per cent per annum it is only forecast to rise to 61 million by 2012. Population in the EU has grown by 17 per cent in the last 35 years to 373 million, but with the average European woman of childbearing age producing only 1.7 children, while 2.1 is required to replace the population, the long-run trend could be downward.

Exam Tip	*Did you know?*

Did you know?
If the German fertility rate remained at its recent level of only 1.3, its native population would actually become extinct by around 2300. Italy's fertility rate has been even lower!

Net migration is now negative due to tightened inward restrictions and a continuous trickle outwards to Commonwealth countries and Europe. Known as the 'brain drain', the latter have tended to be young, enterprising and often disillusioned but highly skilled workers. Births per 1000 of the population have recovered from the low in 1977 and exceed deaths by a small margin.

While the crude death rate has been relatively predictable, the age-specific death rate, defined as the number of people (per 1000) of a particular age cohort that die in a year, is falling, especially for women. The life insurance industry is built on this reliability with actuaries establishing probabilities to determine risk premiums for various customer age groups. The marketer must, however, always be alert to the possibility of unexpected rises in the death rate, whether due to new contagious illnesses, environmental deterioration (e.g. skin and other carcinogens from ozone depletion and pollution) or higher fuel prices.

189

Extending Activity 8.1

Account for demographic transition to lower fertility rates (defined as the total births per 1000 women aged 15–44 years).

You should consider a PEST framework for explaining this and relate it to the experience in your own country. Undertaking this activity will also give you an insight into the importance of socio-cultural factors which are considered later in the unit.

(**See** Activity debrief at the end of this unit.)

A couple's decision to have one more or less child to complete the family is a marginal one for them but will have compounded effects if repeated across the age group. Medical and genetic breakthroughs which may provide the ability to both determine sex at conception and eradicate defects may, if legalized, have far-reaching implications for future births.

Population structure

While aggregate population may be stable this can seldom be said for the various segments that can be identified. The dimensions of a population structure include:

- Age
- Gender
- Marital status
- Region
- Ethnic group
- Occupation

The age and gender distribution in Britain may be seen in Figure 8.4. The indentations are significant, as we have seen already, for the economy in general and specific markets in particular. Change the base line to 10 and it indicates the numbers in each cohort as of 1998.

Activity 8.2

Study the histogram in Figure 8.4 or derive one for your own economy. Note that a developing economy will tend to have a broader base, due to higher birth rates, and a narrower neck, due to lower life expectancy arising from less mature health and welfare systems.

What marketing opportunities or threats will be faced by the following:

- A recording company?
- A university?
- A firm of undertakers?
- A cosmetic surgeon?
- Private health insurers?

One implication of Britain's ageing population is the corresponding shrinkage in the number of school-leavers by nearly a quarter to 1996. The impact of this so-called 'demographic timebomb' has been much reduced in Britain by the effects of recession, investment in technology and contraction in the armed forces. However, many businesses, particularly services, responded positively to economic upturn and the prospect of future labour shortages. East Asian economies have also had to deal with tightening labour markets until recently by:

- Greater marketing of the business and its prospects to potential recruits
- Building closer links with local educational establishments
- Tapping alternative workgroups using flexible employment patterns
- Internal marketing for retention, retraining and promotion

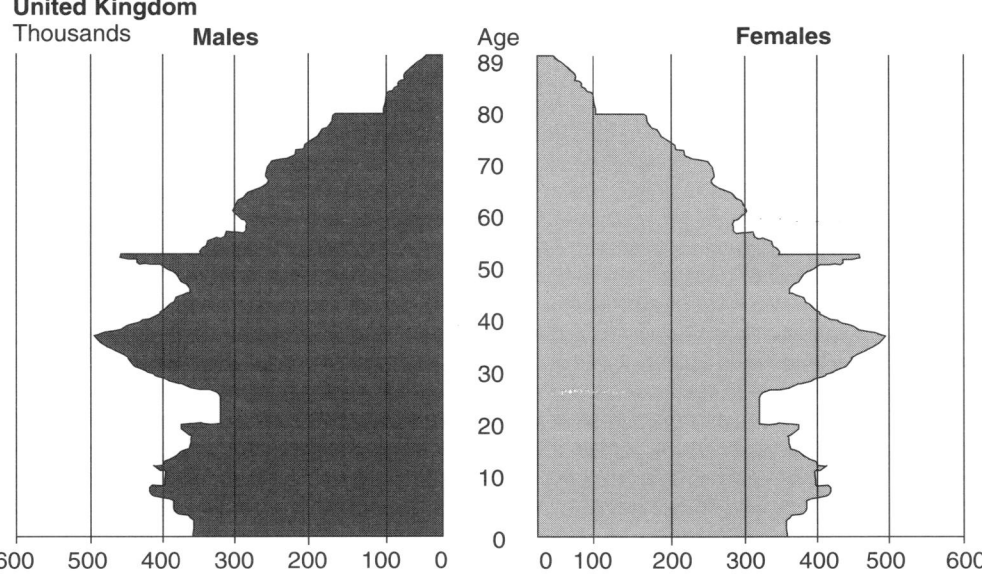

Figure 8.4 Britain's population structure, 1988 estimate. (*Sources*: OPCS, *The Economist*)

- Improving pay and incentives especially for flexibility
- Considering offshore production.
- Selective immigration.

Exam Tip	This environment of social and demographic change offers the examiner a fertile area of trends and changes upon which to build compulsory questions. An example has therefore been provided in the examination section at the end of the unit. So make sure you are aware of the key changes.

Figure 8.5 shows clearly how employers will compensate for contraction in the under-25s by increased employment of married women and older age groups. Women will account for 46 per cent of the workforce by 2006, according to the latest edition of *Social Trends*. Many school-leavers have opted to enter higher education in recent years as a result of planned expansion and the absence of attactive job opportunities elsewhere. This near-doubling, to a third (and more promised by New Labour), implies a

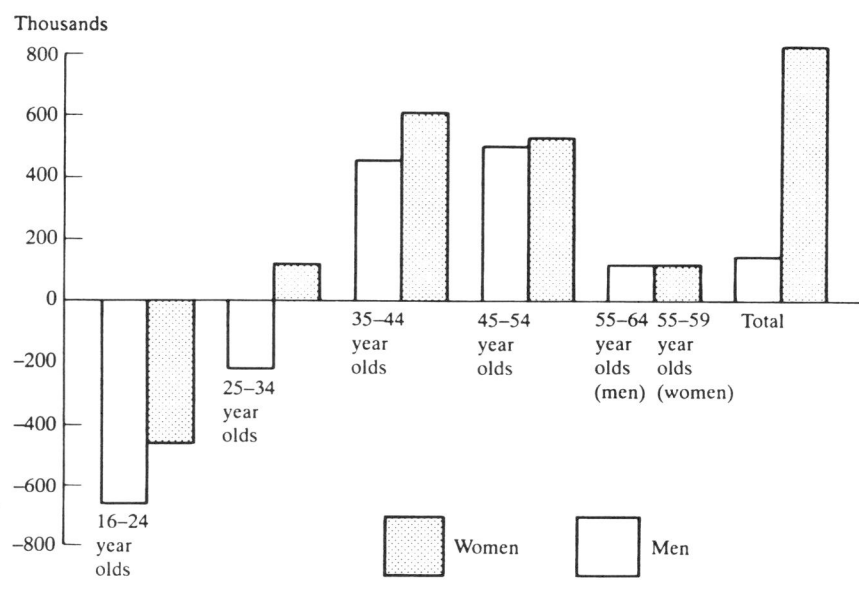

Figure 8.5
Projected change in the UK civilian labour force of working age, 1989–2027. (*Source*: Department of Employment)

much better qualified and well-informed consumer group in future. It may also lead other European Union countries, affected by falling births, to recruit qualified staff from Britain as their economies recover.

The youth-orientated society of Britain in the 1960s is giving way to a more conservative middle-aged culture in the late 1990s. With an average age around 40 and rising and the number of retired about to boom worldwide to an estimated 600 million, the face of marketing is bound to be affected.

Question 8.4

What product values and characteristics will be central to an effective marketing strategy focused on the over-45s?
(**See** Activity debrief at the end of this unit.)

As the old become more numerous, better educated and live longer, so their political and economic power will increase. Financially well endowed and with a greater propensity to vote, they will exert more pressure on decision makers as well as constituting an important but discerning market segment. The marketer must also recognize, however, that the retired at present also include among the poorest in society, with nearly 2 million qualifying for supplementary benefits and a further 1 million qualifying but not taking it up. Also, many of the supposedly attractive 'empty nesters' have ageing relatives to support which may curtail their ability to consume. On the other hand, nursing homes may be the grateful beneficiaries.

Marital status and household structure

This is undergoing considerable change in Britain due to later marriage, rising divorce rates and remarriages. As we have seen, the fertility rate has fallen below the replacement ratio of 2:1, causing the traditional marketer's assumption of 2 adults + 2 children to become the exception rather than the norm.

Divorce rates of 40 per cent in Britain are the highest in Western Europe especially among those marrying young. Earlier marriages have fallen sharply in recent years but cohabitation has increased, as have illegitimate births. Remarriages, already accounting for a third of the annual total, and may produce 'composite' family groups, combining different children and ages from previous unions. The rise in single households is accounted for by the rising number of elderly, greater independence among the young, people staying single for longer, and rising divorce rates. This clearly forms a complicated tapestry for marketing analysis, but also a rich seam of potential segmentation.

Activity 8.3

Analyse Table 8.1 and suggest marketing implications that may arise.

Table 8.1   Percentages of people living in different households (UK)

Households, %

	Married couple*	Cohabiting couple*	Lone parent	Other multiperson	One person	All house-holds***
Estimates						
1971	71	1	2	7	18	15,942
1981	64	3	4	7	23	17,306
1991	55	6	5	7	27	19,215
Projections**						
1996	51	7	6	7	29	20,177
2001	49	7	6	8	31	21,046
2006	46	7	6	8	33	21,897
2011	44	7	6	9	35	22,769
2016	42	7	5	9	36	23,598

*With or without children. **1992 based projections. ***Thousands
Sources: ONS, *General Household Survey.*

(**See** Activity debrief at the end of the unit)

Regional distribution

The marketer must be aware of the shifting distribution of population across regions and localities arising from both natural increase and net migration. The broad movement affecting all industrialized societies has been the steady drift from rural to urban living. Economic decline and depopulation has left a relatively old and poor residue in many parts of the North, Wales and Scotland. For example, overall population in the UK has risen 11 per cent over the last 35 years, whereas Scotland's has actually fallen by 1 per cent.

There has also been reverse flow from the inner cities to suburbia and, more recently, the ribbons of development along the motorway and rail routes radiating away from city centres. As young couples move into these dormitory urban fringes to escape either inner-city decay or rural remoteness, so births increase to reinforce the process. East Anglia in particular has registered an annual growth of over 1 per cent while the major conurbations, including London, have lost 0.5 per cent per annum for two decades now.

Despite a near-static population overall, redistribution will continue along similar lines. The marketer must also identify where target populations reside, especially the retired, with localities on the South and South-west coasts benefiting significantly. The rise in single households is also putting pressure on rural land with 4.5 million new homes projected to be required by 2010. A new town is already being planned in Hampshire, for example.

Question 8.5

In Britain, one-third of the population live in the South-east while only one-sixth inhabit the much larger areas of Wales, Scotland and Northern Ireland combined. In the light of this or similar disparities in your own country, assess the implications for marketers seeking to serve the needs of these populations.

(**See** Activity debrief at the end of this unit.)

Ethnic groups

Many populations are diverse in their origins and therefore their buying patterns. Countries like Malaysia and Singapore will have a strong mix of Malay and Chinese, while Britain reflects its European and Commonwealth heritage. Ethnic minorities account for around 5 per cent of the total with Indians, West Indians and Pakistanis comprising the largest groups but with Chinese, Africans, Bangladeshis and Arabs well represented.

These groups tend to be younger than the indigenous white population with only 4 per cent over 60 (compared to 21 per cent). This produces a very different pattern of needs which must be accounted for by marketers and local authorities alike. Where ethnic concentrations occur (e.g. London and the South East at 9 per cent) the number of births have therefore been more buoyant than elsewhere, although West Indian experience, the oldest New Commonwealth immigrant group, exhibits rates little different to the overall average.

Question 8.6

Why have ethnic minority-owned businesses been able to exploit profitable niche markets among these populations without attracting substantial competition from established businesses?

(**See** Activity debrief at the end of this unit.)

Occupational structure

At the outset of the Industrial Revolution over 60 per cent of the employed workforce were engaged in the *primary sectors* of agriculture, forestry, fishing, mining and quarrying. A century of industrialization saw 60 per cent in the *secondary sector* of manufacturing, construction and utilities such as electricity. By 1980 a further transformation had occurred, with over 60 per cent employed in the *tertiary sector*, including transport, financial, retail and personal services.

The current position is shown in Table 8.2 with a significant contraction in both primary and manufacturing industries. Indeed, Professor Stonier, in his book *The Wealth of Information*, predicted continuing contraction in manufacturing to half the 1992 total by the year 2000.

Table 8.2   Employment status by industry group

Britain (%) Industry group	Self-employed			Employees		
	Men	Women	All	Men	Women	All
Primary, energy and extractive	11	7	10	10	3	6
Manufacturing	11	9	10	26	12	19
Construction	27	2	21	7	2	5
Services	51	81	59	57	83	69
All industries (thousands = 100%)	2321	770	3091	11,182	10,171	21,353

Source: *Labour Force Survey*, Autumn 1992.

The workforce in employment

This has been relatively stable over the three decades to 1996 but with deep recessions in 1980–1983, and 1990–1993, when it fell to 23 and 24.25 million respectively. Between 1983 and mid-1991, however, over 3 million net new jobs were created, contributing to an overall rise of 6 per cent over the last decade. By 1999 it stood at a record 27.3 million, and is projected to increase further with two-thirds of the growth being part-time women.

Manufacturing employment has continued to contract to under 4 million while service employment has been creating net new jobs throughout.

There are now over 12 million women (46 per cent of the total) in the workforce and increasing relative to male employment. This reflects the decline in full-time industrial employment where men predominate and the rise of services and part-time work, where women are mainly found. Forty-eight per cent of women as against just 12 per cent of men work part-time. The latter percentage is, however, rising as male employment attitudes alter.

The increase in jobs as Britain recovered from recession has been in part-time employment. Over the decade, part-time employment has risen by a dramatic 43 per cent while full-time has contracted, little wonder that male part-timers have nearly doubled while female part-timers rose by a third.

One revealing employment trend is shown in Figure 8.6. There has been a dramatic decline in labour market participation among the over-50s males. The proportion of 50–64-year olds outside the working population has risen sharply from 12.5 per cent to 27.5 per cent. Older people have been targeted for employment in the retail sector due to their skills and experience, relatively high regard for customer service and stability. The government has demonstrated concern by introducing a credit scheme for helping over-50s back into work. However, its scale pales next to the £5 billion devoted to the current five-year New Deal Welfare to Work Programme for the under-24 long-term unemployed.

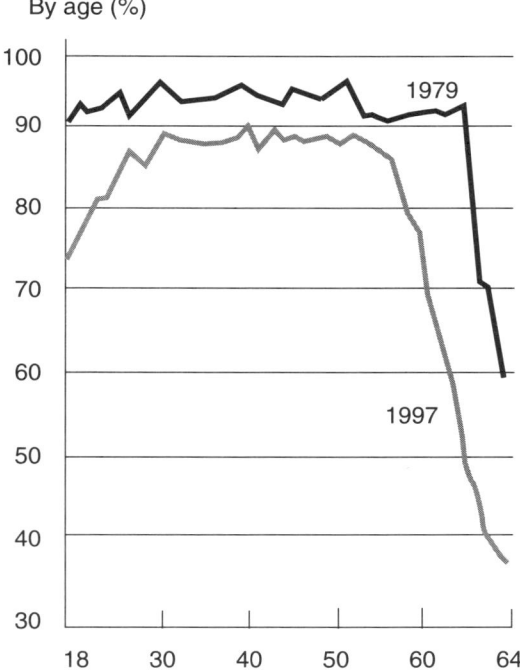

By age (%)

Figure 8.6
Male employment rates

Question 8.7

Normally as an economy emerges from a deep recession there is a long lag before unemployment falls. Employers are cautious about the outlook and prefer to use existing resources more intensively.

In the light of the recent rises in part-time employment, what are the attractions of this mode of work to:

- The business?
- The employee?
- The government?

How might recent legal developments affect this assessment?
What are the implications for marketing of these work patterns?

(**See** Activity debrief at the end of this unit.)

Some important employment trends

We have already identified a number of important developments:

- *The decline in full-time employment* The 'norm' of a 9a.m.–5p.m. 40-hour week may cease to be the norm in the new century.
- *The corresponding rise of part-time employment* This has risen from just under 5 per cent to nearly 30 per cent of all employment in just 25 years.
- *Hours are lengthening for those working full-time* A quarter of all males work over 50 hours, against just 5 per cent of females – 48 hour week legislation will affect this.
- *Self-employment is rising* The percentage has risen sharply to 12 per cent in recent years and is projected to increase by a quarter in the next decade. The incidence varies widely between industries, being especially high in building and construction. Hotels and catering are understandably above average while manufacturing records only half the overall rate. Table 8.2 reflects this distribution as well as the predominance of services for women.

Activity 8.4

Conduct a survey of men and women who are self-employed to ascertain the following:

- What are the main reasons for being self-employed?
- Are there any differences in the reasons given by those recently becoming self-employed?
- Are there difference between reasons given by men and women?

(**See** Activity debrief at the end of this unit.)

- *A rise in contractual and temporary employment* As many businesses have faced an increasingly competitive environment in recent years they have been forced to concentrate on core activities. Unless specialized resources can be fully utilized it has become more efficient to contract-out services or contract-in labour as and when required. The convenience of a large directly employed labour force has become a luxury not even the public sector can afford. Transport and distribution may be contracted-out to third-party operators while specialized marketing skills are hired or 'outsourced' through agencies as and when required.
- *The emergence of flexible organizations* Charles Handy in his book *The Age of Unreason* suggests that more and more organizations employ *a core* of full-time scientific, technical, marketing and managerial employees with company-specific skills and proprietary knowledge to coordinate and direct the fundamental activities of the business. A flexible workforce is utilized to achieve this, composed of readily adjustable groups including:

  High turnover semi-skilled full-timers
  Part-timers
  Temporary workers
  Job sharers
  Staff on short or temporary contracts
  Student industrial placements
  Government trainees
  Homeworkers
  Subcontractors

- *The rise of the knowledge worker* Under 45 per cent of the total employed are now officially classified as manual. Since only a third of those employed in manufacturing are likely to be on the shopfloor, well over half of the workforce may now be designated as knowledge workers. This includes those occupations that produce, process, use and distribute knowledge as well as maintain the infrastructure for its transmission. Since most jobs will require brains rather than brawn in the next century, the government is belatedly expanding vocational and higher education in an effort to avert critical skill shortages from inhibiting high-technology growth opportunities. With the Japanese pattern of educating virtually all its highly motivated 18-year-olds being emulated by the other emerging countries of East Asia, they appear potentially much better equipped to effect the transition to post-industrial society than is the case in Britain. Malaysia, for example, aims to have tripled its students on scientific and technical courses by the year 2000. New Labour has responded by reviving its 'lifelong learning' scheme especially that based around computer literacy.

Activity 8.5

Classify all of the people working in your organization into manual or knowledge workers using the criteria given above.

You will find that it is not so easy in practice since most jobs have some knowledge components involved in them.

- *Flexible work lives* The need for flexibility to match working hours to operational requirements in business today is producing a kaleidoscope of working patterns for the marketer to observe:

Flexitime enabling employees to plan their own time allocation

Staggered hours lengthening but spreading the 'rush hours'

Flexible work years to match seasonal patterns of activity to personal circumstances of key staff

Flexible shifts and rosters to effectively cover customer service requirements

Longer days but shorter weeks to maximize actual working time

2 × 12-hour weekend shifts to maximize utilization of plant

Planned reduction in hours towards retirement

Working from home telecommuting through office computer intranet links.

Use of such flexibility, especially when combined with part-time work, can produce higher productivity, lower turnover and absence rates and much reduced costs. It is not surprising that many employers are recruiting women returners to meet their staffing needs.

This flexibility is in both employee and business interests. It is underpinning much less standardized life styles and demanding a marketing response to cater for three day weekends, all-night and even all-day entertainment as well as the late-night banking and retailing we increasingly take for granted.

- *The self-service economy* Non-standard work patterns imply non-standard leisure patterns and more of this leisure time is being absorbed doing tasks which were previously undertaken by business. Self-service is already well established on much of the high street while home-shopping cable and video systems take the process one step further. Interactive computer systems linked to databases offer dramatic potential to transform the way in which many services are currently marketed, sold and performed. Home banking, direct insurance and distance learning are just a sample of leading-edge applications.

The changing role of women in work and society

The situation of men and women at work in Britain during the 1990s remained very much one where the different genders are employed in different sectors, different industries, different occupations and different levels in the hierarchy. Women usually have family responsibilities yet over half now go out to work, at least part-time. Domestic duties combine to ensure that they often work harder (an estimated 10 hours a week on average) but they are promoted less often and are generally less well paid than male counterparts. Despite a four-point improvement since 1987, women in Britain earn, on average, only 77 per cent of men's wages. This is up to 10 percentage points less than in most other European countries. The gap is even greater in terms of weekly pay because men generally work longer hours, attracting overtime rates.

Women are under-represented in manufacturing but dominate in many of the expanding service industries. Caring occupations such as health and primary education register a ratio of 80:20 in favour of women overall but, interestingly, men still dominate the top positions.

The rising proportion of women in higher education, to nearly half by

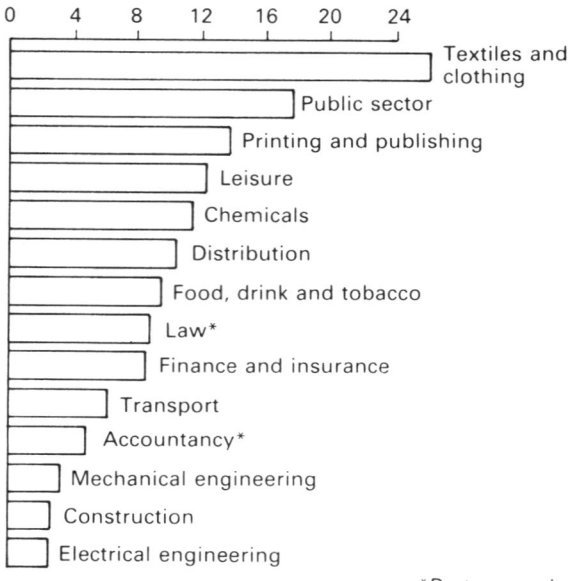

Figure 8.7

Percentage of British managers who are women (by industry). (*Sources*: British Institute of Management; *Remuneration Economics*)

the 1990s, has contributed to an improvement in their representation in managerial and professional occupations. This is now over 25 per cent but is not reflected in senior management, where they form just 2–3 per cent of the membership of large company boards. This is highlighted in Figures 8.7 and 8.8, which also show women predominating in people- or service-centred staff functions rather than line positions, contributing directly to profitability.

Activity 8.6

- Identify the areas, in an organization of your choice, in which women appear to be under-represented.
- Investigate the causes of this situation.
- Consider the ingredients of a 'positive action plan' to improve the utilization of women in the organization.

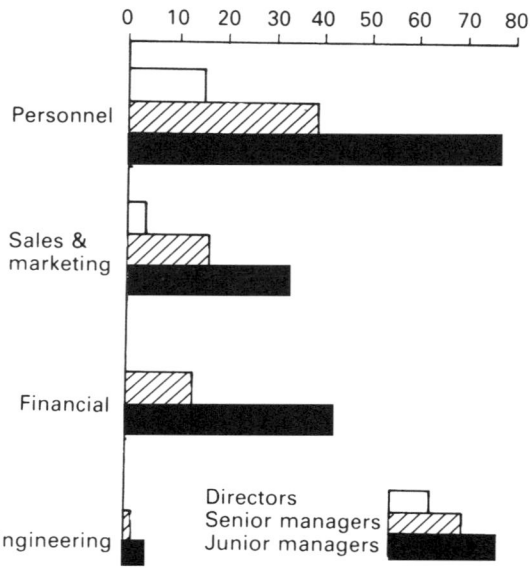

Figure 8.8 Percentage of British managers who are women (by function and status). (*Sources*: British Institute of Management; *Remuneration Economics*)

Since women already account for half of the educated workforce and form the only credible source of untapped labour potential, how should business respond? Relatively high unemployment may have relieved the pressure until recently, but sustained growth has begun to expose critical shortages. The British government showed its concern by launching Opportunity 2000, an initiative encouraging major organizations to set targets for employing more women in senior positions by the end of the decade. This included the NHS, largely run by men but with women comprising 80 per cent of its 1 million workers. New Labour's attempt to introduce 'all women' lists for selecting Parliamentary candidates, however, fell foul of sexual discrimination legislation although over 100 female MPs were returned at the 1997 election. The policy responses have included:

- Career break keep-in-touch schemes
- Flexible working patterns
- Women-friendly recruitment, selection, appraisal and promotion procedures
- Attitude retraining and training in 'core' activities
- Common pay and conditions – equal reward for work of equal value.

It must be recognized, however, that the Civil Service adopted similar policies some years ago to allow women to mix family and career. The result has been an actual decline in those prepared to dedicate themselves to get to the top. One of the main comparative advantages of the male executive is that they have the support of a wife, a luxury denied to the latter!

The actions women require organizations to undertake, to allow them to fulfil the demands of higher positions, would include:

- Positive retraining after career breaks
- Flexible work hours
- Workplace nurseries or
- Financial support for private child care

Unfortunately, only less than a quarter of companies in a recent survey provided career breaks, and only a small percentage provided workplace nurseries. Private childcare is very expensive, although the Labour government's replacement of vouchers with guaranteed places for 4 year olds should improve matters.

One other problem is the tendency, identified by Kantor, for those in large organizations to hire and promote those who resemble themselves. Women who are promoted may be only token gestures for public relations purposes and not treated seriously. Such feelings will tend to make women less forceful.

An Institute of Directors study in 1992 found that three-quarters of female directors believed that they were discriminated against in the workplace while an Institute of Management study in the same year found men's club networks, prejudice and harassment to be three of the top four barriers women encountered. Most respondents opposed positive discrimination as a solution however, with selection on merit the preferred option.

Recognition of so-called 'glass ceilings', preventing women's advancement, has begun to stiffen government resolve for more positive action. Pressure groups are also becoming more active and some shareholders are asking questions at AGMs. However, the most effective catalyst for fundamental change remains a diminishing labour supply which confronts businesses with the choice between hiring more women or lower-quality men.

- Obtained feedback on your answer from a tutor or practitioner? and . . . will you be making the time to undertake the complete paper provided at the end of the workbook *under timed examination conditions* and *before* studying the model answers?

Do not make the mistake of making the actual examination the first opportunity to practise your answering technique. The outcome is likely to be an expensive, time-consuming and confidence-sapping resit. As in other skill areas, practice makes perfect, so do not be tempted to skip answering the specimen questions.

Summary of implications for marketers

- Demography is an important demand condition, helping the marketer to predict both size and change in target markets by population, age, gender, region, family size or ethnic group.
- Predicting volatile birth rates are more difficult than the relatively stable death rates.
- The original baby boomers are approaching retirement age (around 2010) while the more numerous 1960s boomers enter prosperous middle age.
- The scope for demographic segmentation is considerable since consumer needs, wants and usage rates are often closely correlated. As we will see later, the *family life cycle* is a means of adapting marketing approaches and product offerings to match changing needs at the different stages of life. Holiday companies like Club 18–30 or Saga have a clear life-cycle focus.
- The regional dominance of the South East, with nearly a third of total population, is compounded by above average income creating a marked contrast in consumption patterns and a magnet for luxury producers.
- Population growth is potentially more serious if economic development is slow, or arises from increased longevity which ages the population.
- Organizations must market themselves effectively in the face of potential skill shortages. The labour market must be researched and segmented to target potential employees. Their needs must be analysed and matched to those of the organization, and marketed accordingly.
- Greater flexibility is required in recruitment, particularly among married women.
- Marketers must respond to the consequences of demographic trends: flexible finance, mortgages and pension plans to match more flexible but less secure working lives; home based services to meet the needs of home workers; car dependence in knowledge-worker rural retreats.

The social and cultural environment

The difficulties experienced by women in employment compared to men outlined above are largely a reflection of societal attitudes in general and male-dominated corporate cultures in particular. The marketing executive can exert little influence on this aspect of the environment but understanding is vital, if the buying behaviour that results from it is to be fully understood.

Our culture moulds and regulates daily behaviour through constant conditioning and reinforcement. We learn what is and what is not appropriate behaviour in different social situations. Our attitudes, beliefs, values and language derive from such cultural influences as the family, community, religion and education.

Our culture, then, is reflected in what we eat, how and where we live, our life styles and buying preferences, not to mention our humour, art and music. The international marketer, especially, must become aware of the social mores of any country in which they seek new markets. When in Rome, do as the Romans do is apt advice since the accepted norms of business behaviour in, say, Japan are very different compared to those in Europe. Business and general societal customs must also be observed if offence is to be avoided. Language translation is another pitfall to beware, particularly for global enterprises. Nova doesn't go as a brand in Spain but neither would the Spanish 'Bum' snacks do too well in Britain.

Activity 8.7

The social mores or norms of accepted behaviour in Islamic or East Asian countries are radically different in many ways from those of Europe. Under the various headings mentioned in the paragraphs above, research all the main differences you can identify.

Prepare a short report comparing and contrasting the two cultures and provide behavioural guidelines for an international marketer trading between the two.

The marketer must recognize that while many social mores and customs are deeply rooted, others are in the process of change:

- *Role of women* The primacy of the domestic role has declined with developing opportunities for work and career. Smaller families and enhanced parental aspirations have freed resources for girls to pursue higher education. Changing female stereotypes are reflected in advertisements where the subjects are less likely to enthuse about the relative merits of detergents and more prone to be confident and assertive. However, there has been some reaction to the behavioural changes involved, not least in respect to the degree of 'political correctness' now required in this area. For the marketer, the full- or part-time working woman has provided extra discretionary purchasing power to the household and over which disposal she has had increasing influence. Demand for property, consumer durables and holidays have been sustained by these incomes. Work and domestic pressures have also put a premium on time and its effective management. Convenience foods, time-saving appliances and the combined versatility of the freezer and the microwave have transformed food preparation. Central heating and instant warmth at the flick of a switch have extracted the drudgery from another basic household function. Life style and mail order catalogues and one-stop shopping are other necessary innovations to enable the management of enlarging household consumption within the declining non-work time available. The need to be satisfied here is to enable the household to maximize work and leisure by economizing on the non-productive time required to service them.

Exam Tip

A high proportion of CIM candidates are women, so on the premise that the examiner will wish to appeal to all constituencies of the target candidate market, from time to time, expect an occasional question in this area.

- *Religious values and Sunday observance* Church attendance has fallen sharply in the last twenty-five years partly reflecting declining religious values among post-war age groups and secularization. The latter supposes continuing belief, but the absence of its formal expression in places of worship. The increasing mobility of households and an array of possible family activities on Sundays have provided alternatives and the means to satisfy them. The rising ownership of cars and television and a parallel decline in the cohesion of many local communities have also contributed to the erosion. Eventual success in the Sunday Opening campaign in late 1993 was the culmination of these forces for change, opening a vast new market for large retailers and do-it-yourself stores. On the other hand, fast-growing membership of new 'religions' may reflect a trend of individualism and diversity in cultural terms.

- *Healthy living and fitness trends* Concern for health and natural foods was mainly the realm of eccentric hippies up to twenty years ago. Smoking was also the norm and thought to symbolize maturity and sophistication. Attitudes are markedly different today with widespread concern over heart disease, cancer, obesity and lack of exercise. Significant marketing opportunities have developed as a result not least in the markets for low-fat foods, trainers, leisure clothing and fitness clinics. Although jogging as an activity may have waned, the pseudo-image provided by designer sports wear is a symbolic substitute. 'Appearances' are increasingly important to all generations and offer complex but profitable marketing opportunities. The younger age groups, in particular, have a strongly developed image consciousness.

Question 8.8	What other examples of socio-cultural change over the last twenty years can you think of? List them and brainstorm their implications for marketers and sales managers: e.g. animal rights and vegetarianism. (**See** Activity debrief at the end of this unit.)

Social class

One way of classifying groups within society is according to the class or strata they occupy. A class comprises individuals with a defined status and who share common characteristics including wealth, occupation, level of income, educational background and various aspects of life style. For the marketer it is not always the actual social class an individual belongs to that is significant but rather the class they identify with or to which they aspire.

The young in particular may adopt life styles that differ from those of their parents. Open educational access, mobility and rising incomes for all classes has facilitated this class movement.

Class and class aspirations are important since shared values, attitudes and behaviour will be reflected in purchasing preferences and form one of the most widely used methods of segmenting product markets. Examples of widely used categorizations based on class include the JICNAR social grade definitions:

Social class category	*Occupation*
A (upper middle)	Professional, administrative, top management, e.g. directors, barristers
B (middle)	Intermediate professional, managerial, e.g. marketing manager, lecturer.
C1 (lower middle)	Supervisory, clerical and lower management
C2 (skilled working class)	Skilled manual, e.g. crafts
D (working class)	Semi- and unskilled manual
E	State pensioners, long-term unemployed, etc.

An upper class based mainly on wealth is superimposed on this classification. It is important to the marketers of luxuries since it accounts for a quarter of total wealth in the hands of 1 per cent of the population.

Question 8.9	• Critically appraise the usefulness of the above classification system. • Can you think of an alternative approach to segmenting socio-economic groups that would be more appropriate? • Is your buying behaviour more related to your income or the social class to which you aspire? (**See** Activity debrief at the end of this unit.)

In mass urban centres where people are unable to get to know one another with the closer intimacy possible in small communities it is perhaps unsurprising that symbols are adopted to signal who we are and where we stand in society's pecking order. We classify those we meet on the type and quality of clothes they wear, the cars they drive, their sports and social activities, the houses and localities they live in as well as their manner, speech and the type of job they do. These are, in effect, badges of class membership and therefore vital pattern indicators for the marketer to recognize and mobilize in focused promotional campaigns.

Activity 8.8	Select one of the following sectors and research how spending patterns vary by class (look for Mintel market research reports or the most recent copy of ONS's *Social Trends* to assist you in this):

- Eating out
- Holidays and weekend breaks
- Arts and entertainment

Reference groups

Related to class is the concept of the reference group whose actions and behaviour influence the attitudes and values of large numbers of others who seek to imitate them. Reference groups may be large or small and include:

- The family
- Student peer group
- Work colleagues
- Club members

Since most individuals wish to 'belong' to certain preferred groups they will tend to conform to the norms of dress and behaviour laid down by them. Those within the group whose influence over what is and is not acceptable is substantial are known as opinion formers or leaders. Their influence may be based on expertise, knowledge or perhaps a charismatic personality. If a business can persuade such leaders to adopt their product then 'opinion followers' will also tend to purchase. Little wonder that sports equipment manufacturers secure endorsements from top players; use their product and you can be a winner too! Movie makers are also getting in on the act, although Reebok's legal action arising from an altered film ending suggests potential conflicts between art and commercialism.

Marketers must identify the relevant reference groups in the segments they have targeted, especially where expensive purchases (relative to the group's income) involving conspicuous consumption are concerned. The need to 'keep up with the Jones' or emulate members of a reference group to whom the consumer aspires is a powerful basis upon which to charge premium prices, not least to reinforce the implicit snob appeal involved.

The family

The family is a close and influential reference group. It conditions behaviour and values from birth and continues to influence buying decisions throughout the individual's life. As we saw earlier this has led to the identification of a *family life cycle* made up of different stages or phases in family life with significant implications for buying behaviour:

Exam Tip

Are you still keeping those files on Units 1–7 up to date? Revision is so much easier if you do this as you proceed through the course.

- *Young unmarried* Young and footloose with relatively high disposable income due to limited commitments. Fashion and entertainment orientated.
- *Newly married/no children* Dual income with expenditure focused on home building, consumer durables and holidays.
- *Young married/children* Home and family expenditure orientated. Limited scope for entertainment / luxury items
- *Middle-aged married/teenage children* Approaching maximum dual earnings, high replacement expenditure on quality durables
- *Older married/children left home* Disposable income at a peak and focused on retirement planning and luxuries. Well-established tastes and preferences in many cases
- *Older retired/single* Reduced disposable income but increasingly numerous and affluent. Conservative tastes and less susceptible to marketing campaigns. Important purchasers of one-off items like cars, holiday homes and expensive garden equipment.

Activity 8.9

Scan the advertisements in newspapers and magazines and classify their appeal according to (a) reference groups and/or (b) family stages.

In understanding the family and its spending decisions marketers must seek to identify not only who makes the final purchasing decision but also the influence exerted by other family members. Only in this way can they be sure as to whom they should direct their promotional messages. Who is it that decides the type and location of this year's family holiday? Do parents decide on style of dress or their teenage children? Are changes taking place in the distribution of this decision-making power as more married women work and men share the domestic responsibilities?

Stereotyped notions of the male deciding the type of car and home improvements while the female decides the food and furnishings may be increasingly suspect and the business must keep a finger on the changing social pulse if the marketing mix is to remain relevant and effective. That said, the most recent edition of *Social Trends* saw little evidence of 'New Man' emerging among younger age groups. The division of roles in households persists, with mothers spending six times as long cooking and cleaning and twice as long shopping.

Life style

Life styles are defined as the patterns in which people live, spend time and money. They are a function of the individual's motivation and prior learning as well as class, personality and other variables. They are measured by analysts using *attitude, interests and opinions scales* (AIO) alongside demographic factors to establish market segments with clusters of common characteristics.

The central idea is to build a picture of how individuals interact with the environment around them by identifying their behavioural patterns. This will then allow marketers to more effectively segment the market and tailor campaigns designed to appeal to particular life-style types. The presumption is that these groups will respond to different marketing mixes which can then be exploited to advantage.

Companies such as Laura Ashley, Next and Habitat have used such analysis to drive their marketing communications and encourage readers of their catalogues to identify with a particular cluster and therefore focus their purchasing behaviour on the products offered.

The marketer must, however, avoid oversimplified categorization. Individuals may exhibit multiple life style characteristics or evolve from one type to another as time and circumstances alter. Companies may wish to customize their own lifestyle segments or use generic categories such as strivers, aspirers, achievers and suceeders.

Activity 8.10

Consider the realism of the following life style trends and their implications for niche furniture manufacturers and retailers:

- *Instant gratification*   Live now pay later
- *Easy credit attitudes*   to finance the good life
- *Time conservation*   critical resource constraint on consumption
- *New work ethic*   working to live, not living to work
- *Consumerism*   concern for price/quality/service/environment
- *Personal creativity*   desire for self-expression/improvement
- *Naturalism*   return to nature but retaining material comforts.

What other life style trends can you currently identify in society?

(See Activity debrief at the end of this unit.)

A summary of segmentation bases in consumer markets

The main types of segmentation considered so far have been:

- Geographic:
  Region, climate, density
- Life style
- Demographic:
  Age, gender, race, nationality and religion
  Income and education
  Family size and life cycle
  Occupation and social class

The final aspect to consider is geodemographic segmentation based on *neighbourhood and type of dwelling*. As a composite index of factors relevant to buying behaviour this is thought to represent a more accurate assessment than those based solely on one factor such as class or income. A well-used example of this approach is the ACORN system (i.e. A Classification of Residential Neighbourhoods), which classifies households into one of eleven major groups and thirty-six specific neighbourhood types and is used by companies such as IKEA, the Swedish furniture retailer, to analyse its customer base:

A Modern family housing for manual
    A1 local authority and new-town housing: high wage
    A2 mixed housing, young families
    A3 recent council housing
    A4 modern low cost private
B Modern family housing, higher incomes
C Older housing of intermediate status
D Very poor quality, older terraced
E Rural areas
    E13 Villages with some non-farm employment
    E14 Rural areas with large farms
    E15 Rural areas with own account farmers
F Urban local authority housing
G Housing with most overcrowding
H Low-income areas with immigrants
I Student and high-status non-family areas

J   Traditional high-status non-suburbia
K   Areas of elderly people
U   Unclassified (e.g. hospitals and prisons)

Other examples of such database include PIN (pinpoint identified neighbourhoods) and MOSAIC.

<table>
<tr><td>Question 8.10</td><td>Some of the specific neighbourhood types (A1–A4, E13–E15) have been included in the above. How would you subdivide the other groups in a meaningful way?

Which of the above groups would you estimate contains the highest proportion of British households? Which has the lowest?

To what extent do you feel ACORN will be a good indicator of purchasing behaviour?

(See Activity debrief at the end of this unit.)</td></tr>
</table>

Final thoughts on culture

- As we have seen above, culture is a complex blend of acquired values, beliefs, attitudes and customs which provide context and behavioural guidelines for life within a given society. It is an important part of our social conditioning.
- A national culture is usually composed of subcultures based on such considerations as origins, religion or some basis of shared outlook and values.
- Subcultures form important bases for segmentation whether on a regional (e.g. Welsh), urban (e.g. Bradford, Pakistani) or locality (e.g. Jewish community, North London) grounds.
- Individuals from different cultures are likely to respond to different imperatives in terms of what, where, when and how they buy goods and services.
- Ample data exist for analysis of purchasing variations related to regional cultural differences. *Regional Trends* is compiled by the ONS and may be supplemented by market research often derived from the regional television companies.
- While the South-east with its concentration of higher-income households may provide useful insight into future buying trends in other less prosperous regions the marketer must also recognize the degree to which purchasing behaviour is culturally driven.

Implications for marketers

- Much of this chapter has been concerned with classifying people into different groups or segments for marketing purposes. Care must be taken, since many of the divisions and behavioural assumptions are generalizations and subject to change.
- If it is an individual's perceptions and aspirations that drive purchasing decisions, rather than their objectively defined status, then prediction is much more hazardous.
- Complex family structures mean it may no longer be appropriate to use the occupation of the so-called head of the family as an indicator of purchasing potential. Flexible work patterns will compound these difficulties.
- Society is becoming progressively better educated, with lifelong learning the dawning reality. Marketers must adjust their attitudes and communication methods accordingly.
- Social, cultural and demographic factors influence incomes, tastes and preferences, all important demand determinants. Equally they may inhibit purchase decisions.
- The marketer should distinguish a customer's beliefs, i.e. conclusions based on available objective facts and subjective experience, from their values. The latter are more generalized, deep seated and enduring.

Greens are good for you, may be a belief, but vegetarianism values life itself.

- Products can acquire cultural meaning through the marketing process, e.g. designer clothes or a BMW in an achievers lifestyle.
- The changing role of women is making more promotional spending gender specific, as seen, for example, in car advertisements.

Summary

In this unit we have seen:

- The importance to the marketer of monitoring and understanding the implications of demographic changes. These change slowly over time but their cumulative impact over a period can have immense consequences for buying patterns.
- The relevant factors in population structure and their effects on both the supply and demand sides of the market.
- Some of the important employment trends, with particular emphasis on the drive for greater flexibility by businesses.
- The changing role of women in work and society and the ongoing impacts of this transformation.
- The meaning of the term 'culture' and its relevance to successful international and regional marketing.
- Some of the more important social trends and the marketing lessons to be learnt from them.
- The significance of social influences such as class, occupation and life style as bases for segmentation, with particular attention to reference groups such as the family.

Activity debrief

Question 8.1 Those retiring will have state pensions supplemented by private pensions. They will have planned financially for retirement and may have inherited valuable properties in recent years. They will form a market segment with clear ideas regarding their requirements. They will still be fit and active. The mix must reflect this, especially in terms of the product and the financing arrangements. Promotion must address their wants.

Question 8.3
- New technology improved agricultural productivity; industrialization; opened up the lands of the New World; emigration; refrigeration; demographic transition, etc.
- No unexploited continents; global competition; immigration laws; pollution consequences of modern agriculture. A lot therefore rests on development of sustainable technologies and overseas aid. Population growth does not necessarily mean market opportunities because it tends to correlate with very low or falling income per head.
- An optimum population allows full advantage to be taken of resources. A growing population can revitalize and bring larger markets and more mobility. Excessive population as seen in parts of Africa and Latin America can unbalance the ecology through overgrazing and deforestation.

Question 8.4 Quality, service, value for money and greater durability. Over-45s will be renewing household effects after child-rearing and will look for design, not functionality.

Question 8.5 Apart from logistical considerations, life styles will be different. Outlying areas poorly served by public transport will have higher car ownership and infrequent, high-spending trips to retailers.

Question 8.6 The culture, attitudes and buying habits of these groups differ significantly from the indigenous population. The entrepreneurial abilities of some of these minorities are also outstanding: 17 per cent of the Indian community are self-employed against 11 per cent for all groups.

Question 8.7
- For business the main attraction is flexibility to employ when the labour

is required (e.g. retail shopping peaks). Wages tend to be lower and other wage costs are avoided. Exemption from employment legislation and National Insurance also contribute.

- For employees, especially married women, it may fit well with other responsibilities and needs. It also suits the semi-retired.
- For government it reduces the overall unemployment rate.
- Recent legislation has put part-time workers on equal employment status to full-time.
- A change in work patterns implies changes in buying and shopping patterns. One-stop shopping and convenience purchases are reflections of this trend. It is also more likely that the male is more involved in routine shopping decisions.

Question 8.8 Examples may include changing attitudes to:
- *Credit* previously disapproved of but now an accepted part of marketing activity.
- *Single-parent families* even the term 'illegitimate' is losing social stigma.
- *Virtue of hard work* unemployment experience may be causing a swing back in this direction not least as companies downsize their management numbers, putting pressures on those that remain.
- *Concern for quality of life* green products, outdoor life styles, demand for the 'good' things of life.
- *Less formality* reflected in dress and decor.

Question 8.9
- The classification is based solely on occupation and ignores the fact that changing wage relativities have altered comparative purchasing power. Some C2s are better off than many C1s and Bs, for example, and this is reflected in purchases. Others are not easy to fit into the classification (e.g. those living on inherited wealth).
- An alternative classification would be to select specific classes (e.g. upper middle, lower lower, etc.) and define the households concerned in terms of source and size of income, place of residence, type of work, core attitudes and so forth.
- Social classes tend to have distinct and recognizable product and brand preferences which symbolize their position.

Question 8.10
- J includes modern private housing/high income; medium status interwar private; established suburbs of high status and very high status areas.
- J and F both account for around 20 per cent each while G is less than 2.5 per cent.

Activity 8.3 Implications are many and varied. Perhaps mortgage lenders should focus on single people and promote accordingly. Married couples should feature less as the norm particularly since those with 1 or 2 dependent children has declined from 30 per cent to 20 per cent. However 75 per cent still live in some type of family and this is the focus of recent government budget measures.

Activity 8.4 Factors might include independence, lack of paid employment, redundancy payments provided, opportunity, encouragement through tax measures, lack of promotion or recognition in paid employment, etc.

Activity 8.10 Other trends might include health and fitness; novelty and change; energy and environmental friendliness; value for money; supranational or global orientation.

Extending activity 8.1 The factors you may have identified are:

Political	Economic
Provision of welfare services	Rising real incomes
State pensions	Cost of housing
Equal-opportunity legislation	Rising opportunity cost of children
Erosion of family allowances	Recession/poor employment outlook
Social	*Technical*
Children no longer an insurance for secure old age	Decline in child mortality via medical advance removes need to have more
Changing religious attitudes	Birth control advances
Cultural norms changing on women's role in society	Media influences
Concern for health/figure	Marketing influence – nuclear family and promotion of consumer
Decline in marriage and rise in illegitimacy rate (28 per cent!)	durables

We have seen in the previous unit (specimen Question 3) that a broadly based choice question may be set on the macro-environment. Other possibilities include a question on the environmental set or SWOT analysis. These provide ample scope for the examiner to select at least one factor or trend from the social, demographic and cultural environment. Question 3 in Unit 7 required social and demographic trends to be identified.

Clearly, any of the aspects discussed above could form the basis of a question and you should prepare accordingly. Note that a question may test not only your understanding of the trend but also its impact on, or implication for, the business concerned.

Optional question 1 – illustration only

(a) What is the significance of the social environment for the marketer.

(6 marks)

(b) Select two significant social trends and discuss their marketing implications for either a grocery retailer or a bank. (10 marks)

(c) Provide a bibliography of relevant sources on social trends.

(4 marks)

(CIM Marketing Environment paper, June 1996)

Optional question 2 – illustration only

Discuss the impact of **two** of the following environmental elements on the marketing operations of a large retailer:

(a) Changing lifestyles of women
(b) Population begins to age rapidly
(c) Falling real cost of computers and telecommunications
(d) Sharp increases in the membership of consumer pressure groups.

(20 marks)

(CIM Marketing Environment paper, June 1997)

Optional question 3 – illustration only

(a) What do you understand by the following terms:

    (i)   Lifestyle
    (ii)   Reference groups
    (iii) Family life cycle (6 marks)

(b) Comment on how lifestyle may vary over **three** stages of the family life cycle. (14 marks)

(CIM Marketing Environment paper, June 1998)

Compulsory questions may also be posed, as the following shows:

PART A:
Compulsory question

With a greyer picture of the future in mind

While there are few trends which can be forecast with confidence over decades, there is one prediction that can safely be made about the industrialized countries – their populations will grow older over the next 40 years.
In the 18 western European member states of the OECD, the number of people aged 65 and over will rise from 50 million to more than 70 million between 1990 and 2030. During the same period, the number of people of working age will fall. The result is that, by 2030, there will be fewer than three people of working age in these countries for each person over 65, compared with five now.
Similar trends can be seen in other leading world economies such as the US and Japan. The populations of the tigers of the Pacific rim, such as

209

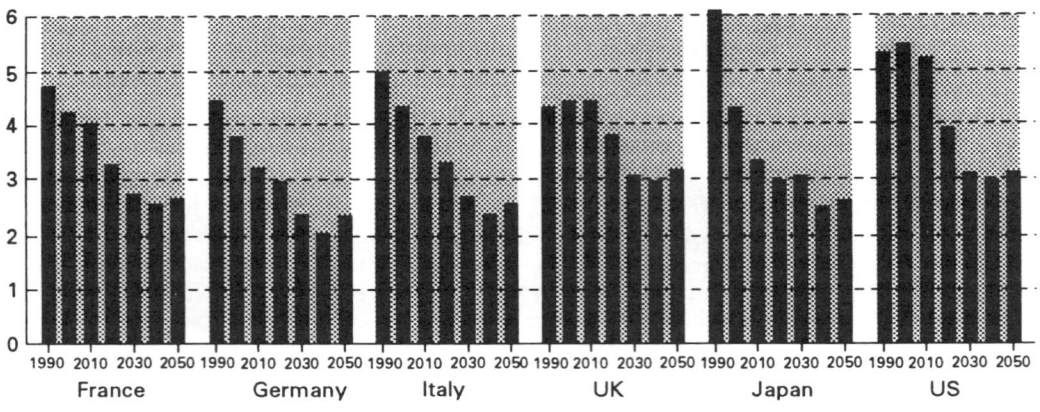

Age structure switches towards the elderly
Ratio of the number of people of working age, 15 years to 64 years,
to support each person aged 65 years and over

Singapore and Taiwan, are also ageing fast. In contrast, developing countries such as China, India and Brazil, will have a much lower share of elderly people.

Economists predict that ageing will have an enormous impact on economies and their international competitiveness, but there is little agreement over the precise nature of the change. Dr Paul Johnson states that 'demographic restructuring could alter patterns of consumption, employment, saving, investment and innovation, but because of the interactions between these separate elements, it is impossible to be sure of either the scale or, in some cases, the direction of the economic impact. Our understanding of the processes of economic growth and of innovation are too primitive to make long-term predictions.'

This uncertainty extends even to the question of whether an ageing population will save more (to provide for old age) or save less as nest-eggs are cashed in for retirement. Lower savings rates could threaten economic growth, although the evidence so far from all over Europe is that ageing populations save more.

The economic consequences of a changing demographic structure will be felt unevenly, as some countries face more radical demographic change than others. The greatest impact in the EU will be felt in Germany where the population will decline by 15 million between now and 2030. Today a fifth of the population is aged 20 or younger; by 2030 only 16 per cent will be. Ageing will be less in the UK and US but globally it would be the NICs, such as China and Brazil, which would gain the greatest competitive advantage by virtue of their much younger populations.

(Source: *Financial Times*, John Williams, 8 March 1994)

1 (a) Write short notes on the following term used in the article briefly summarizing its economic significance to the marketer:
   - Demographic structure   (6 marks)

Either

   (b) Discuss the likely impact of ageing on the labour market. What recommendations would you make to a business currently reliant on recruiting large numbers of school-leavers to meet its labour needs?
                                                                    (16 marks)

Or

   (c) 'Businesses will have to cope with changes in demand patterns as older consumers become more significant in their markets and younger people less so.'
   Explain, with examples, some of the opportunities provided by these changing demand patterns and how the marketer should address this buyer segment.

                                                                    (16 marks)

   (d) 'Ageing is one of the few trends that can be forecast with confidence.'

Briefly explain why this is so, and suggest **two** forecasting approaches, showing how they might enable the marketer to forecast the future with greater confidence.

(12 marks)
(CIM Marketing Environment paper, June 1995)

Hints: Indicative content and approach
Question 1(a)
- Note the tendency for compulsory questions to take terms from the text and require you to explain their meaning and significance (see sample compulsory question in the Guidance on revision and examination unit at the end of the workbook for another example).
- When short notes are asked for, produce notes and keep them short! (i.e. 6 marks warrants only 10 minutes).
- Divide the bullet points into notes on meaning and significance.
- Demographic structure relates to age, sex, distribution, etc., not patterns.

Question 1(b)/(c)
- Choose carefully between the optional parts to make the best use of your demographic knowledge.
- Relate the impact of ageing to the mobility, fluidity and efficiency of the labour market – new blood and ideas.
- Concentrate on recommendations and use a good example such as the National Health Service or the armed forces who recruit large numbers.
- Adopt a broad approach, e.g. recruitment policies; alternative labour forces; substitute technology; relocation; retention strategies, etc.
- The alternative is a more marketing oriented question combined with economic analysis of changing demand patterns.
- Provide examples of expanding older segments and shrinking younger segments.
- Remember that purchasing power depends on discretionary income as well as numbers.

Question 1(d)
- Attempt this question after you have completed Unit 10.

The technical environment and turbulent change

In this unit, which examines not only the all-embracing effects of the technological environment, but also the dynamic and complex nature of change itself, you will:

❏ Investigate the nature and characteristics of technology.

❏ Understand some of the mechanisms responsible for producing change in this environment.

❏ Assess its impact on the marketer in different types of business.

❏ Recognize some constraints and limitations on the pace and quality of change in this important environment.

❏ Examine the concepts of dynamism, complexity and turbulence.

By the end of this unit you will have:

❏ Understood the role of business as the main medium for the development and diffusion of new technology.

❏ Appreciated the factors driving change.

❏ Recognized the importance of technical monitoring and forecasting.

❏ Assessed the absorptive capabilities of the natural environment, as limits to the nature and direction of future change.

❏ Accepted the central importance of change and considered arketing priorities for a turbulent world.

We live in a technological society whose effects impact on all aspects of our life. Our work is particularly subject to such influences and major transformations have occurred in recent years in the majority of industries and occupations. Other aspects of our life have also been increasingly affected; our means of transport, how we shop, the ways we spend our leisure time, how we learn, the houses we live in and the way our health is monitored. Only our sleeping habits seem relatively unaffected, although even here new drugs, insulation, bed designs and environment control are affecting the lives of many.

We will also consider the nature of change in more general terms during this unit. Change is occurring not only in terms of technology, but in all environments and the majority of organizations. Change is therefore multi-faceted and in most cases inter-active. Change in one part of the system causes reactions elsewhere. Consequently we will see that change is both complicated and turbulent in nature. Marketers must strive to understand the complex processes at work and if possible be part of the change itself rather than merely responding belatedly to its confusing effects.

With regard to the technological environment it is an area which can generate a diversity of examples as context for examining its impacts. This unit will therefore concentrate on general themes and leave you the responsibility of finding relevant applications from your own experience and reading.

As you will see from the past examination question at the end of this unit, the examiner may require you to select technologies of your own choosing and discuss their effects or define the general meaning and implications of terms such as 'software' or 'multi media'. You do not necessarily have to select typical areas such as information technology, cars or drugs. Relevant applications from your own industry are more likely to interest and impress the examiner, since it shows you are seeking to relate your studies to your work situation. Do make sure, however, that you have a working knowledge of technical terms affecting the work of marketers (see the Glossary for some of these).

A very useful supplement to this unit are Chapters 5 and 12 in *The Business and Marketing Environment* (third edition) by Palmer and Hartley, which deals in detail with specific applications of information technology to the marketing context.

This unit again accounts for around 10 per cent of the total syllabus, inferring that a question might be expected in alternate exams. Do not bank on a full question, however, and remember that the compulsory question may provide scope for part-questions. To expedite your studies in this area you will require a file sectioned into at least five parts:

- The technological environment
- Technology and change in your own industry
- Marketing impacts: (a) general, (b) own industry
- Resistances to change
- Understanding the nature of dynamic change

Definition of terms

The successful development of new technology comprises a number of distinct stages:

KNOWLEDGE – RESEARCH – INVENTION – DEVELOPMENT – INNOVATION – DIFFUSION – REFINEMENT

New technology represents new production possibilities and therefore the means of satisfying consumer needs and wants, more efficiently and effectively. It allows more and better value-for-money goods to be produced with given resources. It is one of the primary means of shifting out the *production possibility curve* (PPC), as seen in Figure 9.1. If the change only affects, say, the production of consumer goods then the PPC will pivot outwards since no impact will be felt on investment goods.

The state of technology is a function of resources and the knowledge and skills to use them while technical change is the result of changing resources, increased product and process knowledge and the accumulation of applications experience. Knowledge of the current state of technology is

Figure 9.1
Innovation and the production possibility curve

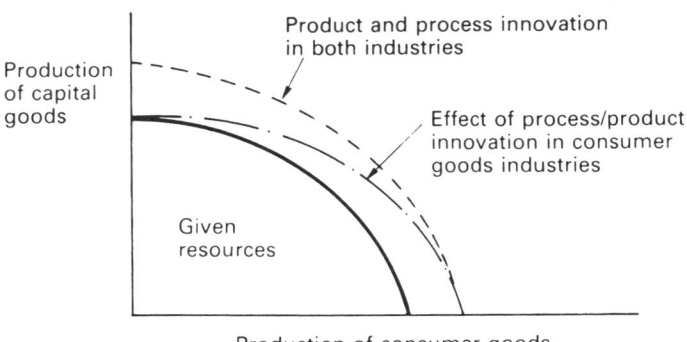

the foundation upon which research takes place. New ideas and developments in sciences often form the basis of advance and synthesis in others. Research and invention is the generation of new ideas, or improvement of existing ones, while development is their useful application to specific products or processes.

Innovation relates to the actual commercial exploitation of a development while diffusion refers to the rate of its adoption through the potential target population concerned. Refinement exploits the full potential of the technology and often forms the basis of product differentiation in the growth and early maturity stages of the life cycle.

It may be noted that continous innovation is probably the only strategy that, if successfully implemented, would ensure a firm earns excess profits over time. New products that more effectively satisfy customer needs and wants will increase profits as will cost-saving processes and technologies. However, only by ploughing back profit into maintaining technological or design leadership can long-term profits be ensured. Competitors will seek to enter the market and imitate the innovations, but they will always be aiming for a *moving target*.

Characteristics of technology

This environment is not just about hi-tech and computers but it is all-pervasive. Change is affecting virtually all industries and sectors, e.g. Courtauld's new fibre, Tencel. Some advances are relatively simple, such as adhesive message pads, while others are more complex, as in new packaging technologies.

Question 9.1

- Think of at least six examples of industries that have had significant cost-saving innovations over the last five years.
- Can you think of at least three examples of industries that have *not* had significant cost saving innovations over the last 10 years?

(**See** Activity debrief at the end of this unit.)

As one of the major macro-environment variables it has a breadth of impact that affects all the other elements. The stock market crash of 1987, for example, was triggered by automatic computer sell signals. Increased employment of married women has been facilitated by the development of labour-saving, controllable and convenient technologies in the home. The political complexion of Eastern Europe and China has altered beyond recognition, with exposure of their material expectations to the telecommunication broadcasts of Western democracies. Perhaps the biggest potential impact of all arises from our dependence on programmable chips. The millennium bug problem, where computer programs do not recognize the year 2000, may involve significant worldwide costs ranging up to £400 billion (UK £31 billion). The UK government has recently made such costs tax allowable.

According to Alvin Toffler in his book *Future Shock*, technology involves not only change but accelerating or exponential change. He illustrates this in a number of ways, including the 800th lifetime:

- The first 650 were spent in caves
- Effective communication in the last seventy
- Printed word to the masses in the last six
- Measured time in the last four
- Electric motor in the last two
- Mass material affluence in the last one

Technology progressed in phases until industrialization, when a marked acceleration occurred. Technology has always extended human capabilities and industrialization massively extended human musculature. Just three lifetimes have seen transformation from agricultural through industrial to service economy and the pace is not slackening as developed countries enter a post-industrial 'information/communication' society. This is based on:

- Technology as the primary driving force for social change
- Convergence of computer/telecommunications media technologies
- A high and rising proportion of communications/information technology ownership
- Extension of the powers of the human nervous systems of sight and sound via TV, telephone, mobile telephone, fax and other information systems such as the Internet
- Development of digital super-highways unifying communications technologies
- Credit transfer rather than cash-based society, e.g. Switch cards
- A high percentage of knowledge workers
- A diverse, decentralized and differentiated society.

Question 9.2

What was the typical life style twenty-five years ago? What products and services that are taken for granted today did not exist then?
(**See** Activity debrief at the end of this unit.)

The role of business

Business is the main conduit by which science and technology impacts on society. Most change is incremental and progressive in nature but breakthroughs can and do bring sudden and dramatic change. Organizations must therefore give as much, if not more, attention to monitoring their technological as other macro-environments. If a rival succeeds in achieving a technological advantage it is a much more significant competitive edge than any other, due to the time, difficulty and resource commitments required to counter it. You may recall the damage inflicted on the Swiss watch industry by Japanese microprocessor-controlled timepieces, or more recently the impact on Apple of the Microsoft Windows '95 launch.

Most businesses are in a position to partly shape the threats and opportunities of their own technological environment by inventing and developing new ideas. Some industries compete on the state of their technology whereas others exhibit little innovation. This disparity is related to a number of factors:

Exam Tip

Have a look at the compulsory question posed at the end of this unit. Plan out an answer as you work through the remainder of this section.

1 *Stage of the product or technology life cycle* The introduction and growth stages of any new invention will be characterized by creative product innovation which will continue until the technology matures.
2 *Size of the firm* Studies suggest that small firms provide a more productive climate for invention but lack the resources and organization to diffuse it quickly and effectively. Small firms tend to specialize and the risk of failure is high. Even large firms must beware of overcommitment (e.g. Rolls-Royce RB211 engine).
3 *Nature of competition in the market* Considerable debate surrounds the best market structure for encouraging innovation. The drive is powerful in fragmented markets but the resources and size to exploit them successfully is often lacking. Financial resources and control of the market exist in monopoly but innovation would make obsolete previous investments. The ideal combination is in concentrated industries, where size

and market share is combined with considerable rewards if innovation can undermine rival product offerings. Interdependence, therefore, ensures that each company will maintain considerable research and development capability as a precaution against rivals obtaining such an edge.

4 *The pace of change in consumer tastes* If the existing market is static then new products supplied to new consumers in new ways may be the only strategy for growth.

What are the technical imperatives?

We live in a technological era where such knowledge and expertise confers status and societal approval. The Japanese and other Asian economies are admired for their ability to emulate and improve on Western technology. In their turn, European and American companies such as General Motors (Saturn project – robotized production), Fiat and Volkswagen have invested staggering sums in an effort to counter the lower wage costs and team-based productivity of Asian competitors. *Global competition* is clearly one of the imperatives forcing technological change.

Technology can also be viewed as a Pandora's box which, once opened, can never again be closed. Advances in one sphere of science provides the catalyst for a dozen others in adjacent fields where time, money and human expertise provide the only limits to the expanding frontiers of knowledge.

The development of global information networks such as Internet, for example, eliminates the constraints of national boundaries and allows small companies, students and researchers to access vast international databases. So-called web sites offer a value added means of providing further information to existing and potential clients. However, a survey of web site operators in 1996 suggested less than 60 per cent were happy with the business they had won and one in five had had security breaches. As communications companies invest to widen and commercialize these networks into 'information super-highways' so they will be capable of delivering not just research capability but a myriad other services. Similarly, organizations are linking subsidiaries and micro-environment stakeholders in so-called 'intranets'.

Fifty-year innovation cycle

Another technology imperative may be provided by this long-wave cycle. It has been observed that economic development since the Industrial

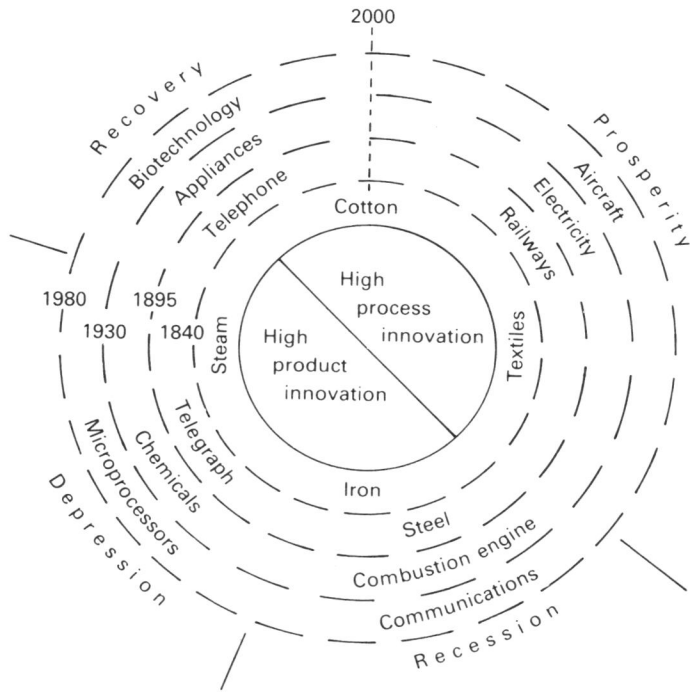

Figure 9.2
The long-wave cycle

Revolution has progressed in fifty-year cycles based on successive clusters of critical innovations.

As can be seen in Figure 9.2, steam power and textiles formed the basis of the first wave, railways and steel the second and so on. As each product or technology innovation cluster matured so their ability to generate further growth and jobs declined. Economies then tended to suffer an unusually severe depression as occurred in the 1880s and 1930s.

Businesses initially responded by cost cutting and retrenchment but as depression continued were forced to consider more radical solutions to declining sales and profitability. A new wave of innovations therefore occurred, as businesses became prepared to risk resources on new and existing inventions.

Considerable debate exists as to whether a long-wave depression was experienced in the decade following the oil crisis in the 1970s. Certainly, a cluster of technologies underpin current growth and development based on, among others:

- Microprocessors
- Satellites
- Biogenetic technology
- Materials
- Fibre-optics
- Lasers
- Digital communications

Activity 9.2

Taking the above state-of-the-art technologies, brainstorm as many product innovations based on them as possible. Can you think of any product or process innovations that represent fusions of these separate technologies?

Creative destruction

Schumpeter viewed innovation as the source of creative destruction whereby dominant established firms and industries based on mature technology are challenged by new firms, using substitute products or processes, often from a different industry. Such entrepreneurial initiatives

217

constantly threaten to shake up monopoly and oligopoly market situations, keeping them on their toes (e.g. IBM and Compaq in PCs). The joint venture between Mercedes-Benz and Swatch provided an interesting example of this in the urban electric car market until the latter's stake was bought out in 1999.

Technological change is part of the *dynamic of capitalism*. The expectation of new and improved products is part of our culture and businesses are rewarded when these needs are satisfied. Businesses are motivated by the need to survive and make profits, governments to promote growth and people to improve and change. This produces a drive for technology which feeds on itself, rippling through society as one advance triggers other applications in a technological *multiplier–accelerator effect*.

New generations of products are introduced with progressively reducing lead times, stimulating the planned obsolescence of current offerings. The power of snob appeal conferred on pioneer consumers and the requirement for followers to 'keep up with the Jones' reinforces the treadmill of constant novelty and change.

Question 9.4

What are the opportunities and threats of technological change as far as the business organization is concerned? What steps can the business take to minimize the threats and maximize the opportunities?

(**See** Activity debrief at the end of this unit.)

Microprocessors: a metatechnology with universal applications

This has become the most important technology of the late twentieth century. Despite a progression from valves and transistors, it represents a 'technological leap' innovation. This has allowed the enhancement of design and performance in a wide diversity of products and services.

The technology has also significantly contributed to the efficiency and effectiveness of communication systems, information services and other infrastructures (e.g. computerized traffic signals and electronic-based road-pricing systems to relieve congestion).

Microprocessors both extend and increasingly displace a wide range of intellectual and intuitive skills. In effect it constitutes the most rapid and dramatic industrial change in history and is still proceeding rapidly with the latest Pentium chips manufactured by Intel.

Question 9.5

Suppose that an unusual electrical storm unaccountably disrupted the workings of all microprocessors that have ever been produced. What would be the immediate effects on the following:

- The motorist?
- The household?
- The shopper?
- The marketing department?
- The individual?

(**See** Activity debrief at the end of this unit.)

A number of characteristics have accounted for the cost and technical effectiveness of microprocessor-based technology as seen in Figure 9.3. When applied to manufacturing processes these characteristics have led rapidly towards the development of computer-integrated semi-automated plants. These are self-organizing systems that learn from their environments as well as from their experience. It may be noted, however, that the limits of power and performance that can be packed on a chip are being

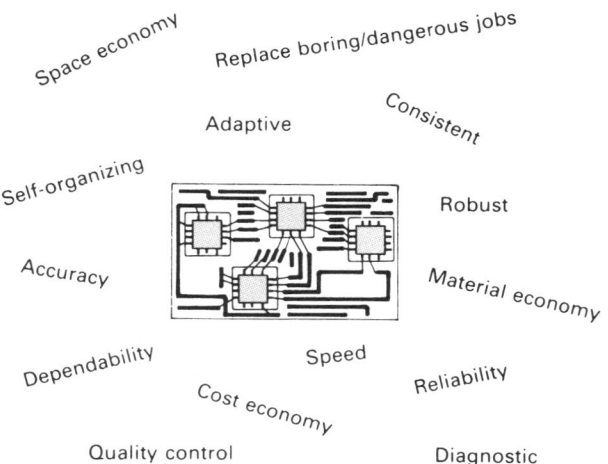

Figure 9.3
Characteristics of the microchip

approached. Alternatives currently being used or considered include parallel processing and even DNA-based 'living' computers. Workstations currently capable of processing 25–100 million instructions per second (MIPS) could rise to 500–2000 MIPS using wide bandwidth computer networks.

The technological diffusion process

Adoption of new technology by businesses involves both cost and risk as well as the prospect of return. The rate at which firms adopt innovations, appropriate to their industry and market, is known as the rate of diffusion.

As can be seen in Figure 9.4, the process is similar to the product life cycle. Factors which determine whether the rate is rapid or slow include:

- *Profitability* The rate of return will depend on a number of cost and revenue factors. The larger the impact on these of the new technology, relative to what is currently in use, the more rapid the diffusion.
- *Deterrence* This measures the consequences of *not adopting* the new technology. If a serious loss of sales is likely due to the superiority of the new technology then diffusion will be rapid as producers are forced to jump on the bandwagon or go out of business.
- *Scale of investment* Hi-tech generally means large financial outlays on both hardware and software aspects of operations. Businesses have limited internal resources and access to external risk capital, causing diffusion to be slower in such cases.
- *Market structure* It has been argued that oligopoly is the the most effective structure for rapid diffusion. Multinationals in particular have the organizational ability and resources to effect this globally.
- *Characteristics of the new product or process*
- *Potential range of applications* Clearly the greater the number under both of these headings, the greater the profitability and sales potential of the technology.
- *Environmental acceptability* As we will discuss later in this unit, the actual and perceived impacts of a new technology on the natural environment

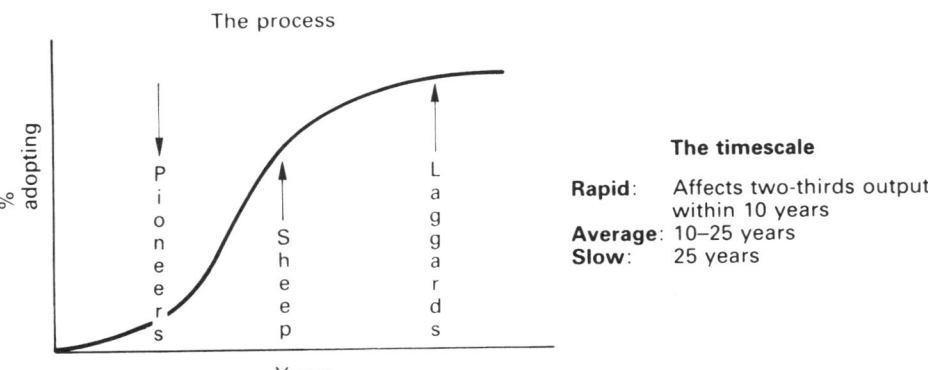

Figure 9.4
The diffusion process

219

will affect diffusion due to legislation and liabilities that may arise. The cost of verifying drugs, for example, is said to account for the halving of R&D expenditure growth in the early 1990s compared to the 1980s.

- *Change agents* For a new idea to succeed in a business it needs a champion to challenge the status quo and persuade decision makers of the need for change. Much is invested in the current way of doing things and resistance to change occurs among management, customers and the workforce. The government is often a change agent through initiatives to support innovation or willingness to place orders. Equally, teenage computer networks were thought responsible for the 20 million Tamagotchi sold worldwide.

Activity 9.3

Using the above diffusion factors, conduct a comparative analysis of some of the following technologies:

- Information technology
- Biotechnology
- Nuclear technology
- Satellite technology
- Synthetic materials technology
- Supersonic transport technology
- Automated surveillance (CCTV)

Do your conclusions bear out the actual rate of diffusion of these technologies?

(**See** Activity debrief at the end of this unit.)

Technological transfer

Another aspect of diffusion is the transfer of technology from:

- Basic research to practical applications
- Military/aerospace applications to industrial products
- Hi-tech to consumer goods and services
- Developed to less developed countries

Fundamental new technologies originate from a number of sources, including universities and research institutes, military establishments, government agencies as well as businesses. Despite its record of Nobel Prizes, however, Britain has only a third to a half the number of scientists and engineers as a percentage of its population as the USA and Japan. Future trends bode no improvement as declining numbers opt for science and technology subjects at 'A' level and university.

An alternative is to license technology from the inventor, or encourage leading-edge multi-nationals to locate high-technology subsidiaries and transfer expertise into the economy. American and Japanese computer companies have been attracted to locate plants in Central Scotland, for example, providing opportunities for third generation indigenous companies to prosper.

Question 9.6

If your firm has invested large sums in developing a revolutionary new product or service idea, what actions would you advise it to take in order to generate maximum returns?

(**See** Activity debrief at the end of this unit.)

Technological forecasting

This idea is not new since good managements have always intuitively kept a cautious eye on the pace of change in both their own and adjacent industries. However, this has tended to be a 'defensive' eye to the danger of being overtaken by substitute technology rather than with a proactive intention to achieve competitive advantage.

A shifting balance of trade has meant that Britain, in particular, has had to learn to cope with rigorous competition from advanced, high-technology high-wage, capital-intensive economies first in Europe and latterly in East Asia. Insufficient resources force Britain to specialize in areas of greatest expertise and comparative advantage: chemicals, aerospace, pharmaceuticals, oil and financial services. Research and development spending as a percentage of sales is high by international standards in pharmaceuticals, for example (20–30 per cent, nearly double the average), but is static and low in manufacturing as a whole. British Telecom spends only 2 per cent of sales while oil companies spend even less.

The government is partly the cause since it decided, in the late 1980s, to progressively reduce subsidies, tax concessions and direct spending on civil R&D, forcing companies to assume more responsibility for product and process development. Short-termism (demands for profits today) among City analysts might also have worked against it.

A technological forecast should be the foundation block of long-term plans, based on effective collusion between the technologist, designer and marketer. This is necessary to achieve the essential balance between creating and satisfying the needs of the customer.

Exam Tip

The technological environment is one area where you must keep up to date in the examples you provide to illustrate your answers. A useful strategy would be to list and summarize those changes which are currently impacting on the marketer's role.

Break this down into the various aspects of the marketing mix in your file and make short notes on current developments in each:

Product e.g. CAD/CAM and design cycles
Place EDI with intermediaries, satellite tracking of vehicles
Promotion interactive TV, computer-designed samples, database marketing
Price barcode scanning, electronic pricing

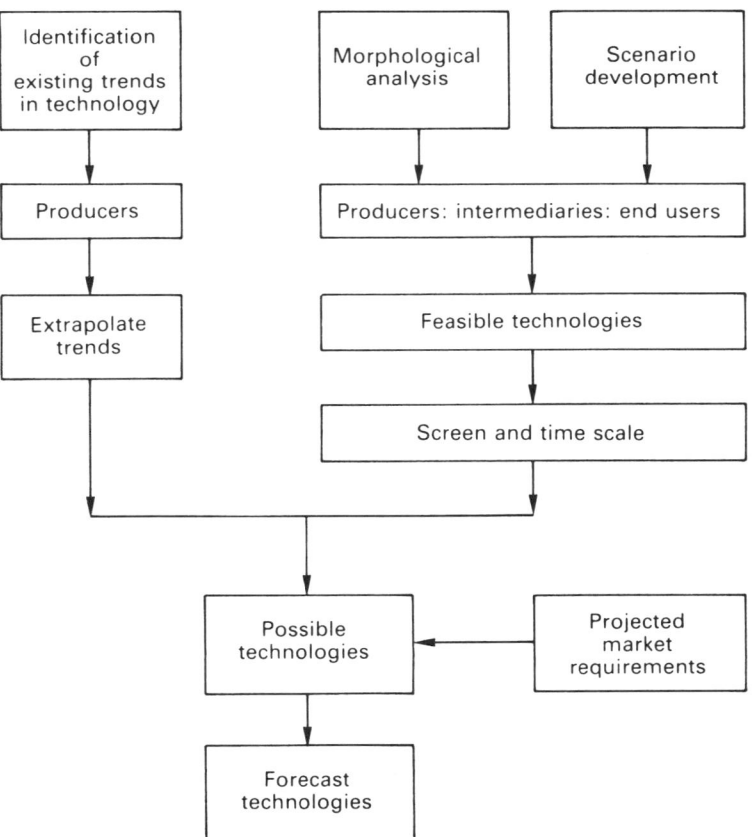

Figure 9.5
A framework for technological forecasting

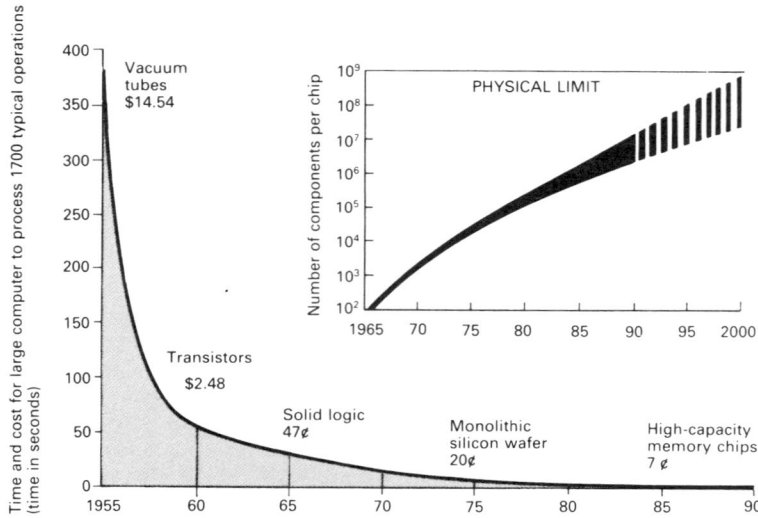

Figure 9.6
Advances in computer technology

A basic forecasting approach for a business is shown in Figure 9.5. Forecasts of technologies are the product of two types of analysis:

1 Evolution of the current technology must first be ascertained. Many such forecasts are made for key technologies often using extrapolation of trends. Figure 9.6 from a *Financial Times* industry survey is such an example (see Unit 10 for a discussion of forecasting methods).
2 Alternative or substitute product or process technology is more difficult to forecast and requires a more qualitative analysis. Morphological analysis explores technological opportunities by systematically defining the basic features of current technology, identifying the known alternatives to each and then looking for feasible alternative combinations.

A car, for example, can have alternative fuels: petrol, diesel, battery, gas, solar; alternative body materials: steel, plastic, aluminium, fibre-glass, etc.; alternative braking systems: friction disk, air, cable, etc. These can then be combined in different formulas to produce alternative-concept cars (hybrids are also possible, e.g. diesel/battery). This provides a fresh perspective on customary technologies and a fruitful basis for brainstorming feasible product alternatives.

Scenarios provide broader views of the future and insight into more diverse developments. Alternative personal transportation systems, for example, might include microlight aircraft systems but equally, developments in interactive video, teleworking and virtual reality might make many such journeys unnecessary in future.

Activity 9.4

Taking either the industry in which you work, or one of your choice for which information can be accessed (see below), undertake an outline technological forecast.

You might find it useful to consider the prevalent technology in various time periods: short term (say, up to 2 years), medium term (5 years), long term (10 years) and very long term (10+).

Potential impacts must be identified, not only for the industry itself but also for channel intermediaries and end users. Feasible technologies are then screened to remove improbable options due to considerations of cost, environmental safety and so forth and a time scale determined for the remainder. This might be done by the use of Delphi techniques, drawing on the expertise of practitioners in the field.

Possible technologies must, however, be set against marketing forecasts of what the demand will be. Timing is also critical in achieving innovative success and avoiding technological failure. An innovation which is right for its time must have not only all the requisite technical building blocks in place but also receptive users, with the need, income and strength of preference to demand it in profitable volumes.

Can you put a time scale on the following applications?

- A chequeless society
- Virtual reality holidays
- Five per cent of residences with interactive access to databases
- Videophones in normal business use
- Drive-by-wire electronic systems for congestion-free motorways
- Speech-responsive computers
- Windscreen maps in cars

Technology and marketing applications

In this section we will briefly summarize the main applications for marketers arising out of information technology. More detailed coverage may be found in the text mentioned in the study guide. As already indicated, you should keep abreast of all developments that potentially facilitate the effective execution of the sales/marketer's task.

The logical order to consider this is from product conception through to after-sales service and eventual disposal. German companies like Mercedes, for example, must now maintain computerized records of all vehicles sold so they may be tracked and accounted for in compliance with recycling legislation.

- *Product development* This is based on forecasting and the use of various databases to assess customer requirements and tastes. Marketing research is facilitated through the use of computerized analysis packages such as SPSS.
- *Product design* Product development times are falling sharply through the flexibility, versatility and time saving involved in CAD/CAM/CAE. New cars which once took seven years from drawing board to production line now take less than four with computer-aided technology. The main implication is a shrinking maturity and decline stage for many products combined with a geometric expansion in models and parts numbers. Virtual reality offers further possibilities in terms of computer simulation.

Match up the following acronyms with their definitions:

- CAD/CAM/CAE
- FMS
- CIM
- JIT
- EPOS
- EFTPOS
- EDI
- CD-ROM

1 A just-in-time system of stock control which involves delivery of parts directly onto the shop/sales floor when required.
2 Computer-aided design, manufacture and engineering of products.
3 Electronic cash registers at the point of sale to the customer.
4 Systems to link up the computers of different businesses allowing the interchange of electronic data between them.
5 A flexible manufacturing system that allows small batches or units to be produced as efficiently as large runs.
6 A point-of-sale register which also allows for the electronic transfer of funds from the customer's to the retailer's account, e.g. Switch.
7 Computer-integrated manufacture automates all aspects of customer order, purchase, supply, manufacture and distribution.
8 A compact disk storing large volumes of information and images which can be read and reproduced by a computer.

(**See** Activity debrief at the end of this unit.)

- *Manufacturing operations* Integrated computer control has enabled production to become increasingly flexible and versatile. Whereas cost efficiency used to demand large production runs, due to long set-up times, these can now be altered in seconds. Waiting time is eliminated and small batches produced at near-equivalent speed and cost. This is of great significance to the marketer in terms of product availability and the ability to respond to increased demand arising from promotional initiatives. The spread of the JIT stock control concept from Toyota has also transformed volume production and distribution systems. Responsibility for delivery of parts onto the shopfloor, as they are required for assembly or processing, is transferred to suppliers. Work in progress is therefore minimized. Similar systems have been adopted by retailers in order to maximize selling areas and sales per square metre. Range can be extended by minimizing the stock that has to be carried.
- *Warehousing and logistics* Service levels for fast-moving consumer goods are improving progressively through the automation of storage and handling facilities. Maximum availability and rapid response to changing tastes and preferences now require a system which can instantly capture changing sales trends and translate them into the necessary supply and stock adjustments. EPOS systems using product barcodes and increasingly sensitive laser readers provide the sales data for stock control, sales analysis, automatic replenishment or new-order placement. More and more businesses are linked through EDI systems to facilitate such automatic computer linkage. Linked systems allow interrogation of stock and order status together with the transmission of marketing mix-details. Delivery now often takes place around the clock to avoid traffic congestion and conform to JIT requirements. Computerized transportation programmes plan optimal routes while satellite beacon systems and radio links allow flexible redeployment. Digital technology via cable, satellite or computer similarly eases the delivery of a wide array of 'home' services and offers opportunities for targeting customer segments.
- *Point of sale* EFTPOS has transformed the potential of retail outlets in terms of not only additional sales area and frequently replenished demand related stock ranges but also speedier and more accurate customer transactions, shorter queues, improved cash flow and enhanced security. Some supermarkets have introduced trolleys with mini-scanners, enabling customers to process their own transactions as they shop and avoiding the need for checkouts. The internet is transforming direct marketing as well as improving customer relationships through accessible web-sites.

Future applications of technology

Although it is difficult to be specific about the timing of particular developments it is clear that there is still considerable scope for new applications of relevance to the salesperson and the marketer. It is important to recognize that technology does not operate in isolation from the individual, relationships or the wider organization.

Activity 9.5

Conduct a Delphi study of relevant internal and external stakeholders on their views and predictions regarding innovations thought likely to affect relationships between themselves and your organization.

Do not restrict this to stakeholders in different functional areas of the business. Contact suppliers, distributors, third-party contractors, banks, local authorities and so forth where possible.

Teleworking

Alternatively known as telecommuting or the electronic cottage, this involves working from home using telecommunications and computing equipment. A 1993 Department of Employment study on teleworking in Britain concluded that over 5 per cent of employers employed such workers. The most frequently cited occupations expected to figure in future plans were data entry, sales or marketing work and computer-based activities.

The main benefits of teleworking include:

- Flexibility
- Reduced cost
- Solution to travel problems
- Employ staff with care responsibilities
- Convenience
- Space saving
- Retain skilled staff

Other benefits include savings in travel time and stress; greater productivity due to fewer distractions and ability to work in preferred locations. The falling cost of technology and increasingly versatile equipment that is available makes this option attractive as office and non-labour costs soar in urban centres. Global telecommunications will also allow teleworkers from less developed countries to compete with high-wage equivalents in affluent nations. Telework may be processed in India or Pakistan at one-tenth the cost of London.

There are, however, a number of drawbacks to teleworking:

- Management and communication difficulties
- Social isolation
- Losing touch with the organization
- Unavailability for meetings

Technical and security problems may also arise as well as difficulties in ensuring quality control. Many workers find work discipline a difficulty and miss the creative spark provided by fellow-workers. Employers have therefore often taken steps to increase social integration by providing more communication with colleagues, managers and customers. One societal development of note is Hong Kong's plan to test interactive television in 88 000 homes by the end of 1998 and to have 90 per cent of its 6.5 million population connected by 2001.

Question 9.8

Technology now allows a vehicle to be fitted with the equivalent of the electronic office (i.e. portable computer, fax, carphone, etc.). With regard to marketing, do you think the future lies with mobile or residential teleworkers?

(**See** Activity debrief at the end of this unit.)

Electronic meetings

Meetings can take up to two-thirds of a manager's time. It is therefore essential that such time is used productively, especially where clients are involved. If, say, ten people meet for an hour then the average contribution of each is just 6 minutes. Since 20 per cent of those present tend to speak 80 per cent of the time the contributions of the majority are actually restricted much further.

Technology can not substitute for brain power and human interaction but it can vastly increase contributions. Given appropriate technology, participants can type their ideas and contributions onto a network of screens and react to those provided by the others. Brainstorming and evaluation can take place quickly and anonymously if necessary.

Remote metering

New electronic meters and remote-sensing devices now allow a competitive transformation in UK utility markets such as gas and electricity. Since 1998 it has been possible for consumers to buy power from competing companies by virtue of these devices. The system is operated by British Gas, but rival marketing companies will be responsible for supplying sufficient gas through it to meet customer demand. Fierce and sometimes questionable competition has marked this radical restructuring of the market. In Finland mobile telephone manufacturers are pioneering a home management system where dialled instructions activate various domestic appliances.

Database marketing

The ability of the computer to capture, store, communicate and process vast amounts of data opens up massive opportunities for the far-sighted marketer. Database marketing involves the fusion of information gathered on actual and potential customers; actual and potential competitors; as well as internal cost and sales data. This can be used to screen then select target customers and fine-tune the marketing mix offered, in order to achieve maximum profit contribution in the light of operational and financial constraints.

Activity 9.6

Refer to the company reports you were asked to obtain in Unit 1 and study them for references to the technological environment.

Companies often take the opportunity presented in reviewing the past years performance and future plans to outline new technology initiatives and achievements. This provides a very useful insight into their research, development and capital expenditure.

Resistance to change

Technology has been the major engine in the development of mass affluence yet it has always been resisted. From the Luddites, who smashed the knitting frames that threatened their livelihoods at the outset of the Industrial Revolution, to print workers displaced by computer typesetting and more recently miners made redundant by cheaper alternate fuels, the outcome has always been the same: beneficial advance may have been delayed but never prevented.

The short-term impact of technologically induced unemployment has frequently been considerable, not least on communities dependent on the industry in structural decline. In the long run, however, there has been a growth in demand for labour that has broadly paralleled the growth in the labour force.

Process technology has substituted machines for labour to minimize costs but new *product technology* has created employment opportunities in so-called sunrise industries. Adaption has been difficult, however, because the new jobs have generally required higher-order skills than the ones they replaced.

It is not only employees who resist change, but also consumers, distributors and managers themselves. Changes in method and organization are as readily resisted as in technical processes, although change in one normally requires change in the others.

Question 9.9

Management is about the efficient allocation of resources to match changing consumer needs and wants, yet British management has frequently been criticized for its reluctance or inability to bring about change. Identify factors, the lack of which, may account for this weakness. Identify conditions which enable management in your own country to become effective change agents.

(**See** Activity debrief at the end of this unit.)

Customers may resist product changes out of force of habit, prejudice or conservatism born of age. Product revivals may succeed on similar grounds as adults relive their youth or bring their children up consuming equivalent goods and services. Market understandings may also make the business reconsider introducing changes that disrupt competitive relationships.

Change might also be resisted by external forces such as pressure groups, concerned with the impact on the environment. Laws and regulations also constrain what is possible. The Data Protection Act, for example, required that mailing list organizations register and abide with its provisions, thereby limiting their scope for use by direct marketing businesses. Provisional EU legislation will forbid unsolicited fax transmissions unless prior permission is obtained. This will inhibit the activities of many direct marketers and provide resistance to the growth in corporate junk mail.

The symptoms of resistance to change

The marketer should be aware of why people resist change and take steps to minimize it. This applies as much to marketing staff as to affected stakeholders in the micro-environment. An important first step is in the identification of resistance to change as evidenced by:

- Increased turnover rates
- Illness and absenteeism rises
- Reduced productivity or operational effectiveness
- Failure to cooperate or communicate
- Head-in-the-sand attitudes
- General loss of morale
- Increased membership of unions or staff associations
- Action up to and including actual sabotage of operations.

Question 9.10 What would be the symptoms to look for among the customer base as evidence of an adverse reaction to a change in order-processing procedures initiated by your organization? What steps might you have taken to reduce this resistance?

(**See** Activity debrief at the end of this unit.)

'All the forces which contribute to stability in personality or in social systems can be perceived as resisting change' (Goodwin Watson). Such forces work to the advantage of established brands, for example, since consumer behaviour is also governed by:

- *Habit* In purchasing patterns.
- *Primacy* The first successful means we find of solving a problem or meeting a need is used again in future. Hence a firm keeps using the same advertising agency.
- *Selective perception* Evidence that conflicts with preconceptions is ignored (e.g. Buy British despite the fact that some foreign alternatives are now superior in quality).
- *Dependence* This relates to buying patterns to maintain our sense of belonging to a group or a class (e.g. keep up with the Jones).

Change is also resisted if it is against our best interests. Indeed, it is not the change itself but the results and consequences of it that are often the cause of the problem. We have also seen that the interests of both individuals and stakeholders do not always coincide with those of the organization. The individual will therefore be concerned not only with economic and security needs but also social and status considerations when technological change takes place. Other factors increasing resistance to change might include:

- *The nature of past experience of change* If this has been negative and prejudicial then resistance will be stronger.
- *If apprehensions are unanswered* If people mistakenly fear that they will not be able to cope with change then misapprehensions arise, producing unnecessary resistance.

227

- *The manner of the change* Resented if autocratic.
- *Lack of consultation or participation* If a supermarket alters its layout without reference to its customers.
- *Where change is infrequent* Experience and confidence are therefore lacking.

<table>
<tr><td>**Extending Activity 9.1**</td><td>Identifying the symptoms and causes of resistance to change is one thing, but managing change to prevent them arising in the first place is a more effective strategy. Undertake research into how either Japanese management or excellent Western companies have succeeded in accommodating turbulent environmental change. Indicate how their approach addresses each of the sources of resistance outlined above.</td></tr>
</table>

Conclusions

Technological change is very much a double-edged phenomenon. It has so far prevented the dismal predictions of both Malthus and Marx by enabling rising productivity and real living standards but at the cost of high transitional unemployment. Its accelerating pace has enabled a sharply rising population to be accommodated but has produced 'future shock' among many seeking to cope with the myriad changes involved. It has provided convenience through increasingly intelligent products and services but also unforeseen consequences as the effects have rippled through society. Genetic technology, for example, may cure inherited diseases and enhance crop quality and consistency, but might equally release uncontrollable mutations and steralize wildlife.

<table>
<tr><td>**Question 9.11**</td><td>Identify some unintended consequences of the following product developments:

- The car, e.g. the RAC claims that the average motorist spends five days per annum stuck in traffic – this could rise to 14 days by 2005!
- The telephone
- The television

How have they changed the nature of marketing?</td></tr>
</table>

The nature of turbulent environmental change

The marketer is concerned with the future. This concern is fundamental given the importance of identifying and anticipating future needs and wants. Profitable realization of this aim, however, means the marketer is confronted with the task of understanding the nature of this environmental change and coping with its consequences. So, having devoted nine course units to the study of specific environments, let us now consider its overall nature from an integrated viewpoint. It has been a consistent theme of this workbook that the various environments are in a continuous state of change. Indeed some writers suggest that the marketing environment is not only ever changing but inherently turbulent. What does this mean, and what is the evidence to support it?

- The term 'turbulent' suggests an environment in a degree of turmoil, buffeted by uncontrollable forces which continuously disturb any tendency towards stability. We have seen that the macro-environment is made up of largely uncontrollable elements and that virtually no organization operates in static conditions. What can be debated is the degree of turbulence which may vary from industry to industry and environment to environment.

- Turbulence suggests confusion and a state of flux. The increasingly competitive nature of many markets could fit such conditions as could the current outlook for stock markets or the Euro.
- Turbulence also implies uncertainty and discontinuity, but is not as strong a term as chaos or revolution. One could argue, of course, that genetic engineering is potentially revolutionary, or that a youth and gender revolution is currently underway, but the time scale seems sufficiently long to remove much of the unpredictability. On the other hand it could be argued that the process of invention and innovation is inherently unpredictable along with the extremes of weather and natural disasters that have seemingly increased in frequency over recent years.
- What is clear, is that an array of variable environmental forces are operating to produce a degree of ambiguity for the marketer as to the probable patterns of the future. As we will discuss more fully in the next section, greater dynamism and complexity are synonymous with turbulence in the marketing environment.
- Apart from technological forces there are other trends including globalization, religious fundamentalism and variable economic growth rates to drive the turbulence. The uncertain state of Russia, China, East Asia and many emerging countries, together with the doubtful outlook for continued boom conditions in America provide a basis for current volatility.

Turbulent conditions do not necessarily imply adversity for organizations. Opportunities as well as threats are created and businesses vary in their ability to 'ride' the market rapids. Equally, much of the associated cost may be shared with, or transferred onto, the consumer (in higher prices), the workforce (redundancies), competitors (lower sales), suppliers (lower prices), the government (subsidies/bail outs) and other stakeholder groups.

Dynamic and complex conditions

These are the two critical dimensions by which marketing environments may be judged, the dynamic and the complex. There is a spectrum of market possibilities ranging from completely static to extremely dynamic conditions in a given environment. Similarly, there is a degree of environmental complexity from the very simple (i.e. a single clear cause and effect), to the extremely complex (with many and varied interdependent causes).

Activity 9.7

Locate on a matrix of increasing environmental complexity and dynamism the following organizations: a funeral director; a computer software manufacturer; a university; a biscuit manufacturer; a pop group; an advertising agency; your own organization.

(**See:** Activity debrief at the end of this unit.)

Dynamic conditions are associated with high energy driving forces within a wider environment with relative few frictions and that often produce rapid change, growth and development. It therefore suggests markets where significant and potentially powerful environmental forces are in motion and these drive the situation in which the organization finds itself. Emerging markets driven by invention, accelerating innovation and an explosion in information technology are clear examples of such change. Globalization with its flows of direct investment responding to changing exchange rates, labour market conditions and economic performance is another source of creative energy in the world economy. Dynamic conditions can be unleashed by a catalyst such as deregulation, the burgeoning internet, new entry into a market or the changing needs, wants or demands of a stakeholder group. Government policy tends towards the creation of a dynamic economy. Enterprising management is encouraged, red tape curtailed, information technology learning centres introduced and incentives to work and succeed are enhanced. Competition policy may also be sharpened to encourage the process of creative destruction.

Complex conditions suggest a market context upon which diverse influences are exerted and is complicated. Many variables are involved and these are either interdependent or inter-react through both positive and negative feedback loops. Systems theory has demonstrated the intricate complexity of economic and social systems. These are extremely difficult to model. British weather forecasts, despite sophisticated computer analysis and simulation, are frequently criticized for their imperfections, but we are much further away from convincingly modelling societal change.

Complexity is very much like a 'black box', we observe flows in and out, we apply trial and error and make predictions but we don't fully know how it works! We have seen that most markets are not simple and that analysis requires consideration of at least five forces. Alternative outcomes are likely due to the interdependence of rivals. They may seek to manage the complexity through agreements and understandings but the tension created by pursuit of competitive advantage and the potential for a zero sum game (I win–you lose) create options and complex uncertainties.

Complexity therefore means that marketers are faced by a succession of non-routine problems and situations demanding action. Few will be simple or repetitive and therefore amenable to standard policy responses. Predictability is likely to be low, the environment dynamic and any action will cause reaction through a highly interconnected system. The fall in retail sales which brought M&S to crisis has resulted in corporate actions which have not only reverberated within internal departments and along the supply chain, but also to downmarket competitors (as prices have been cut) and upmarket designers.

Adaptability – the proactive response

Some argue that it is people's 'ability to change' that is the critical limiting factor in exploiting the full potential of information and other new technologies. We have already discussed the potential forces of resistance to change earlier, and these can arise anywhere in the internal, connected or even macro-environments. Management can be the countervailing force in reducing resistance or driving change, but may equally form a constraint. What is it that makes for an adaptable organization in the face of dynamic and complex change? Points to consider would include:

- Management must actively confront a difficult environment, not acquiesce or passively accept it.
- Reliance on accumulated experience and perceptions only allows reaction.
- Management must forecast change if it is to act proactively – this is a function of the variety of media channels used, the richness of the data collected, the speed of feedback and the openness of internal sub systems.
- One approach is to 'read the environment' and adapt by making business and marketing changes that resonate with it. This continuous adaption achieves a dynamic equilibrium between internal strengths and capabilities and external opportunities.

- Burns and Stalker argued that dynamic environments required 'organic' organization favouring decentralization of decision-making power to where they need to be made, and fewer organization levels to allow rapid communication up and down the chain of command. Bureaucratic or mechanistic structures were only workable in relatively static conditions.
- Contingency plans are a means of dealing with future uncertainty. This approach could be informed by so-called risk analysis to assess the probability and likely impact of possible environmental changes. Further development could involve executive training in crisis, or shock management, e.g. simulate the consequences of an oil tanker running aground or an explosion.
- Adaptability demands flexibility in the redeployment of scarce resources to meet new threats and opportunities. We examined this concept in Unit 8.
- Organization's must embrace change and innovation and not wait until the maturity stage of the life cycle. The success of current product lines can create powerful resistance and inhibit necessary adaption to the products of the future. Companies like 3M formalize continuous innovation in their policies, including the encouragement of intrapreneurship.

Definition 9.2

Match up the following definitions:

- Entrepreneur
- Intrapreneur
- Change agent
- Champion

1 A risk taker and creator of new enterprises.
2 An individual with a fresh perspective who acts as a catalyst in helping the organization find new solutions to old problems.
3 One who believes in the value of an idea or approach and supports or advances it in the face of numerous possible obstacles and opposition within the organization.
4 Individuals who are encouraged to fulfil entrepreneurial roles within a large organization.

(**See** Activity debrief at the end of this unit.)

Note: The entrepreneur and his or her equivalents have been viewed as the vital spark that has ignited the economic engine ever since the Industrial Revolution. Resources are little use in themselves unless they can be creatively and innovatively combined to generate new and improved products and processes. The economist J. A. Schumpeter viewed the entrepreneur as both a positive and a disruptive force which:

- Kept existing businesses on their toes
- Broke up the old economic order by innovating change
- Created wealth through new factor combinations to better serve the market.

The marketer may conclude that even the most sophisticated environmental scanning and forecasting techniques will prove unable to cost effectively consider more than a very small proportion of the total of potentially useful information available. Many organization's decide that the change is too difficult to manage proactively and choose instead to shadow the actions of competitors as a strategy against being isolated and caught out. An alternative approach, adopted by many of the more successful organizations, is to plan to create your own environment based on your own view of the future. Action is taken to share this vision with stakeholders and build relationships that allow a flexible response to turbulence throughout the micro-environment. The organization sets the market agenda and competitors are left to follow.

Summary

In this unit concerning the technological environment we have:

- Identified some of the main characteristics of technology and its main phases, culminating in the information or communications era which developed economies are currently entering.
- The critical role of business was examined and the factors that caused some firms to be more innovative than others.
- Technical imperatives driving the pace and diversity of technological change were identified and explained. The capitalist dynamic and the source of fifty-year long-wave cycles were studied in some detail.
- The microprocessor, as the key enabling technology in the information revolution, was described in terms which accounted for the all-inclusive impact it has had on all aspects of contemporary society.
- The diffusion process was explained and the need for technological forecasting emphasized. Sources of information by which a business can keep track of potential developments were outlined.
- Various applications to sales and marketing were discussed with reference to the supply chain. Some future applications were assessed including telecommuting and marketing databases.
- The symptoms and sources of resistance to change of the customer and employee were explored.
- The marketing environment is increasingly complex, dynamic, uncertain and turbulent for many organizations and their stakeholders.
- The nature of the environment demands adaption from organizations, although standard strategic planning responses may prove less effective in turbulent circumstances.

Activity debrief

Definition 9.1 2, 5, 7, 1, 3, 6, 4, 8.
Definition 9.2 1, 4, 2, 3.
Question 9.1
- Industries affected by innovations are numerous, especially where information technology has been applied. Others include pharmaceuticals, chemicals, car design, financial services, etc.
- Unaffected sectors are difficult to find since most have been affected by IT systems. Craft goods and personal services of various types provide possibilities.

Question 9.2 None of the information technology-based consumer products and services were available – colour TV, video, calculators, cash dispensers, microwaves, camcorders, computer games, etc.

Question 9.3
- A super-highway involves the laying of fibre optic cable which allows high-speed transmission of a variety of information services. BT is laying a domestic system while Cable and Wireless is providing transPacific services.
- Interactive TV, on-line shopping, video-conferencing, database access.

Question 9.4 The main threats involve the loss of market share/profitability as a result of technological surprises; when to invest since rapid technological change will make premature investments obsolete; hi-tech may involve highly specialized plant and inflexibility in the face of changing consumer tastes; high cost of investment (e.g. microchip plants currently cost $1 billion); risk and loss of failure (e.g. Sinclair C5 car, Phillips videodisc). The main opportunities involve excess profit, competitive advantage, lower costs, faster growth, greater flexibility. See also the benefits of microprocessors.

Question 9.5 Example: the *motorist* would be stranded since microprocessors control ignition, steering, braking and in-board control systems on modern cars. Traffic lights would cease to function as would petrol pumps. *The marketing department* relies on 'information systems' defined as the products, services, methods and people used to collect, store, process, transmit and display information. It also relies on the telephone now controlled through digital exchanges not to mention televisions that receive advertisements. Product information derived from bar code scanners would be lost and banking and credit systems would fail.

Question 9.6 Clearly, an array of marketing strategies are relevant here including price skimming and penetration. Licensing and franchising are other possibilities to consider in achieving rapid coverage of the national/international markets.

Question 9.8 Portable computers are already transforming the capability of the sales force, giving them the opportunity to access the corporate database to answer customer queries regarding product availability, order status, promotions, etc. They could also enter orders immediately ensuring that stock is allocated. Intelligence regarding competitors could be input into the system. These combine through the power of the computer to offer massive potential to the sales force of the future. Legislation may limit mobile phone use.

Question 9.9 Factors include lack of: competitive pressure, incentive, finance, support from the board, champions, a risk-taking culture, long-term horizons, skills and experience of change, awareness of potential.

Question 9.10 Resistance may lead to loss of orders in the extreme, increased returns, more queries and complaints, a rise in errors, etc.

- You may have suggested such things as joint consultation over the proposed changes or, more importantly, involving customers in formulating them in the first place. Communications and incentives also have a role to play.

Activity 9.3 Information technology rates highly on nearly all counts. The scale of investment is high, however. Supersonic transport rated highly on change agents due to the impetus provided by government defence spending and subsidies but low on environment, safety and scale of investment. Nuclear has a similar pattern. Biotechnology has intermediate scores.

Activity 9.7 A funeral director (Low/Low), a computer s/ware (H/H), a university (M/M), a biscuit manufacturer (L/M), a pop group (H/L), an advertising agency (M/L).

Extending activity 9.1 Such companies achieve a culture favourable to change; single status; suggestions welcomed/acted upon; atmosphere of trust; involvement; security needs recognized; retraining and support; support from the top.

Examination hints and specimen questions

Technology, as we have seen in this unit, is an all-pervasive aspect of the business environment. It also knows no boundaries and companies of every nationality will be seeking to exploit its potential for competitive advantage. It is therefore likely to be a popular aspect of the macro-environment for examination questions, given its general applicability to all CIM international centres. Refer to the compulsory question below for an example of a compulsory question from this area.

1 (a) What is the significance of technical change to the marketer?

(8 marks)

(b) Comment on the impact of technical change on the natural environment and suggest what direct action marketing activity must take if future growth is to become sustainable.   (12 marks)

(CIM Marketing Environment paper, June 1995)

2 Write notes on the implications for marketing of two of the following environmental factors:

(a) Technological forecasting
(b) Turbulence
(c) Complexity   (10 marks)

(CIM Marketing Environment paper, June 1998 – amended)

Hints: Indicative content and approach

Question 1(a)
- This is a relatively straightforward question.
- Deal with both opportunities and threats arising.
- Product and process innovation impacting on costs, design and development.
- Refer to creative destruction, diffusion, substitution and potential competition.
- Examples to illustrate significance, e.g. intelligent products.

Question 1(b)
- See Unit 10 case 4 for relevant material.
- Impacts would include emissions, effluents, solid wastes and resource depletion.
- Identify particular issues arising out of industrialization and mass consumption, e.g. the greenhouse effect, ozone depletion, acid rain, etc.
- Comment on the double-edged nature of change with examples, e.g. nuclear power releases no greenhouse gases but involves toxic waste.
- Define sustainability.
- Provides an opportunity to develop green marketing strategies based on cradle-to-grave approaches to product design and development.

Compulsory Marketing Environment question – illustration only

On-line for speedy sale

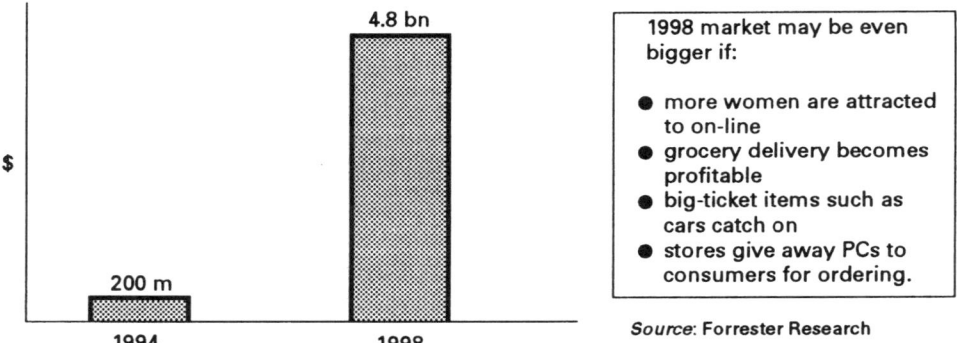

Source: Forrester Research

Do you want to send roses to your sweetheart, buy a new car, choose a cookbook for your mother's birthday or purchase computer software? One of the quickest, if not the cheapest, ways to make these purchases in the US and increasingly Europe and East Asia is via on-line computer information and communications services.

On-line computer shopping has been around for several years, but until recently most of the products available were aimed at computer hobbyists. Now the proliferation of home computers, with about one third of US households equipped with a personal computer, is attracting the attention of a broad variety of retailers to on-line shopping as a potentially important new sales channel.

An on-line service jointly owned by Sears Roebuck, the US retailer and IBM offers products from 150 merchants while America On-line allows subscribers to offer their homes for sale. Shopping centres are also being built on the internet, a global network that links an estimated 20m computer users offering software, hardware and related products.

While no-one is predicting that computer retailing will replace every trip to the local shopping centre, on-line merchandising is expected to grow rapidly over the next few years as the installation of communication 'superhighways' makes multimedia technology both cheaper and more accessible to consumers. To date this technology has generated only modest sales of less than $200m in the US compared with total retail sales of $1500bn. Of this, mail order accounted for $53bn and home shopping channels, placing orders by phone, a further $2.5bn. However as the chart shows, some market researchers are predicting dramatic increases driven by a swelling potential customer base, improved product presentation and the low comparative costs of selling on-line.

In San Francisco, consumers with the necessary software can shop at their local Safeway supermarket without leaving home. On-line shoppers can either wander through the 'virtual reality' supermarket aisle by aisle or go to specific locations. Personal shopping lists carrying regular items can be created and special offers highlighted. The grocery order is then delivered at the customer's convenience.

Currently prices are no lower and the transmission of pictures to the home computers is slow but multimedia PCs are transforming this. One company has launched a CD-Rom catalogue to supplement its on-line shopping service with pictures and videos of available products. Even this combination is primitive compared to the 'interactive' shopping planned by US cable television companies. These services will require substantial investment but would supply full video and sound and may even provide customers with 'assistants' to help armchair shoppers with their fashion choices.

(Adapted from Louise Kehoe article in FT 23/6/94)

1 (a) Write short notes **two** of the following technical terms used in the article and briefly comment on their wider significance for the marketer:
   (i)   Multimedia technology
   (ii)   Virtual reality
   (iii) CD-Rom
   (iv)   Interactive television shopping
   (v)   Communications superhighway
   (vi)   Computer software   (6 marks each Total 12 marks)
   (b) Draw on your understanding of the marketing environment to explain why no one is predicting that computer retailing will replace every journey to the shopping centre.   (7 marks)
   (c) Suggest further reasons why growth in on-line retailing may expand more rapidly than predicted.   (7 marks)
   (d) Provide an outline structural analysis of your grocery retailing market. What recommendations would you make to a traditional retailer like Safeway?

(14 marks)
(Total 40 marks for question)
(CIM Marketing Environment paper, December 1995)

Meeting the challenge – managing the future environment

This unit is intended to be integrative since much of the content is in the form of a series of case studies on current and future challenges in the marketing environment. In this final study unit of the workbook you will:

❏ Appreciate the complex and dynamic nature of the external environment and consider how it might best be managed in marketing terms.

❏ Understand the key problems associated with forecasting change in the marketing environment.

❏ Distinguish between quantitative and qualitative forecasting methods.

❏ Examine other means of assisting the marketer to cope with future challenges.

❏ Consider a variety of current and future issues.

By the end of the unit you will be able to:

❏ Undertake an environmental audit for an organization.

❏ Assess the probable impact of significant opportunities and threats.

❏ Draw on a toolbox of techniques to meet the challenge of change.

❏ Recognize the complex nature of the marketing environment.

❏ Be able to discuss the significance of relevant and topical environmental challenges.

This concluding study unit is central to managing the future environment. It considers three aspects of coping with the future. The first aspect develops a theme introduced in Unit 9, that of key problems confronting the business in dealing with the dynamism and uncertainty of future change. The second aspect surveys the tools and techniques available to the marketer in establishing the nature and significance of the challenge. The third aspect involves consideration of a number of cases of current and future environmental change to which the marketer may have to adapt. In common with most of the preceding units, this one accounts for around 10 per cent of the syllabus content. Although some elements were contained in the old syllabus, its re-formulation here makes this whole area entirely new. As such there are no previous examination questions to use as a guide for future papers. Some specimen questions have been prepared at the end of the unit to provide insight into their possible form. Others are provided at the end of Unit 11.

One important point to note is that while the syllabus includes examples, it does not confine you to specific issues to address in this part of the indicative content. Questions will normally allow you some latitude to discuss any relevant current/future issues rather than designating, for example, the Euro or genetically modified foods. This unit considers a number of cases, but there are many more that could have been selected. Many, indeed, have been discussed in earlier units.

You should therefore have a two part file: one part for the description of various tools and techniques, with a sub-section for each, and the second part for cuttings and articles on interesting issues, again divided into sub-sections. These would be the type of issues that would find their way into the environmental set of a company. Possibilities, not included in the cases in this edition (i.e. they will change as editions are annually updated), may be drawn from any of the environments. Examples might include the implications of the employment bill, the ending of duty-free allowances, the introduction of new telephone numbers, the impact of digital television and so forth.

Coping with the challenge: the key problems

Since the determinants and resulting shape of the future market for a product may be significantly different from the past, most forecasting techniques that rely on historic information and the projection of past and current trends will tend to be misleading. Even highly sophisticated forecasting based on computer models, as used by the UK Treasury, has been prone to considerable error. One cynic suggested that economists had successfully forecast nine of the last five recessions!

The long-awaited green shoots of recovery in 1991/1992, for example, took 18 months longer to germinate than predicted and led to the resignation of the Chancellor of the Exchequer . The long-term consequences of the sharp tax rises then required and the persistence of the 'feel bad' or at best 'feel insecure factor' implied a change in government at the next election. Businesses may fare little better. Many have a planning horizon of five to ten years, but to make strategic plans over such a time period implies a reasonable degree of certainty regarding significant environmental trends and developments. However, as seen in Unit 9, turbulence undermines predictability making such an approach questionable. Consider Siemens decision to close its £1.2 billion state-of-the-art semi-conductor plant in Tyneside just a year after its opening. Why? Because it had failed to foresee the Asian economic collapse and a fall in chip prices from $55 in 1995 to under $3 at the time of closure. Such are the potential consequences of bad forecasts and any business must address the following problems:

- *Which are the right forecasts?* There are often a variety of independent economic forecasters, but how can a business know which to rely on in advance?
- *How significant are the different trends?* Think about this question in reference to green consumer attitudes. Are concerns strengthening or tending to ebb and flow with recession and boom?
- *How long before a pattern of events become a trend?* Is teleworking – working from home via a computer/communications link with your employer, a trend yet or not?
- *Where are the turning points?* Many aspects of life have rhythms, not least buying patterns, where seasonal or cyclical movements occur. The important requirement here is timing of the upturn or downturn. Failure to anticipate and prepare for it will result in either lost sales or unsold stock, depending on the error.

- *Which are the discontinuities?* This is one of the most difficult areas to forecast since it implies a reversal or even disappearance of a trend. The significant shift from cheap to dear energy caused by the OPEC cartel in the 1970s was a discontinuity. With commodity prices, including oil, at an all time low is another in prospect? A change in government with a very different economic philosophy can also have this effect. The demise of the nuclear family (2 adults + 2 children) as the norm is another.
- *What is the pace of change?* Knowing the direction of change is one thing, but knowing the speed of its development is the key to an effective response. Who predicted the frightening pace of contraction in the British coal mining industry? From 170 deep mines employing 175 000 people in 1985 to just seventeen operational pits employing a mere 11 000 in early 1994. Suppliers and local traders who failed to anticipate this and adjust will also have suffered the consequences.

Many distinctive trends have reversed or discontinued in recent years. The power and significance of trade unions has declined greatly, house prices have fallen while inflation in general has decreased to negligible rates not seen for over twenty-five years. With falling birth rates Britain's youth culture has also given way to an affluent ageing one.

Disagreements over the answers to the key problems outlined above produces very different views of the future with no guarantee as to which will turn out to be the most accurate one. The possible business responses to such forecasting problems are as follows:

- *Abandon all forecasting pretensions* This would be a naive response to such difficulties. Every action involving plans or preparations for tomorrow requires some forecasting to be effective. The essence of managerial decision making involves forecasting future conditions. Even day-to-day operational decisions, involving a much shorter time horizon than strategic decisions, require a clear view of the future if such matters as stock levels, sales targets or advertising budgets are to be effectively set.
- *Concentrate on short-term adaptive planning* If the further the manager peers into the future, the murkier the view becomes, then this is a great temptation. Focus on the year ahead but establish a flexible management system that allows rapid adaption to environmental change. This may be possible for some businesses in relatively static markets, but what about a water company, a telecommunications supplier or a pharmaceutical business? A new reservoir must be planned over ten years ahead, while technological change is so rapid in telecommunications that a reaction strategy, no matter how effective, would come far too late. The drug company must be planning its product life cycles in the knowledge that testing and verification procedures will take a decade. All companies considering acquisition, modernization or diversification must forecast the medium- and longer-term future, if only in broad terms.

Remember that the examiner may set the question in the context of your business communications skills. Instead of a straightforward essay question you may be asked to prepare a brief or write a report. Read the question carefully, and if this is the case then follow the instructions given. Remember *up to 10 per cent* of the marks *may* be awarded for presentational effectiveness.

If a report is required then the format would normally include:

- Title
- Summary
- Contents
- Introduction
- Findings
- Conclusions
- Recommendations

Do not get carried away with the format, however, and forget to answer the question itself which counts for at least *90 per cent of the marks*. Set the points out clearly and break up the text using lists of short, key points rather than long sentences.

- *Improve the quality of conventional forecasts* Forecasts normally refer to objective, quantitative techniques which seek to extrapolate or project historical data into the future. Effective forecasting involves the following stages:

  - Select the critical environmental variables as future indicators.
  - Identify relevant sources of information on the variables.
  - Evaluate forecasting techniques.
  - ntegrate forecast output into strategic plans on a continuous basis.
  - Monitor and evaluate with particular reference to possible discontinuity of time series, meaning that the 'rules of the past' no longer apply.

The problem is not a lack of the necessary statistical techniques but rather the quality and availability of the necessary data. As with computers, the principle of garbage-in garbage-out applies and the resulting projection will only be as good as the input. Sophisticated statistical methods such as multiple regression, moving averages and exponential smoothing will be of little value if the data collected is suspect. Be warned by the wry response to the question 'why did God create economists?' – answer, 'To make weather forecasters look good!'

Definition 10.1

Match the following terms to the definitions:

- Demand function
- Depth interview
- Multiple regression
- Moving averages
- Exponential smoothing
- Probability

1 Best estimate of the outcome of each decision alternative.
2 Unstructured, usually face to face and intended to elicit meaningful information from a respondent.
3 A technique used to calculate the explanatory value of a number of independent variables affecting a dependent one.
4 The factors that determine the quantity demanded of a good per period of time.
5 Change in the average of, say, sales values over a number of time periods, by adding the most recent value and dropping the earliest in the series.
6 When weights used in the averaging process decrease progressively for values further into the past.

(**See** Activity debrief at the end of this unit.)

- *Use the combined view of experts (Delphi technique)* This is a subjective and qualitative technique relying primarily on human judgement rather than statistical method. They are essentially intuitive techniques, deriving, from the expert's blend of knowledge, experience and judgement. The experts may include academics, consultants, relevant stakeholders as well as key directors in marketing, operations, finance and non-executive board members. Each may make an independent forecast of sales, for example, or respond to an initial prediction. These may be fed back for further comment in the light of each expert's contribution. The resulting forecast reflects the collective 'informed view' of those who are in the best position to judge developments. The consensus achieved will 'smooth out' extreme views and should carry credibility with those who use it. Unfortunately it is a time-consuming process and therefore costly in the expert's time. It may also fail to capture the possibility of radical change due to a similar mind set of the experts involved.

Activity 10.1

It is said that decisions should be taken closest to the customer affected. It is also suggested that the day-to-day operative knows most about the process involved. In the light of this, conduct a Delphi study within the sales force of your company with a view to forecasting sales on a product-by-product basis. Alternatively, survey the expert views of counter/shelving and support staff in your college library on improving customer service.

List the *advantages* of using the sales force to build up forecasts.

List the *weaknesses* of this approach.

(**See** Activity debrief at the end of this unit.)

- *Use judgemental analysis to identify a desired future* We all engage in goal-orientated planning if we wish to progress in life. It is a relatively successful approach so long as the world around us remains relatively stable and predictable. A young boy or girl who decides that becoming a renowned doctor is their goal will plan to get good GCSE grades, particularly in maths so they can progress to 'A' level, where good results are required in the various sciences if they are to gain entry to a university with a record of excellence and so on toward their goal. The organization may also map out its future towards a desired goal given the current environmental landscape. Lack of perfect foresight, unexpected obstacles and changing conditions might force changes in direction along the way, but the goal is clear and an outline map is better than no map at all!

Extending Activity 10.1

Have you identified your desired future and made a map?

The fact that you are reading this workbook suggests that you have given some thought to your future, but have you really planned it out?

- Where do you want to be in five years' time?
- Where do you want to be in ten years' time?
- Where would you like to be at the peak of your career?
- What do you need to do to ensure that you reach these milestones?
- What are your personal and intellectual strengths?
- What are your areas of weakness?
- Are these going to inhibit you from achieving your goals?
- If so, how are you going to remedy them and when?
- What qualifications, skills and experience will be necessary?
- Where are the gaps and when and how are you going to fill them?

- Is your job leading somewhere you want to go?

The list could go on, but the important thing is to try to control your own future and not drift along on a hope and a prayer. The environment will change and the unexpected will occur but a future-orientated plan provides a framework for successful adaption.

Mintzberg argues against centralized corporate planning and suggests that turbulent conditions demand decentralization and devolved responsibility. An evolving or incremental approach is advocated with adjustments made within a broad vision of the organization's future. He also reminds us that every generation believes its environment to be more turbulent than preceding ones and that the best way forward is to avoid over-formal planning processes and to put the emphasis on 'learning and flexibility'.

- *Use scenarios* These are alternative views of the future and have been developed by organizations such as Shell to assist prediction in uncertain times. The best way of understanding scenarios is by comparing them with quantitative forecasts:

A scenario	*A forecast*
A description of the future based on mutually consistent groupings of determinants.	A statistical synthesis of probabilities and expert opinion.
Says here are *some* of the key factors you have to take into account and this is the way they could affect your business.	Accounts relevant factors to yield *the best answer* – what is most likely to happen. This tends *to dictate final decisions.*
Designed to be considered with other scenarios – it is valueless on its own.	Stands alone.
A tool to assist understanding. It forms the backdrop to decision making, not an integral part of it.	Intended to be regarded as an *authoritative statement.*
A means of placing responsibility for planning decisions on the managers concerned.	A means of removing much of the responsibility for the final decision – managers tend to rely on the central forecast
Essentially qualitative.	Fundamentally quantitative.

Forecasts are therefore based on the belief that the *future can be measured and controlled*, whereas scenarios are based on the belief that they cannot be. Shell warns all corporate planners that the forecasts they know, love and rely on are based on this fallacy. It likens decisions based on them to pursuing a straight line through a minefield, and views much economic and business theory as a 'pretend world' in which people act as if they had knowledge where it can not exist. Planners seek firm answers and optimum solutions, as if uncertainty and change can be assumed away.

Activity 10.2

Identify key variables in the PEST environment and vary your assumptions about them in order to produce two alternative futures for the year 2002. Variables might include such factors as the outcome of the next general election, the stage of the economic cycle, demographic trends, trade factors and so forth.

You should also use the same exercise to produce two alternative industry scenarios based on the key variables operating in the specific market concerned. You may wish to label the scenarios to reflect the view of the future they suggest (e.g. business as usual or rapid recovery).

Coping with the challenge: the main approaches

The marketer has a toolbox of techniques available to assist understanding of a turbulent environment. Forecasting methods have already been considered and form a component among other techniques including: external audits; impact analysis; PEST/SWOT analysis; and the product life cycle. Other techniques have been described in context, such as: five-force and competitor analysis; leading indicators and morphological analysis. In this section we will consider some of these techniques.

Environmental audits

Knowledge is power and audits are the means of acquiring this power through the regular identification and collection of relevant information on the current situation.

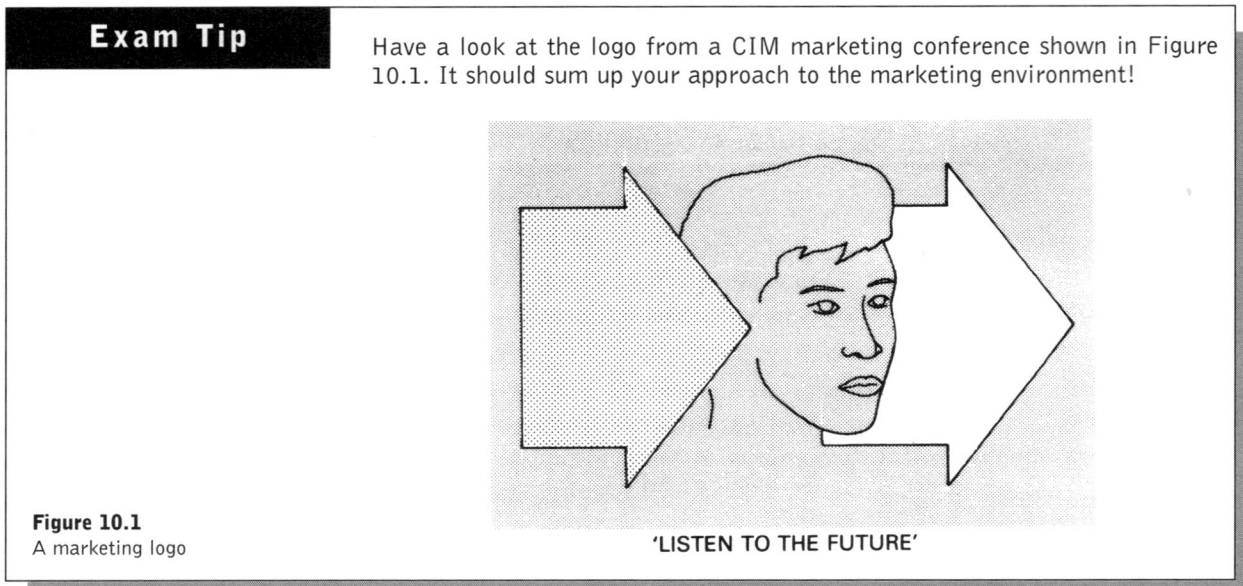

'LISTEN TO THE FUTURE'

Figure 10.1
A marketing logo

Audits are the formalized means of taking stock of the marketing environment. They require the marketer to undertake a detailed examination of external opportunities and threats:

- Markets, connected stakeholders and competitors.
- The economic environment and key macro-economic indicators.
- Other external environments.

It enables the organization to systematically understand what is happening in its environment and adapt accordingly. It is a critical input into the strategic planning process and underpins any projected diversification or extension to foreign markets. An external audit would normally be complemented by an internal or marketing audit to assess effectiveness in meeting marketing objectives. To determine how well the marketing activities and actions matched the opportunities and constraints of the environment requires a sound marketing information system covering all aspects. Some organizations will invest in the services of a consultancy firm to undertake the audit in the interests of objectivity. Explicit questions would be framed about the environment to independently verify or challenge any critical assumptions the organization had been making. Stakeholder perceptions could also be investigated regarding future trends. Audits, therefore, are a foundation stone in the process of coping with environmental change.

Impact analysis

This is a simple but applied approach to forecasting and assessing the probable impact of a specific environmental change on an organization or

Environmental future	Sainsbury's	Tesco	Asda	Kwik Save	Aldi
Edge-of-town planning restrictions tighten	– –	– –	– – –	–	– – –
Food Agency set up	–	–	–	–	0
Serious recession	–	–	0	+	+ +
Genetically modified foods backlash	– –	– –	+ +	0	0

Figure 10.2

its competitors. In effect it is measuring the sensitivity of key parameters to changes in environmental variables. A number of impact grids may be constructed to provide a more informed view of the implications of environmental change:

- *Competitor impact grid* – Figure 10.2 shows the effect of potential/probable environmental changes on direct competitors in multiple groceries. The effect is rated on a scale ranging from, say, +++ to – – – with 0 representing a neutral situation. A positive score suggests opportunity and improvement in profits, sales or overall competitive position, and visa versa.

Competitors vary in their ability to withstand threats or exploit opportunities. In the above example, most are affected by tightening planning regulations, but some more than others. Aldi is a relatively new entrant to the market and is short of sites for expansion. Asda is concentrated in the North of England so the regulations may prevent correction of this imbalance. A serious recession tends to advantage the cost focused retailers at the expense of Sainsbury's and Tesco, while Asda with its cost proximity should weather the storm. A boycott on GM foods would advantage those who have publicly declared GM free zones against those who will merely label ingredients. This analysis enables the marketer to assess the effects of environmental change in advance and adapt accordingly. A competitor analysis, as discussed in Unit 4, is a prerequisite for effective comparison in the use of this technique.

- *Environment impact grid* – this is designed to enhance the marketer's understanding of the specific impact of environmental forces on critical elements of the business. The marketer identifies environmental forces relevant to the business and then awards a weighted assessment ranging, say, from 0 (neutral) to 7 (critical impact). Figure 10.3 provides an outline of the technique using the case of cross channel ferries.

Environmental Factor / Impact on ferries	Duty free removed	High speed rail link in place	Exchange rate falls sharply	UK joins Euro	Low cost airlines wins Paris landing slots
Car passenger demand					
Foot passengers					
Lorries					
Ferry prices					
Marketing costs					

Figure 10.3

Question 10.3

Using your own knowledge and/or common sense, complete Figure 10.3.

- *Trend impact analysis* – this is a straightforward development of the environment impact grid. Any trend, in say commodity prices or household composition, is plotted up to date, according to its impact on revenues or costs, and then projected forward. This might draw attention to a prospective change in impact.

- *Cross impact analysis* – as the title suggests, this approach recognizes that the impact of a change in one variable may cause consequential impacts on other variables producing either positive, i.e. reinforces initial impact, or negative feedback.

- *Influence diagrams* – these are designed to provide the marketer with a clearer perception of the critical environmental influences on the business. These can then be closely monitored in order to provide early warning of threats or opportunities. A response to the contingency can then be planned and executed. A positive relationship in the influence diagram means that a change in any direction by the independent environmental variable will bring about a corresponding movement in the same direction by the dependent variable. A negative relationship applies the pressure in the opposite direction. In Figure 10.4, each environmental factor is designated by a box, a direction arrow and a + or – sign. A firm marketing Jacuzzis would recognize that sales volumes were influenced by private sector luxury house building, modernization and refurbishment trends and growth in health and fitness facilities. These will in turn be influenced by factors such as consumer confidence, house prices and the numbers moving house. Influences on these factors include interest rates, real incomes, employment and activity levels and so on. A rise in interest rates would therefore depress consumer confidence and in turn the demand for new luxury houses causing demand for Jacuzzis to fall.

Question 10.4

Can you fill in the lower part of the influence diagram relating to environmental influences affecting new health and fitness facilities? These are currently expanding rapidly in Britain causing Jacuzzi sales to rise. There are a number of + and – influence movements to identify.

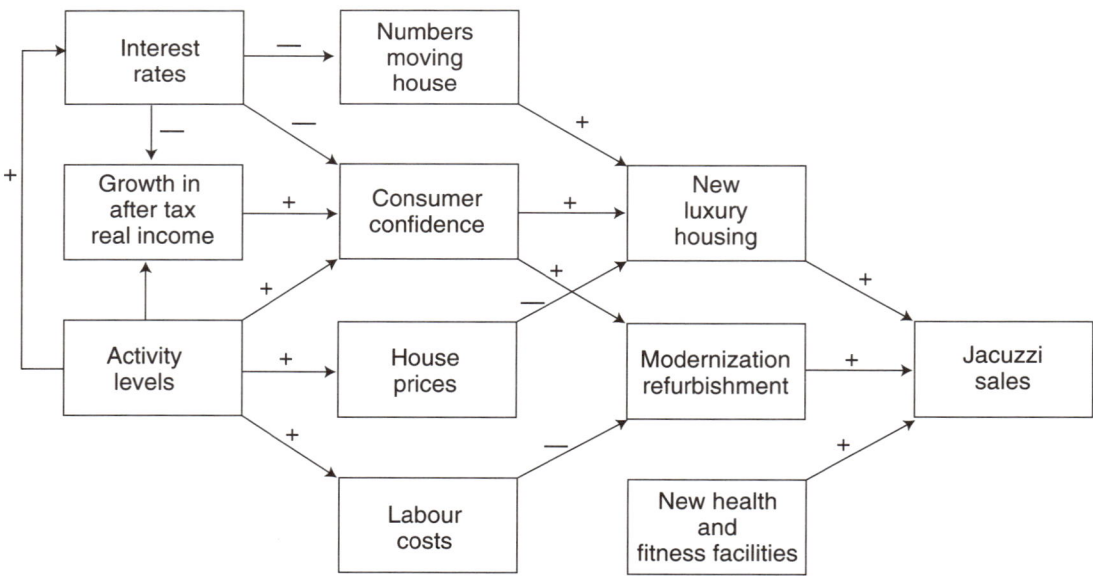

Figure 10.4 Influence diagram for sales of Jacuzzis

244

SWOT analysis

This analysis distils the results of the internal and external audit. When combined with impact analysis, it allows the organization to focus on its critical organizational strengths and weaknesses relative to the threats and opportunities faced in the environment. The whole purpose of the technique is to encourage the marketer to be outward looking. This means they must anticipate and understand important environmental developments and their impact on the business. An opportunity represents an area or development which, with appropriate marketing, would enable the organization to achieve a competitive advantage. Conversely, a threat has been defined as a challenge posed by an unfavourable trend in the environment, that would lead in the absence of marketing action to the erosion of the organization's competitive position. Much of this workbook has been concerned with the identification and discussion of threats and opportunities associated with the various elements of the marketing environment and will not be repeated here. However, every marketer is confronted with a unique array of such forces and these require some means of differentiation.

SWOT analysis provides a framework for the collection and systematic classification of information. Not all threats demand the same degree of concern and attention since the probability of impact and extent of consequential damage varies. The marketer naturally wishes to focus on the more threatening or potentially costly ones. Similar thinking applies to the range of emerging opportunities to which the organization's resources could be committed. Resources are scarce and have opportunity costs. The marketer requires some means of ranking opportunities according to:

- Potential attractiveness/prospective rate of return.
- Degree of matching with the organization's critical success factors (i.e. its strengths and weaknesses in key areas for exploiting the opportunity relative to competitors).
- Feasibility of alternative courses of action to exploit them.
- Probability of success – based on risk analysis/assessment.

Kotler suggests that if strengths and weaknesses represent where the organization is now, and opportunities and threats represent where it wishes to be at a given time in the future, then the role of the marketer is to supply the creativity to fill the gap between the two.

One classification technique to assist in the above process is the construction of an *environmental threat and opportunity profile*. As can be seen in Figure 10.5, both opportunities and threats can be located in matrices. Opportunities are located in the matrix according to their probability of success on the one hand and their relative attractiveness on the other. The latter is weighed in terms of, for example, potential profitability, projected growth rates and actual/potential competition, while the former is based on assessment of relative strengths. Threats are assessed by judging the likelihood of them happening against the scale of the potential damage if they do.

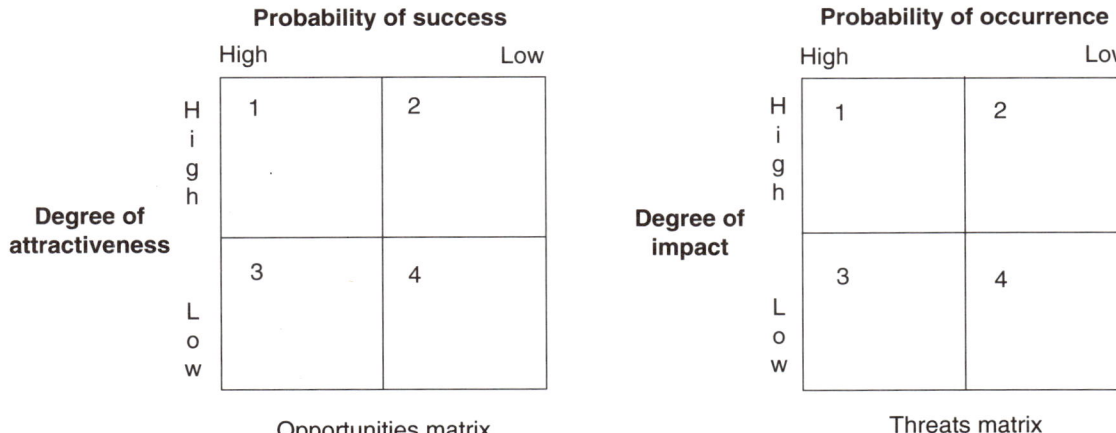

Figure 10.5   Opportunities and threats matrix

245

Each box in the analysis provides a ranking of significance. Marketers will clearly be more interested in opportunities located in Area 1, since they are both attractive and provide a good fit with organizational strengths. Area 1 threats will also require more serious consideration than those residing in Area 4. The analysis can be applied with varying degrees of sophistication through the use of calculated probabilities, weights and so forth. However, at the end of the day the role of the analysis is to concentrate marketing minds on future plans to exploit the 'right' opportunities and/or defuse serious and imminent threats to the continued success of the business.

Product life cycle (PLC)

This concept will be more familiar to candidates of Marketing Fundamentals than the Marketing Environment. However, there are aspects of this fundamental concept that have value in appreciating the future environment. The PLC is, after all, a trend projection but with a familiar S shape as seen in Figure 10.6. The shape of individual product PLCs can vary significantly due to the characteristics of the market environment an/or the marketing commitment of the firm.

The concept can be applied to product categories, e.g. washing machines or to more short-lived brands. To plan for the future an organization needs to project its revenues and costs for all its product lines. This applies as much to a college or a consultancy as to a fmcg manufacturer. The current stage the product has reached needs to be determined along with the profile of future contribution. This will partly depend on micro-environment factors (e.g. strength of rivals/changing consumer tastes), partly on the macro-environment (e.g. substitutes/legislation/demography) and partly on marketing decisions on the costs and benefits of product extension and promotional strategies.

The technological environment is particularly relevant to the PLC since it underpins both product development (Stage 1) and decline (Stage 5). Acceleration in technology, and particularly in the manipulation of information, images and ideas, has meant ever shortening product design and development cycles. A succession of new generation products is the norm for brands of cars, computers and other lifestyle products as rapidly changing customer tastes, fashions and preferences reinforce this desire for something new and better. Decline often comes from technological substitution and must be anticipated. Are the days of the personal computer numbered

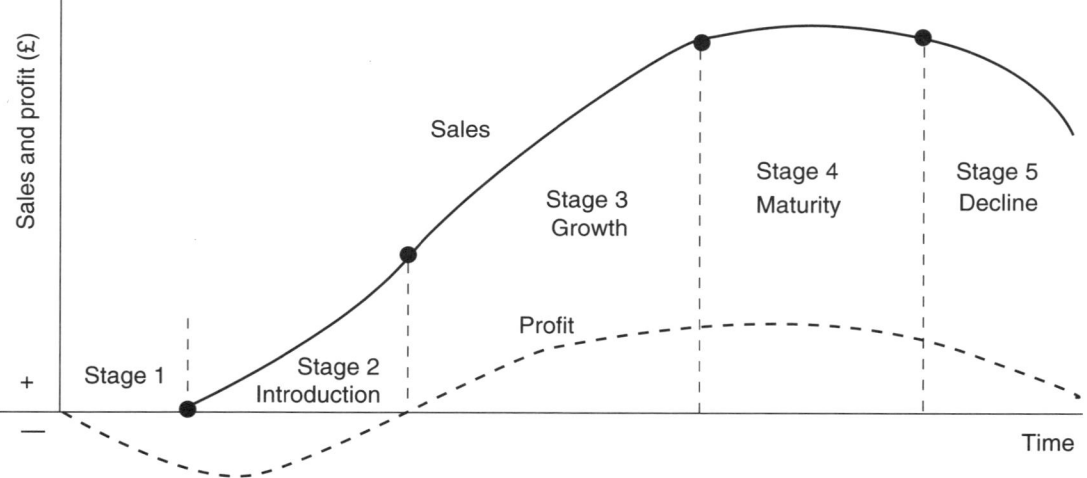

Figure 10.6 The product life cycle

246

by the development of more powerful and versatile laptops and notebooks, more cost effective workstations and interactive television? If so then marketing action is required. Impending maturity also signals the need for innovation and regeneration as competition intensifies and profits decline. An organization requires a regular audit to assess the portfolio and trigger the need for action. We have already discussed the importance of change agents and intrapreneurs in providing a catalyst for this process.

Marketing information system (MIS)

A final tool of analysis requires re-statement and that is the crucially important MIS. Unless internallly and externally generated data is collected, processed, disseminated and promptly acted upon, all other techniques will be of limited benefit to the marketer. Processing data into meaningful information is the critical activity for marketers. Piercy has even argued that 'processing information' should be regarded as an additional P in the marketing mix. A MIS provides the equivalent of the pieces of the jigsaw that depict the ever changing marketing environment and is an important sub-system within the organization.

It is important that the marketer sets the information agenda rather than the other way round. A clear focus is required so that the data gathered fits the intended purpose. There are large amounts of readily accessible information in the public domain and this can be economically mined by the MIS. However, since much of the required environmental data is company specific, so resources need careful targeting. Market research can provide some important specific feedback, but a marketing intelligence gathering system is the main means of identifying emerging trends. A balance has, of course, to be struck between the benefits of additional information and the costs of collecting it. Equally the marketer must weigh the costs of inaccuracy arising from insufficient data, not least because of the constraint imposed on the use of the techniques discussed in this section.

Coping with the challenge: current and future issues

This final section reviews the potential significance of a number of marketing challenges that are currently emerging as issues for the coming century. You should note that the environmental cases that follow do not equally apply to all industries or all parts of the world economic system. For example, marketers in worldwide manufacturing industries would rank the rising level of competition in general and price competition in particular as the external issue of greatest concern. In contrast, service industries rate price competition as a lesser concern because rivalry tends to focus on other dimensions. High technology firms, in particular, have suffered from shorter product life cycles and faster commoditization of once well differentiated products, while only high profile chemical and allied industries put green issues near the top of their checklist. Similarly, businesses in Africa or East Asia are less troubled by the development of a single currency in Europe than by the trend toward globalization. Consequently, it is not possible to please all of the marketers all of the time in the selection of relevant issues to discuss. Space is limited, but the challenges that follow provide a brief insight into the marketing significance of a representative cross section.

Activity 10.4

As suggested in the study guide at the outset of this unit, select one or two of the following alternative themes/challenges and collect sufficient information to write a brief on its significance for the marketer:

- Rising government regulations.
- Growing power of distributors.
- Traffic congestion.
- Consolidation into fewer larger businesses.
- Changing customer requirements.
- Flexible lives.

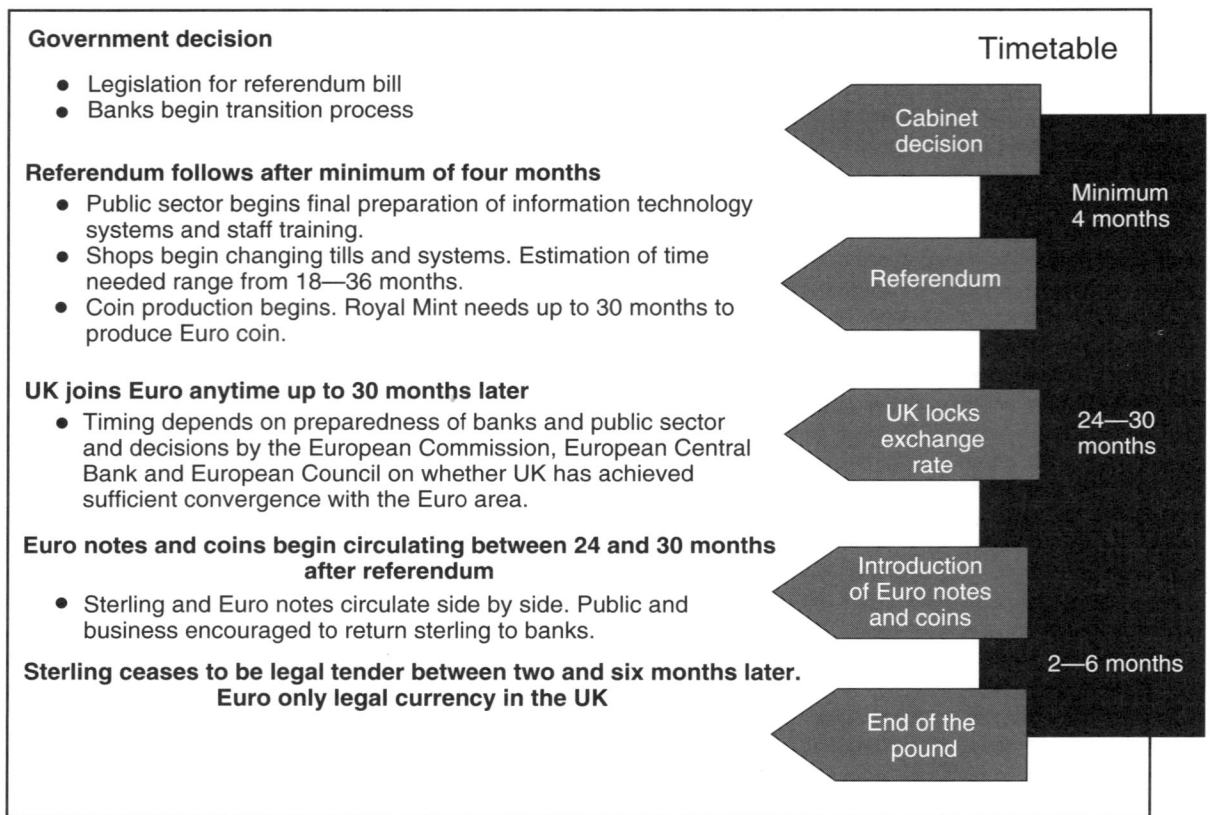

Government decision

- Legislation for referendum bill
- Banks begin transition process

Referendum follows after minimum of four months
- Public sector begins final preparation of information technology systems and staff training.
- Shops begin changing tills and systems. Estimation of time needed range from 18—36 months.
- Coin production begins. Royal Mint needs up to 30 months to produce Euro coin.

UK joins Euro anytime up to 30 months later
- Timing depends on preparedness of banks and public sector and decisions by the European Commission, European Central Bank and European Council on whether UK has achieved sufficient convergence with the Euro area.

Euro notes and coins begin circulating between 24 and 30 months after referendum
- Sterling and Euro notes circulate side by side. Public and business encouraged to return sterling to banks.

Sterling ceases to be legal tender between two and six months later. Euro only legal currency in the UK

Timetable

Cabinet decision

Minimum 4 months

Referendum

UK locks exchange rate

24—30 months

Introduction of Euro notes and coins

2—6 months

End of the pound

Figure 10.7

Marketing challenge 1 – a single currency
Background

The Euro became the major transaction currency for the thirteen governments and corporations of participating countries on 1 January 1999. Coins will enter circulation on 1 January 2002 and displace existing national coinage six months later. The single currency complements the Single European Market, introduced to facilitate and encourage open and free intra-EU trade. The UK ruled out joining in the first wave and is unlikely to do so until the single currency proves sufficiently successful so that a clear case may be made for joining. The government, however, supports entry into the Euro 'in principle', and has launched a national changeover plan. Funds are to be spent supporting this commitment with preparations, explanations and a provisional timetable. It is estimated that the UK could enter the Euro by the Autumn of 2003 if the timetable was followed. This may have to be preceded by a two-year period when the pound shadows the value of the Euro.

Uncertainties

- The government will only recommend monetary union if five economic tests are passed. The tests are very broad and open to interpretation since they include beneficial effects on foreign direct investment and on the financial services industry, as well as broader concerns such as the impact on growth and employment. These tests are already passed.
- New Labour has to win the next election followed by a referendum supporting entry. Public opinion, the Conservatives and the media are currently against, while the CBI and TUC are for. A positive government recommendation is predicted to move the balance of public opinion to within ten points of acceptance but considerable uncertainty remains.
- Economic cycles are out of alignment meaning that a 'one policy fits all' approach might disadvantage UK firms unless there was sustainable convergence.
- The economy has to be judged flexible enough to adjust to the probable shocks of being in the Euro.

- The cost of changeover is difficult to determine but will impact significantly on domestically focused businesses.

Advantages

- Currency uncertainty and transaction costs reduced.
- The most powerful trading bloc with over 350 million largely well off consumers.
- Independent European Central Bank (ECB) should stabilize inflation/assure low interest rates.
- Members will be forced into deregulation/structural changes to put their economies in order.
- The single market should take-off reducing costs and expanding activity and trade.

Disadvantages

- Lack of adjustment mechanisms for individual countries may cause tensions.
- A unified monetary policy can not meet the needs of fifteen separate countries. A divergence already existed in 1999 between booming Eire and Spain and the static Italy and Germany.
- Europe is not as open, mobile or flexible as the USA and there is limited transfer of funds from booming to depressed regions.
- The EU has unresolved structural problems: widespread state ownership, excessive subsidies, generous welfare, powerful unions, rigid labour markets.
- Pressure might develop to unify other aspects of policy, e.g. taxation.
- There is no mechanism for leaving the Euro but there is a stability and growth pact that may fine irresponsible governments for budget deficits in excess of 3 per cent of GDP. What will the ECB do if, for example, it is faced with a choice of depreciating the Euro or raising interest rates causing recession and forcing a member off the Euro?
- Britain is the only oil exporter and has a higher proportion of non-EU trade.

Significance

- Most small companies have not even thought about the Euro and estimates suggest a cost equivalent to 2.5 per cent of turnover.
- Cumulative loss of foreign direct investment if we don't join, e.g. warnings from Rover and Toyota
- Winners are businesses with high cross-border revenues.
- Losers are those who deal in cash to a large domestic customer base.
- Marketers of slot machine producers gain, slot machine operators lose.
- Losers are those currently pricing above EU levels since Euro 'transparency' will allow comparisons.
- Winners are those who adapt most successfully. Relocation and restructuring will be required.
- Local markets will become Euro-wide markets and marketers in small firms must face up to more competition. Market extension strategies must be considered to exploit niches.
- Marketers must assess the impact of integration on each product market and anticipate change.
- Marketers should review price lists and differentials, competitor reactions and promotional lead time.
- Marketers should work actively with partners for an agreed and timely transition.
- Marketers need to review training and adjust business systems for currency conversion.
- The hidden economy will have to convert from sterling into the Euro – the tax man cometh?
- International marketers should recognize that the Euro has become a world reserve currency so creating the potential for volatility, e.g. 5 per cent real depreciation in early 1999.

Conclusion

The outlook is one of continued uncertainty regarding UK entry, the consequences of not entering and the ultimate prospects for the Euro. There is no doubt, however, that the Euro presents a marketing challenge whether the UK enters or not. Turbulence will continue in Europe while the new currency beds in and the financial markets judge the resolve of the authorities. While benefits should flow in the longer run, the current uncertainties can only be intensified by disagreements over the redefining of EU finances, the proposed enlargement to the south and east and uncertainties arising from the resignation of the Commission.

Marketing challenge 2 – globalization
Background

This is a process by which the world economy is becoming a unified interdependent system involving multinational businesses adopting worldwide strategies which apply the same or similar marketing mixes in all markets. The process has been facilitated by the progressive development of communications and information technology and enabled by mass media and travel creating similar patterns of consumption in otherwise diverse cultures. Globalization is characterized by international flows of capital and information and increasingly mobile labour. The key agents in the process are international firms, which conduct a significant proportion of their business in foreign countries and the multinational that designs, produces and markets its products and services directly. A global marketing perspective implies a centrally coordinated plan directed towards a worldwide audience rather than the usual decentralized focus on local or regional markets. Global products include the likes of Rolex, Coca-Cola, Sony, Nike, McDonald's, Airbus, Xerox, Virgin and Microsoft.

Although in many senses a global economy was established in the nineteenth century, it is in the last fifty years that we have witnessed dramatic growth rates in world trade and multinational sales turnover. Multinationals now account for a staggering one third of total global trade and their global revenues exceed the GDP of all but the largest countries. Other factors accounting for this trend include:

- Continuous progress in reducing tariff barriers through trade rounds and the formation of the WTO.
- Over 130 countries in membership and a new system for settling disputes.
- Development of regional free-trade zones as seen in Figure 10.8. These represent attempts by countries with similar interests to obtain the benefits of free trade, on the one hand, while retaining the advantage of some protection against the outside world on the other. These may represent the building blocs to eventual global free trade.
- Many emerging countries in Africa, Latin America and Asia now see open economies and direct investment as the better route to development than protectionism.
- An infrastructure of international institutions is in place to support sustainable global growth. These include the:
  - *International Monetary Fund*, which is responsible for supervision of the world financial system and provides lending support and structural reform programmes for countries in difficulty, as recently in the case of Russia, Indonesia and Brazil.
  - *World Bank*, which provides long-term capital for development purposes
  - *Organization for Economic Co-operation and Development*, which represents the richest and most powerful governments in the world. Its main role is to coordinate economic policies to avert any possibility of mutually reinforcing inflation or deflation that would damage trade.
  - *World Trade Organization*, which encourages multilateral trade and seeks to resolve trade disputes.

Advantages

- Enhanced scope for specialization and standardization of production and distribution.

The main regional trade groups

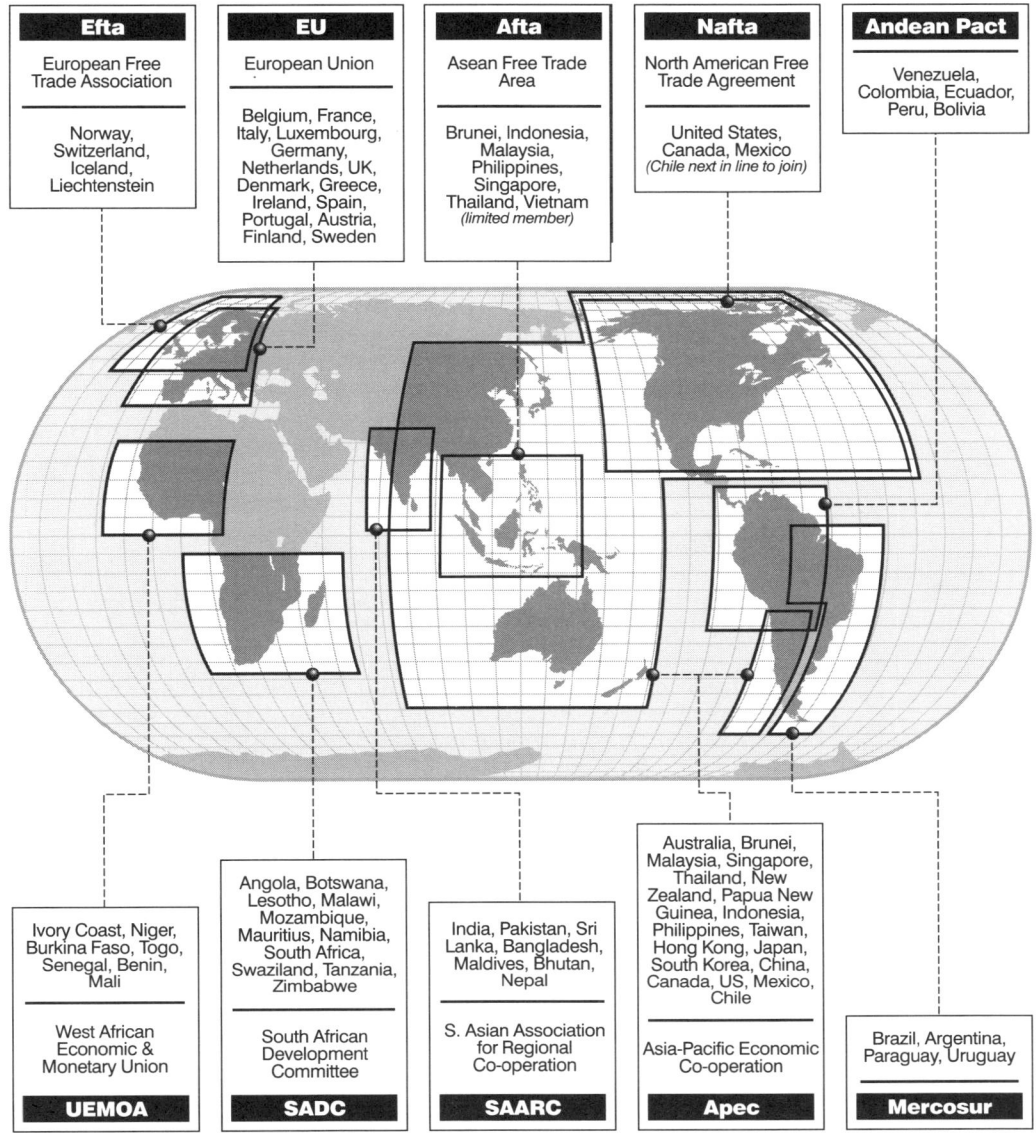

Efta	EU	Afta	Nafta	Andean Pact
European Free Trade Association	European Union	Asean Free Trade Area	North American Free Trade Agreement	Venezuela, Colombia, Ecuador, Peru, Bolivia
Norway, Switzerland, Iceland, Liechtenstein	Belgium, France, Italy, Luxembourg, Germany, Netherlands, UK, Denmark, Greece, Ireland, Spain, Portugal, Austria, Finland, Sweden	Brunei, Indonesia, Malaysia, Philippines, Singapore, Thailand, Vietnam *(limited member)*	United States, Canada, Mexico *(Chile next in line to join)*	

Ivory Coast, Niger, Burkina Faso, Togo, Senegal, Benin, Mali	Angola, Botswana, Lesotho, Malawi, Mozambique, Mauritius, Namibia, South Africa, Swaziland, Tanzania, Zimbabwe	India, Pakistan, Sri Lanka, Bangladesh, Maldives, Bhutan, Nepal	Australia, Brunei, Malaysia, Singapore, Thailand, New Zealand, Papua New Guinea, Indonesia, Philippines, Taiwan, Hong Kong, Japan, South Korea, China, Canada, US, Mexico, Chile	Brazil, Argentina, Paraguay, Uruguay
West African Economic & Monetary Union	South African Development Committee	S. Asian Association for Regional Co-operation	Asia-Pacific Economic Co-operation	
UEMOA	**SADC**	**SAARC**	**Apec**	**Mercosur**

Figure 10.8 The main regional groups (*Source: Financial Times*)

- Cost effective R&D, product design and promotion – attractions of universal image advertising combined with the scope to adapt to suit local conditions.
- Shorter new product planning cycle via learning/comparison/feedback from global experience.
- Faster reaction to customer preferences and superior marketing potential.
- Transport cost savings, improved supply chain efficiency and leverage.
- Direct investment gives tariff free access to trade blocs given that local content requirements are met. Direct access increases local market knowledge and customer confidence.
- Rivals derive competitive advantage out of their network of global activities.
- Greater political stability through the developing web of multinational subsidiaries and development of 'common' commercial interests.
- Pressure on governments to conform to stable economic management as a condition for continued direct investment and favourable reaction from global financial markets.

251

Disadvantages

- Cultural sensitivities require adaption of 'global products', e.g. Big Macs in India.
- Divergence in language and stage of economic development implies differentiation.
- Concern over the American / Western cultural domination undermining national identity.
- Risk of strategic dependence on foreign controlled multinationals whose strategy is globally not nationally driven.
- Powerful companies can play one country off against another to secure incentive packages and competitive advantage compared to established producers, e.g. Nissan's new greenfield plant versus Rover at Longbridge or Ford at Halewood.
- Multinationals are criticized for avoiding taxation via transfer pricing (i.e. the internally set prices on components transferred between subsidiaries in different countries – profits can be varied by setting these higher or lower) and using their leverage to secure favourable treatment.

Significance

- The marketer must monitor a worldwide marketplace and the global environment.
- The threat of competition in domestic markets is significantly increased.
- Interdependence between economies rises with every direct investment creating the potential for rapid communication of shocks throughout the system. Figure 10.9 demonstrate the scale of the trade flows and the potential for disruption.
- The negative impact of the East Asian crisis on the growth projections of the German and British economies and the heavy specific consequences for manufacturing in general and industries such as textiles in particular serve as a warning to marketers.
- Any slowing in national or trade bloc growth may produce a protectionist response, as discussed in Unit 6. Countries remain concerned with national competitive advantage and governments will face pressure from affected interest groups.

Conclusions

No marketer can remain insulated from this dynamic global economic system. It represents a major arena for profitable opportunity but equally a significant source of potential volatility and threat. The international environment cannot be ignored and as we saw in Unit 6, it must be closely monitored and carefully assessed. Fortunately, the international institutions mentioned above collect a wealth of information on the evolving state of

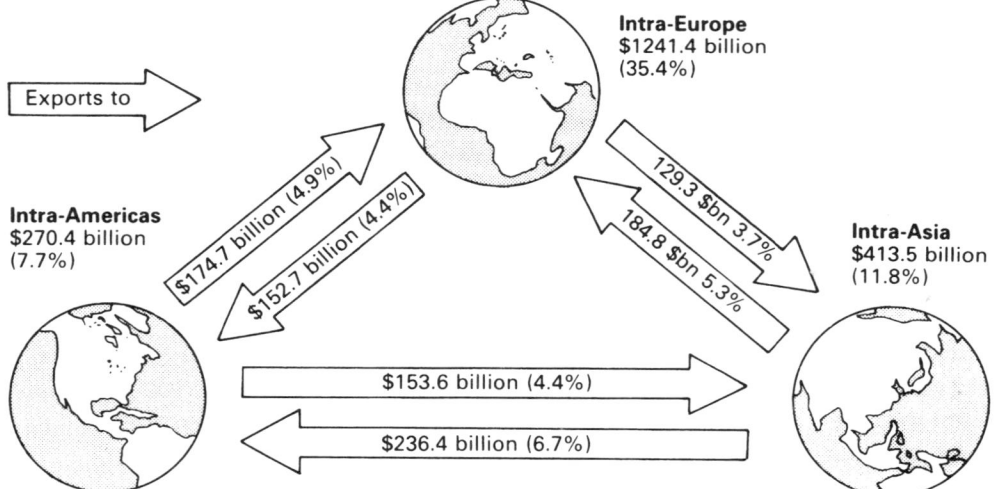

Figure 10.9 How the trade winds will blow. Merchandise trade in US$ billions and as a percentage of world trade. (*Source: Financial Times*)

the world economy and its constituent blocs, providing a database for marketing research on both trade potential and competitive risk.

Marketing challenge 3 – information technology and the millennium (Y2K) effect

Background

An imminent challenge to all businesses who rely on electronic software is the so-called millennium bug. Since virtually all enterprises use power supplies, banking services, suppliers and intermediaries, transport networks and communications systems, it is inconceivable that a business will not be potentially affected. The challenge originates from the 1960s when programmers economized on expensive computer memory by utilizing just the last two digits of a given year. It was not foreseen that this would make it impossible for the year 2000 to be identified, meaning the computer would treat it as 1900 and shut down completely. With most of the world's essential systems controlled by computer software, the risk of 'failure' is critical, particularly for military applications, hospital equipment or air traffic control. A breakdown in such systems could lead to economic disruption and even public disorder. A lot of equipment has embedded computer chips which may cause them to malfunction. This even includes many recently sold PCs which are not compliant. Most software has evolved through incremental change over many years and few, if any, records remain. Also, staff have moved on.

Advantages

- High risk businesses, such as banks, have spent up to £1 billion tackling the issue and in the process have updated and improved the effectiveness of their systems.
- The government has funded schemes for recruitment and training, so adding to the skills base.
- Compliant systems will provide a competitive edge plus opportunities for suppliers.

Disadvantages

- A recession could be triggered not just by failures, but by the effect on business and consumer confidence. Precautionary behaviour involving stocking of essentials and withdrawing cash could cause instability.
- Loss of sales and customer information would disrupt marketing effectiveness and revenue flows.
- Law suits for consequential losses may result. These would be particularly damaging because insurance companies have inserted exclusions in policies for electronically related losses.
- Impacts are being felt in the run-up to 2000, e.g. on 1 September 1999 and 1 March 2000 (leap year). Companies have already experienced problem with credit cards expiring or warranties being rejected in 2000.
- Rectification costs have been high due to the pressure of demand for programming skills.
- No automatic rectification programme has been developed, meaning laborious reading of affected computer code, written in a language no one learns any more.
- A ball park minimum of £30 billion could represent the total cost to the UK ($4–600 billion worldwide) but doubts as to the ability of cash strapped public sector agencies and smaller businesses remain.

Significance

- Affected software is often the oldest, but also the most vital since critical systems have evolved over time with Y2K problems at their core.
- Marketers need to put not only there own house in order but also that of suppliers and intermediaries.
- Many smaller companies could go out of business due to the costs involved.
- Alternative scenarios may be developed, with some business slowdown the likely outcome.

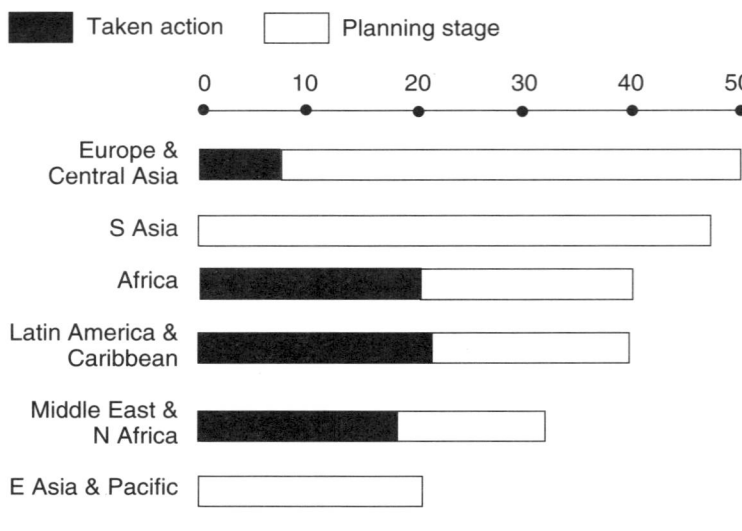

Unprepared
% of emerging markets taking or planning
action on Y2K

■ Taken action   □ Planning stage

| | 0 | 10 | 20 | 30 | 40 | 50 |

Europe & Central Asia

S Asia

Africa

Latin America & Caribbean

Middle East & N Africa

E Asia & Pacific

Figure 10.10

Source: World Bank

- Many emerging countries (see Figure 10.10) are either not aware of the problem or don't have the skills to rectify imported software. A negative impact on world trade is probable.
- Another area of uncertainty is the impact on the internet. This is particularly significant since a recent survey suggested that the internet, together with online information and e-mail, was the main factor contributing to the reduction of information overload among managers.

Conclusions

The millennium bug is but one example of the wider challenge of computer security. It has already been established that modern systems are dependent on computers. The potential commercial damage arising from computer breakdown is almost inestimable for businesses such as travel companies and financial institutions. Consider the possibility of global economic meltdown if a computer virus even temporarily disabled electronic dealings. Hackers continue, almost as a matter of course, to gain access to 'secure' computer facilities. How long will it be before their services are coordinated by revolutionaries? Such thoughts should at the least prompt the marketer to audit their computer systems, ensure back-up is in place and that manually based contingency plans are potentially operational.

The millennium could also be the origin of some expansionary developments. President Clinton has suggested a new trade round, for example. Many consumers and businesses may make significant spending commitments due to the 'new start' it may represent.

Marketing challenge 4 – environmental decline: the impact of technology
Background

Economic growth has inflicted a significant cost on the natural environment. This has arisen, in part, because of externalities that have been borne by third parties other than the producer or consumer involved. Declining environmental quality has been the unavoidable result, unless the state has intervened to make the polluter pay. Similarly there has been a tension between technology as a force for good or a force for evil in its impacts on the natural environment.

We looked at the relationship between the business and environmentalists in Unit 4. In this section we will consider the impact of technology and business activity on the environment in future terms. Three fundamental constraints limit the pace and nature of technological change and the continuity of economic growth:

- *Social and institutional* Reflected in customs and legislation intended to curb the appliance of science in ways felt to be undesirable to society (e.g. a moratorium on nuclear programmes after Chernobyl, bans on animal testing, controls over GM foods).
- *Depletion of non-renewable resources* This includes fuels, minerals, fertile lands through overgrazing, tropical rain forests and biological diversity in terms of animal and plant species extinction.
- *Pollution of the ecosystem* Ecology is the study of plants and animals and their interaction with each other and the environment as a whole. Ecosystems include bio-degradation processes which decompose wastes to provide nutrients for renewed growth. Problems arise only when their absorptive capabilities are overloaded due to the volume and/or nature of the wastes concerned:

Industrial	Effluents, emissions, solid wastes
	Toxic and chemically complicated wastes
	Plastics and non-degradable materials
	E.g. *Sea Empress* spillage, Milford Haven, 1996
Consumer	Vehicle emissions
	Disposable packaging
	Human wastes, e.g. after Christmas British households throw away an estimated 6 million fir trees, 85,000 miles of wrapping paper and 2.5 billion cards – enough to go around the globe nine times

Definition 10.2

Many terms are used frequently in discussion of the environment. Can you match up the following terms to the brief descriptions below?

- Effluent
- Emissions
- Acid rain
- Ozone-layer depletion
- Greenhouse effect

1 Carbon dioxide absorbs and radiates back heat which would otherwise escape into space, causing temperature rises.
2 Liquid wastes discharged into seas or watercourses.
3 Discharges of sulphur dioxide from power stations or vehicle exhaust gases combine with water vapour in the atmosphere.
4 Release of gases into the atmosphere.
5 Caused by the discharge of CFCs in aerosols, solvents, foam plastics and fridges allowing through dangerous ultraviolet rays.

(**See** Activity debrief at the end of this unit.)

The source of the decline

The natural environment has found no difficulty in coping with the wastes created by our economic development, at least until recently. Natural disasters have also been easily accommodated, be they bush-fire, volcano or hurricane, because their impacts have been both localized and reversible. However, the cumulative effects of the nineteenth century's industrial development has involved a different order of 'impact magnitude and irreversibility' in many of the effects created. Figure 10.11 shows the main factors responsible.

While any one of the three factors identified will cause environmental problems, their combined and interdependent effects are much more serious. Three-quarters of the world's population still live in less-developed countries and should they wish to emulate the high resource-consuming life styles of already industrialized countries, the environmental consequences are likely to be unsustainable. If every Chinese household merely aspires to own a fridge, for example, then the impact on the ozone

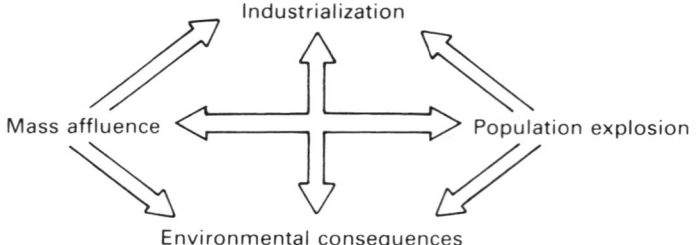

Figure 10.11
Key factors in environmental degradation

layer would easily offset current international attempts to reduce CFC emissions.

The effects of the above are compounded by the pressure of competition and the pursuit of economic gain. Many natural resources are neither privately nor corporately owned but are subject to common exploitation with little regard to environmental costs and benefits. We have also recognized the political imperative of economic growth in all countries.

Belated recognition of these consequences has mobilized both government and business interests to seek solutions. The immediate reaction of halting or even reversing economic growth has, however, quickly given way to a more pragmatic concern for achieving *sustainable* development.

This involves meeting the needs of the present generations without compromising the needs and requirements of future generations. In effect, the objective is to achieve the relationship between GDP and pollution shown in Figure 10.12.

Since pollution and resource depletion do not observe boundaries, they are global problems which can only be solved by global initiatives. The Montreal Protocol, for example, agreed to cap CFC production but with reduced targets applying to less-developed countries.

Significance for marketers

- Business is central to the problem of environmental decline but also to the solution.
- Environmental consciousness is rising under a variety of stakeholder pressures.

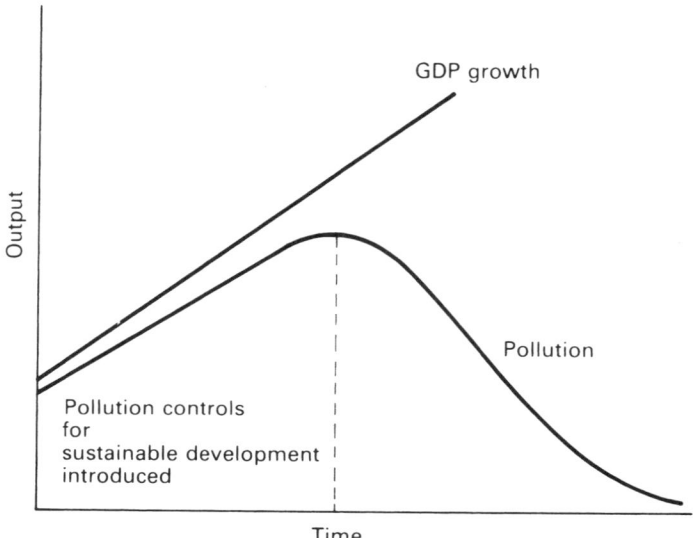

Figure 10.12
Desired relationship between GDP and pollution

256

- Few consumers budget on environmental performance alone – just one element in the mix.
- Local publics seek information, reassurance, improving performance and a risk-free future.
- Agreed objectives need to be set and supported by top management/trading partners. The latter will prefer to deal with a business with standards.
- A competitive edge may be available through ethically sound practices and cleaner products and technologies.
- The effects of depletion can be offset by technical change, redesign, reduction, re-use, recycling and substitution, linked to quality initiatives.
- An environmental strategy needs to be based on sound ethical principles, an audit and impact assessment, action based on benchmarking of best practice.
- Stakeholders must be involved and educated into good environmental practice.
- Pay-off in a sense of security, improved image/relationships, avoidance of fines/litigation.

Conclusions

It is clear that a heightening concern for society and the natural environment will require that new technology is only introduced with care and foresight as to its likely impacts. Society still divides into technical optimists who see salvation and sustainable development through accelerated research and development and pessimists who view unforeseen threats to the ecosystem as unavoidable, no matter how enlightened the technological intent. It is therefore an area which society already views as too important to leave to business decisions alone and is likely to become increasingly regulated as a result.

From the marketing point of view the environmental market in the UK alone will be worth an estimated £140 million in the year 2000. This is not a very consistent market, however, as action–awareness gaps arise between what green consumers profess to want and what they actually buy. Awareness also cuts across segments, with children and women being more environmentally aware than men.

Another important point to be noted by companies is that up to 30 per cent of graduates and managers view this aspect as very important.

Finally, it should not be assumed that environmental impacts are primarily the concern of large firms. A recent OECD study concluded that it was small and medium enterprises (SMEs), accounting for less than 10 per cent of GDP, that were responsible for 70 per cent of pollution. A strategic response is clearly required from such firms with the addition of *packaging* and *people* to the marketing mix as a useful first step!

Marketing challenge 5 – genetically modified (GM) food
Background

This is food made from crops whose genetic code has been altered or manipulated in some way. The aim is to develop strains which produce higher yields with more consistent quality, nutritional value and appearance. Further objectives are to enable the crops to grow under hardier conditions with greater resistance to disease and parasites so that fewer chemical-based weed killers or herbicides need to be applied. In effect, it is a high tech development of what agriculturalists have been doing for centuries through selective use of crop strains and breeding. GM foods are already big business in America where multinational chemical companies, such as Monsanto, supply resistant soya seed. Well over a quarter of the total crop is genetically modified and much of this is mixed with natural soya at the processing stage. In the UK the crops are at the experimental stage but will shortly be seeking approval. Only four GM products have so far been licensed for human consumption: tomato paste, soya, maize and vegetarian cheese, but these are found in a large variety of supermarket foods which until March 1999 had little or no labelling information to guide the consumer. Following critical research findings, pressure groups have called for a three-year moratorium as a precautionary measure so that further research may be undertaken.

Advantages

- Regulation is strict in the UK and the EU.
- The government wishes to promote the UK biotechnology industry as an emerging sector.
- GM offers massive potential to the third world, particularly those affected by soil erosion or unable to afford expensive fertilisers and chemicals.
- The environment would benefit since less inorganic additives would be required.

Disadvantages

- There may be long-term side effects arising from artificial gene combinations which once out of Pandora's box cannot be contained, e.g. are human immune systems at risk?
- They could wreak environmental havoc on adjacent plant species, e.g. pollination from herbicide resistant plants could create super resistant weeds; insect resistance could transfer destroying wildlife.
- Crops made resistant to a certain company's herbicide create a monopoly for its sale.
- Memories of BSE are very fresh in the public mind.
- Modern farming methods have already driven species toward extinction, e.g. skylark, grey partridge – more for the farmer means less for wildlife.

Significance

- GM foods have won the label 'Frankenstein food', constituting a marketing nightmare for staff responsible for its future promotion.
- The political pressure exerted through the media led to hasty and emotive regulations. Immediate labelling requirements on supermarkets, to be followed by restaurants and cafes, represent a legal minefield given the problems of ascertaining origin down a long and often foreign supply chain. Any ban on GM imports would breach WTO rules.
- Monsanto, with GM sales approaching $8 billion and a big contributor to the US president's campaign funds is a powerful lobby. It has already spent £1 million on advertising GM food in the UK and contributed £140,000 to an 'independent' research institution. There is a clear tension between being first into the market and the time devoted to consumer testing.
- The competitive reaction amongst supermarkets saw Iceland, with the only initial outright ban, quickly joined by M&S and Asda as fears of a boycott grew.

Conclusions

There are no natural plants since genetic modification has been proceeding for thousands of years. The only real difference is that GM replaces trial and error with control and systematization. The US Food and Drug administration have subjected GM crops to unprecedented scrutiny, not least because of fear of litigation over unsafe foods. There are risks, as seen in the failures over thalidomide, but there are also substantial rewards from successful drug and genetic developments. While not proceeding with GM tomatoes may have limited impact on affluent consumers, the same may not be said for an emerging third world where half the population is under 25. Freezing research and development of GM foods may indeed represent a tyranny of the pressure groups and media if fears prove unfounded, but it will surely be the poor of Africa and Asia who foot the final bill. Technology has always generated great benefits which have been partly offset by misuse and misunderstanding. Perhaps there is an important role here, for business and the marketer, in promoting the necessary knowledge and managing the inevitable risk. Our future may depend on it.

Marketing challenge 6 – ageing
Background

Ageing is an increase in the average age of the population. It was discussed in Unit 8 so we will only briefly expand on its nature here. It is potentially the most important population trend in the UK and represents a considerable challenge for the marketer.

Opportunities

There are opportunities with the 'young old', who are fit and healthy and intent on staying that way for as long as possible. The travel industry will benefit, as will health related products, security equipment and secure dwellings, quality furniture/other durable replacements, cars, financial services and nostalgia products.

Disadvantages

- Danger of overlooking other important demographic developments.
- The dependency ratio will worsen from five to less than three to one.
- Those of working age will have less discretionary income due to the need to repay university loans, purchase unsubsidized housing and provide for private pensions.
- Labour shortages could develop with a shrinking workforce unless working lives extend.
- Savings ratios could fall progressively as a rising proportion of elderly dis-save.

Significance

- Emerging economies could gain a competitive edge by virtue of their younger and more energetic age structure – flexibility and a willingness to change should result.
- The centre of gravity of the population is creating a critical mass of the so-called third age. In life-cycle terms it represents an increase in empty nest 1 and 2 as well as single households.
- The greying of the population may bring about a cultural shift within society.
- Consumer needs and wants change with age and marketers must practice carefully researched age and life-cycle segmentation to exploit it.
- The over 50s, after the year 2000, will form a more dynamic group due to improving health and education. Increasing life expectancy will make them the prime target for the leisure industries.
- Discretionary spending power will be greatest among the 50–65 year group due to completed families, repaid mortgages, peak earnings and possible inheritance.
- Responsibility for ageing relatives may increase, reducing both time and income for spending.
- An ageing market is not a 'maturity' market although the members may be age conscious and smartly dressed.
- Value for money and quality may be important but so is the opinion that they are deserving of a little luxury. If so, then the marketing message must be altered accordingly.
- BA's 'We'll take good care of you' strikes a valid chord.

Conclusions

- Imminent labour shortages are being countered by the use of alternative workforces, such as married women and ethnic groups. There is also further scope for encouraging delayed retirement through tax incentives. New technology, flexible contracts and a developing culture of continuous learning will also help to alleviate any skills gap. Marketers should in any case form partnerships with educational institutions, market attractive recruitment packages while developing a positive image as a responsible employer. As the number of retired people rise sharply from 2010 so will their power as an influential pressure group. More educated and articulate, they will constitute a demanding and service oriented customer. They may represent a distinct marketing challenge since up till now they have been too busy earning to flex their latent bargaining power. On retirement they will possess the wit, the time and the means to use search and comparison technologies, such as the internet and teletext. So marketers may find the days of fat margins and easy profits become an ever dimming memory.

Summary

In this unit we have seen that:

- It is crucially important for the marketer to monitor change in the marketing environment.
- There are problems in making accurate forecasts when the environment is turbulent and unpredictable, but scenarios can provide management with useful alternative views of the future.
- Scenarios can provide the basis for effective contingency planning.
- There are a number of useful tools and techniques available to the marketer to assist in classification and analysis of the changing environment.
- Audits should be conducted on a frequent basis to provide the necessary inputs for impact and SWOT analysis.
- The marketer must be future oriented and beware of the patterns of the past.
- Issues and environmental challenges should be scanned for continuously with a view to determining the ones that constitute potential threats or opportunities for the organization.
- A number of challenges are of current significance for marketers including globalization, the single currency and critical technological concerns.

Activity debrief

Definition 10.1   4, 2, 3, 5, 6, 1
Definition 10.2   2, 4, 3, 5, 1
Question 10.1 Forecasts are necessary whenever resource decisions affecting the future (e.g. investment in plant and equipment, new product research and development, etc.) require a view to be taken of future supply and demand conditions. Factors affecting supply and demand must be forecast, which in effect means all relevant factors in the micro- and macro-environments.
Activity 10.1 First-hand experience of customer base. Realism if believed to feed into budgets and targets but may corrupt if bonus payments related to them. Too close to market.

Examination hints and specimen questions

As mentioned in the study guide at the beginning of this unit, there are no past questions due to this being a wholly new section to the syllabus. There are some sample questions at the end of Unit 11 and you should refer to Questions 1 and 3. There is a strong probability of at least part of a question on this important syllabus area, not least because it can be linked in with other areas of the macro- and micro-environment. You will notice that this is the case with specimen Question 3 referred to above. A number of other questions have also been produced below. You should note that the challenges section is open ended in terms of relevant issues and so therefore should be the questions posed. It is clearly important that you prepare at least two or three challenges for the examination and be prepared to analyse their significance for marketers within a stated context. Remember that even if you don't prepare a full answer to each question, you should at a minimum prepare a plan.

Specimen questions

1 Most marketers work in businesses operating under cyclical conditions.
   (a) Discuss the importance of forecasting to successful marketing under such conditions.   (6 marks)
   (b) Giving an example of each, provide a brief assessment of **two** of the following:
      (i)   quantitative forecasts
      (ii) qualitative forecasts
      (iii) scenarios   (14 marks)

2 Understanding why things happen is the key to making things happen. Taking this statement as your theme, prepare notes for a presentation on **three** approaches available to marketers to meet the challenge of change.

(20 marks)

3 Choose **one** of the following issues currently faced in the marketing environment plus **one** other of your own choice and summarize their meaning and significance in a selected organizational context:
(a) globalization
(b) ageing
(c) the Euro   (20 marks)

Hints: Indicative content and approach
Question 1(a)/(b)

- Define the meaning of cyclical conditions.
- Focus on the importance of forecasting as it relates to marketing.
- You could refer to new product development issues, pricing pressures at different stages, promotional requirements and accounts of other supply chain member positions.
- Be sure to only address two parts and conform to the brief format.
- Provide examples, e.g. trend projection, delphi, industry scenarios.
- Focus on an assessment rather than a description – comparison provides a good basis.

Question 2

- Explain the meaning of the statement in terms of gathering information on, and analysing environmental change as the basis for planning.
- Provide the format in the form of headings and bullet point notes.
- Work on the assumption of 6 marks for each approach – provide a balanced contribution.
- Supply a cross section of approaches: forecasting, classificational, analytical.

Question 3

- This is a representative type of question for this section of the syllabus.
- It requires that you have prepared an alternative issue of your own choosing.
- You must provide examples within an organizational context for full marks.
- Divide your answer to each part into meaning and significance. Marks will probably be allocated on a 4:5 mark basis with the balance of 2 marks for format.
- Be sure to select a current/future issue.

Marketing Environment – test question
(a) Distinguish between a scenario and a forecast.   (6 marks)
(b) Using a bullet point format, provide:
    (i) One scenario based on the assumption that your government wins the next election.
    (ii) One scenario based on the assumption that the main opposition party wins the next election.   (10 marks)
(c) Identify **two** important marketing implications of either scenario (i) or scenario (ii).   (4 marks)

Hint
Attempt this question having read this unit but also the policy section of Unit 7. It is a challenging question and requires you to understand the policy differences between the two parties and how these would impact on the marketing environment. Note that only 5 marks are available per scenario so only a limited number of bullet points need be provided.

Unit 11 Guidance on revision and examination

As you will be aware, throughout the workbook, examination tips and specimen questions have been provided to help you relate the course content to the examination requirements. In this short unit a brief summary of the *key elements in learning and examination success* will be outlined. These should be studied well in advance of the date of your examination to obtain maximum benefit from them.

There is no specimen paper available from the CIM to complement the updated syllabus due to the limited number of changes that have been made. Transitionary papers will be set in December 1999 and June 2000 following publication of this workbook (three either/or style questions to be set in Part B tailored to address areas of the old/revised syllabus plus three questions on areas of commonality). At the end of this section, you will find a full examination paper which you are advised to attempt under controlled examination conditions. Unfortunately, Questions 2, 3 and 7 do not relate to the new syllabus and so have been supplemented with equivalent questions from the December 1997 paper. In the final section you have been provided with one or two 'specimen' questions covering the new areas of the syllabus not previously examined.

It would be a great advantage if you could find someone appropriate to provide feedback on your attempt since only the exceptional candidate can perform excellently on the first try. A tutor, your marketing manager or a previously successful candidate may be able to give you invaluable pointers in improving your focus and technique in subsequent attempts.

To help you further, a set of *model answers and commentaries* have been provided. *It is important that you do not consult these until you have attempted the question paper*. The commentaries concentrate more on structure and approach to the questions while the model answers provide detailed substantive content which you may readily supplement from the various units. Remember that *practice makes perfect* and the more practice you can have at actual past questions, the better.

As further examination papers become available it is essential that you obtain copies not only of the papers themselves but also the senior examiner's report on how candidates had fared (a summary of recent examiner's reports is provided below and you should study it carefully) and perhaps copies of the specimen answers, obtainable from CIM Direct and in future over the internet. Attempt these questions before you read the report and model answers and compare how well you did. Then analyse why you did not do better!

- Had you revised enough?
- Did you choose to do the right questions?
- Did you focus on what the question asked for?
- Did you run out of time? and so on.

Perhaps you should consider doing a SWOT analysis on yourself and the examination based on where you went right and where you went wrong in attempting the paper. Recognize your strengths and exploit them fully. Acknowledge your weaknesses and work to improve them. Consider the shape of the paper, what the examiner was looking for and the opportunities this presents for the next paper you sit. Look for the threats in terms of failure to adopt the right format, failure to revise sufficient topics, failure to keep up to date with environmental developments and even failure to answer the required number of questions.

The subject knowledge contained in this workbook is a necessary but not a sufficient basis for passing the examination. You must also supply the following:

- A high proportion of the activities and further reading completed
- The necessary effort put into revision of the material
- Effective communication of your knowledge to the examiner
- Efficient management of your examination time.

A businesslike approach

Approaching a CIM Marketing Environment examination is like confronting a business problem. Your *primary objective* is to *pass first time*, in the shortest study time duration and with an A or B credit or distinction standard. Your *strategy* involves revising in good time, allocating your time between different syllabus areas, deciding which topics to concentrate on and, in the exam, which of the optional questions to actually answer.

Market research involves study of the course material, the activities, awareness of developments in the marketing environment and comments in examiner's reports. *Planning* will require a revision schedule and a framework of understanding about the marketing environment and appropriate concepts to apply in solving examination problems.

Implementation will necessitate effective use and distribution of your time between and within questions, set in a constrained examination situation, where the emphasis must be on supplying well, structured and professionally presented answers.

As a candidate your role is changed to presenting information rather than absorbing it as a student. You now have a customer and must respond clearly and concisely to questions posed.

Key elements in learning

There are three elements involved here:

1 *Learning* Many students do not know *how to learn*! You should not fall into this category if you have used this workbook correctly. You learn very little if all you do is passively read the course material, memorize some and then try to regurgitate it in the exam. Our minds do not react well to such a passive approach, we are easily distracted and nothing much sinks in. We can waste many hours in this way, pretending to study!

For learning to be truly effective it must be active and applied. You must involve yourself in the learning process by thinking about it, testing it against your experience, making links with your existing knowledge and developing it further. There is an old adage that suggests we 'learn by doing' so do not be tempted into passive learning but instead apply active learning techniques such as:
- Make your own set of notes, in words you understand, combining all sources of information and activities.
- Whenever an example is provided, always stop to think of one of your own, preferably from work/company experience.
- Try to develop an environmental way of thinking about business and marketing and relate concepts to your own experience.
- Make sure you can define *all key terms* concisely.
- Make revision notes using headings/bullet points possibly on 'prompt cards' since these will provide the framework for answers in the exam.
- Do not try to memorize ideas but work on understanding and applying them. This way you will remember them automatically.
- The exam is about the environment, so make sure that you are *well briefed* on current developments *in your own economy*.
- Think about relevant and topical questions that might be set.
- *Do* attempt all the sample questions provided in the workbook since

these are vital tests of your active learning and understanding. Don't treat them as a chore, but as a cement that will fix knowledge securely in your mind and strengthen your confidence for the 'real thing'.

2 *Memory* Active learning will fix knowledge, understanding and application in your 'long-term memory'. Passive learning will, at best, fix it in your 'short-term memory'. Memorizing parrot-fashion is also unlikely to be effective because examiners are experienced at recognizing such a tactic. Such a technique is, in any case, unlikely to match the exact question posed since a tailored response to the 'slant' of the question is necessary and this means real understanding is required, not an 'off the memory shelf' answer. It is, however, useful to use memory aids such as SLEPT and SWOT to ensure that you recall all key points when under the considerable pressure of exams.

3 *Revision* This should be an ongoing process rather than a panic measure implemented just before the exam itself. You should be blending a set of notes that are comprehensive and easy to revise from as you proceed through the syllabus. For each concept you should generate two or three examples and link ideas as you go along. Knowledge is a building process and you must lay solid foundations upon which to construct your understanding and application of the material.

Key revision skills include such things as:
- Keeping your file well organized, easy to reference and updated.
- Practise defining key terms from memory. These are an essential ingredient of exam question introductions.
- Progressively refine and condense your revision notes into key word clusters.
- Prepare topic outlines and essay answer plans, then prepare some more. Get them checked out to make sure you are on target.
- Read your concentrated notes the night before the exam and immediately before going to sleep. This should help to fix the notes in your short-term memory throughout the following day. Do not overdo it and get a reasonably early night so that your mind will be fresh and alert for the exam itself!

Key elements in examination success

There are five main elements involved here.

Spotting topics

Any good salesperson or marketer will want to forecast the future and the examination questions are no exception! However, as you will already have learnt, it is one thing to forecast accurately in a stable, predictable and known environment, but quite another where new product development is involved.

With a relatively new syllabus and a subject area which is substantially different from what most candidates have experienced before, it is vital that you must absorb *all* the examination hints and tips provided in this workbook.

You already have a good idea of the likely distribution of questions across the syllabus and a set of past examination questions set by the senior examiner. Study these carefully in terms of form and style of presentation.

As past papers become available, the task of forecasting becomes a little easier. You can construct a grid relating the syllabus areas to questions arising in successive exams to get a feel of patterns and topic areas with a higher probability of occurrence. The examiner will be setting questions to cover the whole syllabus area over a run of years, so be prepared for a topic that has not come up for a while.

Remember the lead time in preparing exam papers and do some market research on current events a year before yours is due. It is *not advisable*, though, to try to spot specific questions and prepare for these in detail. Your chances of predicting the precise question format is remote, but having invested considerable effort in 'preparing' a model answer you may be tempted to show the examiner what you know under the pretext of answering the actual question that has been set. Do not be tempted to do this since *you must answer the question set,* not the one you hoped for, otherwise all you might get is a red line through your work.

Examiners – the nature of the beast!

It is often quite a revelation for students to learn that examiners are on their side. They would like you to pass and derive no satisfaction or benefit from failing candidates. Indeed, it is psychologically much more difficult for them to fail you than to pass you. The CIM also has systems in place to help ensure that fairness and consistency prevail across the team of examiners. However, one of the primary responsibilities of the examining team is the maintenance of standards and to ensure that those who gain the CIM certificate are worthy of the qualification in the eyes of both actual and potential employers.

Why not take a leaf out of the marketer's handbook of success and:

- *Be examiner-friendly* and orientate your answers to what *they* need. With a lot of other scripts to mark as well as your own, make life easy for them!
- Provide them with *value for money* by understanding and answering precisely what the question requires. Read their needs (i.e. the question) very carefully and don't provide unwanted frills (i.e. waffle).
- Make the job of marking your script straightforward by answering the right number of questions, clearly and concisely in well-laid-out report-type style with white space separating the points made.
- Deliver the answer in the format requested in the question.
- Give the examiner something to mark. If you do not attempt a question or write very little then the examiner is in a fix in terms of awarding any marks. Even if you have not prepared the topic use your common sense, define the terms, provide a couple of examples, etc. The extra mark or two this generates may make all the difference!
- The examiner is your ultimate consumer so use your 'marketing mix' to meet his or her needs. Provide a strong sense of enthusiasm and professionalism in your answers supported by relevant examples and applications where appropriate. Try to 'differentiate' your product from run-of-the-mill scripts, consider critical success factors and make it a pleasure to mark. Your reward will be substantial.

Examination practice

This has already been heavily emphasized as the means of getting it *right first time*! Make the effort to practise papers under exam conditions and sketch out outline plans to as many questions as possible. Time is a scarce resource and you must use and distribute it between questions effectively. Writing at length on three questions and then penning a note of apology to the examiner that your time has run out for the fourth will cut no ice at all. If, however, you have badly mistimed the previous question then provide the examiner with your outline answer plan in note form with a list of bullet point conclusions.

Examination technique – planning the answer

Planning is the keystone of success in examinations. You must:

- *Plan* to cover the majority of the syllabus.
- *Plan* to prepare more topics than you will need.
- *Plan* an orderly revision schedule with time built in for unforeseen personal, social and work pressures on your time.
- *Plan* for emergencies which might disrupt your schedule.
- *Plan* your sample questions and learn from your mistakes.
- *Plan* to be fully informed on the time and venue of the exam.
- *Plan* to be fully prepared, fresh and relaxed for the exam.
- *Plan* to avoid nervous colleagues prior to entering the exam.
- *Plan* to channel natural examination nerves into alert awareness.
- *Plan* out which three questions to answer from the six options.
- *Plan* all your answers at the outset since one might trigger ideas for the others. Do not be rushed into writing because others around you are. Your plans are the key to a good pass! Make simple single trigger word

plans, not detailed ones. Each word represents an idea, then number the order you are going to develop them.

- *Plan* to allocate time equally between questions.
- *Plan* to allocate time within questions according to the marks.
- *Plan* to relate what you say to the question posed. Do not insult the examiner (who might have set it!) by not specifically addressing it.
- *Plan* to read the questions *very* carefully. Underline key words, identify the context, the marks allocated, the number of parts and the problem being posed.
- *Plan* the structure of your answer – provide an introduction, define the terms, signpost your approach, adopt the required format, supply reasoned arguments, draw conclusions.
- *Plan* to label diagrams correctly if you use them, and only use them if you can!
- *Plan* to focus *only* on what the question asks for and not to waffle.

Writing a plan forces you to focus on the question as well as making the writing of answers easier and faster to implement. However, as with all these skills you must practice.

Examination technique – presentational effectiveness

This is an often overlooked but critical aspect of examination success. How do you judge people or companies you have dealings with? First impressions often condition our reactions, and so it is with examiners. If they pick up a scruffy, near-illegible script which is poorly structured and presented they will immediately develop negative feelings whatever the actual content. Examiners do recognize, however, that for many candidates English is their second language and will make some allowance for this. There is no excuse, though, for an unprofessional script!

If you do not appear to care, then neither will the examiner! Marketing students should in any case be adept at presentation and persuasion and you should seek to demonstrate these skills. The key requirements here are:

- *Compliance* answer the exact question set and
- *Clarity* in layout, legibility and presentation

Practise laying out answers in a report rather than essay style since this is what is adopted in business. Headings, a list of bullet points and a paragraph of explanation and discussion is far easier for the examiner to absorb than big blocks of solid text.

Activity	

As a final activity take the past paper on page 272 and, once you have answered it under examination conditions, go through the following checklist of points. Better still, ask a friend or your tutor to do so on your behalf. If any are answered in the negative then work out an action plan that will guarantee a positive outcome in the actual examination itself.

Yes   No

1 Is your layout professional?
2 Is it clearly legible?
3 Have you used semi-report-style format?
4 Is there white space between points?
5 Have you numbered the questions clearly?
6 Have you saved time by *not* writing out questions?
7 Have you used black ink/biro?
8 Have you avoided/deleted crossings out?
9 Are diagrams relevant, clear, labelled and explained?
10 Did you answer the questions posed exactly?
11 Did you define all relevant terms in the question?
12 Did the amount written reflect the marks allocated?
13 Did you answer the compulsory question?
14 Did you finish in time?
15 Would you have given it a pass mark?
16 Was it really up to the standard required by CIM?

In the sub-section 'Spotting topics' it was suggested that you construct a grid relating syllabus areas to questions arising in successive examinations. With nine series of Marketing Environment examinations now complete and one in progress it is helpful to examine such a grid. The table that follows has been adapted for the new syllabus but incorporates the pattern

Syllabus ref.	Syllabus area	June 1996	Dec 1996 (old)	June 1997 (old)	Dec 1997 (old)	June 1998 (old)	Dec 1998 (old)	June 1999 (old)	Dec 1999 (new)	%
3.1.1	Internal environment Public, voluntary private organizations			*a,b		✓p				**The organization**
3.1.2	Mission, differing organizational objectives internal/external influences	*6	✓p			✓p				
3.1.3	Marketing interface Systems and contingency approaches			New syllabus area						10%
3.2.1	Micro-environment and marketing process Key sources of information	✓p	✓p	✓p		✓p ✓p	*a,b			**The micro-environment**
3.2.2	Stakeholder concept Perceptions and expectations Societal marketing, social responsibility, ethical issues	✓p	✓			✓p				
3.2.3	Role/importance suppliers intermediaries. Partnerships and relationship marketing	✓			✓	✓p	✓p			30%
3.2.4	Publics: consumerists environmentalists. Role of marketing	*d *a	✓p	*a	✓	✓p	*c			
3.2.5	Monitor competitors, 5 force analysis, competition policies	*a	✓p	✓	✓	✓	✓p			
3.3.1	Macro-environment Key sources of information	✓p	*a✓p	✓p		✓	*a,b			**The macro-environment**
3.3.2	Social-cultural environment	✓		✓p	✓	✓	✓p			
3.3.3	Economic-international environment/implications	✓	✓	✓		*a,b,c,d	✓✓p			
3.3.4	Political-legislative environment/implications	*a✓p	*b	✓	✓p✓p	✓p	✓			45%
3.3.5	Technical environment: impacts on organizations		*a	✓p	✓p	✓p				
3.4.1	Turbulent change, complex/dynamic conditions	New syllabus area								**Managing the future environment**
3.4.2	Environmental approaches audits, forecasts, SWOT	✓p	✓p				*6			
3.4.3	Environmental challenges and issues for the future	New syllabus area	*d		*c					15%

Figure 11.1 Marketing Environment Examination grid

Specified format	Dec 1994	June 1995	Dec 1995	June 1996	Dec 1996	June 1997	Dec 1997	June 1998	Dec 1998
Appendix		✓							
Appropriate/Own format					✓				
Bibliography		✓		✓					
Brief/Outline [0]	✓		✓	✓	✓O	✓		✓✓O	✓✓O
Bullet points		✓		✓			✓	✓	
Checklist/list	✓	✓	✓			✓			
Cite industry example	✓	✓		✓	✓				
Commentary					✓	✓		✓	
Debate							✓		
Memorandum					✓		✓	✓✓	✓
Notes	✓	✓	✓✓	✓			✓	✓	
Other, e.g. Article [A], Booklet [B], Draft [D], Resume [R]	✓R	✓D✓B	✓R	✓A	✓A	✓D		✓D	
Reports/Submission [S]	✓				✓✓S		✓	✓	✓
Slides/Presentation	✓	✓	✓	✓	✓	✓	✓	✓	✓
Space-limited response				✓1 page ✓700 words	✓ 2 page				
Summary		✓			✓	✓	✓		

Figure 11.2 Business format requirement grid

of questions posed on the aspects of the old syllabus that continue to apply. The table starts in June 1996, the first series to use six optional questions, and summarizes the syllabus areas. The proportions allocated to the main sections are highlighted and the series when the changeover from old to new scheme is made. Ticks represent the location of optional questions and compulsory parts are shown from (a) to (d). The letter p designates part questions. A word of warning, however, some questions draw from across the syllabus so the location of the tick only represents the primary focus.

The grid provides a useful overview of the question pattern within and across the examination series. Empty columns have been left for you to extend the grid as papers become available. You might also wish to indulge in some predictions of your own. Such a process should carry candidate health warnings since the risks of depending on 'bankers' have been mentioned and *all* sections of the syllabus appear to be examined regularly.

Month/Year	Title
June 1995	With a greyer picture of the future in mind – implications of ageing
December 1995	On line for a speedy sale – technological potential and the marketer
June 1996	New line of attack in Great Soap War – non-price competition and regulation
December 1996	US ranked as most competitive nation – sources of competitiveness and consequences
June 1997	Body Shop and the franchise concept
December 1997	Small turns out to be profitable
June 1998	The joys of synchronized growth
December 1998	The importance of the marketing environment

Figure 11.3 Cases or articles used in past examinations

A useful supplement to the above exercise is to construct an equivalent grid for format requirements specified in questions. As you know, marks are allocated for providing answers within the context of these and might represent up to 10 per cent of the total marks in some cases. Such a grid not only allows you to review the patterns across papers but also the variety used. Make sure you are familiar with all these format types and note recent developments such as space-limited responses where you must restrict your answer to, say, one page or 700 words. You will lose marks if you ignore this requirement, which in effect means the examiner wishes you to be concise and to the point.

Finally, you may wish to survey the types of articles used in past papers. They cannot be predicted in advance but do give you a feel for the nature and spread of topics covered and underline the importance of practising evaluating similar articles in the context of your studies.

Key point summary from the senior examiner's reports

December 1994–1995 series
- This subject is not a 'soft option' but a demanding and important area of knowledge for the marketing practitioner. Centres must ensure candidates are aware of this, have access to the appropriate texts and cover the whole syllabus at least in broad terms.
- Overseas candidates frequently ignored the requirement to provide an industry context or examples. This might have been due to failure to read the question carefully enough. It might also suggest the need for greater effort to relate their understanding to business and marketing applications.
- Distinctions were achieved by candidates who focused on the question posed in a well balanced manner, adopted the required business formats and effectively demonstrated their knowledge and understanding of the marketing environment by convincingly relating it to marketing practice.

June 1995 series
- Improvement was most noticeable in home Centres while overseas performance was rather patchy.
- Candidates are advised to read the whole paper very carefully and make clear precisely which question they are answering. It is not necessary, however, to write out the question in full causing valuable writing time to be lost.
- Candidates should avoid the folly of writing up to two sides of notes before commencing the actual answer. Notes and plans that do not form part of the answer should be crossed out.
- Candidates should beware of adopting a wholly 'marketing' perspective without explaining the environmental aspects first.
- Formats were adopted in the main but candidates must take care not to provide all report format without the necessary content to answer the question. Only a framework format is required.
- Plan all questions before writing to provide structure and avoid unnecessary repetition of points in different questions.

December 1995 series
- A steady, consistent standard across *all four* answers in the examination was the surest route to a pass.
- Avoid the temptation of writing *too much* on the first question/part question. Relate the amount you write to the marks available. A compulsory question worth only 6 or 8 marks should not have more written than for a whole optional question worth 20 marks! The rule of thumb is 17/18 minutes for each 10 marks.
- Much less care was taken in adopting the appropriate and required business formats this series. Requests for appendices, résumés, note or presentational form should not be ignored. Candidates *must* aim to answer the question within the spirit of the required format.

June 1996 series

Home centres
- A disappointing slippage in progress to a higher pass rate occurred, although it was comparable with other Certificate subjects.
- Consistency across all answers remains the key. Weak performance in just one or two parts may produce an overall marginal fail.
- One or two questions were surprisingly unpopular, suggesting some Centres were omitting significant sections of the syllabus, e.g. the political environment.
- Some candidates were relying too much on 'breadth' and 'appreciation' and too little on real depth and understanding. Centres must work hard to get the balance right.

Overseas centres
- Marred by an inability to conform to the required format:
  - Overhead projector slide format was poorly attempted in question 1(d).
  - The requirement for a one-page brief in question 2 was largely ignored.
  - A number selected one from each of the four pairs of terms rather than two pairs as directed.
- Even after allowance is made, communication skills sometimes fall below the standard that would be acceptable in business.

December 1996 series

Home centres
- The need is to improve the tail of weaker candidates up to the standards of the better ones in some Centres.
- Some candidates continue to rely on their marketing knowledge when attempting marketing environment questions.
- The main source of weakness is the failure to address the precise question posed. One question clearly asked for an evaluation of opportunities or threats, yet many candidates addressed strengths and weaknesses, or policy recommendations rather than what was required.
- Use of required format improved but should not be provided if not asked for.

Overseas centres
- Despite a fair paper relating to candidates' own experience and country a degree of needless misinterpretation occurred.
- Reading time allowance did not prevent a number of candidates answering less than the required four questions – two candidates scored over 40 per cent from just two questions but only answered two questions and so failed.
- One candidate wrote eight pages of essay plan notes but only ten pages of answer.
- Many continue to write far too much on the first question attempted or those where only a few marks are allocated.
- Format requirements continue to be either ignored *or* provided to the exclusion of actual answer content.
- There is insufficient evidence of reading recommended texts or workbooks such as this.

June 1997 series
- A marked improvement in grades, particularly in home Centres.
- Fewer candidates omitted questions, with fuller answers the norm.
- Critical weakness is inability to focus on question requirements.
- Candidates should be more examiner-friendly in the structure and layout of their answers.
- Overseas candidates should avoid the temptation to write all they know about examination topics.
- The characteristics of weaker candidates and Centres tend to be:
  - not well prepared;
  - limited evidence of using recommended workbooks;

- short answers on the compulsory questions;
- comparatively poor examination technique;
- unnecessary overlap of points suggesting lack of planning;
- real difficulties in reading or understanding questions;
- general observations and background provided, which earns no marks;
- poor handwriting and untidy, unprofessional scripts.
- Concern that the full syllabus is not being taught.

December 1997 series
- A challenging paper with pitfalls for the unwary.
- Excellent scripts received from candidates who focused carefully on the questions.
- Case questions posed the greatest difficulty *but* more due to lack of attention than lack of overall knowledge. Knowledge without understanding and application will not suffice.
- Fully answered scripts are now the norm.
- Tendency to answer 'organizational' questions from a marketing perspective.
- Poor interpretation. In one question weaker candidates discussed market structure in detail instead of using it to explain the trend of intensifying competition.
- Improvement in use of format, but do not use it when not required.
- Don't jump to conclusions, for example, where five factors are called for don't assume it's 5-force analysis!
- PESTitis has been overtaken by PORTERitis with some candidates managing to introduce it into every answer.
- Don't pose questions, provide answers.
- The key message is to *read and re-read* the question.

June 1998 series
- Improvement in pass rates despite a challenging paper.
- Address format requirements precisely, e.g. beware of writing at length if an outline/brief is required.
- Aspiring marketers should be customer oriented, yet some fail to apply key principles of their craft:
  - question numbers not recorded on front cover of answer book – meaning the examiner has to do it!
  - question numbers recorded but not in the order answered – marks are easily placed wrongly;
  - questions started, seemingly completed, then resume again without warning – marks have to alter!
  - continuation pages tied in backwards or not in order, leading to confusion/wasted time;
  - writing is difficult to read – if so consider breaking text up into 'bites' or use bullet points;
  - 'waffling' rather than addressing question – excessive reading time for the examiner!
  - answering sectionalized questions as if they were one – examiner left to divide it up.
- Candidates were warned that in the future marks may be lost if candidates make no effort to comply with reasonable standards of script presentation.

December 1998 series

- Candidates advised to spend more time interpreting past exam questions.
- Underline key words and briefly justify your interpretation of the question if you are in doubt.
- Don't provide formal report format for each and every question – just when required.
- *Do not* add personal notes of any type for the attention of the examiner.

Specimen exam paper   December 1998

Certificate in Marketing

The Marketing Environment   3 Hours' Duration

> This examination is in two sections.
> **Part A** is compulsory and worth 40 per cent of total marks.
> **Part B** has six questions, select three. Each answer will be worth 20 per cent of the total marks.
> **DO NOT** repeat the question in your answer but show clearly the number of the question attempted on appropriate pages of the answer book.
> Rough workings should be included in the answer book and ruled through after use.

PART A
The importance of the marketing environment

The CIM defines marketing as … the management process which identifies, anticipates and supplies customer requirements efficiently and profitably.

This focuses attention on the importance of the marketing environment for practitioners and students alike. Identifying and anticipating customer requirements is impossible unless the organisation looks outward from itself, to understand its external environment and the implications of changes taking place on its current and future profitability.

No organisation, whether small or large, public or private, profit or non-profit making can afford to ignore its environment. As the strategist H I Ansoff observed,

"… the firm is a creature of its environment. Its resources, its income, its problems, its opportunities and its very survival are generated and conditioned by the environment."

It is the generally uncontrollable forces in the macro-environment that create a succession of potential threats and opportunities for the business. These broad trends and changes are extremely important in shaping the competitive situation and the actions and perceptions of relevant stakeholder publics.

Societal concerns are often translated through the legislative process to impact on the freedom of business to manage. The marketer must always be aware that the environment reflects the pressures from a range of interested groups to which a positive response may be called for. It is also the domain of actual or potential competitors, and is consequently ignored at the organisation's peril.

"But tomorrow always arrives, it is different and then even the mightiest company is in trouble if it has not worked on its future."

Large firms, particularly multinationals, may be able to exert greater influence over their business situation, but small firms may have the advantage in responding to the need for change more flexibly. Both must recognise they are on the equivalent of a moving conveyor belt, they must move fast just to stand still as tastes, technology and competitive forces alter.

(Extracts from the *Sales and Marketing Environment*, Butterworth-Heinemann).

PART A
Question 1
a. *"... the firm is a creature of its environment. Its resources, its income, its problems, its opportunities and its very survival are generated and conditioned by the environment."*
Using examples, fully explain your understanding of this quotation.

(15 marks)

b. What can organisations do to effectively keep abreast of environmental changes?

(15 marks)

c. Explain the term **relevant stakeholder publics**.
Use an example to show how stakeholder perceptions may impact on the marketer.

(10 marks)
(40 marks in total)

PART B – Answer THREE questions only

Question 2
Write a report to your Marketing Manager which examines the relationship between the size of organisations which comprise an industry and the nature of competitive activity within it.

(20 marks)

Question 3
Government regulation can impact on companies and their activities in many different ways. In the context of a country of your choice:

a. Explain the role of Government regulation and identify **three** objectives it is currently pursuing through such means.

(5 marks)

b. Briefly explain the way in which these three objectives might influence the marketing behaviour of firms.

(6 marks)

c. Discuss the relative merits of **either** self-regulation **or** legislation as the best means of achieving improvement in environmental quality.

(9 marks)
(20 marks in total)

Question 4
a. What is the business cycle, and why must the marketer have an understanding of its phases?

(12 marks)

b. Define the turning points of the business cycle and suggest two ways in which they might be forecast.

(8 marks)
(20 marks in total)

Question 5
"If demography has its way, Asian and other developing economies should continue growing for decades to come." (Economist 13/9/97)

a. Prepare a brief for a group of international marketers on the long-term importance of demography to the future growth of any economy.

(10 marks)

b. Outline other key factors that determine a country's real rate of economic growth.

(10 marks)
(20 marks in total)

Question 6

You have been asked to prepare a presentation on "Assessing the Prospects: direct investment versus international trade."

a. Identify and justify three sources of information you would recommend in assessing the prospects for any overseas market.

(6 marks)

b. Explain how the existence of trade blocs might affect the assessment.

(6 marks)

c. Using a country other than your own, argue a case for direct overseas investment in the production and marketing of your company's product.

(8 marks)
(20 marks in total)

Question 7

In a memorandum to your Director, make a note of how **three** of the following might have implications for an organisation's marketing activities:

a. A contractual relationship.
b. Relationship marketing.
c. Market power.
d. World Trade Organisation.
e. Scenarios.

(20 marks)

Specimen answers   December 1998

Answer – Question 1
Rationale

The intention of the compulsory question was to provide a broad test of the candidate's understanding of the marketing environment. Unlike previous unseen case material and articles, which have related to specific aspects of the syllabus, this extract was drawn from one of the recommended readings and referred to general environmental concepts. By definition, this approach will have provided a level playing field for all candidates from around the world, since all are expected to have covered the essential reading. The extracts covered both foundation knowledge and concepts of the marketing environment, which are thoroughly covered in this reading. They also enabled very specific questions to be posed on core syllabus material. This is not always as readily achievable in a case written on a specific theme. As is always the case, candidates were expected to draw on their knowledge and understanding of the syllabus to answer the questions set.

There was no element of choice within the three compulsory questions. This was justified because of the very fundamental nature of the questions posed. Essentially they were being asked why is an understanding of the marketing environment so important to the organisation and marketing practitioners; what can organisations do to cope with continual environmental change, and why must the marketer understand stakeholders and the impacts they may have on the business. These are basic questions, presenting an opportunity for candidates to score well on this important compulsory section.

There was no format requirement in any of these questions. The provision of a formal report format, for example, attracted no marks and wasted valuable time.

Question 1a. was based on syllabus reference 3.2.1. and 3.3.1. These are the introductory sections to the two main areas of the syllabus. All candidates who had prepared for the examination should have had no difficulty thinking of content for the answer; the challenge was to address the quotation in a focused way, and to write in a well structured and concise manner. The question explicitly asked for examples, providing an opportunity for candidates to translate syllabus theory into applications of their own choosing, to illustrate the conceptual points they were making. The quotation is a well known one and provided a ready-made structure for the answer. It also provided an opportunity for candidates to express their understanding of the essence of the subject within this framework. It was not intended to be an excuse for candidates to write down all they knew, or had revised about the marketing environment.

Question 1b. was based primarily on syllabus reference 3.3.1. and 3.3.3., but allowed contribution from all the applied aspects of the syllabus. It was intended as a practical question of how organisations can keep abreast of the changes taking place in various environments. It offered a large degree of choice and selection of relevant points, although some reference to environmental scanning, information sources, forecasting techniques and conceptual planning frameworks were to be expected. However, it was also appropriate to discuss factors such as maintaining good relationships with stakeholders, ensuring research and development capability, forming alliances and so on. The aspiring marketer might have been expected to place marketing orientation and an effective marketing department as the centre piece of their answer to this question.

Question 1c. was based on syllabus reference 3.1.2. and to some extent 3.2.2. The first part of the question was intended to test understanding of the stakeholder and publics concepts. Stakeholders may be internal, connected or external, while publics are the main external constituencies, with an actual or potential interest in, or impact on, the activities of the organisation and its ability to achieve objectives. The term 'relevant' was also important since not all publics and stakeholders are equally relevant to all organisations. The second part of the question concerned how stakeholder views and judgements about an organisation may affect the marketer. An example was required and this could have been either a positive or negative perception. Given the limited marks available it was not expected that more than one example would be provided.

1a.
Student answer
A firm is a creature of its environment and must constantly be analysing what is going on around it, in order to experience growth and assure survival. What follows are examples of how a firm is dictated to by its environment, by using the five aspects of the firm described, namely: resources, income, problems, opportunities and survival.

Resources
One resource a company uses is labour. The amount and type of labour used depends on what is being produced and where. For example, in the UK we now have a minimum wage of £3.60 per hour, which enforces a minimum labour cost on the company. This is enforced through legislation. Other resources a company uses are fuels and materials. The availability of these and any by-products arising again depend on the environment. The use of radioactive materials is strictly controlled by government regulations in the UK, but regulations may be less stringently applied in developing economies. Another resource a company uses is the distribution network. There are strict laws in the EU on the number of hours a lorry driver can operate without a break. Good relationships must be established with the suppliers of these resources if they are to be available in the required quantity and quality.

Income
A company's income/revenue may increase if it supplies its products more efficiently and effectively than its competitors. For example, a company with a monopoly or oligopoly position would have a more secure revenue than a company with many competitors. If a company is seen as either environmentally friendly or environmentally damaging this may affect its revenues. People may prefer to buy recycled paper or CFC free aerosols and so the company must respond to their customers environmental con-

cerns. A company may take advantage of cost saving technology to keep retail prices low and so improve income.

Problems

Many problems originate in the macro- and micro-environments. Trade Unions may obstruct technical change or demand higher wages. If a company trades with other countries it may encounter tariffs, making its products more expensive and less desirable in the new markets. New legislation may force changes to product specifications, while competitors are a continuous source of marketing problems.

Opportunities

Opportunities arise in the macro-environment as well as threats. A company like McDonald's takes advantage of global market opportunities. A manufacturer in a developed country may take advantage of cheaper labour in other areas of the world. The technological environment offers good opportunities not only to lower costs but also to provide new and better products to sell. Computer technology provides opportunities to suppliers and users alike.

Survival

If the environment is so competitive that companies feel their survival is threatened, they may seek to merge. Many banks and insurance companies, such as Commercial Union and Guardian Direct, have undergone mergers recently. A firm may be forced to cut costs if its competitors engage in a price war, as has been seen in grocery retailing, with the disappearance of many small high street shops. In times of economic hardship, as in recession, a firm must plan its survival in advance if its long-term survival is to be assured.

Conclusion

A firm ignores its environment at its peril. It is part of the wider environment and must be open to its changes and respond to them positively, be they threats or opportunities.

Senior Examiner's comments

This answer secured a good pass, not because it was exceptional in terms of content or examples, but due to its focus on the key terms in the quotation. The examiner was not looking for 2 or 3 pages on the nature of the PEST environments or relationships with stakeholders. What was required was a well-structured answer explaining the meaning of each key term in the context of the Marketing Environment syllabus. With 15 marks available, this implied approximately 3 marks for each explanation.

The introduction to this answer was somewhat brief, but it did provide focus. It could have developed the 'creature' aspect, in terms of organisations existing in an environment full of potential threats and opportunities. It could exert some control over its micro-/immediate environment but many aspects were uncontrollable, e.g. the political/economic climate, social and technical developments. The organisation will certainly be threatened by other creatures/competitors/rivals and must adapt to unexpected changes in environmental conditions. Creatures must adapt and evolve or risk becoming extinct.

Resources are the lifeblood of organisations and are drawn from the environment. Their quality, availability, delivery, price and productivity are at best only partly controllable for even the largest organisation. Reference might have been made to resource depletion. Income or revenue/funding for organisations ultimately comes wholly from external sources (i.e. sales revenues/service contracts/licences) and depends on the organisation in question effectively meeting the current and future needs and wants of the customer/elector/taxpayer. Examples were needed to demonstrate this, and perhaps the fact that this was partly controllable through the efforts of the marketer. Problems may be seen as threats that still need to be overcome. Change in the micro- and macro-environments alters the status quo and creates potential obstacles to achievement of objectives, as well as opportunities. This candidate might have provided more specific examples of these.

The survival section and conclusions could have been strengthened by reference to the fundamental nature of this objective. Survival requires a competitive edge; a conversion of weaknesses into strengths, and threats into opportunities; a marketing orientation; a proactive approach to change and luck. The candidate might also have placed the firm in an open systems framework of drawing resources in from the environment and converting them into desired outputs of goods and services which are returned to it.

1b.
Student answer
Organisations should:

- Follow current affairs.
- Take advantage of the resources of trade organisations.
- Delegate a person within the organisation to periodically brief it.
- Consider employing an outside consultant e.g. in changing lifestyles.
- Study figures from the Office of National Statistics.
- Subscribe to the services offered by organisations, such as Greenpeace, to highlight 'hot' issues which might damage the company.
- The internet and its discussion groups can highlight issues – some consultancy firms monitor these for free.
- An organisation's public relations department can monitor developments.
- Keep abreast of technical developments in other countries in a strong position within the industry.
- Liaise with a University/Science park.
- Maintain good relationships with journalists.
- Visit relevant trade and industry fairs.
- Develop good but transparent relationships with political parties.

Senior Examiner's comments
This answer has the merit of immediately addressing the question. There was no need to explain why the organisation needed to keep abreast of changes. The approach was, in effect, a brainstorming exercise, but the technique was effective and provided a range of practical suggestions as required by the question. It was also an examiner-friendly format since the bullet points made for easy to assimilate content and ideas. Some of these could have been expressed a little more clearly/fully but overall provided a very good answer. For example, study figures from the ONS could have been developed with one or two specific sources of information, on say the economy (Blue Book/Digest of Statistics) or population (Census data).

Other possibilities included auditing the environment and using techniques such as SWOT/PEST analysis; the environmental set; 5 force analysis; impact analysis and continuous scanning. Notice that this answer referred to building relationships with pressure groups and other stakeholders. Investing time in such partnerships pays dividends in times of change, when their support is important. Other factors would include investment in marketing intelligence/management information systems (e.g. EPOS); investment in training and development of staff; a flexible organisation structure and a proactive organisation culture.

1c.
Student answer
Stakeholders are organisations and groups of people who may be deemed to have a legitimate interest in the way that an organisation or company conducts its business. They are also effectively in a position to help it achieve its aims, or to hinder it. It is therefore vital to both understand the priorities and needs of those stakeholders and to know how to communicate with them.

Internal stakeholder publics include employees, suppliers, distributors, competitors and customers.

Shareholders are seen by some commentators as internal and by others as external.

External stakeholders include pressure groups, community groups, regulators, local and national government agencies, the media and analysts.

Perhaps the most blatant example of ignoring the importance of stakeholder perceptions in recent times was the statement made by Gerald Ratner, the Chairman and Managing Director of the now defunct Jewellers. This was a rapidly expanding high street multiple, positioned at the low cost, mass merchandising end of the market. Ratner's infamous description of his products and his comparison of their value with that of a sandwich from Marks & Spencer were picked up by the media and widely publicised. This altered the perceptions of both actual and potential customers to one that was highly negative, causing new sales to slump and existing customers to demand their money back. Other stakeholders, such as suppliers, no longer wanted to be associated with the company and top quality sales people quickly looked for jobs with better quality retailers. Despite the efforts of the Marketing Department and Gerald Ratner himself to recover the situation, shareholders and analysts were not impressed. The share value fell precipitously, and a change in ownership, name and positioning became inevitable.

Senior Examiner's comments
With 10 marks available for this answer the candidate could assume that 5 or 6 would be awarded for the first part of the question and the balance of 4 marks for the example. Use of the word explain, rather than define, tends to generate more marks, particularly when there were 3 separate terms in the question.

This answer tends to focus on the term stakeholder rather than the terms 'relevant' and 'publics'. The explanation of stakeholders is, however, fairly comprehensive. The two-way nature of the relationship with the organisation might have been stressed, and the distinction between direct (continuous contribution) and indirect (intermittent/less significant) stakeholders could have been made. Shareholders were included as stakeholders, which in a sense they are, but are often treated separately to distinguish the two concepts. A distinction was made between internal and external stakeholders, but the former could have been broken down further into connected stakeholders.

There was no explicit recognition that an organisation would only be concerned with the stakeholder publics relevant to its operations, rather than all stakeholders. Relevant stakeholder publics are those who are affected by, or can affect the achievement of corporate objectives. Publics would normally be taken to be groups external to the organisation.

The example was a good one, although only familiar to UK candidates perhaps. You will notice that just one example was provided, but the perceptions of a number of stakeholder publics were briefly outlined. Some candidates used Shell as another example of where perceptions altered dramatically. Equally, the emphasis by some companies on ethical values, for example The Body Shop, had created positive perceptions.

Answer – Question 2

Rationale
This question had not been posed in this precise form before, but it did, in effect, ask the candidate to address section 3.2.3. The wording was re-expressed but this was the essence of the question. The candidate was expected to examine a relationship: the relationship between the size of firms in an industry and the nature of competitive activity that resulted. This implied a spectrum of possibilities, ranging from the case where there is just one (monopolistic) firm (competitive activity by definition does not exist except with itself, or to counter potential entrants, or substitutes

which compete for consumer spending); to perfect competition, where there are large numbers of relatively small and homogeneous forms. In between there are situations such as oligopoly. The danger was for the candidate to focus on either 'the organisations which comprise an industry', or to write generally in marketing terms only about 'the nature of competitive activity'. A useful approach would be to discuss the 4 Ps within the context of 3 market structures. Better candidates would make clear their understanding of what constituted competitive behaviour and recognise that size was only one determinant of that behaviour.

A report format was required, which attracted 10% of the overall marks. Relevant headings were required, together with a concise, well-structured layout, using bullet points where appropriate.

Student answer

To:	John Smith, Marketing Manager
From:	A Candidate
Date:	9th December 1998
Subject:	Report On The Relationship Between Organisational Size And Competition In An Industry

Introduction
This report examines the relationship between organisational size and the nature of competitive activity in industry. It will look at three basic types of organisations found in those industry types and how they compete with each other. From this description it will become clear that certain relationships will indeed exist.

Industry types
1. **Concentrated industry:** the two clearest examples of concentrated industries are oil and pharmaceuticals. The industry has the following characteristics:

   - **High barriers to entry:** the need for a great deal of R&D investment; patents protecting revenues; exploration and extraction costs; capital investment. All these contribute significantly to reducing the number of competitors in an industry. They also mean the companies who are in this industry are very big, with vast resources at their disposal.
   - **Economies of scale:** these can be achieved in very large companies. Head Office functions – Administration, Personnel and Finance – are centralised and overheads spread over more products. Equipment in large laboratories can be shared by many staff and does not need to be replicated many-fold. Such cost savings mean that smaller companies would be unable to compete on equal ground.
   - **Little product differentiation:** the customer needs are well understood and competition is more likely to be on the basis of service rather than product or price.
   - **One market leader:** there is likely to be one dominant market leader who will dictate the terms on which the whole industry does business. This company is also likely to be a price maker, setting the going-rate price for all the companies in the industry. Highly concentrated industries may become oligopolies – a market that is characterised by a lack of price competition. If a firm increases its prices, customers move immediately to competitors; if a firm lowers its prices, all firms follow, reducing profitability for the whole industry. This is known in economic terms as the kinked demand curve, with the equilibrium price charged by all oligopolists at the kink. Thus concentrated industries comprise large companies who compete on the basis of service differentiation rather than price differentiation.
2. **Fragmented industry:** this is an industry such as legal advice services, accountants, estate agents and such like. Its characteristics are very different to oligopoly:

   - **Few/no barriers to entry:** it is very cheap and easy to enter (and

279

exit) this market. There are a few set-up costs but investment is recouped quickly.

- **No economies of scale:** there are few economies of scale which can be realised by companies, so they remain small. Small or medium suppliers with <200 employees are the norm.
- **Product differentiation:** customer needs are well understood and are satisfied with tailored products. Customers have brand loyalty reinforced by differentiated products. For example, legal advice has many specialisms e.g. criminal/commercial/conveyancing, etc.
- **Local presence:** companies remain small and offer local services to customers.

Fragmented industries may develop over time into more concentrated industries as firms learn to pursue strategies to improve long-term profitability. Some estate agents have become national chains by acquiring local firms. Economies of scale are realised by centralising services at head office. Competition in such markets is primarily through differentiated products and market segmentation.

3. **Emerging industries:** New industries today would typically be Internet service providers and digital TV. These are the most difficult to classify, as the markets are confused and rapidly changing. Nevertheless some characteristics hold, such as:

- **Limited product differentiation:** at the growth stage of the product life cycle the product is still innovative and the marketing effort is centred round creating awareness. Customers are purchasing because of its newness, so product differentiation is left till later.
- **Highly competitive:** many firms enter and cost economies are achieved, causing prices to fall. An example is the Sony PlayStation, launched at around £300 but one year later retailing at £100.
- **Few barriers to entry:** there are few of these initially but they increase over time.

Emerging industries may be initially populated by a large number of small firms, but as competition intensifies a process of rationalisation and take-over leads to a re-structuring into fewer and larger firms looking to grow their business. It is in their collective interests to erect barriers to form a concentrated industry and come to informal agreements not to compete through price wars.

Conclusion
It can be concluded from the above that relationships do exist:

- Big organisations mean greater market power, a reduction in price competition and an increasing emphasis on brand image and customer service.
- Small organisations mean less market power, greater price competition and a desire to push towards greater differentiation in order to increase market power. This will tend to lead towards a defensible and profitable niche.

Senior Examiner's comments
This was a relatively long answer which could have been more concise without loss of content. It does represent an effective approach to this question. The report format is provided, at least in outline, and there is a good use of heading and bullet points within the text. An introduction, and particularly a conclusion, are important aspects to a well-structured report. There is some confusion in the text, particularly regarding the absence of product differentiation in oligopoly. Better examples might have been chosen, for example, household repair services or personal services, such as hairdressing. Such markets are a mixture of perfect/monopolistic competition.

Some candidates approached this question by referring to Porter's 5 force analysis. This was only acceptable if the 5 forces were carefully related to differing sizes of organisation. It was acceptable to define the characteristics of small and large firms and relate these to the nature of competitive activity. Small firms tend to exploit their specialisation, personal expertise/presence and commitment, adaptability and flexibility to search out and occupy profitable niches that larger firms find uneconomic to serve. Similarly, the candidate could have developed an answer based on smaller firms serving local needs; medium-sized firms serving regional needs; large firms serving national needs and multinationals serving global markets.

It was important to remain focused, as this candidate did, on competitive behaviours related to recognised market structure and conduct. It was inappropriate to assert that large firms were more competitive than small firms without clearly explaining in what sense this might be true. Oligopolists do tend to avoid real price competition in order to optimise margins and avoid mutually damaging price wars. On the other hand, while a store like Tesco's might not react if a small greengrocer opened up in competition close to one of its stores, this would not be the case if a well resourced new entrant such as Aldi located there.

There was a lot of scope in this question for candidates to discuss a range of competitive behaviours in a number of market contexts, but the points relating to differently sized firms had to be justified by reference to syllabus content, not anecdote.

Answer – Question 3

Rationale
This question was drawn from the micro-environment sections, 3.2.6. and 3.2.5. It was concerned with the legal and regulatory environment. This should have been clear to candidates given the specific reference in part c. to legislation. Part a. of the question was intended to allow candidates a broader scope of material selection than a specifically legal environment question would allow. The possibility was there to focus specifically on legal statutes, such as the Fair Trading Act, or to draw more widely from regulations designed, for example, to improve the environment. Only a brief statement of the role of government regulation was anticipated, since only 2 marks out of the 5 were available. Some reference to either the supervision and control by government of the activities of private and public businesses, in the interests of social efficiency and fairness; or the balancing of conflicting stakeholder interests; or protection of weaker members of society; or the provision of a level playing field in business was expected. Three objectives currently being pursued suggested specific applications of regulation to achieve these broader purposes.

Part b. clearly required a very brief summary of implications/impacts on marketing behaviour arising out of the regulations selected in a. Part c. was looking for a discussion of merits of **either** legislation or self-regulation. It was also intended that the merits be illustrated by reference to improving environmental quality i.e. reduce pollution. No explicit format was required, but the allocation of the marks implied brief and concisely expressed points.

3a.
Student answer
UK Government regulation is designed to make the market operate in a more perfect way, and to counteract the tendency of any business to want to control its market to such an extent that it stifles competition and the influence of outside bodies on its activities.

Such an absolute control of a company's environment is seen as harmful to the public interest and, in the longer-term, to the industry of which the company is part, and to overall competitiveness. A firm which has removed competition from its domestic environment, in an increasingly global market, can be very prone to a foreign competitor. Government regulations are often also directed towards protecting public health and safety.

Three objectives

1. Fostering of competition in telecoms, and the development of a keenly priced telecoms infrastructure that will help deliver the information age. This is being delivered through the offices of the regulator OFTEL.
2. Protection of the public interest and maintenance of an effective rail infrastructure.
3. Improvement of the overall competitive environment in the UK and the creation of harmony with European competition law. This is being achieved through the new Competition Act.

3b.

1. Marketers in telecoms companies have had to be careful not to infringe OFTELs policing of the regulations by appearing to act in an anti-competitive way. They therefore have to pay attention to all aspects of their marketing mix, including publicity material, pricing structures and the use they make of the data they hold. BT was recently disciplined because of its telesales staff's use of BT call information to appear to suggest to internet users that they might like to use their 'click' internet connection service.
2. Train companies have to meet performance conditions with regard to the number of trains they run. Without such regulations they might be tempted to cut service frequency, particularly in off-peak times. South West Trains was recently penalised/fined for poor performance. Its Marketing Department offered a day's free service in order to try and deflect the regulators disapproval.
3. When the new Competition Act comes into force the Office of Fair Trading will be able to raid the premises of companies who are suspected of acting against the public interest. Companies found guilty will be liable to fines equivalent to 10% of their turnover. This should prove to be a significant restraint on aggressive marketing. It will also bring the UK into line with the EU, enabling marketers to apply common standards across the single market.

3c.

Self-regulation has the following potential advantages for achieving environmental quality:

- Action can be taken immediately, so no lengthy legislative process is required.
- It is generally better to allow businesses to show that they can do the right thing rather than having to force them.
- It could perhaps impose less costs on business.
- It minimises the need for 'big government'.
- It avoids a PR backlash against the 'nanny state'.
- Industries understand their processes and their environmental effects, so they should be able to introduce the most effective regulation.

Legislation has the following merits in achieving environmental improvement:

- Legislation is transparent – clear to all parties, i.e. business/environmental pressure groups/environmental protection agency, with, for example, the specific limits to emissions.
- Any infringement of good practice can be tested in a court of law.
- Better integration is achieved with international standards, since pollution does not observe boundaries.
- Legislation works – companies spend the funds for environmental improvement because they need to observe minimum legislative standards and they know that their competitors must do the same.
- It provides a checklist for compliance/audit purposes and demonstration to the media.
- Self-regulation has often been found to be wanting, risking a major calamity.

Senior Examiner's comments

This answer tended to write too much on part a. given the marks available. It also tended to focus wholly on 'regulated industries' and so did not adopt a more desirable wider perspective on the role of regulation. The examples of objectives were effective, given the framework selected, and there was some recognition of wider issues, such as health and safety. The answer did focus on regulation and resisted the temptation to drift into the area of policy.

Part b. was answered well, with the use of some good examples and at least an attempt to relate the effects of the regulation to the activities of marketing.

Part c. presented ideas in an easy to assimilate manner. The points presented were accurate and well informed, although they could have been illustrated more relevantly with environmental examples. The focus was excellent, in that only merits were presented. This was in contrast to many weaker candidates who tended instead to provide examples.

Other points that might have been introduced for self-regulation include: industry will be more willing to implement regulations if they have been involved in setting them; self-regulation may provide an edge in marketing terms to green consumers and other publics; they are flexible/more able to adapt to changing circumstances; if self-set they are more likely to be adhered to – peer pressure leads to compliance.

Other merits of legislation include: assurance of level playing field; allows all interested parties to contribute to the legislative process; protects the industry from unfair competition from abroad; provides a means of redress by pressure groups and communities; helps to remove externalities.

Answer – Question 4

Rationale

This question related to section 3.2.2. of the macro-environment together with elements from 3.2.1. It represents a relatively straightforward question on the economic environment and one that is particularly appropriate at this time of global economic uncertainty. Part a. comprised of two elements, the first of which was looking for a basic understanding of the business cycle, and earned 6 of the available 12 marks. This suggested that the candidate should supply a definition, an explanation of cyclical activity, perhaps with the assistance of a diagram, and a brief outline of the 4 main cyclical phases. The second element called for an assessment of the importance of the marketer understanding the phases of the cycle. This could be best integrated with discussion of the phases themselves.

Part b. only required a definition of the turning points and perhaps a recognition of their importance, rather than a full description of associated conditions. These should have been dealt with in part a. The bulk of the marks were awarded for a specification of two forecasting methods. Ideally the examiner was looking for a quantitative and a qualitative approach.

4a.
Student answer

The business cycle is the periodic fluctuation of business activities. Business activity does not proceed in a smooth and continuous trend over time but oscillates through four phases of irregular duration, from boom to boom and recession to recession.

The four main stages of the business cycle are: downturn, recession, recovery and boom. The movement from downturn into recession and the early stages of recovery tend to produce low or negative growth in GDP; this is below the trend rate of growth for the economy. As recovery gives way to boom and in the early stages of downturn the economy is growing strong and tends to be above trend.

Characteristics of downturn

- Business activity slows and confidence declines.
- Investment spending is reduced due to rising spare capacity.
- Profit suffers as competition puts pressure on margins.
- Inflation starts to moderate and interest rates start to fall, but unemployment rises sharply.

What should the marketer do at this period?

- Alter the composition of output in favour of necessities and cut back on luxury lines.
- They should seek markets elsewhere – global marketing will reveal economies not in recession.
- They might consider reducing the prices of their products in order to clear stocks.

Characteristics of recession

- Recession is defined as two or more periods of negative growth in GDP.
- Business activity becomes static.
- Investment is very low as firms wait to see and avoid risk.
- Employment levels fall and incomes are adversely affected.
- Savings tend to rise due to uncertainty, causing retail sales to be depressed.

What should the marketer do?

- Sell off unnecessary factors of production.
- Downsize operations and streamline activities.
- Undertake an analysis of products and customers and remove uneconomic elements.

Characteristics of recovery

- Business activity/sales begin to pick up.
- Some encouraging signs of increased investment spending.
- Business and consumer confidence begins to rise and spending patterns begin to change.
- Unemployment peaks and vacancies begin to rise.

What should the marketer do?

- Market research activity should be stepped up to anticipate consumer needs.
- Ideal time to consider the launch of new products.
- Invest in skills/recruitment in preparation of the coming boom.

Characteristics of boom

- Sharply rising levels of income and spending.
- Increased demand for luxury products.
- Unemployment falling sharply and skills shortages begin to emerge.
- Interest rates rise to curb excess demand and inflationary pressures.

What should the marketer do?

- They should be able to achieve higher margins as well as sales growth.
- Recognise that boom conditions will inevitably come to an end.
- Dispose of unwanted assets at boom prices.
- Control stocks to avoid problems in the downturn.

Through knowledge of the cycle the proactive marketer can obtain an edge over competitors, secure larger markets and gain some economies of scale.

4b.

There are two critical turning points in the cycle. The first occurs when the economy turns from experiencing boom conditions into downturn. This represents a complete sea-change in economic conditions. The economy changes from buoyant and rising growth to progressively falling rates. The lower turning point occurs when the economy turns from recession conditions to recovery. This is the economic equivalent of winter giving way to the first few green shoots of spring.

The turning points may be forecast in the following way:

1. **Boom to downturn** – by monitoring economic policy. Boom leads to rising interest rates as the government tries to contain inflation. The higher these rise under the pressure of increasing wages and prices the greater the chance of a turning point.
2. **Recession to recovery** – by monitoring business confidence the first signs of recovery may be detected. The CBI conducts a regular survey of business intentions. When these start to turn up the turning point has arrived.

Senior Examiner's comments

This answer demonstrates a very well structured approach to the question. The points made are not particularly sophisticated, but they are focused on the key requirements and are presented in a very examiner-friendly manner.

The cycle could have been illustrated showing the phases and oscillation around a trend line. If diagrams are used it is important that the axes are correctly labelled. In this case it would be time and activity/GDP levels. It should also be recognised that the business or trade cycle is an aggregated average of all industries in the economy. Consequently businesses must locate their position relative to the main cycle. Some reference might have been made of the current state of the cycle in the candidate's own economy. Clearly there are other characteristics that could have been listed under the various phases, but with only 6 marks available brevity was required. The need for understanding by the marketer was also worth 6 marks. A consideration of the 4 Ps and People would have provided a useful framework for discussion of the phases. Good relationships with suppliers are important in the boom phase, for example when shortages can interrupt deliveries. Equally relationships are important in recession, so that a co-operative approach can be taken to streamlining the supply chain.

Answer – Question 5

Rationale

Part a. of this question related to the social environment in section 3.3.2. of the macro-environment.

Part b. referred to the economic environment in the same section. There was a clear format requirement in the question i.e. a brief to international marketers. This suggested that a concise and structured approach should be taken to setting out the material, and that the brief would be of interest to international marketers. This was important because the question specifically asked for consideration of the long-term importance of demography to future growth. There was credit for recognition that demography involved the study of population, its structure and composition, as distinct from social, cultural or lifestyle considerations. Positive or negative impacts on future growth were the subject of the brief, rather than structural aspects of population.

Part b. also had a format requirement in that an outline of key factors was required. This may be taken to mean a list of points with brief explanation or justification. The question did not ask for a measurement of economic growth but the causal factors that produce it in real terms. This is of fundamental importance to all economies and particularly those that are coping with the pressures of rapid population growth.

5a.

Student answer

Demography is the study of a country's population base. It consists of the people in the country, their age group, income levels, geographical distribution and gender. The study of demographics is important to the marketer, especially if entry into international markets is being considered.

Brief outlining the importance of demography to the future growth of any economy

- Demography is important for the future growth of a country because every country needs human resources to develop, manage and operate its economic activities.
- It also creates large markets for the economic activities of the country.
- Industrial activity is boosted due to this higher consumption rate; economies of scale are exploited, leading to lower unit costs; higher profits result, yielding both increased investment in capacity and high tax revenues for the finance of infrastructure and welfare provision.
- Higher investment produces multiplier increases in employment and activity levels, which further enhances economic growth.
- It supplies more labour for the firm to utilise but helps to keep down costs of production and inflation.
- Higher population creates the potential for more target market segments e.g. ageing and very young.

All the points mentioned above contribute to long-run growth. However, it must be recognised that excessive population growth may be detrimental, as in parts of my continent, Africa. If population growth exceeds output growth then living standards per head decline. Resources are diverted away from productive investment to support an expanding and dependent population. The result of a larger labour supply might be poverty level wages and underemployment.

5b.

Other key factors that help a country's real rate of growth include:

- Political factors – this is the relationship between a government and its citizens. If it is repressive or continually at war then resources will be drained away. Political stability in an economy can help a country grow by:

  - Increasing investment confidence.
  - Creating favourable working conditions.
  - Attract more foreign investment.
  - Reduces imports and encourages exports.

- Economic factors – stable, non-inflationary conditions, buoyant consumption, competitive exchange rates and rising employment levels all help to positively influence a country's real rate of economic growth.
- Balance of payments – a favourable balance means there is no constraint on the real rate of growth.
- Training and education – this is critical to the productive and competitive ability of businesses. Knowledge based industries like computers are the key to future growth.

Senior Examiner's comments

The format requirement needed to be more explicit in this answer. Poor provision of format requirements is less of a problem in UK centres but continues to be a weakness in some international centres. However, the answer does provide a clear focus on implications for growth, and correctly specifies most of the dimensions of demography. Not enough consideration is given to the use of the expression 'long-term' in the question. Population change has limited effects in the short-term but can dramatically influence the health, vitality and well being of an economy in the longer-term. The brief was intended for an international marketer and this was important. They are interested in market growth and market development. Entry into an international market is a long-term commitment and they will need to be assured as to future numbers, income levels, ages and spending preferences.

The student answer does not refer to the quotation. This quotation suggests that demography will either not operate as a constraint on growth in these countries, or will contribute positively, by providing necessary labour resources to fuel the expansion, and potential customers to purchase the resulting product. The answer does focus on a number of relevant relationships with future growth, although the negative factors are added in hindsight. A UK script would have tended to dwell more on the changing structure of population, and particularly on the progressive trend towards ageing and its potential significance for future growth. A growing dependency ratio means the burden of support on employees is rising. Higher taxes and personal pension contributions will reduce discretionary spending by those in employment. Fewer entrants into the job market might reduce the adaptability and efficiency of labour markets and reduce the flow of new ideas.

Part b. did provide an outline of ideas with effective use of bullet points. Certain of these points were justified. The political factors were certainly relevant, although the other factors were less convincingly stated. The real rate of growth relates to those factors which push the production possibility curve of the economy out. An increase in output can only occur if:

1. Resources are currently under-utilised and better management succeeds in taking output to a point on the curve.
2. The distribution of resources is inappropriate and extra value can be achieved by redistributing resources from less to more productive employment e.g. agricultural labour into industry.
3. If resources are increased i.e. the quantity and/or quality of land/materials, labour, capital, entrepreneurship.
4. If technology improves the productivity of resource use.
5. If resources are given or can be borrowed from outside investors/governments.

Many of the relevant growth factors are the conditions to allow the above to take place. Political stability, deregulation, supply-side policies, an effectively working price mechanism and so on are all examples.

Factors such as the balance of payments or exchange rates, were not acceptable unless it was explained how they contributed to real growth. Lower interest rates, for example, might be suggested because they would tend to encourage higher investment.

Answer – Question 6

Rationale
This question was drawn from all three sections of the global environment i.e. 3.4.1/2/3. The format requirement was preparation for a presentation. Ideally the information needed to be presented in a concise and relevant form. The title of the presentation was intended to provide a prompt to the central focus of the question i.e. whether to export or invest directly in the market. Part a. required a straightforward identification of three information sources (relevant to assessing foreign markets) and a justification of why each was suitable to assessment of prospects. With 6 marks available in total, there were 2 marks allocated to each source.

Part b. referred to trade blocs. This meant countries who co-ordinate their trading activities, such as the EU. Internal tariffs are removed but external tariffs with the rest of the world are controlled. Points were to be related to the assessment of prospects for direct investment versus international trade. Clearly exports would encounter external tariffs, quotas and extra costs while direct investment would avoid these.

Part c. required the candidate to select a foreign location for their company's subsidiary and to argue the production and marketing case for locating it there. In essence it was asking for a statement of the case for multinational operations.

6a.
Student answer

'Assessing the prospects: direct investment versus international trade'
Slide 1: Identifying sources of information

- **Financial Times: Country Reports** – issued monthly, they highlight key industries and economic factors, such as growth and performance. It will list prospective government agencies who can be contacted for further information.
- **Economist Intelligence Unit** – produces books, business reports and periodicals on a range of areas, from regional characteristics, country reports (GDP/inflation/exchange rates) and the state of particular industries in a country.
- **Dun and Bradstreet** – an American firm providing financial analysis on individual companies and industry sectors. This is useful in assessing the strength of competitors and the financial health of potential suppliers/distributors.

6b.

Slide 2: Effects on trade blocs

- A number of trade blocs exist throughout the world – they govern movement of goods into member states. Examples include the European Union (EU) and the North Atlantic Free Trade Area (NATFA).
- On deciding whether or not to invest in other countries, it is worth noting the effect trade blocs have:

    - **Barriers to entry** – the EU may discourage firms from non-member states from exporting there. They can do this by imposing trade tariffs and additional legal requirements.
    - **They may insist** – on a certain number of EU nationals to fill a certain number of posts if they invest directly i.e. by restricting work permits.
    - **Trade blocs may protect** – domestic businesses through direct subsidies or grants from a central body.

6c.

Slide 3: The case for direct overseas investment
The case for direct overseas investment can be split into 2 main areas, namely effects on production and the ability to control marketing. If, for example, we were to try and sell British beer in France, we would do it through direct investment for the following reasons:

Production

- Limit cost of production by buying raw materials cheaper locally.
- Eliminate excessive transport costs by using local transport rather than international delivery.
- Minimise labour costs by employing cheaper local labour/save on relocation from the UK.
- There will be no trade barriers since both are members of the EU, where free movement of goods, services and labour is allowed.

Marketing

- You can maintain good brand image as you do not have to dilute it or replace it with local image.
- You can develop brands and marketing messages specifically for the French market.

The key issue is one of control. By direct investment you can control the factors of production, maintain consistency in quality, product and service across both countries.

Senior Examiner's comments

This answer provided a reasonable format in terms of preparation for a presentation. It was clearly expressed and easy to assimilate and mark. Part a. saw the provision of three sources and some justification for their use. More diversity could have been introduced by substituting governmental or international agencies. Local sources to the market concerned would also have been useful.

Part b. indicated a good grasp of the trade bloc concept but did not successfully differentiate between export and direct investment. There was reference to the use of non-tariff barriers and the ways of giving preference to members. A Japanese firm directly investing in the EU, for example, would need to comply with 'EU content requirements' before the product would be treated as tariff free.

Part c. provided a well structured approach to the question but did not really make the most of the marketing advantages. Location in the market would reduce customer resistance for example, and give them long-term confidence in the future supply of the product. Products would tend to be tailored to local tastes (e.g. McDonald's in India) and the firm could respond quickly to problems and opportunities. Links with stakeholders would be more firmly established and exchange risks would be avoided. The offer of subsidies and supports is also an important factor to consider. It was important that the answer was orientated towards the advantages of locating in the country rather than a summary of how a business should promote and market its products in foreign countries.

Answer – Question 7

Rationale

This question provided an opportunity to cover a wide cross-section of the syllabus, while requiring a degree of depth in understanding. The format requirement is for a memorandum, but there is also clear reference to the need to adopt a note form for the meaning and implication for marketing of the three terms selected. With 2 marks for format, each term was worth 6 marks, giving an indication of the length of answer required.

The question specifically asks for implications for marketing, so the effective answer is one that concentrates on these rather than on an explanation of the terms themselves.

Student answer

Memorandum

To: **Marketing Director**
From: **P. Timer, Marketing Assistant**
Date: **9th December 1998**
Subject: **Implications of key concepts/institutions for our organisation's marketing activities**

7a. Contractual relationship

This is an agreement between two or more parties which the law will recognise and enforce. It could have the following implications for the company:

- **Assured supply** – it allows us to enter markets with the confidence that we can meet our obligations to customers without disruption. Alternatively we will be compensated for any losses arising from breach of the contract.
- **Minimise risk** – we may be able to negotiate a clause which allows for returns if the product does not sell as well as expected.

- **Customer reassurance** – they expect us to be able to offer them a commitment and to have the market standing to do so.
- **Promotional message** – the commitment our two organisation's have made to each other can be a useful secondary message in advertising and public relations. Our mutual standing through this legally binding relationship will be enhanced.
- **Legality** – if the contract is breached we can go to court as a last resort. This may establish our rights but will be costly and may attract negative publicity. Other organisations might hesitate at entering into contractual relationships with us.

7b. Relationship marketing

This is a process of getting closer to a customer/stakeholder by developing a long-term relationship, through careful attention to service needs and their quality delivery. It has the following implications:

- We could promote the relationship as a selling position in itself. Relationship marketing is a popular topic at the moment and by adopting it we will appear modern and sympathetic.
- With a strong relationship forged with suppliers we can jointly develop new products and new niche champions as opportunities arise.
- Coping with high demand: if we need more products than anticipated, in order to meet the demand our marketing has created, we need loyal relationships with suppliers so a committed response would be forthcoming.
- Countering threats: two heads are better than one, and we will be in a better position to counter problems, due to our combined expertise and market power.
- Elimination of potential supplier threats: developing relationships reduces the risk of forward integration by suppliers. It is better to work with them than be taken over.
- Technical innovation: working together and pooling expertise and resources we can stay ahead of competitors.
- Just-in-time: we can minimise our stock holding by giving each other access to our information systems and processes.

7c. Market power

Market power may be described as the ability of the firm to exercise a degree of control over its competitive environment. Its implications for marketing activities are as follows:

- Market power requires that the marketing department achieve a high market share. This applies as much to a small firm supplying a niche, as to a global company, such as Microsoft, seeking to dominate the world software market.
- Market power is associated with monopoly. To maintain a sole supplier position the marketing department must be careful to build effective barriers to entry. Providing excellent service and keen marketing orientation relative to potential competitors may be sufficient, but patents, effective branding and product proliferation will also help.
- Market power is also associated with price leadership and the muscle to enforce price changes on smaller rivals.
- Market power may derive from the marketing department's efforts to build relationships, partnerships and alliances. Both suppliers and customers will seek to enhance their bargaining power to redistribute the added value created along a supply chain.
- Market power also depends on the absence of close substitutes. Customers would then have no real alternative but to buy. Such power arises out of careful positioning in the target market and investment in branding. Alternatively the organisation with the lowest costs and most streamlined operation may have the power, particularly in hard times.

7d. World Trade Organisation

The World Trade Organisation is the successor to the General Agreement on Tariffs and Trade. Its purpose is to strengthen management of the world trade system and global economic integration. Implications for the marketing department are as follows:

- Opportunities are created by the push towards lower tariff and quota levels among member countries.
- Our home market is equally subject to increased competition as tariff levels fall.
- Preferential arrangements and non-tariff barriers are also under threat, so raising the possibility of entry or import competition in our home market.
- In the event of dumping i.e. selling products below cost of production on our markets, we are able to appeal to the WTO to impose anti-dumping duties.
- Emerging economies are now looking more favourably on WTO efforts to reduce their infant industry protections. Greater competition is seen to be the means of attracting direct investment. Such opportunities should be explored, so we can position ourselves to take advantage of the rapid growth potential in these markets.
- Successful operation of the WTO is a guarantee against a return to protectionism and the threat to sales volumes that that would imply.

7e. Scenarios

Scenarios are alternative views of the future upon which contingency plans can be developed. The implications for marketing activities are as follows:

- Potentially a better insight into what the future holds. We can combine this approach with our traditional forecasting to provide a range of possible outcomes.
- A marketing mix can be developed which would be appropriate to the different future scenarios, so that we are prepared for whichever future arises.
- Responsibility rests with what the marketing department judge the most credible scenario. Scenarios are more judgmental, but provide flexible tools for coping with an uncertain future.
- Scenarios are more likely to highlight opportunities in an age of convergence, note the coming together of data and voice communications.
- The beauty of scenarios is that they are not exclusive. Several can be constructed, enabling us to retain the speed of thought and reaction that generally characterises the smaller company.

Senior Examiner's comments

This is a fairly standard question, although candidates had to be careful to address implications rather than meaning. This is the case in the student answer above. Each of these provided good focus on implication, and despite some weaknesses in orientation would have scored highly. Candidates must be beware, however, of being tempted to write too much. Certainly no more than 6 valid points are required. The answer to the contractual relationship was set in very general marketing terms, with only limited reference to concepts such as offer, acceptance and consideration. However the focus was good and relevant implications were provided. The answer to relationship marketing was very specific to the supplier but valid implications were set out. Customer relationships and the importance of building up loyalty and mutual benefit could also have been developed. The concept of switching cost would have been useful in this context. Market power is an idea that is easy to identify with but not as easy to explain convincingly. The implications were focused on how to achieve market power rather than its effects and consequences. High margins and good profits would tend to result, but the interest of the Office of Fair Trading, or its equivalents, might be attracted. Market power may be a by-product of successful marketing or it might be a defensive strategy to achieve control over the environment and deal more successfully with future uncertainty. The answers to the last two terms were fairly comprehensive since there was limited scope to develop any further implications.

New syllabus practice questions

As a final exercise in your examination preparation attempt the following. Questions 1, 2 and 3 are from the December 1997 examination and specimen answers follow.

1 You are to make a presentation to your regional marketing team on the impacts of recent advances in information technology.
    Prepare a bullet-point slide and summary explanation on **two** of the following themes:

(a) Impact on organizational effectiveness.
    (10 marks)
(b) Impact on marketing processes.
    (10 marks)
(c) Environmental factors resistant to change.
    (10 marks)
    (December 1997, Part B, Question 2)

2 (a) Explain the terms:
        i)   Partnership sourcing.   **(4 marks)**
        ii)   Partnership marketing.   **(4 marks)**

(b) Draft a short report for consideration by your Marketing Manager on:
    'The partnership approach – the value of long-term relationships.'
    (12 marks)
    (20 marks in total)
    (December 1997, Part B, Question 6)

3 (a) What are the various 'publics' of an organization?   **(5 marks)**
   (b) Explain, with examples, the importance to the marketer of communicating effectively with **three** of these publics.   **(15 marks)**
    (20 marks in total)
    (December 1997, Part B, Question 7)

4 You are to give a presentation to a group of marketing managers on the topic: 'Challenges and change in the marketing environment.' Prepare notes for this paying particular regard to:

- The nature of change in the marketing environment
- An overview of four or five major challenges
- An outline of the specific marketing challenge posed by two of them
    (20 marks)
    (Specimen question)

5 (a) Explain what is meant by an open system.   **(5 marks)**
   (b) Makes notes on the role of the marketer at the interface of the organization and its environments.   **(10 marks)**
   (c) With examples, provide **two** reasons why contingency management might be appropriate in a dynamic situation.   **(5 marks)**
    (Specimen question)

6 (a) What do you understand by the term *turbulent environment?*
    (4 marks)
   (b) Brief your product managers on the usefulness of **two** of the following approaches in dealing with a turbulent environment:

(i)   qualitative forecasts
(ii)   impact analysis
(iii) environmental audits   **(16 marks)**
    (Specimen question)

Answer – Question 1

Rationale
This question relates primarily to the technological environment aspect of the syllabus. It relates specifically to information technology, which candidates should also have familiarity with from both their employment experience and the Business Communications syllabus. Credit would be given for the recency of the advances referred to.

The format requirement is significant since candidates not only have to provide bullet points, using a slide format but also support the points made with a further summary. This should be brief and concise to earn the full three marks available.

The focus of the question is on the impacts of IT and candidates had to ensure their points related specifically to organizational effectiveness, marketing processes and/or environmental resistance factors. Both positive and negative impacts were appropriate to the answer.

Answer

SLIDE 1

PRESENTATION
TO
**THE REGIONAL
MARKETING TEAM**
ON
**THE IMPACTS OF RECENT ADVANCES IN
INFORMATION TECHNOLOGY**

SLIDE 2
WHAT ARE THE KEY RECENT ADVANCES IN IT?
• Increasingly powerful microprocessors
• Sophisticated software packages based on Windows
• The information superhighway or internet
• Powerful organizational tools: databases/fax/mobile
• Newly IT educated 'knowledge workers'
• New organizational concepts – the remote office
• Voice responsive computers

SLIDE 3
IMPACT ON ORGANIZATIONAL EFFECTIVENESS
• **Improved communications** – internally, via E-Mail and externally via Electronic Data Interchange for mutual stock interrogation
• **Streamlined stock control** – EPOS/scanners/automated warehousing
• **Efficient financial and budgetary control** – data capture and accountancy software packages
• **Routine data processing, storage and retrieval** – cost, time and space saving
• **Time management and use of scarce managerial resource** – via video-computer-phone conferencing; mobile communications; use of computerized diaries to coordinate meetings/locate staff
• **Professional presentation** via computer graphics/powerpoint

Summary explanation
Impacts on organizational effectiveness have been both positive, as outlined in slide 3, and negative. Negative impacts include:
• possible communication overload
• less face-to-face interaction
• concerns over system security, re hackers/fire/disruption
• worry over the impact of the 'millennium bug'
• the cost of upgrading systems to maintain a competitive edge
• the risk and uncertainty in investment timing has increased

- the possibilities of waste and underutilized potential has risen
- other organizations can achieve advantage, e.g. direct banking

Positive impacts have transformed administrative and management systems and are an important weapon in delivering superior service to customers and other stakeholders:
- Effectiveness has improved along most dimensions:
  - Accessibility – improved by networked computers
  - Quicker – transactions processing by more powerful computers
  - Cost effectiveness – Just-in-time systems minimize stock
  - Empowerment of senior management/supervisors – access to on-line databases
  - Quality – via desk top publishing capability

SLIDE 4
IMPACT ON MARKETING PROCESSES
- **Market research** – via computer aided telephone interviews/EPOS sales analysis/automatic reorder
- **Product design** – use of CAD/CAM technology for shorter cycles
- **Pricing** – computerized invoicing/electronic pricing flexibility/loyalty cards
- **Distribution** – satellite tracking/internet orders/telesales
- **Marketing communication** – websites/desktop design and publishing/mailmerge for accurate targeting

Summary explanation
Marketing processes are being transformed by information technology from initial identification of needs to the servicing of 'lifetime' customer requirements through computerized sales histories. Similar negatives apply as in the case of organizational impacts but opportunities appear boundless:
- audience targeting and segmentation analysis is facilitated through database analysis using SPSS type software
- computer integrated manufacturing allows mass customization, e.g. BMW cars, and new retailing methods, e.g. Daewoo
- catalogues and pricelists may be updated on distributor networks
- the internet's potential is only just beginning to be realized, but carries the threat of negative publicity by pressure groups
- such IT is expensive and can be neutralized through imitation, productivity improvement overall appears unimpressive
- retail developments include home shopping and virtual reality marketing of property and holidays; scanners on trolleys

SLIDE 5
ENVIRONMENTAL FACTORS RESISTANT TO CHANGE
- **Pressure groups** – resist 'Big brother' tendencies of centralized computer records
- **Customers** – naturally resist change, laggards v innovators. Society may display a culture which is negative
- **Employees** – fear for security, income and status
- **Partners** – suppliers/distributors fear cost implications and potential competitive disadvantage
- **Shareholders** – may be risk averse with concerns over technical obsolescence
- **Government** – legislate to protect interests of powerful entrenched groups. Dictators may control flows of information and limit access
- **Managers** – prefer to retain a 'comfort zone'
- **Competitors** – prefer the status quo to technological uncertainty

Summary explanation
Information technology may appear threatening, complex and confusing to individuals and organizations alike. Resistant attitudes to change need to be permanently unfrozen if opportunities are to be realized. However much of the resistance is understandable since not everyone gains from change:

- Marketers must be aware of stakeholder resistance and seek to overcome it
- Implies constant training/upgrading of knowledge workers
- Resistance of suppliers and distributors is being overcome through relationship marketing/EDI and ISDN allowing mutual interrogation of computer systems
- Inform and liaise with consumer groups concerned at IT impacts
- Formulate a code of social responsibility practice
- Develop a culture of continuous change based on active participation of all relevant stakeholder groups

Answer – Question 2

Rationale

This question was directed at the role of intermediaries and suppliers within the context of relationship rather than transactional marketing. A definition of the two terms was required together with a brief explanation of their significance. It was important that the candidate did not interpret the reference to partnership as referring to the legal form of organization.

Part b. required a report format addressed to the marketing manager. The emphasis on brevity was reinforced by the use of ... *draft a short report* in the question. The focus in the report was on the **value** of the relationships.

Answer

a.

i) Partnership sourcing

- defined as the close and continuous business relationship built with designated suppliers
- unlike Porter's analysis based on competitive relationships and the use of bargaining power to determine profitability between a firm and its supplier, partnership sourcing is based on a collaborative rather than a transactional approach
- rather than constantly seeking lowest prices from a variety of suppliers this approach is to build long term relationships with one or two of them
- an alliance is formed based on mutual benefits accruing to both partners. A win-win game replaces the win-lose game
- attention focuses on multiple contracts and repeat business in the long run rather than a single contract
- the relationship is therefore built on mutual commitment with account taken of all aspects not just price, i.e. quality/delivery
- the relationship between Marks & Spencer and its independent suppliers is a good example as are the Japanese companies such as Sony and Nissan with their complex hierarchy of suppliers

ii) Partnership marketing

- partnership or relationship marketing is the process of getting closer to intermediaries and final customers by developing a long-term relationship through careful attention to their service needs
- the approach emphasizes retention of customers rather than costly recruiting of new ones
- intermediaries become trading partners and while independent are linked to the firm through open communications and long standing relationships
- the partnership might involve joint promotion campaigns and in some cases so-called piggy back marketing, e.g. Sainsbury's and Air Miles
- the philosophy is one of continuous cooperation with mutual trust as the basis for mutual cooperation in designing, developing, producing and delivering the product or service

b. REPORT

To: Marketing Manager, Automotive Supplies
From: Marketing Assistant
Date: 3 December 1997
Title: The Partnership Approach – the value of long term relationships

1. Introduction
This short report briefly considers the value of the potential benefits arising from long term relationships with our key partners or stakeholders. Attention will focus on our suppliers and intermediaries.

2. Value of long term supplier relationships
- suppliers form the initial links in the supply chain
- critical factors include price, delivery, quality and dependability
- single sourcing can generate considerable added value by:
    - ncreasing volumes and shared cost savings
    - providing schedules of requirements to assist planning
    - joint development and funding of improved components
    - introduction of just-in-time, with stock holding responsibility transferred to the supplier
    - adoption of total quality and zero defects philosophy
    - mutual support and understanding in difficult times
    - mutual access for interrogation of internal databases
    - reassurance to other stakeholders
    - sharing skills, knowledge, resources and expertise
    - savings on the purchasing and quality control functions
    - full benefits from outsourcing to a specialist

3. Value of long term intermediary relationships
- intermediaries are wholesale or retail specialists
- critical factors include stock holding/availability, merchandizing and sales promotion
- long term relationships with key partners can add value by:
    - exchange of key staff to facilitate joint planning
    - matching of special promotions with extra production
    - integrate customer orientated marketing of the brand
    - a long term view can be adopted on basis of repeat business
    - easier to ensure service levels are maintained
    - reduction of risks and costs from the alliance
    - high level contact produces high level commitment
    - improved feedback as the basis for quality improvement
    - exchange of ideas, pooled efforts and joint developments
    - builds goodwill for the bad times
    - denies competitor a distribution channel

Answer – Question 3

Rationale
This was intended as a straight forward question on publics or stakeholders. Part a. required a definition of the term together with examples of external and connected publics.

No format was required but part b. required the use of examples to illuminate the importance of communicating to three of these publics. The candidate had to beware discussing the publics themselves.

Answer
a.
Publics are the main external constituencies with an interest in the activities and impacts of the organization. They are equivalent to many of the stakeholder groups who can affect or are affected by the achievement of organizational goals.

A distinction can be made between connected publics who have a direct and often continuous contribution to the core activities and to whom the business may be held to account and unconnected publics. The former include:

Customers – upon whom the revenues of the business depend
Suppliers – who determine the timing and qualities of supplies
Creditors – who take a keen operational interest in the viability of the business
Distributors – who are key players in the supply chain
Unconnected publics have only an indirect interest in the business. Impacts are intermittent but may be serious.
Local community – concerned with pollution, jobs and amenity
Local government – concerned with conformance with regulations
Media – positive and negative coverage of business impacts
Pressure groups – various cause and interest groups

b.
The marketer has a degree of influence over its publics and much time is spent communicating with them. The general aims of the communication is to:
- assess the actual and potential impacts of the publics
- assess the threats and opportunities involved
- influence and inform the relationships with the publics

Actual and potential customers
Effective communication is important because:
- marketing requires identification and anticipation of customer needs. Without market research this is impossible. Much of this is primary research through interviews/focus groups etc. The CIM uses focus groups in the development of its Syllabus 2000 proposals
- an excellent product by itself is insufficient unless there is marketing communication. The Dyson vacuum was revolutionary and technically very effective but still required advertising to bring its originality to the attention of laggardly consumers
- profitability requires effective use of resources and prioritization. Without customer feedback on holiday destinations and experiences, companies like Airtours would be unable to make the adjustments necessary to sustain their profits growth
- it may be argued that a customer is only a customer when making more than one purchase. Relationship marketing requires on-going communication if the customer is to be retained. Car dealers maintain and build such relationships to achieve this outcome
- contact and understanding at the point of sale, complaint, service or repair is critical

Local community
Effective communication is important because:
- the community is a potential source of sales, employees and goodwill
- the community can generate negative publicity through media campaign, boycotts and demonstrations
- planning permission may hinge on the attitude of local residents
- social responsibility can bring its own rewards
- openness builds goodwill for support in any bad times ahead
- the marketer can achieve positive results through modest means. An agrochemicals producer like Zeneca may use the following to allay concerns over weedkiller manufacture:
  - open days
  - good public relations with local media
  - close liaison with local representative
  - informing interested parties of developments in advance
  - sponsorship and donation to good causes
  - cultivating good relations with the local media

Pressure groups
Effective communication is important because:
- as Shell discovered to its cost with Brent Spar, pressure groups such as Greenpeace can constitute a major threat to corporate image and operations. Boycotts not only lose short term sales but customers may be lost to rival suppliers

- pressure groups can lobby for tighter legislation which is unnecessarily strict and costly
- pressure groups can be very persistent in their actions leading to a progressive loss of community support and hardening of attitudes amongst other critical stakeholders
- the marketer can only deal with such pressure by effective communication. It must focus on those pressures most likely to impact most severely on the business and then:
    - consult with them and listen carefully to their concerns
    - liaise with them and if necessary collaborate to achieve mutual objectives, e.g. dolphin friendly tuna
    - support their efforts where congruent with marketing objectives

Appendix Syllabus

Marketing Environment

Aims and objectives
- To enable students to understand the nature of the marketing environment and its relevance for the organization and marketing practice.
- To examine the various types of organization, their objectives and the interface between marketing, internal functions and external influences.
- To encourage students to recognize the importance of building relationships with relevant stakeholders and publics.
- To enable students to identify and interpret the marketing implications of significant changes in an organization's wider environment.
- To appreciate the complex, dynamic and uncertain nature of the external environment and how it might be best managed in marketing terms.

Learning outcomes
Students will be able to:

- Distinguish between the types of organization within the public, private and voluntary sectors, understanding their objectives and the influences upon them.
- Recognize organizations as open systems and explain the importance of relationships between the organization and its suppliers, market intermediaries, customers and other key stakeholders.
- Appreciate the concept of societal marketing and social responsibility.
- Access relevant sources of information on the marketing environment, undertake a competitor analysis and systematically evaluate forces impacting on market share and profitability.
- Undertake an environmental audit for an organization and assess the probable impact of significant opportunities and threats.
- Recognize and assess the potential impact of key trends in the social, technical, economic, environmental, political, legal and ethical environments.
- Understand the complex nature of the marketing environment in order to discuss the significance of a number of current and future environmental challenges.
- Draw on a toolbox of techniques to meet the challenge of change and communicate the concepts and implications of the marketing environment in a variety of relevant business communication formats.

Indicative content and weighting

3.1 The organization (10%)
3.1.1 Broad appreciation of the internal environment; recognition of various private, voluntary and public sector organizations, their legal status and characteristics.
3.1.2 The meaning and importance of an organization's mission. Appreciation of different organizational objectives and the internal and external influences and drivers for change.
3.1.3 The interface between marketing and other functions and the value of systems and contingency approaches to managing organizations in a changing environment.

3.2 The micro-environment (30%)
3.2.1 The micro-environment within which organizations operate and its importance in the marketing process. Be aware of key sources of information on the micro-environment.
3.2.2 The stakeholder concept and their perceptions of the organization.

299

Assessment of stakeholder expectations and the relative importance of different groups and coalitions. Societal marketing, social responsibility and ethical issues.

3.2.3 The role and importance of suppliers and market intermediaries. The significance of partnerships and relationship marketing.

3.2.4 The variety of publics interested in the organization and potential impacts, particularly pressure groups such as consumerists and environmentalists. Appreciate the role of marketing in communicating with these publics.

3.2.5 Monitoring competitors and analysis of the industry environment using Porter's 5 force analysis. Consideration of the impact of competition policies on the organizational/marketing environment.

3.3 The macro-environment (45%)

3.3.1 The importance of the macro-environment to the marketer. Awareness of the key sources of information on the macro-environment.

3.3.2 The social and cultural environments and, in general terms, their influence on, and implications for marketing.

3.3.3 The economic and international environments and, in general terms, their influence on, and implications for marketing.

3.3.4 The political and legislative environments and, in general terms, their influence on, and implications for marketing.

3.3.5 The importance of the technical environment and its actual and potential impacts on organizations, employment and marketing.

3.4 Managing the future environment (15%)

3.4.1 The nature of turbulent environmental change and the meaning of complex and dynamic conditions.

3.4.2 Appreciate the approaches available to cope with the challenge of environmental change: e.g. auditing the environment; forecasting; impact analysis; strengths, weaknesses, opportunities and threats (SWOT); product life cycle (PLC).

3.4.3 The potential significance of environmental challenges to marketing in the future: e.g. globalization; a single currency; information technology; changing roles; environmental decline; rising competition and a new marketing landscape.

Glossary

This glossary includes all the key terms to be found in the syllabus and past examination papers to date. Further definitions are to be found within the body of the units and these should also be carefully studied. They are not included here since they form part of the workbook exercises.

Ageing is the increase in the average age of the population.

Appendix is a supplement containing explanatory or statistical information attached to the end of a report. To append means to attach an appendix covering some topic in more detail than in the report.

Article is a piece of non-fiction text written for inclusion into a journal, newspaper or similar.

Audit (external) involves a detailed examination of an organization's markets, competition and relevant external threats and opportunities to provide understanding of how it relates to the environment in which it operates.

Balance of payments is a record of all transactions between domestic residents and the rest of the world.

Barriers to entry are economic or technical factors or costs that make it difficult for new firms to enter a market.

Bibliography a list of references or writings related to a particular topic and referred to by the author.

Booklet is a format that involves a small and concise version of a larger text and may be presented in bound or leaflet form.

Brief is a concise and short statement of points pertinent to the topic in question.

Bullet points are a list of key concise factors relevant to the subject under discussion.

Business cycle is the regular fluctuations of economic activity and income through boom, downturn, recession and upturn.

Business values are the philosophical and ethical standards adhered to by personnel in the pursuit of the organization's purpose.

Caveat emptor let the buyer beware.

Caveat vendictor let the seller beware.

CD-Rom is a compact disc with read-only memory forming a cost effective and secure information storage device with multimedia capabilities.

Change is a process involving movement from one state to another and often requires resistance to be overcome. Different types of change arise, e.g. organizational, structural, technological.

Checklist is a succession of important or relevant points or tasks which when duly completed are noted with a tick or a mark.

Communication superhighway refers to the Internet or global information networks linking personal computer users worldwide.

Competition policies are any set of government measures aimed at stimulating competition and protecting consumers against monopoly power.

Competitive activity involves the actions taken by businesses to improve their profitability at the expense of rivals.

Competitive behaviour is the conduct of businesses in market situations involving actions and reactions to achieve advantage over rivals.

Complexity (environmental) refers to a complicated and intricately interacting environmental state or situation.

Computer software is a term for the programs and application packages that make computer hardware useful by storing, sorting, manipulating and retrieving data.

Consumerists are those groups and organizations who exert legal, moral and economic pressure on business to account the interests of consumers over profit.

Contingency management is based on the assertion that appropriate managerial action depends on the particular circumstances of the situation rather than predetermined rules.

Contractual relationship is an agreement between two or more parties which the law will recognize and enforce.

Cultural environment embraces the influences that affect society's basic values, attitudes, perceptions and behaviour.

Current account balance is that part of the overall balance which records both visible trade in goods and invisible trade in services.

Demand patterns are the trends and characteristics associated with consumer expenditure on the various goods and services currently marketed.

Demographic environment embraces the size, structure and characteristics of population.

Deregulation is the removal or relaxation of restrictions on the production, distribution or sale of goods and services.

Dominant firm is one that controls a relatively large share of the market and whose actions tend to be followed by smaller competitors.

Draft a preliminary plan or outline of a topic or report.

Duopoly is a market which is supplied by only two firms.

Dynamism is associated with high energy driving forces producing rapid growth and development and operating in an environment with few frictions.

Economic convergence is a process involving a number of different economies at different stages of development aiming to come together into a union with common legislation, monetary base and policies, e.g. European Monetary Union.

Economic environment encompasses the conditions which determine aggregates such as national income, output, employment and price levels.

Economic forecast is a prediction of future economic conditions.

Environmental change involves alteration to the nature and significance of factors in the organization's environment. The impetus may arise from a variety of sources, e.g. changing attitudes, tastes, technologies, laws or economic circumstance.

Environmental networks are contacts formed and maintained with various individuals, groups and organizations concerned with the environment.

Environmental set is a ranking of the key environmental factors currently impacting on the organization and specific to it.

Environmentalists are individuals, groups and organizations who seek to apply political, economic and moral pressure on business to adopt sustainable operations.

Ethics are a set of moral principles which govern the behaviour of the individual or organization.

Euro is the new unit of account of the European Monetary System introduced in 1999, and to enter circulation in 2002.

Expenditure reducing policies involve increases in taxation and reduced government spending programmes to bring about a general reduction in imports.

Expenditure switching policies involve actions to improve the attractiveness of domestically produced products at the expense of imports.

Fair trading is the supply of a good or service without restriction of competition or choice and in accordance with prevailing legislation.

Family lifecycle describes the stages of formation and progression of a typical family and indicates the types of consumer expenditure most likely to be associated with them.

Feel bad factor is a term used for describing depressed consumer and business confidence which results in flat or falling spending on products and investment goods.

Feel good factor is a term for describing buoyant consumer and business confidence.

Five forces *see* Structural analysis.

Forecasting approaches include quantitative and qualitative estimates of the future.

Global environment embraces world markets and developments including changes in the distribution of economic activity and spending power.

Globalization is a process whereby multinational companies treat the world as an integrated market place and develop relatively standardized products to meet its needs.

Goals provide the broad direction to organizational activities and are the driving force behind its strategies and actions, e.g. to achieve No. 1 market position.

Green environment is a term colloquially used to designate the natural environment and implicitly its protection.

Gross domestic product (GDP) is the sum of the market values of all final goods and services that are produced during a year in a country by domestically and foreign owned firms.

Impact analysis assesses the probable impact of an environmental trend or development on an organization.

Industry structure is the organizational and competitive characteristics of an industry including the number and size distribution of buyers and sellers, the nature of the product and the size of any barriers to entry.

Information needs refer to areas of knowledge required in order to make an informed and effective decision.

Information sources refer to the locations or holders of the knowledge required for a particular purpose. They may be secondary (published) or primary (research) sources.

Information technology is the science applied to the generation, processing and dissemination of data.

Innovative technologies are radically new methodologies, processes or machines which are developed into commercial use.

Interactive television shopping provides the marketer with a two-way cable or computer link with the customer, allowing purchases to be made in the convenience of the home.

Intermediaries include any organization in the supply chain between the business and its final customers. Such firms help to distribute, promote and sell to final buyers.

Internal markets are established by government within public sector organizations to encourage efficient and effective resource management in the absence of external competition.

International environment embraces all the trade and payment activities or relationships between the buyers, sellers and governments of different nations, as well as supra-national organizations.

International institutions are organizations designed to maintain global trade and payments stability and encourage the development of Third World countries, e.g. IMF, IBRD.

International markets include any target customers located outside domestic or trade bloc frontiers. Domestic sellers will seek exchange transactions with these potential buyers.

International trade is the exchange of goods and services between countries and arises out of comparative cost advantages.

Inward investment is direct investment by overseas organizations in premises, plant and equipment in the domestic economy.

Keynote address is one that sets the tone and focuses on the key issues.

Labour markets are where wages, salaries and conditions of work are established by the forces of supply and demand for labour.

Large business normally a company employing over 200 employees and having a significant share of the market.

Legal status is the standing of an organization in the eyes of the law, e.g. a sole trader is unincorporated.

Legislation is the enactment of new laws.

Lifestyle is a person's pattern of living as expressed in his or her activities, interests and opinions. It may be measured through a technique known as psychographic profiling.

Macro-environment includes those forces which impact on the business, creating opportunities and threats, but over which it has no real control or influence.

Managing director is appoined chief executive by the board and is responsible for the day-to-day running of the business.

Market forces refer to supply and demand and embrace all conditions and influences upon price and quantity.

Market power is the ability of the firm to control its competitive environment.

Market size is the total value or volume of turnover/sales for a product.

Market structure classifies the competitive characteristics of a market in terms of the number of firms, the nature of the product and barriers to entry.

Marketing environment embraces not only competitors, customers and supply chain participants over whom the business can exert some influence but also the wider SLEPT factors. These factors or forces in turn affect marketing management's ability to develop and sustain successful transactions with its target customers.

Marketing orientation places servicing of the customers' needs and wants at the centre of the whole organization's attention and activities.

Memorandum is a means of recording and retaining information which is worthy of note. The heading cites the intended recipient, sender, others who have received copies, what it refers to and the date.

Micro-environment includes the groups and organizations close to the business that affects its ability to satisfy its customers. They have a two-way operational relationship with the business and may be influenced by it to some degree (see Stakeholders).

Mission is the statement of the organization's overall purpose that expresses what it stands for and wants to accomplish in the wider environment.

MMC was the Monopolies and Mergers Commission set up to investigate monopolies. It was replaced in April 1999 by a Competition Commission which has stronger powers.

Multimedia technology integrates text, sound, animation, music and moving images with a computer providing the user with a variety of communication possibilities for business applications.

Multinationals are enterprises engaged in simultaneous manufacture/operations in a number of countries and which take decisions from a global perspective.

Natural environment embraces natural resources including land, vegetation, wildlife, air and water and the amenity which they confer.

NIC's are newly industrializing countries such as China.

Non-tariff barriers are standards and regulations to which imports must conform.

Note form involves setting out information in brief points, comments or explanations.

Objectives are specific ends or achievements to be realized at a future time to fulfil the goals of the business, e.g. to increase sales by 10 per cent over the next 12 months.

OECD is the Organization for Economic Cooperation and Development and includes as members the affluent industrialized economies.

OFT is the Office of Fair Trading established by the Fair Trading Act to monitor and investigate trading practices and refer any monopoly situations to the Monopolies and Mergers Commission.

Oligopoly is an industry with a small number of relatively large sellers, who have some control over price but recognize that competitor actions will affect profits.

On-line means that a computer is linked to a wider area network and can interact with the real time or updated system.

Opportunities are changes in the external environment which provide the organization with the ability to achieve its goals.

Organization describes the relationships which arise when two or more individuals agree to coordinate their activities to achieve common goals. It is the vehicle for achieving stated goals.

Organization structure represents the distribution of tasks, power and authority within the business and the relationships involved.

Pacific rim includes the countries around the shores of the Pacific ocean including Japan and the western seaboard of the United States and Canada.

Partnership marketing involves close collaboration and mutually advantageous relationships with linked distributors in the supply chain.

Partnership sourcing is the use of a supplier with whom the organization has a long-term relationship including new product development and efficiency improvements.

Political environment embraces the activities of the state in setting national objectives, legislating, policy making and implementation.

Pressure groups are composed of people with common interests or attitudes who seek to influence relevant decision makers to act on their concerns.

Price war is a systematic reduction in the price of a good or service by two or more competing firms, often occurring after the breakdown of an agreement.

Primary/connected stakeholders include customers, employees, suppliers and creditors (see Stakeholders).

Private sector is the part of the economy in which productive activity is carried out by privately owned/run enterprises and includes the household and personal sector as well as businesses.

Product liability refers to the legal obligation on companies to avoid acts or omissions that could have reasonably been expected to cause harm to consumers.

Profitability is the rate of return on capital or the excess of revenue over total cost of production.

Public relations includes all forms of planned communications between an organization and its publics with the aim of establishing mutual understanding.

Public sector includes the activities of central government departments, local authorities, public corporations and nationalized industries.

Publics are the main internal and external constituencies with an actual, or potential, interest in, or impact on, the activities of the organization and its ability to achieve objectives.

Quangos are executive agencies established by governments to supervise or regulate a variety of public activities and services.

Recession is a stage of the business cycle where GDP has fallen for two consecutive quarters.

Red tape is the unnecessarily complex and time-consuming rules and procedures laid down by bureaucracies.

Reference groups are the groups in society with which a person interacts. They are a point of reference for consumers in making their decisions through their knowledge and influence.

Regulation is the supervision and control by government of the activities of private and public businesses in the interests of societal efficiency and fairness. A regulation is a rule set out to govern the behaviour of those it applies to.

Relationship marketing is the process of getting closer to the customer by developing a long-term relationship through careful attention to service needs and their quality delivery.

Report is a formal business communication presenting a summarized record of investigations into some topic. It will utilize headings to lay out material.

Responsibilities arise out of a duty or an obligation placed on an individual who holds a position of authority and trust or an organization accountable to various stakeholders.

Restrictive trade practices are agreements between two or more firms designed to control prices, quantities or qualities of products supplied or on the intermediaries used.

Résumé is a summary of a longer piece of text, e.g. a report.

Scenarios are alternative views of the future.

Secondary stakeholders include local community, pressure groups, media, analysts, government agencies, other firms, etc. (see Stakeholders).

Size is a concept which relates to the relative scale of turnover of a business. Concentration ratios measure relative size by calculating the number of firms accounting a given proportion of sales.

SLEPT factors include the social, legal, economic, political and technical environments which may impact on the business in the form of threats and opportunities.

Slides are prepared acetates or photographic material used on overhead projectors. They may also be generated directly from computers.

Small businesses are independently owned and operated with only a limited slice of total sales.

Social costs are imposed on the rest of society and equal the difference between the total cost to society of an activity and the private costs of production.

Social-cultural environment embraces changes in the nature, attitudes, behaviour and values of society which affect employment and buying patterns.

Social responsibility is the acceptance by an organization of obligations to protect and improve the welfare of society as well as its own interests.

Societal marketing is an approach to marketing which aims to combine profitable satisfaction of customer needs with the maintenance or improvement of both the consumer's and society's welfare.

Stakeholders are any group or individual, other than shareholders, who can affect or are affected by the achievement of organizational goals. Primary stakeholders make a direct and often continuous contribution to core activities of the business. The impact on or by secondary stakeholders is more intermittent and normally of less significance.

Standards are established by government agencies or the firm itself and normally set a weight, design, quality or process specification to which all production must conform.

Statute is a law passed through Parliament by a government as a means of implementing its policy programme.

Structural analysis refers to M. Porter's five forces of industry rivalry, the threat of new entry and substitutes and the bargaining power of suppliers and customers. These combine to determine the long-run profitability of an industry.

Submission means putting forward proposals for consideration by higher authority.

Suppliers are those who provide resource inputs to specification at an agreed price.

Sustainable growth is that which meets the needs of the present generation without compromising the needs and requirements of future generations.

SWOT strengths, weaknesses, opportunities and threats.

System is an organized combination of parts/sub-systems which form a complex entity, with interrelationships or interactions between the parts, and between the system and its environment.

Taxation includes payments to the government from the private sector and constitutes the primary source of revenue to finance state expenditure. Levies are made on income, property and expenditures.

Technological environment embraces changes to products, processes and methods of business which impact on the organization.

Technological forecasting involves the extrapolation of existing trends or identification of feasible technologies within a given timeframe.

Threats are changes in the environment whose impact may prevent the achievement of a firm's objectives.

Trade blocs involve groups or countries who coordinate their trading activities. Internal tariffs are removed but external tariffs with the rest of the world may (customs union) or may not (free trade area) be controlled.

Trade descriptions is legislation requiring that products perform to the specification stated or implied, i.e. they are fit for their purpose.

Trade mark is a brand name, symbol or logo, which is registered and protected for the owner's sole use. The Trades Marks Act brought Britain into line with the EU by allowing smells, sounds, product shapes and packaging to be registered.

Trends are general tendencies to move or extend in a specific direction.

Turbulence is a confused environmental condition where continuous and largely uncontrollable forces disturb any tendency towards stability in the system.

Values reflect the worth, significance or importance we attach to human actions and behaviour.

Virtual reality recreates a desired environment using a computer and headset allowing sensual experience of simulated situations, e.g. of a retail display or motor vehicle handling capabilities.

Vision is the ability to imagine or foresee the future prospects and potential for the organization.

Voluntary codes are freely adopted guidelines to encourage desirable modes of behaviour.

Voluntary sector is made up of not-for-profit organizations which promote good causes by raising funds through donations.

Weighted index is a numerical means of measuring a price or volume series by allocating weights or values to the items comprising it and comparing current changes to a base year value equal to 100, e.g. Retail Price Index.

Index

314